QUEER
COUNTRY

Music in American Life

A list of books in the series appears at the end of this book.

QUEER COUNTRY

SHANA GOLDIN-PERSCHBACHER

**UNIVERSITY OF
ILLINOIS PRESS**
Urbana, Chicago, and Springfield

Publication supported by a grant from the AMS 75 PAYS
Fund of the American Musicological Society, supported
in part by the National Endowment for the Humanities
and the Andrew W. Mellon Foundation.

Library of Congress Cataloging-in-Publication Data
Names: Goldin-Perschbacher, Shana, author.
Title: Queer country / Shana Goldin-Perschbacher.
Description: Urbana: University of Illinois Press, 2022. |
    Series: Music in American life | Includes bibliographical
    references and index.
Identifiers: LCCN 2021046889 (print) | LCCN 2021046890
    (ebook) | ISBN 9780252044267 (hardback) | ISBN
    9780252086335 (paperback) | ISBN 9780252053221 (ebook)
Subjects: LCSH: Country music—History and criticism. |
    Gender identity in music. | Gay musicians. | Transgender
    musicians.
Classification: LCC ML3524 .G64 2022 (print) | LCC ML3524
    (ebook) | DDC 781.642—dc23
LC record available at https://lccn.loc.gov/2021046889
LC ebook record available at https://lccn.loc.gov/2021046890

CONTENTS

Acknowledgments   vii

Introduction   1

CHAPTER ONE: Queer Country and Sincerity   25

CHAPTER TWO: Genre Trouble   70

CHAPTER THREE: Rurality and Journey as Queer and Trans Musical Narratives   125

CHAPTER FOUR: (Mis)representation, Ownership, and Appropriation   153

CHAPTER FIVE: Masks, Sincerity, and (Re)claiming Country Music   172

Notes   201

Discography   229

Bibliography   235

Index   251

ACKNOWLEDGMENTS

I am extraordinarily lucky to have been encouraged by my extremely generous and loving parents. They took me to concerts and suggested we go backstage to talk to the musicians I admired. In addition to helping me try a multitude of endeavors, they arranged, drove me to, paid for, and sat through lessons, rehearsals, instrument repairs, auditions, and concerts at all hours of the day and night and have been an enthusiastic audience. They have cheerfully extended this encouragement for my scholarship, attending the occasional show with me and learning in detail about the musicians, history, and concepts I'm studying. My sister, Maya, has been a friend and enormous help, and her young family has provided me great joy.

When Nadine Hubbs offered Gender and Sexuality in Popular Music during my senior year of college, I was thrilled to find a way to explore social, emotional, and ideological relationships to music making. Dean helped me find my way to a graduate program at the University of Virginia's Department of Music that modeled everything I wanted to be as a scholar and has continued to be an inspiration and support. The wisdom of UVA's program and thoughtful, honest, motivating mentorship from Fred Maus, Susan Fraiman, Richard Will, Michelle Kisliuk, and many others has continued to be a blessing. I hit the jackpot with the warm and generous intellectual camaraderie of my classmates and colleagues, especially Liz Lindau, Mary Simonson, Lee

Bidgood, Vilde Aaslid, Allison Robbins, and Kelli Joseph, which has nurtured me and my scholarship and teaching for twenty years.

George Chauncey and Joanne Meyerowitz hired me for my first academic job as lecturer of LGBT studies at Yale University, a thrilling start for which I will always be grateful. Stanford University's Andrew W. Mellon Fellowship of Scholars in the Humanities, directed by the kind and wise J. P. Daughton and Lanier Anderson, encouraged my research with insightful company, introductions to scholars and publishers, reduced teaching, and funding during a recession when academic jobs were disappearing. Heather Hadlock generously created a role for me in both feminist studies and the music department, allowing me to dream up new courses, working with me to host an identity studies–themed faculty retreat, and funding the first of many musician visits to my classrooms over the last ten years. Jesse Rodin and Daphna Davidson have offered over a decade of friendship, advice, and encouragement.

I'm grateful to Robert Stroker for hiring me at Temple University, allowing me to take a sabbatical to focus on writing this book, granting me research funding, and contributing toward hosting Rae Spoon at the International Association for the Study of Popular Music (IASPM) conference. Kevin Delaney granted me summer research funding. My department contributed toward funding my conference presentations and honoraria for musicians to visit my classes. As Director of Gender, Sexuality, and Women's Studies, Heath Davis contributed generously to paying my musician guests. My department extended the extremely helpful opportunity to develop courses in American Roots Music, Queer Country, and Intersectional Identity Studies and offer them to multiple populations at Temple. My music majors, honors students, and graduate students in these courses participated in class visits and calls with several of these musicians, attended concerts and a film screening with me, and offered mature, insightful comments on portions of the book manuscript in progress. In particular I'd like to thank Melissa Acheson, Elizabeth Bergman, Julius Brown, Ben Burch, Daniel Carsello, Christina Colanduoni, Marquise Cruz, Emily DeWoolfson, Renée Ray Drezner, Emiko Edwards, Zach Gallagher, Matthew Gatti, Elysia Hempel, Tom Reynolds, Bexx Rosenbloom, Ben Safran, Hannah Strong, Candace Truitt, and Vivien Wise. I have had several opportunities to share my research at Temple, including at the Center for Humanities at Temple, the Institute for Dance Studies thanks to Mark Franko and the dance department thanks to Sherril Dodds, and my own department. Responses to these lectures were enormously helpful to my thought process. A number of colleagues have offered a variety of assistance: Beth Bolton, David Cannata, Marcus DeLoach, Alex DeVaron, Rollo Dilworth, Ed Flanagan, Anne Harlow, Jan Kryzwicki, Ted Latham, Wendy Magee, Noriko Manabe, David Mindich, Steve Newman, Alisha Nypaver, Elizabeth Cassidy Parker, David Pasbrig, Devon Powers, Adam Vidiksis, Elijah Wald, Lindsay Weightman, Stephen Willier, Maurice Wright, and Asta Zelenkauskaite. Thanks in particular to Michael Klein and Steve Zohn for mentorship.

The Wolf Humanities Center at the University of Pennsylvania included me in a year-long study group organized by Heather Love and facilitated by Jim English. This working group invigorated my intellectual life at a crucial moment while I was writing, offering feedback and questions, particularly from Anne Balay, whose insight, enthusiasm, and friendship have aided me in writing this book.

Presentations at the Feminist Theory and Music Conference have prompted crucial feedback throughout my career, including in 2014, when I presented an early draft of research that would become this book. Stephan Pennington's questions and comments there were and have continued to be very helpful. I benefited from presenting portions of this book in earlier forms at the annual meeting of the American Musicological Society and also in its LGBTQ Study Group, as well as in the Queer Resource Group of the Society for Music Theory, the Society for Ethnomusicology, the Society for American Music, the US and Canadian chapters of IASPM, and the Trans* Studies Conference. Lectures at Rutgers University, the University of Virginia, Westminster Choir College of Rider University, Dickinson College, and West Chester University provided me with important outlets for developing material and answering thoughtful questions.

Chip Tucker and Jahan Ramazani extended a thrilling publishing opportunity with *New Literary History* to produce an essay that helped me begin writing this book. They generously offered detailed questions and editorial suggestions. I was so deeply touched and buoyed to receive the Marcia Herndon Award from the Society for Ethnomusicology for that essay. Fred Maus also invited me to publish an essay that led to crucial insights for this book.

I have been working with Laurie Matheson on this project since 2015. Her calm, incisive, thorough, and encouraging feedback, including reading and commenting on an earlier version of this manuscript at a crucial moment, helped me shape and deliver this book. My two peer reviewers offered deep, detailed comments that inspired important improvements throughout the book. Jennifer Argo helped me stick to the deadlines to get this into print. Mary M. Hill's careful copyediting has offered beautiful polish to this labor of many years. Jennifer Fisher took my collection of inspirational ideas to craft the perfect cover, which Orville Peck and Jeff Henry generously allowed us to use. Megan Rainwater also kindly contributed her photo. My friends Emily Gale and Renée Ray Drezner helped me prepare the bibliography, filmography, and discography. Roberta Engleman helped me with the index. Thanks to the American Musicological Society for its subvention in costs associated with publishing this book. As I was completing the book, my friends in the Antiracism in String Band Music working group offered insight, energy, and camaraderie.

I'm grateful for the wisdom, insight, humor, and compassion of Karen Smith, who discussed with me the process of researching, writing, and teaching about these subjects. Katy Hawkins's moving poetics classes have been an inspiration and comfort. I am extraordinarily lucky to have friends who are loving, hilarious, brilliant, and generous. Kathy Nigh has been a kind friend and source of good cheer. Since 2001 Brad Rogers has been a constant source of humor, wisdom, and camaraderie through this long process, sharing manuscripts and discussing various decisions. Liz Lindau has patiently and insightfully helped me see what I'm trying to say, rescuing me from so many challenging moments over the last two decades, and providing inspiration, wisdom, and fun. My dog, Rufus, has been the most loyal, patient companion that a writer could hope for. Finally, there is no way that this book would exist without the courageous, creative, generous, and brilliant musicians about whom I have written.

INTRODUCTION

Why queer country music? Because sometimes you
love a culture that doesn't love you back.[1]

The Gay Ole Opry is hosted in a Brooklyn bar, unlike its famous namesake, which has its own large, dedicated venue in Nashville. It does not air live on the radio on Saturday nights, nor does it elect musician "members." These days it occurs once every few months and is thus referred to as Queer Country Quarterly. But since April 2011, queer country musician and wealth-redistribution activist Karen Pittelman has been a dedicated host of the Gay Ole Opry, inviting musicians from all over the United States to perform. And in 2015 queer transgender Bay Area roots musician Eli Conley started a sibling West Coast series. The music varies widely, from renditions of classic old-time tunes to Dolly Parton covers, traditional as well as original Appalachian labor songs, original pop country as well as embodiments of older country styles, and country blues and folk singer-songwriter activism. What the musicians have in common is a perceived otherness that has, in almost all cases, prevented the Grand Ole Opry and the mainstream country music industry from taking notice of their music.

While country is rarely considered as a music that queer and transgender people would enjoy, let alone spend their lives making, this music's history should include many lesbian, gay, bisexual, and transgender people. But their stories have not made their way into the narrative. In the mid- to late twentieth century, lesbian and gay country musicians were considered anomalies, if considered at all in the history of country music—musicians such as the 1960s lesbian country musician Wilma Burgess, who recorded hits without gendered pronouns and who also opened the first lesbian bar in Nashville; Patrick Haggerty, who, with friends, created the first gay-themed country album, *Lavender Country*, in 1973; and the 1980s multi-platinum-selling artist k.d. lang, who began her career as a country artist. Of all of the out queer and trans contributors to country music history, the only one depicted in Ken Burns's eight-part 2019 PBS documentary series about country music was lang, and she was not discussed: her photo appeared on-screen in a montage of musician photos. Nineties star Chely Wright, the first modern mainstream country musician to come out, describes in her documentary nearly killing herself over keeping the secret of her sexuality and says when she came out she was met with closed doors, including the Grand Ole Opry.[2] Mary Gauthier, the first out lesbian to play the Opry (where she appears regularly), is still more often described as a "folk" artist than "country," a distinction that seems to have less to do with her preferences or style than with the industry's. Amy Ray, of the Grammy-winning famed (lesbian) folk rock duo the Indigo Girls, active since 1985, plays smaller shows with her stellar country band than she does with fellow Indigo Girl Emily Saliers. But their former mentee, lesbian Americana singer-songwriter Brandi Carlile, has won multiple Grammy Awards and was the 2019 Americana Artist of the Year. When Carlile played a September 2019 sold-out show at Philadelphia's outdoor venue, the Mann Center, the half of us in the audience without sheltered seats remained in the fifty-degree rain for the entire show. Meanwhile, although *Billboard* record-setting gay artist Lil Nas X won two Grammy Awards in 2020, his hit song "Old Town Road" was the subject of a viral journalism and social media debate about genre that raised the issue of racism and exclusion of Black artists from the country music industry.[3] While most mainstream country venues and country radio stations have not (yet) welcomed these musicians, the twenty-first-century North American populace's growing awareness of and support for queer and trans identification has led audiences to value out musicians playing country and related genres in greater numbers, including *Ru Paul's Drag Race*–winning drag queen country singer Trixie Mattel; masked gay country crooner Orville Peck; lesbian "Southern Gothic" musician Amythyst Kiah; "Fabulachian" Sam Gleaves; transgender singer-songwriter Joe Stevens; nonbinary country (now indie pop) musician Rae Spoon; post-coming-out comebacks by Chely Wright, Ty Herndon, and Billy Gillman; and over a hundred more artists. Most but not all of these musicians make gender and sexuality a central part of their musicking, even as or, perhaps more precisely, *because* it affects their careers.[4] This book centers on these musicians and their work, continually reflecting on what it means to interpret a genre through musicians marginalized from its history. My theory is developed through my ethnographic, analytical, and historical work with them and their music, drawing out themes that musician and organizer Karen Pittelman engages in describing her early Gay Ole Opry events:

> So many queer people who grew up on country music connect to it and its meanings, yet feel there's no place for them. . . . They're not welcome. There's a lot of homophobia in country—all of the themes and the way that gender is approached in the songs. I realized that I wasn't the only one who wanted to love the music and the culture in a place they felt welcome. . . . When the [ticket sales] numbers started to go up, I was worried. Sometimes in Brooklyn things can come off as ironic, and I was scared people would think it was like "Hee Haw" or something. Or somehow it might look like we were appropriating it instead of treating it with respect. But when people showed up for the music in all their country finery, I realized they were serious too.[5]

Through country, these musicians tell stories of where they're from and how they understand themselves. As Pittelman says, "Country music is a vehicle to tell the truth about your life. That's what I love about it."[6] Country music's storytelling shapes what they share and how they represent themselves. It's important for their performances to be heard as sincere, because queer and trans people are more at risk than straight or cisgender people for being misunderstood or mistrusted due to the sense of personal revelation of queer and trans identification and the question of revealing this understanding to others. (Yet irony is also important to many queer and trans people, for example, the camp humor that has long been a crucial coded language of camaraderie, as well as a way to disarm the hatred and fear of some straight and cisgender people.) This experience and how it is relayed raise questions of authenticity and sincerity both crucial to and at odds with queer and trans experience: important for their humanizing power, yet problematic for their essentializing of "truth." Yet this tension is also at the heart of country music. Country sends conflicting signals of real and fake, a juxtaposition that the country industry and audience are sometimes able to laugh about (for example, in relation to *Hee Haw* or Dolly Parton). But because queer and trans musicians and listeners have often been othered and excluded by both country music and US identity norms, they tend to have special insight about the politics of authenticity, sincerity, otherness, representation, and appropriation.

WHY COUNTRY?

When music scholars write about genres that appeal to North American queer and/or transgender participants (or appeal to us as scholars for making the sorts of claims we're interested in exploring about trans and queer identities), we have tended to look to almost *any other* type of popular or art music besides country. Country music, connected in theory if not always in practice with the rural, is often assumed by nonlisteners to be conservative, if not also bigoted. Country and its listeners are regularly assumed to invest in concepts of tradition, naturalness, Christian religiosity, heteropatriarchy, and white supremacy, ways of structuring life that make existence difficult for many trans and queer people. Music, gender and sexuality, and class studies scholar Nadine Hubbs's 2014 study, *Rednecks, Queers, and Country Music*, complicates these assumptions, discussing the appeal of mainstream country music as a "queer" music. Hubbs's argument reveals that the rural and working class, who are often themselves stigmatized as nonnormative, were at one time more accepting of queerness than the middle class; it was only in the 1970s and 1980s, when middle-class people shifted from elitism to cultural omnivorism, that they projected their own former intolerance onto the working class. Hubbs's work challenges the demographic biases the mainstream media has invented and demonstrates the close relationship between working-class identities and queered gender and sexuality across the history of commercial country music.

Yet there are biases in this genre. Recent statistical studies of women performers' participation in country music, as well as lyrical depictions of gender and race, suggest that the top hits in country music often include sexism and racism. In a statistical analysis of the lyrical content of country hits from 1980 to 2019, Braden Leap argues that mainstream country hits objectify women and represent race as homogeneous. Similarly, Jada Watson's "Gender

Representation on Country Format Radio: A Study of Published Reports from 2000–2018" and the Annenburg Inclusion Initiative's research brief "No Country for Female Artists: Artist and Songwriter Gender on Popular Country Charts from 2014 to 2018" demonstrate decreased play of women-fronted bands by country radio stations, fewer women receiving major awards, and clear ageism impacting women in this industry. Musicians regularly mentor one another and speak out about this discrimination.

If (mostly straight-identified cisgender) women singer-instrumentalists have had a difficult time maintaining long-term country music careers despite their musical brilliance, out queer and trans singers and instrumentalists have had almost no support from the mainstream country industry in developing careers or maintaining careers after coming out, regardless of their musical creativity, skill, and insight.[7] However, this lack of support has not stopped over one hundred out queer and trans musicians from recording and performing country and related genres of music since at least 1939, when the Sweet Violet Boys (later revealed to be a pseudonym of the Prairie Ramblers) released "I Love My Fruit" on OKEH Records.[8]

As Patrick Haggerty told me when we first met, "Why country?" is the wrong question.[9] There are many reasons why country music appeals to queer and trans musicians and listeners, despite the lack of encouragement from the industry. The old and new tunes of country and folk music often explore life from the vantage point of the everyday concerns of ordinary folks. They tell stories of a working class that includes the gender and sexually nonnormative: itinerant laborers, cowboys, drifters, strong and sassy women, proud as well as sensitive men, sex workers, alcoholics, outlaws, community organizers, and the elderly. These are narrators who may not otherwise get much attention in North American life and who are not always trusted as having valid or truthful stories to tell. Country music is an important vehicle for telling their stories.

Esteemed country songwriter Harlan Howard was known for saying that country music is "three chords and the truth."[10] This music is thought to truthfully and simply explore the lives of ordinary working-class people, their yearning, suffering, and regrets, their pride about a set of values different from that of middle- or upper-class people, and their romantic, familial, friend, and even animal relationships. At the same time as it presents itself as truthful and simple, this music is also often funny and over-the-top, embraces outmoded styles, and spins tall tales. With this context, it may seem more understandable that some queer and trans musicians and listeners, who may be in exile from their own families and/or who love line-dancing to a gutsy female singer wearing sequins and cowboy boots, would relate to country. When scholars and journalists address transgender and/or queer people's musical performances, we have tended to focus on camp aesthetics or rebellious styles as opposed to sincerity or adherence to tradition. For example, k.d. lang's country music performances have been widely discussed for their camp appeal. While lesbian fans worldwide adored lang's country music, it was frequently viewed with suspicion by both journalists and the country music industry, despite her repeated declarations of honest appreciation for country music and her view that loving a genre included having a sense of humor about it.[11] But queer and trans musicians have developed sincere and politically activist aesthetics in their performances of country and related styles. While a scholar such as sociologist Richard Peterson demonstrates the fabrication at the heart of country music's cherished relationship to the concept of "authenticity," I argue that attention to queer and trans country musicians' sincerity reveals a crucial aspect of their performances of self. What we can draw from often-repeated quotes such as Howard's is a sense of how country music tells its story, as well as why someone like the creator of the first out gay country album might want to use country music to communicate about being gay when there were few sources of affirming narratives, especially in this style.[12]

Issues of authenticity and sincerity are often of special importance to North American transgender people, who may be deemed "deceitful" by discriminatory cisgender people.[13] Their gender identification seems to demand constant explanation not asked of most people about their identity.[14] As acclaimed transgender author and professor Jennifer Finney Boylan wrote in response to debates about transgender people's bathroom usage and other rights, "I'm all done explaining my humanity."[15] But cultural notions of what honesty entails have also created problems and danger for people with marginalized gender and/or sexuality. The narrative of the "out and proud" urban coastal queer has made life difficult for rural queer and trans people, as ethnographer Mary Gray found in her study of queer and trans teens in Kentucky at the turn of the twenty-first century. Although the rural is often situated rhetorically as the "closet" of North America, if not a space of death for queer and trans people, Gray and other scholars have found that rural queers develop different ways of surviving and, in some cases, thriving in their settings.[16] While today, gender- and/or sexually diverse people are expected to move to an urban and especially coastal area and to visibly and audibly differentiate from straight (and, for some, also cisgender) people, Gray argues that this narrative creates problems for a core structural value of rural life, "familiarity." In rural areas, residents depend on one another for the basic services that would be provided by large institutions and government in a city. Sam Gleaves, an out gay musician from Southwest Virginia, invokes rural familiarity directly in the title of his debut album, *Ain't We Brothers*.[17] The title prompts an imagined listener to reconsider the relationship between himself and his gay neighbors based on the rural ethics of familiarity.

Listening to queer and trans musicians sing their own and others' country music can offer glimpses into their life experiences and how they engage with ongoing debates about identity. In featuring country's themes of rurality and journey, these musicians explore debates about sincerity and humor, nature and nurture, minority assimilation or rebellion, and appropriation and (mis)-representation. But these debates, common in discussion of queer and trans life, are not the only themes this book listens for. Paying attention to these typically marginalized voices also offers insight into country and folk music as genres and how they forge a sense of place, history, community, and values.

Old-time musician and American studies scholar A. J. Lewis started off his September 2016 Queer Country Quarterly set at Branded Saloon in Brooklyn by saying, "I think death and destruction is a cool lens through which to explore the queerness of the old-time genre—because these are all songs by and for misfits, social outcasts, social outsiders, people who lived their lives outside of heterosexual kinship structures, who refused dominant norms of capital accumulation, health, longevity, happiness." After a medley of morphine songs he introduced the "omnipresent" old-time song "The Cuckoo" using queer and trans lenses to view this bird's practice of laying its eggs in the nests of other species of birds. "I like to think of the cuckoo as a queer bird, in the sense that its primary allegiances are not those of biological kinship. It refuses the cult of child-rearing. And as a transsexual I have a special affinity for the cuckoo, because as we all know, when that cuckoo egg hatches, it flouts whatever biologized expectations that the rest of us have projected onto it and ends up being something else entirely."[18]

But while Lewis's brilliant stage banter makes immediately clear why old-time and related music offers queer and trans resonances, these interpretations, as well as queer and trans musicians, tend not to be included in discussions of old-time, country, and related genres of music. And so many people missed appreciating the queer and trans stories told in country music and what insights these stories might offer to those who listen to, play, and write about this music, as well as how it contributes to queer and trans people's lives, and, finally, how queer and trans voices in this quintessentially North American music might depict their sense of place, community, and values during a period of enormous social change and political instability from the middle of the twentieth century to the present.

GENDER AND GENRE

Focusing on queer and transgender musicians who make country and related music reveals genre trouble, a theme of this book (and a musical riff on Judith Butler's foundational queer scholarship).[19] To understand the particular intersections of identity and music that result in the phenomenon of queer country, we need to consider the histories of the taxonomy of identity and music. The categories of "gender" and "genre" may seem quite different to discuss at once: one pertains to living things, the other to artwork; one is often assumed to be entirely "naturally" assigned,[20] while the other is understood as invented and applied by humans; one is often assumed to offer only two "opposite" choices, while the other seems to have endless options. But actually, these words have significant etymological overlap, and both categories have roots in the nineteenth-century impulse to categorize all things. In "c1125 Old French" *genre* meant "kind [or] sort," could refer to "sex, race, [or] people," and is translated into English as "gender."[21] "Genre" in its present usage developed in the mid-nineteenth century as a category of creative work (originally literary and visual art—"genre painting" described scenes depicting "ordinary life").[22] Queer and trans studies scholar Jack Halberstam reminds readers that flora and fauna classification systems, while seemingly benign and standard ways of labeling living things, are inherited from colonialist practices of "discovering" and managing "new" populations and species.[23] While "gender" had been used to refer to "sex difference" for hundreds of years, the late nineteenth century supported a proliferation of scientific study and categorizing of sexual desires and activities to consolidate these into *identities.* As philosopher, historian, and social theorist Michel Foucault famously explains, "The sodomite had been a temporary aberration; the homosexual was now a species."[24]

Lesbian, gay, and queer studies scholarship has vigorously explored and debated the repercussions of this invention of a type of person based on the gender of that person's object of sexual desire. Lesbian and gay scholarship has tended to value this new awareness of type of person. Historian John D'Emilio notes that the development of gay identity happened alongside the shift to capitalism and industrialization: with the opportunity to earn a wage instead of working as a family member on a subsistence farm, individuals had free time in which they could develop new identity-based sexual communities (often, but not always, in cities).[25] Activism and scholarship have often supported greater visibility of sexual and gender minorities as a means of demanding the right to exist and to thrive. Yet queer scholarship and activism have tended to resist labeling, whether binary or multiple, as a form of control and oppression.[26] Thus, Halberstam argues that while the recent proliferation of gender and sexuality categories (and the possibility of choosing these on social media and online dating services, for example) seems to offer more freedom to describe one's identifications, this impulse to be classified is a legacy of colonial violence, and the new categories may not be providing the assumed liberation from the binary (nor from the colonialist legacies).[27]

Genre and gender are both taxonomies based in style, form, function, and discourse. These categories seem to predict content and usage. The category of gender presumes a feature of animal and plant life that forms a central facet of the way humans interpret the worth and function of a living thing. And, interestingly, musical genre also assumes a type of person. As is explored in this book, the relationship between gender and genre has been so strong for some of these musicians that they have experienced a shift in identification of both at the same time, the lens of each clarifying their relationship to the other. In music scholarship, discussion of musical form often attributes significance to parts of a musical work as completing a unified whole. While discussion of unity in music is typically assumed not to be sinister, these same sorts of discourse are used in limiting ways to discuss human identity: the assumed reproductive use value of a body part is often employed to construct a life narrative that supports the most simplistic version of heteronormative categories and makes invisible deviations from these norms.

Musical categories are also shaped by discourse, including artistic conversation, reception, and "community validation."[28] Genre implies decisions about marketing music and finding an audience, a choice that has to do with presumptions about different kinds of people. Thus genre can be limiting to musicians in terms of reaching different listeners and also exploring their musical interests and facets of themselves in their public artistic personae.

In the past, people assumed that genre and gender were fixed, if not essential, categories, but now, both are understood to be shaped by social factors.[29] These categories are felt to be "pragmatic and necessary," and they "condition our understanding of the world."[30] Yet this definition of genre reveals some tension in the invention and use of these categories. Pragmatic means "practical" and "based in reality." If these categories condition how we see the world, then they shape how we perceive "reality," and they affect the conditions under which we decide what the "practical" and "necessary" categories might be.

Like identity categories, musical classification systems may also seem benign to some, but they have been shaped to (mis)identify and (mis)manage populations. In the late seventeenth century, philosopher Johann Gottfried von Herder categorized some music (*Volkslieder*) as traditional to the *Volk* of a particular region. Their identity was shaped by language, music, and stories, which were influenced by the very topography of the landscape. While this philosophy allowed for communities without wealth or an army to consider themselves "a people," it also placed different groups in a hierarchy measured against a European standard. Colonized or soon-to-be-colonized groups were imagined to be less "developed" people, based on European comparisons. Those seeking to define American folk music inherited this essential problem with the category, with many folk song collectors listening only to white locals wherever they traveled while avoiding Black locals.[31] As musicologist Marcia Citron argued in her groundbreaking work on the near total exclusion of women from the canon of classical music, if women composed at all, they were long limited to composing certain genres as a result of societal oppression that prevented their access to education, musical rehearsal spaces, legal rights regarding artistic creations, and more. Given these constraints, women in some cases composed other types of music that did not require extensive education, a large ensemble rehearsal, and publication. Simultaneously, the genres that men tended to compose were lauded as much more "important."

Popular music genres have experienced similar patterns of gendered exclusion or ghettoization, such as women being welcomed as vocalists but not as instrumentalists, engineers, or producers; women being sexually harassed in musicking spaces; women not being taken seriously as songwriters; and the physical design of some instruments creating challenges for some women to play or transport them.[32] The history of American popular music is shaped by its racialized stereotypes, inherited from blackface minstrelsy, and then through racialized, class-based, and regional stereotypes used to market early country music, despite (or perhaps because of) the diversity of musicians who played this music. The distinctions described by the genres of "hillbilly" and "race music" were projected racial stereotypes and did not correspond to real musical differences.[33] As historian Diane Pecknold argues, musical genre categories help define and maintain identity categories: "The stakes of analyzing the relationship between music and racial identity are at least as much about our own investments and the dynamics of contemporary racial hegemony as they are about originary musical traditions or the degree to which such traditions reflect a consistent cultural essence or sensibility."[34]

Genres set the stage for performances of self, interactions with listeners, types of instruments, and styles of production. They allow entry into certain kinds of venues and involve creating particular moods and telling different stories. Perception of an artist's musical persona, as well as the identity of the audience, is shaped by notions of genre. Sociologist Jason Toynbee points out, "Genre is seen to express the collective interest or point of view of a community," and thus the "social process" of genre formation measures the "validity" of music by its sense of "grass-roots values and identity."[35] Drawing from such understandings, some practitioners feel that folk and country music are "valid" by their "grass-roots values and identity," developing from presumed anonymous tunes shared orally. Yet in the United States these genres were not solidified and proliferated by grassroots activity but rather through the (mis) perceptions and directions of outsider folk song collectors and record industry employees, as Richard Peterson and historians Benjamin Filene and Karl Hagstrom Miller argue. This music was then later reenvisioned by revivalists, as Filene, Neil Rosenberg, Robert Cantwell, and Elijah Wald discuss. The notion that this music was somehow pure because of its presumed noncommercial origin "romances" a much more complex situation, hiding intervention from a variety of forces that led to the development of folk and country as genres.[36]

Some artists have sought to distance themselves from genre boundaries or accompanying image stereotypes and in some cases have referred to themselves as "post-genre." Philosopher of music Robin James argues that those who claim to be post-genre are often drawing from the problematic concept of "post-identity." She notes that the only people who could consider themselves post-identity are those who benefit from being in the dominant, unmarked group of their culture, who have the luxury of not considering group identity categories as central to their sense of self. White privilege allows them to shed the racialized, regionalized genre categories and claim to have risen above them, purportedly making music that is more widely appealing and artistically free.[37]

While queer and trans people might listen to and play all types of music, there are some genres and scenes that have been especially welcoming of queer and trans participants. For example, gay dance clubs and women's music festivals have often attempted to create safe spaces and craft alternate worldviews via music, dance, and sociality, as well as through the business of the scene.[38] Other genres might be appreciated by queer and trans people for gender or sexual rebelliousness and/or irony. Such rebelliousness is written into the genre itself, as sociologist Simon Frith argues about rock and punk: "The rules (and the comic or shocking possibility of breaking them) are always on the surface of performance itself." Meanwhile, he argues that folk genres' rules are "naturalized" for fear of drawing attention to the "peculiar" features of their performance events.[39]

Cultural ideas about identity have been central in the creation of musical categories, and these musical categories have, through their centrality to life, reinforced social understanding and policing of identity. Exploring examples of people who do not fit all of the expected stereotypes of a genre and yet make that particular style of music is informative for understanding the cultural acceptance (or questioning and rejection) of these stereotypes, as well as the flexibility for the types of identity performances and storytelling of each genre to relate to a perhaps unexpected group of people. Queer and trans artists in this study profoundly experience the relationships between identity and genre and often discover that in order to find an audience they must create an understandable relationship between their identity category and a musical genre—a requirement that inevitably involves engaging in some way with the biased identity stereotypes built into these genres in the face of contemporary identity politics. But no matter what they try, their genre is difficult for mainstream industries to categorize, and thus I discuss queer country not as a subgenre but as a socioaesthetic phenomenon.[40] Likewise, I employ "queer and trans" as more ambiguous and overarching terms that do not specify a particular gender or sexuality formation, as this level of identification is also difficult and political to pin down (as discussed below).

QUEER COUNTRY

The country music industry polices the borders of what counts as country.[41] Musicians' identities, especially singers' identities, affect these outcomes. For the most part, country has not welcomed outwardly lesbian, gay, bisexual, or trans musicians. This industry has, of course, included untold numbers of closeted or quietly queer and trans producers, instrumentalists, deejays, songwriters, publicists, stylists, journalists, and singers. (While I would have liked to credit each and every one of them, out of respect for their privacy this book will not "out" or speculate about anyone.) But out country musicians have, until very recently, lacked support to maintain a career in the mainstream country music industry (defined as the music played on country radio). For a long time, these musicians have had no clear alternative: they could either remain closeted or scramble to find a way to reinvent themselves in a new genre or a new career.

Some have found the folk music industry more welcoming to out queer and trans musicians. Folk musicians often consider country an outgrowth of folk, and some facets of that genre seem to be open to a wider range of musician identities, as well as musical styles, than the mainstream country industry. Yet folk has far less market share and selling power. And those out queer and trans people who entered into folk-related music are still considered marginal in this genre, fighting for inclusion, relevance, and publicity, despite, in the case of the Indigo Girls (discussed in chapter 2), for example, becoming worldwide stars.

The Americana industry (also called roots or alternative country) emerged in the late 1980s, developing a country-rock-punk sound and embracing certain country artists as "roots" of its country-rock-punk amalgam. They market to middle-class, urban and/or coastal, Democrat or progressive-identified listeners, pitched in contrast to the perception of country styles as appealing only to working-class, rural and suburban, and Republican listeners. Only since around 2014 have many queer and trans country-style artists experienced any burgeoning sense of interest from the main power brokers in the Americana, folk, and bluegrass industries.

While this book explores what some musicians and journalists call "queer country," this is not an official musical category. The musicians I write about cross musical boundaries in a way that makes definition of their genre difficult. While many musicians are happy to cross genre boundaries—for reasons of musical growth and enjoyment, financial gain, or otherwise—out queer country musicians, I argue, have little choice but to cross musical boundaries in search of opportunities, audiences, camaraderie, safety, and promotion. So not only are their gender and sexual identities queer, but their relationship to genre is also queer. Out queer and trans musicians have participated in country, folk, Americana, bluegrass, and old-time music as much as they have been welcomed to, which, until very recently, was not at all. So, many queer and trans country and folk musicians have made an enormous effort to network and support one another to create an independent scene through series such as Homo Latte in Chicago and Queer Country Quarterly in Brooklyn and San Francisco; organizations such as Bluegrass Pride; the podcast and web magazine *Strange Fire* and its successor, *Country Queer*; self-created, coalitionally supportive labels such as Daemon and Coax; queer and trans-friendly venues such as Club Passim in Harvard Square, People's Voice Cafe in New York, and Freight and Salvage in Berkeley; and sustained internet journalism and social media attention from the *Bluegrass Situation* and *Country Queer*. Another area of support for some of the musicians has been the women's music scene (which was also created out of an urgent need in the face of discrimination and exclusion). In particular, the Indigo Girls flourished with early support from the women's music community and have, in turn, mentored several musicians in this study, most notably, Brandi Carlile and Chely Wright, in developing musical careers as out lesbians. They have also welcomed Coyote Grace and Amythyst Kiah as openers. Likewise, Toshi Reagan has been an important presence in women's music and a mentor to many, including Amythyst Kiah. (I overheard Reagan introduce herself to then-not-yet-well-known Kiah at Queer Country Quarterly, her New York City debut, and offer to feature her in Reagan's annual Birthday concert, which she has hosted for over thirty years and which is a celebration of and support for women of color musicians.) Recently, the "middlemen" of Americana, folk, and even bluegrass genres have realized the marketability of "progressiveness," which they can demonstrate by visibly including queer and trans musicians in their festivals, by allowing a "Diversity Showcase" at IBMA and a Newport Folk Festival gay roots showcase, and by offering awards to musicians from marginalized identity categories. But it still remains to be determined whether the mainstream country music industry will ever fully embrace queer and trans musicians.

A WORD ON TERMINOLOGY AND DEMOGRAPHICS

Scholarship on nonheterosexual and/or noncisgender people prompts care in how individuals from different time periods and communities describe their identities. The historical range of the book, from 1939 to 2021, covers a period of rapidly changing terminology. Not all these terms are embraced and people who use the same term to identify themselves may not agree on its definition. When referring to the entire range of musicians in the study, I have chosen "queer" and "trans" in order to be inclusive and succinct. I intend the inference of "queer" as an "umbrella" term that includes lesbian, gay, bisexual, transsexual, transgender, intersex, asexual, two-spirit, nonbinary, and other nonheteronormative identifications, but I also employ its meaning as a radical politics of refusing institutionalized categorization and assimilation. But since studies of "queer" subjects sometimes focus more on sexuality than gender, I also employ "trans" to include people who identify as transsexual, transgender, nonbinary, two-spirit, and intersex. Focusing on trans as a category also serves as a reminder that not all trans people consider themselves queer (either in terms of the communal LGBT grouping or queer's implied radical politics, or both). Engaging these identifications together is not unproblematic, as people who identify with these terms may strongly disagree with one another's identity politics (for example, regarding gender legibility, identification as trans versus as a man or a woman, and aims regarding assimilation versus social revolution). Thus, I include examples of different musicians' identifications, music, and politics, analyzed intersectionally with reference to region, class, religion, race, and age, among other identifications. When referring to individuals, I use the terms each musician prefers (to the best of my knowledge). Some of the included musicians have come to understand and describe their identifications differently during the course of the study. My own theorization of this music has followed musicians' engagement with this discourse of gender and sexual identity and how these perspectives influence their musical aims and vice versa—how the politics of the music they play influences their sense of gendered and sexual identity. Not all of the musicians intended to make their music "political" in terms of gender and sexuality. But that intention makes no difference to the mainstream country music industry, which has excluded those who were happily making country music before they decided to come out and were forced to explain their identification to any intolerant listeners, as well as those who have long identified as out queer or trans musicians and always intentionally included radical politics in their music. Musicians from these groups have, at times, allied with one another and at other moments diverged in message. This book is an attempt to understand these musical messages.

The demographics of the musicians included in this study skews toward white lesbian, gay, and trans musicians. There are many lesbians (cisgender as well as some transgender), a handful of cisgender bisexual women, several trans men (some straight and others gay), and nonbinary people (more of whom were assigned female at birth than male). There are many cisgender gay men, one of whom performs his country music in drag. I know of no straight transgender women playing this music. Some bands include straight and/ or cisgender collaborators. The musicians come from many parts of North America, rural and urban, and grew up in socioeconomic classes ranging from working class to independently wealthy. Many of the musicians were raised observing one or another form of Christianity and a few continue to practice. There are a small number of Jewish queer country musicians. Most of the participants in this scene are white, although there are several Black queer country musicians, at least two prominent Latinx queer Americana musicians, at least two Asian American queer country musicians, and one part-Ojibwe gay country musician.

SINCERITY, GENRE AMBIGUITY, AND QUEER AMERICANA

In late March 2004 I saw an ad in Charlottesville, Virginia's *The Hook*, a now-defunct free weekly paper, for a band called Girlyman. They were playing on a Sunday night at a venue called Gravity Lounge, which was a bookstore, café, and concert space on the Downtown Mall in operation from 2003 to 2009 that hosted touring and local musical acts and was queer friendly. I remember that the ad offered limited information about the band but that it quoted a reviewer who said something like, "Girlyman's music is so cheerful it makes me not want to kill myself."[42] What a dark and personal way to offer a positive review, I thought. How much was the writer joking? I figured that I needed to see this show, as I was in the third year of the University of Virginia's PhD program in critical and comparative studies in music, and I had been especially interested in studying gender and sexuality in music. I had never been to the Gravity Lounge nor heard of Girlyman. Given their name and my lack of much knowledge about the venue other than its queer and trans-friendly atmosphere, I wondered if Girlyman might be lip-synching drag queens. As the words of the ad stuck with me, I thought about what made drag feel life affirming for some people and perhaps inauthentic and confusing to others.

That night the audience met three earnest singer-songwriters around my age and decades younger than some of the folkies in the audience. They sang their own songs in sophisticated three-part harmony, accompanying themselves on baritone guitar, acoustic guitar, ukulele, banjo, and djembe, trading the instruments back and forth. They explained that two of them were best friends from childhood in New Jersey, and the three had become friends at Sarah Lawrence College. (In later years, the band added a drummer.) They explained to the audience that the band had been formed after 9/11, their band name quoting then California governor Arnold Schwarzenegger's critique of what he framed as Democrats' weak masculinity. Girlyman described themselves as a group of misfits: one Jewish butch, one white man who wore makeup and bleached his hair, and one tattooed feminine Japanese American woman. They weren't all clear about their sexuality, but it seemed like any or all of them could be queer and that they intended that understanding. Onstage they cracked endearing, self-referential, dorky jokes, enveloped their audience in thoughtfully choreographed vocal harmony, and shared poetic and poignant insight about what it was like to be a young adult in the early twenty-first century. Their repertoire was almost entirely self-authored, offering a broad range of stories about human experience, including being the first-generation child of immigrant parents who do not relate to how their child sees the world, having one's heart broken, looking back on the simple thrills of childhood adventures, navigating the complexities of friendship, coming to terms with a family member's suicide, having a crush on someone who does not yet know that she's queer, singing as a bullied butch from the 1950s who sees themselves as a "young James Dean," being concerned about environmental destruction, and protesting a lying president's war in Iraq and Afghanistan. They wove references to American culture and geography into their songs—a gospel song collected by John Lomax, fragments of Emily Dickinson's poetry, a phrase of a nursery rhyme or famous pop song, and references to topographical features of the country and stories of travel. Band member Ty Greenstein would joke that they were making the most of their high school English reading list. For lack of an obvious genre, they called their music "vocal harmony–folk–pop," a description that revealed their difficulty using the marketing labels of the American music industry. Their music had exciting rhythmic drive that sometimes recalled the bluegrass influence of Greenstein's father, often drew from the longing expressed in country music, engaged current and historical social justice concerns more typical of folk music, and sometimes revealed ambitions that at times led them toward the "pop" end of their self-label, such as filming a music video directed by co-median Margaret Cho. Their label and band name worked well enough for the thirteen years they toured the US and the UK, with a loyal following everywhere they performed.

My memory of this performance and subsequent rethinking of my reactions in the years since as I learned about the history of queer and trans people's relationships to folk and country music eventually inspired the themes that shape this book. When I heard the name of the band and the queer friendliness of the venue, I anticipated drag and irony but was met that night with folky sincerity peppered with critical, queer, social-justice, savvy humor. This striking realization led me to theorize about the sincerity of queer country music. Sincerity seemed at odds with then-common understanding of identity as socially constructed. And I was intrigued about the relationship between sincerity, humor, and gay "camp" aesthetics. Further, Girlyman's struggle to define its genre highlighted a trouble I associate with musicians whose sexual, gender, and racial identities create problems with the identity performances expected from a genre. Their genre conundrum chafed with the racially, socioeconomically, regionally, and sexually marked divides between country, folk, and popular music. This theme of genre trouble also profoundly impacted my theorization of queer country. Despite or perhaps because of this trouble, Girlyman and so many other queer and trans country and folk bands sing music with themes that can be understood as stories of American experience. At times they explicitly engage with normative people's expectations of them as sometimes "othered" people. These songs are especially striking during a time when issues of accurate representations of minoritized people and questions of appropriation have become urgently disputed.

The sincere yet also at times critical or humorous appeal of country music to queer and trans musicians and listeners is illuminated by critical theorist Eve Kosofsky Sedgwick's reframing of camp as reparative rather than paranoid:

> As we've seen, camp is most often understood as uniquely appropriate to the projects of parody, denaturalization, and mocking exposure of the elements and assumptions of a dominant culture. . . . To view camp as, among other things, the communal, historically dense exploration of a variety of reparative practices is to do better justice to many of the defining elements of classic camp performance: the startling, juicy displays of excess erudition, for example the passionate, often hilarious antiquarianism; the prodigal production of alternative historiographies; the "over"-attachment to fragmentary, marginal, waste, or leftover products; the rich, highly interruptive affective variety; the irrepressible fascination with ventriloquistic experimentation; the disorienting juxtapositions of present with past, and popular with high culture.[43]

Sedgwick seems to be defining exactly what makes country and folk music appealing to so many queer and trans musicians and listeners. Country and folk musicians lecture from the stage about the history and interpretation of country and folk music. (In this book, AJ Lewis's "startling, juicy display of excess erudition" about the queerness of old-time music is a perfect example.) Heated debates about which of a famous, allegedly straight, contemporary but old-fashioned artist's songs seems most gay display a "passionate, often hilarious antiquarian" interest in a type of country music most fans no longer favor and for a cheeky, unintended purpose. Even the common interest some musicians have in old-time music and Baroque, Renaissance, and medieval music begins to make more sense as "passionate, often hilarious antiquarianism." Folk and country genres are rife with "alternative historiographies"—this book serves as one that centers queer and trans voices. The obsession for the history of old songs some enthusiasts display in blog posts, journal articles, and stories from the stage in order to make sense of the disparate verses of a song created via collage or to reveal the oral history through which the musician learned this song makes sense as "'over'-attachment to fragmentary, marginal, waste, or leftover products" (only excessive to outsiders who don't also enjoy this obsession). These genres also encourage "rich, highly interruptive affective variety" in musical performance, leading listeners to laugh, cry, protest, and joyfully sing along during performances. Covering songs made famous by older stars and the tradition of drag queens dressing like Dolly Parton (who encourages this practice) are both examples of "fascination with ventriloquistic experimentation." And these genres absolutely "juxtapos[e] present with past, and popular with high [and, I'd add, folk] culture," merging the African banjo with the presumed "high culture" mandolin and fiddle and the "popular" electrified instruments and then playing old and new music that flirts with presumed boundaries between folk and popular culture, which infuriates the hypotheses of the songcatchers of yore and delights present queer and trans audiences who are thrilled to recognize a line of Shakira in an original queer country song by My Gay Banjo.

METHODOLOGY

My revelations about Girlyman's performance and experiences after it also shaped my methods for coming to understand this music. My interactions with this and other related bands and the issues of identity politics with which their music engaged inspired how I worked to understand them. There wasn't a list of out trans and queer country and folk musicians, so I started by going to the shows of the out queer and trans musicians I did know of, talking to them and their listeners, and slowly learning about musicians to study. During this period, the format of social media exploded, and I then had the opportunity to follow and/or befriend musicians not only through emailed newsletters but also on Facebook, YouTube, Spotify, Patreon, and Instagram. In order to execute this project, I amassed an archive of queer and trans musicians' country and folk music and material about these musicians. I attended local and out-of-state shows regularly from 2004 to 2021, as well as many virtual shows, both before and during the Covid-19 pandemic. (Some artists had used the virtual format prior to the pandemic in order to earn money through performance without incurring the expense, time commitment, or risk of going on tour.) In addition to regularly attending shows (often I arrived early to observe the unloading of equipment and to interact with venue operators, and I remained at the show to watch merch table interactions) and speaking with musicians, listeners, and other industry participants, I was also able to spend longer stretches of time with some musicians by hosting them on my campus and/or at my home, attending another queer or trans musician's concert with them, or joining the band for more than one concert on tour. This experience created intimacy and built trust between us, as they got to know me and my aims, saw how I interacted with my students regarding the concepts I write about in this book, and had the opportunity to interact directly with students. In some cases we have become friends and gotten to know one another's social worlds. I believe that it's important to pay for artists' labor, especially when my own research benefits from their creative work. And so I have purchased every album these artists have created, and I have, in almost every case, paid for my concert ticket. I have employed musicians as guests at my university and at an academic conference, and I attempted to pay artists as much as possible. In many cases, I have contributed a small amount financially over many years to their projects and livelihoods, often via Patreon or Kickstarter. I was able to help a filmmaker with grant applications to complete her film about two of the musicians, an interaction that happily led to a much longer relationship in which she consulted me to comment on different prerelease cuts of the film and allowed me to host a screening with her and one of the musicians at Temple University after the film was released. As I was completing this manuscript, several different media avenues and community groups began to offer more coverage of queer and trans country (and related genre) musicians, including *Country Queer*, a terrific dedicated site with a podcast started by Kevin James Thornton under the name *Strange Fire*, passed to Cindy Emch, and eventually transformed by Dale Henry Geist. During that same period, the nonprofit Bluegrass Pride took shape and held concert fundraisers. There are now many more out country musicians than I was able to include in this book.

My methodology has been also influenced by my own identity and musical experience. I am a white, cisgender, queer, middle-class, Jewish woman who was raised in a town in New England listening to folk, classical, and popular music. I studied classical viola performance from age seven through college.

My PhD coursework merged historical, ethnographic, analytical, and critical approaches to studying music of many kinds (my dissertation focused on popular music). I took a graduate seminar on bluegrass music during which I explored the role of the fiddle, but I never became proficient. I am more familiar with folk music, as my mother taught our Girl Scout troop songs from *Rise Up Singing,* and our family attended folk concerts and festivals and ventured backstage to meet Pete Seeger, Tom Paxton, Tom Rush, Arlo Guthrie, Kris Kristofferson, and others. I did not grow up listening to or playing music that was defined to me as country music. I have studied and participated in feminist, queer, and transgender activist and scholarly movements since 2001. I am both an insider and outsider in these communities. I have dated transgender men and nonbinary people, as well as cisgender men. And as a single, childless adult who has shaped her life around scholarship, I disidentify with the prescribed path that feminine-appearing, middle-class, white women are often expected to follow. Yet while I have some sense of shared experience with a portion of my research subjects, I by no means presume to fully understand their lives and identifications. Thus I have tried to be consistently aware of my preconceived notions and to be open to what each musician communicates is important to them, to correct any of my earlier misperceptions, and to adjust the theory that I develop in relation to these insights. My prose is typically not focused on the ways that I interacted with the musicians but rather uses observation and interviews as two methods among many to explore these musicians and how we might understand the music they make and the stories they tell about themselves, as well as the larger issues raised by considering their existence at the intersection of this genre and identification. When it seems important to the larger point to discuss my role in a situation, I do so.

CHAPTERS

Chapter 1 explores the centrality of sincerity to country music and the problem of sincerity's ties to essentialism (the notion that aspects of self are inherent). Listeners expect truthfulness and insight about life from certain musical performances, but at the same time, most listeners also understand that any performance is always partly fictional. What makes a performance sincere? And how is that criterion impacted when the musician's identity is considered nonnormative? What do the results of this conversation tell us about how we as a culture understand truthfulness in art? What does this tell us about how we interpret sincerity and truthfulness from marginalized identity groups? I identify several key moments in queer country history and analyze these in the context of sincerity: *Lavender Country*, the first out gay album (which prioritized sharing truthful information about gay life); Canadian star k.d. lang, the first major country musician to seem very queer (and whose sincerity was called into question); and an early twenty-first century transgender take on sincerity by Canadian musician Rae Spoon.

Chapter 2 explores the history of queer and trans artists' negotiations with country and related genres. Musical genres come with particular expectations for credible identity performance, as well as for the message and use value of the music. Often queer or trans identification puts a musician at odds with the stereotypical identities expected of a genre. A musician's inability to be understood as a particular genre can make a musical career close to impossible. Many queer and trans musicians find themselves with what I call "genre trouble," not finding an easy name for what they play or why. Thus, this book includes musicians who play styles of music that might not be grouped together if the musicians were straight and cisgender, but because of their coalitional politics, as well as their professional difficulties being accepted in some of these genres, they often cross paths if not regularly work together and get featured together in queer media. In this chapter I develop a theory of identity and genre as cogenerative and then deliver an alternate history of country and related music narrating this genre history from the perspective of out queer and trans musicians. Finally, I explore three transgender musicians (Namoli Brennet, Lucas Silveira, and Rae Spoon) who transitioned gender and genre simultaneously.

What can we understand about the United States and Canada by listening to stories about rurality in these regions told by queer country musicians? Chapter 3 moves to explore how these musicians engage the themes of journey across North America and journey to discover self that are part of the mythology and history of this music. In their navigation of these themes, they also bring up contemporary trans and queer political issues, including "the trans narrative" (the idea that all transgender people's experiences follow a certain journey) and queer and trans people's relationships to ideas of revolutionary queerness versus a compelling ordinariness that allows for ease of living. A number of queer and trans singer-songwriters craft songs that use rurality and journey as frames for exploring some trans and queer experiences and rurality to demonstrate a sense of groundedness and ordinary life that may not typically be associated with queer and trans characters. They develop the theme of lifelong personal journey (one way of understanding gender). The chapter explores the country music of Amy Ray (of the Indigo Girls); Rae Spoon's "Keep the Engine Running" and "A Message from the Queer Trans Prairie Tourism Co."; Actor Slash Model's "TN Tranny Two-Step"; Joe Stevens's musical career; and Dolly Parton's Oscar-nominated song for *Transamerica*, "Travelin' Thru," as well as the film's overall crafting of its transgender heroine's identity through a country music soundtrack that humanizes her character after a century of cruel trans stereotypes in film.

Chapter 4 considers concerns of appropriation and misrepresentation. This chapter explores Rae Spoon's "Stolen Song" and the music video that inspired it, engaging the history of folk and country music's impacts on North Americans' understanding of identity and, more broadly, the questions of artistic sincerity in the context of Otherness, accusations of misrepresentation, and questions of belonging.

The book concludes with discussion of six queer country acts who have been successful in the latter part of the second decade of the twenty-first century. I first attend to three gay male musicians who use drag, masking, and cowboy costuming as strategies for developing queer sincerity in the face of a history of exclusion from the mainstream industry. The chapter then moves to explore Our Native Daughters, the Indigo Girls, and the Highwomen in comparison—three all-female collaborations that allowed lesbian musicians to write courageously vulnerable songs. In 2020 Trixie Mattel's, Orville Peck's, and Lil Nas X's embrace of gay camp humor, fashion, and irony allowed them to forge a sincerity with their audience, one that is framed through the understanding of a postmodern critique of essentialism and its ties to identities and musical categories and one that, as we shall see in chapter 1, follows in the footsteps of the truthfulness of an early pioneer of gay country and activism, Patrick Haggerty.

CHAPTER 1

QUEER COUNTRY AND SINCERITY

Nobody ever *dreamed* of accusing *Lavender Country* of being invalid. . . . [I]t was honest information about the topic.[1]

The first openly gay country album came about because Patrick Haggerty, the son of white Irish Catholic tenant dairy farmers in rural Washington, put together a band of gay and allied friends in 1972 to get out what he called "honest information" about homosexuality and Marxism.[2] Despite growing up in what he later realized was an unusually progressive and loving family for a gay child in the 1950s, he had at times experienced confusion and trauma and lacked sources of knowledge and advice from other gay people, and the mainstream media of his youth did not offer happy representations of being a gay person. Haggerty was sent to India with the Peace Corps but was kicked out for falling in love with his roommate. The situation was considered so serious that the head psychiatrist of the army questioned him and blamed his homosexuality on his working-class upbringing. Traumatized by the experience, Haggerty returned home depressed. His family doctor had him institutionalized, until a prescient night nurse told him, a week into his stay, that he was simply gay, and there was no point to him being institutionalized.[3]

Passing on "honest information" felt like a crucial project to Haggerty. The record *Lavender Country* was released in 1973 in a pressing of one thousand copies sponsored by Gay Community Social Services in Seattle (figure 1). The band advertised in gay bookstores and underground magazines and sold the record from a post-office box.[4] When asked, forty years later, to account for the album's significance, he responded, "I would like to say it's remarkable because it's such a *fabulous* album, but that would not be the truth—even though it may be. What's truer is how thirsty all of us were for any kind of information at the time. We were coming up with information, out of whole cloth, by ourselves; nobody was telling us anything about what it means to be gay. Any kind of information we could get from anywhere, we were just gobbling it up. That's what happened with *Lavender Country*."[5] To get a sense of how few out gay people there were in this period and how important their camaraderie was, Haggerty explained that in 1970, "when I met Faygele [ben Miriam]," his activist friend who would become the producer of the album, "there weren't all that many people out in Seattle—like, maybe 40 or 50. So, the circle was small, and I was in the circle and eager to meet anyone. . . . Faygele was also a radical. He wasn't just out. He was a radical. I have a very similar personality."[6] What Haggerty notes about Faygele and other collaborators in this protest movement right after the Stonewall riots of 1969 is that they were radical and intersectional in their critique of structural oppression. They did not advocate for tolerance or assimilation—they envisioned a totally restructured society not only in relation to homophobia but also regarding capitalism, racism, and sexism: "Before the gay movement was subsumed by the Democratic Party there were a lot of radicals. [One slogan was] 'go left, go gay, go pick up the gun!' It was a little ultra left [laughs], but that's what we were thinking. I was surrounded by people who were coming from a deeper appreciation for the situation we were in than just the general liberal struggle for acceptance in a capitalist world. A lot of us were after a bigger fish."[7] As for the genre he chose, Haggerty said, "I stuck with country because that's what I knew best."[8] "Maybe it was a brazen thing to do, to come out with a gay country album. On the other hand, why not? I think we forget that gay people come from everywhere. And I came from Dry Creek."[9]

To me, the most striking features of this story are that Haggerty prioritized music as a medium for sharing desperately needed knowledge.[10] His choice of genre was practical and also felt like a way to truthfully deliver "honest information," and his album was produced not by a record company but by a gay community center, with 60 percent of the proceeds donated "back into community-oriented projects for the sexual minority communities."[11] These priorities are not typical of a band trying to make a career of music.

But sharing marginalized people's stories, working for social justice, and investing in community over profit, fame, and genre norms are common values for many of the queer and transgender musicians playing the country, folk, old-time, bluegrass, and Americana music featured in this book. And, as this chapter will explore, these seemingly unusual priorities and the sense of authenticity they offer to country music are precisely why *Lavender Country* experienced a renaissance forty years after its initial release. This chapter analyzes the first out gay country album and several since then, considering the importance of sincerity in queer and transgender people's country music, including how the musicians have navigated tensions that the ideal of sincerity invokes in regard to essentialism and the role of humor and irony, particularly gay camp, in relation to their sincerity.

Haggerty's voice is both earnest and playful, invitingly singing "You all come out, come out my dears to Lavender Country," a phrase that served as the name of the band, the song, and the album, as well as suggesting an imagined genre and a physical or metaphorical space. The LP's back cover reads, "We'd like to tell you about Lavender Country. For many, it means a

Figure 1. Cover, *Lavender Country*, 1973.

27

land of fear, confusion, and loneliness; for the rest of us, it means a life of struggling towards liberation and an affirmation of Gayness."[12] Offering a mix of love and protest songs, the album intersectionally critiques white supremacist patriarchy, homophobia, and capitalism and calls listeners to rise up against the period's psychiatric mistreatment of gay people. For Haggerty, the album's central song has always been "Cryin' These Cocksucking Tears," a frank critique of homophobia that stings with the suffering and fury of being relentlessly stigmatized. Haggerty's nasal, evocative voice expresses sadness and anger in this song. Meanwhile, his lesbian band mate Eve Morris passionately sings, as *Pitchfork* writer Jayson Greene describes, in the "most earnest Joan Baez voice you've ever heard the name of the song over and over again like it's 'Blowin' in the Wind.'"[13] Both "Cryin'" and "Blowin'" offered political critique important to members of their generation, yet Bob Dylan's 1963 song was turned into the anthem of its era by folk trio Peter, Paul, and Mary, while Haggerty's 1973 song was banned from the radio and guaranteed the album's obscurity.[14]

"Cryin' These Cocksucking Tears" uses a homophobic slur to evoke a real sense of the pain being stigmatized causes gay men and in singing the slur reclaims it to fight both homophobia and misogyny. As gay drag queen country singer Trixie Mattel interpreted in 2020, "It's almost like he's using their words, like, 'Oh don't worry, don't feel too much for me, I'm just a cocksucker, right?' That's sort of the vibe, like—'this is real feelings, real hurt, and it's . . . *your word.*'"[15] The title, while evoking a typical country music theme of "cryin'" over a lost lover, is, atypically for country, both explicitly gay and also includes a word that has been debated in terms of "decency" by the United States Court of Appeals for the District of Columbia Circuit, as well as being famously lampooned by comedian George Carlin in his 1972 monologue, "Seven Words You Can Never Say on Television."[16] ("Blowin'," incidentally, is also a popular sexual term, although it has another meaning.) Haggerty's voice and lyrics evoke anger, sadness, wry gay humor, and fright. As he explained, "I was really pissed off at straight men when I wrote this song in 1972," but he also said that their hatred was "making me cry!"[17] Haggerty, who said to me that he can hear the fear in his voice on this record, explained that everyone in his activist circle was terrified in this moment but felt compelled to protest intersectionally and create artwork.[18] And among the ways he and his friends protested, this album came about to give a voice to experiences that weren't typically explored in music, especially not country. As Greene notes, the record conveys a sense of "humanity" and getting to know Haggerty. Yet Greene also pokes fun at the solemn earnestness with which Morris sings—the classically trained, well-educated, and activist singer originally from Miami sounds deadly serious as her solo voice rings out enthusiastically on the chorus "cryin' these cocksucking tears," as though as a song narrator she also identifies as a "cocksucker." As Haggerty explained over the phone to my students, Morris was a lesbian feminist and at first took offense at this song. But she eventually grew to appreciate this lyric in solidarity with gay men.[19] (One can imagine her finding feminist solidarity, since part of the reason cocksucking is considered horrifying when performed by men is because it is assumed to be "women's work.") Morris's vocal style sounds strident and courageous, reminiscent not only of Baez but also of women's music pioneers, who were sometimes erroneously depicted as humorless.

Considering this context, Greene's laughter over Morris's earnest Joan Baez–style vocal affect is striking. The comparison is reasonable. So why does it seem funny to him to use that sort of vocal style to sing this chorus while it seems solemn in the case of Baez? Or perhaps Baez's solemnity seems fabricated? What does this question have to do with the histories of folk and country music, women's music, and queer activism? Joan Baez is an icon of her generation who inspired many people to activism but also crafted a fictionalized biography to enhance her audience's awe of her difference and authenticity. She even came out as bisexual in 1973, though that identification seems little known in literature and conversation.[20] Baez's Mexican-born physicist father and her mother, who had Scotch English ancestry, raised her in a middle-class household in Palo Alto, California. After dropping out of college she became a folk star by 1959 while still a teenager, developing a riveting stage persona. Her musical performances of folk songs from working-class and racially and regionally othered peoples were consumed with utter seriousness and appreciation for her artistry and commitment. Unlike some of her fellow folk stars, Baez regularly attended protests, even in dangerous situations, such as helping integrate a Birmingham school in 1963. It's possible that Eve Morris's passionate seriousness, singing in brave recorded protest of homophobia and patriarchy, was met by a contemporary music journalist's laughter at the comparison between an unknown out lesbian singer and an iconic folk singer whose songs, though often arguing for social justice and nonviolence, rarely addressed homophobia and patriarchy.[21] But it also seems possible that Greene found Baez's earnestness laughable and Morris's adoption of Baez's style a welcome comic relief, perhaps even a gay camp send-up of Baez's famous solemnity. Meanwhile, he appreciated that Haggerty sounded "human" and "sad," "like a person alive in his own record."

This book considers the ostensibly "othered" examples of queer and transgender country and folk music since the earliest example I found, from 1939, in relation not only to relevant sexual politics of its time(s) but also to the complicated politics of folk and country music, which privileges some identities and songs and attempts to silence others. Greene's comparison of Morris and Baez brings up questions about authenticity and the purpose of folk and country music: Whose stories should be told? What sort of activism is expected or surprising in folk and country music? Who is a reliable folk or country narrator? What musical approach best conveys these messages? When are distinctions made between folk and country music, by whom, and why? In considering these questions, one might look back to the ways that early folk song collectors, publishers, archivists, and promoters, nearly all middle-class white people from coastal cities, collected music. Their goals often centered on finding a national music, one from Britain carried to the United States and preserved through presumed isolation, or finding a newly emergent US-centric folk music by those citizens presumed to be living more "primitively" than middle-class coastal city dwellers. The song collectors were often selective about what sorts of songs they wanted to collect from the targeted population. Some collectors omitted verses with language deemed "crude." Others omitted "popular" music. Many collectors initially ignored Black Americans. Their motivations for excluding different groups depended on the goal of the collection—but the effects on how the country understood working-class and rural people, whether people from Appalachia, southern prisoners, cowboys, and so on, showed evidence of nationalism, regionalism, classism, and racism. Contemporary folk and country music inherited this history, as I discuss further throughout the book.[22]

Haggerty's band sold out of records and could not afford to print more, and so after many performances during the 1970s, the band members moved on to other endeavors. Haggerty ran for office, became a social worker, formed a family, adopting a Black female friend's baby, and fathering another child with a white lesbian friend. Later he fell in love with and was eventually allowed to legally marry a Black, Philadelphia-born, career navy man. He reissued *Lavender Country* in 1999 and released a five-song follow-up in 2000, *Lavender Country Revisited*, which included three rerecorded songs from the first album and two other songs. While then professionally (for example, by Goldenrod, the women's music distributor), *Lavender Country* remained largely unknown. He was nearly seventy and performing locally to people in assisted living when he received a totally unexpected phone call from a record label asking to reissue his album. Someone had uploaded "Cryin' These Cocksucking Tears" to YouTube (a platform that Haggerty had not heard of), and Jeremy Cargill, an "aficionado" of "unheard-of Americana," found it and contacted Paradise of Bachelors, an Americana label that specializes in reissues.[23] When Haggerty received the phone call, he thought the speaker was a con artist, but after cashing his first $300 check from Paradise of Bachelors he began to cry, feeling overwhelmed that after forty years, someone in the music industry was finally taking his project seriously. Even recalling this day to me, his eyes welled with tears.

Figure 2. Lavender Country members Patrick Haggerty and Bobby Innocente. Photograph by the author, September 22, 2017, Brooklyn, NY.

Figure 3. Post:ballet dance artist Scott Marlowe. Photograph by Natalia Perez.
Lavender Country Ballet, San Francisco, 2017.

In a turn of events that has "kick[ed] [*Lavender Country*] into the strato-sphere" and reversed Haggerty's stance on the song's sweeping critique of straight white men, "Cryin' These Cocksucking Tears" has unexpectedly be-come the very reason that the album resurfaced and attracted a much larger audience.[24] Haggerty has re-created the Lavender Country band with new members (figure 2) and performed across the country. Between the 2014 re-release and the present, Haggerty has collaborated with straight, cisgender, progressive country musicians Jack Grelle, Ryan Koenig, and J. P. Harris (for the 2018 Newport Folk Festival); had a viral animated StoryCorps interview; and is featured in a South by Southwest award-winning documentary short. Post:ballet of San Francisco has created a *Lavender Country* ballet (figure 3). Producer Rob Connolly is planning a Hollywood feature film about the al-bum and his life.[25]

Haggerty agreed to an interview before his headlining performance with Brooklyn Queer Country band Karen and the Sorrows, a show in honor of their September 2017 album release (depicted in figure 2).[26] We have contin-ued to be in touch since, including two five-to-ten-hour days spent together around a June 2018 concert in Philadelphia that I helped to organize, breakfast at my home with his husband and a sister-in-law, attending Rhiannon Giddens's concert (featuring out queer Black southern gothic musician Amythyst Kiah), and regular text messages and phone calls.

During our first meeting, a two-hour interview before his 2017 Brooklyn performance, he explained his interpretation of the dramatic shift in his album's reception:

> The point is that the culture, the music culture in America flipped, it turned into its opposite. It's a dialectical thing where it's like a Marxist dialectic . . . turned into its opposite. "Turned into its opposite" is a theme throughout this whole *Lavender Country* story. "Cocksucking Tears" was the bane of *Lavender Country* for forty-five years. It was the defining song that kept it dead for forty-five years, and it was the very song that brought it rushing to life. I couldn't make any headway at all in Nashville because the straight white men in Nashville were not having a thing to do with *Lavender Country*, and they were running away from it as fast as they could. And it flipped. And now those guys wanna be seen with me. They wanna work with me. And it's not because my voice is so melodious, and it's not because my musical expertise is so fantastic—it's because I'm doing a fight, and they want to do the fight too. And they see me as an authentic, real fighter, as opposed to somebody who watered themselves down to get into Nashville. They're all sick of that. Sick to the heart of playing that game. These straight white men in country music, one after the other after the other after the other, are basically coming up to me and saying, "We are so sick, we are so desperate for any goddamn thing that shines authentically," because it's so steeped in phoniness and glitz and glamor and making sure that you say the right things today.[27]

Haggerty witnessed this major shift in cultural values in response to the album's most provocative song. He pointed out that the element that originally repelled industry stakeholders (that the album critiques patriarchal, heteronormative, and capitalist society and promotes the well-being of nonheteronormative people) is the same reason why it now appeals to certain industry stakeholders.[28] His album, which had previously seemed unacceptable as country music, now beckons to some industry insiders as truly "authentic." While these music industry insiders might deem other current country music as phony and watered down for being influenced by market research or conservative sponsors, they see Haggerty as a hero for continuing to fight the good fight.[29] These debates about country authenticity prompt reflection about why country appealed to Haggerty in 1973 and what it means for this particular album to be revived today as part of a political and aesthetic battle. To describe this development, he uses the term "Marxist dialectic," meaning an element that contains its opposite and that draws truth from understanding the relationship of the contradiction it holds. So in this case, although the song was initially written as a rebellion against straight culture, within the song were opportunities to *both* repel *and* attract straight white male music industry stakeholders. Their reactions to this critique depended on their outlook and the timing.

Haggerty's understanding of why some music industry workers began to want to join his "fight" stems from his observations of changing reactions to the bigotry of the mainstream country music industry and the election of Donald Trump as US president in 2016. Haggerty says that the country music industry CEOs he has encountered are bigots and crass opportunists who are insincere about their relationship to Christianity, the religion that is deeply tied to country music for many mainstream listeners. He describes some of the executives he encountered as closeted gay people, and he notes that he knows that they have worked to stifle his projects (for example, a withdrawn invitation to play in Nashville Pride and the suspicious timing of the firing of an author who had just published an article about out country musicians). Meanwhile, his impression has been that the musicians are not bigots. And he also gets the sense that they're frustrated with being limited in their political expression, especially given that they can barely make a living in this industry by toeing the line: "Most of them aren't making any money—they're jerking lattes—*and* they have to follow the [bigoted, conservative, watered-down] script."[30] He explains that the people in the music industry who have been reaching out to him are in their late thirties and forties and grew up with more progressive views of identity and difference, and they now find themselves in a state of disgust during the recent years of backlash against progressive changes in US culture:

They're [referring to the progressive music industry employees] all on board. They all get it about human rights; they all put their shit together about gay and lesbian rights in the eighties and nineties. They're not threatened by it. They're not threatened by people who aren't white, because they know the best music comes from Black people. Any half-baked idiot knows that, so how can you be a fuckin' racist and be a musician when the best music is coming [from] that dynamic, right? Anybody who can think knows that. And they know when they're sixteen, "Well, I can't be a racist and do this music." It's easy to put together. So that's who's there. Now, here comes Trump. And all of these straight white men in the music industry are going, "Fuck this. I want to do battle. We have to take up this cause. I need to distinguish myself from the industry by showing what side I'm on, because I'm sick of this shit, and I want to stand up."

It took the interest of these straight people who had not seen themselves as activists until recently to propel Haggerty's 1970s gay Marxist critique into the spotlight forty years after its first release. For some progressive music industry professionals connected with country and Americana, Haggerty's message seemed authentic because he had not watered it down in order to be accepted by the industry. But he took pains to explain to me that this new popularity of his album does not make him the most radical or important contemporary queer musician:

It's not that gay people don't love *Lavender Country* and haven't loved *Lavender Country*, they do, and it's not that lesbians didn't know about *Lavender Country*, and a lot of them love *Lavender Country*, they do, but we never did have the power, nor does the gay community now have the power, to turn someone into a star. It's not how the gay community operates. The mechanisms are not in place to do that. You understand all that, right? . . . You can't misquote me on this, because it's really important, because transsexual, transgender, creative people of color are leading the pack in radical music right now. The point is that these two straight white men discovered *Lavender Country*, and so they ran a label, and so when you put out something on your label, you call the press, and you call your buddies, and you tell them what you're doing. That's what happens. One straight white guy in the music industry went to the next one and the next one and the next one.

In Haggerty's experience, gay listeners and industry insiders do not have the power to propel gay acts to stardom. In fact, he mentioned that the gay venues often ask him to perform for free and that he more typically makes money

35

playing shows at straight venues. These venues and industry members have become much friendlier to him lately. With the surge of interest in democratic socialism fueled in part by Bernie Sanders's 2016 presidential campaign, straight cisgender progressive white men in country and Americana looking to collaborate musically to make a political and artistic statement found Haggerty's sustained Marxist, antiracist, and feminist critique appealing. He realizes that his whiteness, maleness, and advanced age made him appear a less threatening choice for them than allying with queer and trans artists of color. He told me about his longtime collaborator and friend Blackberri, a Black, gay, award-winning, Bay Area activist and singer-songwriter who is Haggerty's age. Haggerty and his husband, J.B., wanted me to know that Blackberri's music is more revolutionary and musically sophisticated than Haggerty's.[31] Haggerty teared up telling me that Blackberri's music has not received the attention that Haggerty has. But through his second album, Haggerty was able to feature Blackberri's cheerful Marxist blues song "Eat the Rich."[32]

Haggerty is certain that his Marxism repelled "the gay Democrats" (whom he identifies as "petit bourgeois"), who ignored and refused platforms for his music and his message for forty years, preferring to feature musicians whose message was based in notions of visibility, tolerance, and assimilation into heteronormative society.[33] He cites several instances, including a proposed gig in Nashville, where one person approached him to do a show, and that person's (often closeted) gay or lesbian boss quashed the idea. Haggerty noted that Chris Dickinson, the author of an article on gay country, was fired from her position as editor of the *Journal of Country Music Studies* three months after the article was published in 1999. Haggerty has found more camaraderie and support from some straight white cisgender men in country and Americana and "anarcho punks" who do not care what genre he plays than he has with "the gay Democrats." When Paradise of Bachelor's Brendan Greaves and Christopher Smith were preparing *Lavender Country* for rerelease, they asked Haggerty if they should approach anyone in "the gay community" about this project to get their blessing. Haggerty was relieved that they asked him, because he anticipated that, if they were asked, the gay Democrats would silence his message yet again.

Further, Haggerty needed the support of straight white men. As he explained, gay people have never had the power that straight white men have had in catapulting someone to stardom. And in fact, I saw this at work in my attempts to book a show for Lavender Country, My Gay Banjo, and Paisley Fields in Philadelphia in the summer of 2018. The one local band, My Gay Banjo, approached me for help booking a venue and explained that they had never had luck being able to book a show at a venue in Philadelphia. (This explained why in Philadelphia I had only previously heard them at house concerts or, once, in a warehouse, whereas in Brooklyn they play at two different bars that regularly host queer country events.)[34] I wrote to every popular and folk music venue I could think of and heard back from just two, and neither was the usual space for queer performances. The first was the Philadelphia Folk Song Society, which ultimately failed to follow through, despite my urging that it could use this event to attract new young queer listeners. The second was PhilaMOCA (the Philadelphia Mausoleum of Contemporary Art), a former mausoleum showroom repurposed by famous popular musician Diplo to be run as a nonprofit arts space. The concert was ultimately held there, hosted enthusiastically by the venue's married cis-gender straight white manager. Turnout was mostly comprised of roughly twenty of Haggerty's Roxborough-based in-laws, twenty of my students and friends, and twenty of My Gay Banjo's local audience, who are mostly West Philadelphia–based queer and trans activists in their twenties and thirties.

Haggerty makes a point to remind himself of his continuing political goals in order to stay focused during this newfound fame, in which his collaborators and audience have wanted him to emerge as an elder gay icon.[35] This stardom impulse risks making invisible the communal effort that originally created the band and the album:

> It was a few months ago when I incorporated all this buzz, which is basically bourgeois buzz, about *Lavender Country* and all that it's done to me and how it's warped my personality and all that other bullshit people in my position go through. I'm laying in my bed, and a solid peace comes over my body when I realize all that is incidental fluff. Stardom really, truly is a capitalist plot, it reeks of traps, and you wrote *Lavender Country* to get the movement going and to transform society in the first place. That's why you thumbed your nose at Nashville and wrote *Lavender Country* instead. You made that decision to make *Lavender Country* to help change the world. That's why you did it, that's why you denied yourself a career in country music, that's why you've led the life you've led, that's the reason that you wrote *Lavender Country*. And that's the reason that people wanna hear it.

And it's like, "Oh. I get to do *Lavender Country* for the damn reason I wrote it in the first place. Let's go!"

Haggerty's experience of suddenly being sought after in his seventies by members of an industry that for forty years wanted nothing to do with him has been life altering. He had a sense of who he was and what he was doing at this stage in his life, and this new attention has changed that. While thrilled to be able to have this much larger platform for the political critiques he's developed over his lifetime, as well as to pay tribute to his late father for his loving acceptance of a gay son, he is concerned about how a Hollywood film or touring with a more high-profile musical act might affect his political message or its reception.[36]

Haggerty's unlikely success story confirms to him that the Nashville executives' pressure on musicians to conform to the lucrative conservative image feels empty to many of these musicians. (He felt especially bad for those working as baristas while also feeling compelled to deliver the industry's message.) But while he feels that the mainstream country music industry stifles its musicians, he also pointed out that his choice of genre was crucial in terms of setting the tone of his radical Marxist gay politics and for the resurgence of this album decades later:

> And frankly, the genre that I picked was another reason that *Lavender Country* lay fallow for forty-five years, but it's also squarely one of the reasons why it's being jettisoned from the pack. That dialectic turned into its opposite, too. The fact that it is country sets my radicalness so far apart, because I wasn't trying to act like David Bowie. Don't get me wrong, I haven't a thing against David Bowie. He did a huge amount of work. He moved a weight a distance for all of us, and he was very brave to do it. He still came at the subject obliquely, . . . and he got away with it! Well, honey, I wasn't oblique, so I might as well've been country. It's a genre where you get to tell the truth. Or it used to be.[37]

"COUNTRY MUSIC IS THREE CHORDS AND THE TRUTH"

In saying that country is "a genre where you get to tell the truth," Haggerty drew on a common understanding of this music as a genre in which honest communication is expected and songs represent real people, places, experiences, and values. He described his 1973 album in terms of its message's validity and honesty, saying, "Nobody ever *dreamed* of accusing *Lavender Country* of being invalid. It was valid information; it sure was. It still is, for that matter. That's what people loved about it—it was honest information about the topic."[38] Sincerity is a central facet of country music, but this value is also rife with contradictions, particularly given sincerity's ties to essentialism, the belief that identity is fixed from birth. Country music is a performed art, and any performance, even an autobiographical one, is also partly fictional. Yet this essentialism is in such demand that musicians take pains to demonstrate their connections to rural, working-class culture, whether that's the culture they were born into or not. Esteemed country songwriter Harlan Howard is famously thought to have said that "country music is three chords and the truth."[39] This often-repeated appraisal of country music is attractive for highlighting an accessible simplicity and appealing sincerity. Country writer Jimmie N. Rogers refers to the expectation that country music communicates honestly with listeners as "the sincerity contract."[40] This belief is long-standing and tied to an understanding that this music addresses working-class and rural life. As influential midcentury singer-songwriter Hank Williams said, "[The hillbilly] sings more sincere than most entertainers because [he] was raised rougher than most entertainers. You got to know a lot about hard work. You got to have smelt a lot of mule manure before you can sing like a hillbilly." Williams repeated elsewhere: "You have to plow a lot of ground and look at the back side of a mule for a lot of years to sing a country song."[41] The first statement addresses the issue of sincerity in country music, claiming that its singers must have personally experienced hardship from working-class, rural life in order to be able to "sing like a hillbilly." Both quotes mention farm labor, setting up a tension, because throughout his life Williams suffered from a painful condition called spina bifida occulta that made even standing painful, and so he would have been unable to complete the plowing he describes as requisite for country music performance. In fact, this condition was one of the reasons he pursued music as a source of income (an occupation that certainly requires "hard work" in its own right).[42] Yet it seems likely that for a number of reasons, including poverty, back pain, and addiction, he experienced enough agony and exhaustion to be able to sing from experience about rural, working-class suffering.

Williams's statements helped solidify an important piece of the rhetoric of country music, as sociologist Richard Peterson argues in his influential book

Creating Country Music: Fabricating Authenticity. Early in the development of the country music industry, records were often produced by people who had no direct knowledge of (or, sometimes, appreciation for) country music and also were not familiar with the region in which they were recording. Thus their expectations of the musicians' identities were shaped by stereotypes of working-class, rural, and mountain people and an impression that they were entirely different from the producers' imagined stereotypes of Black southern people, whose music was sold as "race records."[43] As Peterson details, industry encouragement of over-the-top costumes of "old mountain men" and, later, "hillbillies" fueled these stereotypes. Yet early country musicians arrived from across the region, including from city homes, in studios and performance venues dressed in several different ways but often in their best professional clothing. Jimmie Rodgers, for example, appeared early on dressed in a suit, later as "the singing brakeman" railroad engineer (despite not having worked in such a role in real life), and finally as a cowboy. In Peterson's view, Williams's iconic career marked the establishment of this music as a major commercial genre based in Nashville with an industry of professionals working to support it, and so Williams helped strengthen the contradictory rhetoric surrounding authenticity and sincerity in the heart of this genre.[44] As Joli Jensen elaborates, country music has always been an urban music about rural living and a commercial music attempting to hide that it was commercial, so it has always provoked anxiety about its authenticity.[45]

As ideals for human existence, "authenticity" and "sincerity" describe dimensions of realness, honesty, and human value that are perceived to be unchanging and apolitical. These concepts are deeply appealing for engaging some of the representation, storytelling, and wisdom people hear and see in musical performance. Yet marginalized people are often distrusted, devalued, and scapegoated by these paradigms. As typically understood, authenticity rests on assumptions of bodily essentialism that defend often-harmful stereotypes, creating problems with some popular ways of understanding human identity and culture. These stereotypes are thus of interest (and potential threat) to country musicians and queer and transgender people, especially to queer and transgender country musicians.

"Sincerity's claim is precisely that it is a mode of self-expression generally held to be nondiscursive, transparent, and outside of ideology," performance scholar and playwright Jane Taylor writes. She prompts us to consider "what is being masked by that set of assumptions."[46] This chapter has already addressed two cases of country music's concealed ideologies of sincerity—the case of early folk song collectors' selective archive and its legacy of what sort of person and song and story counts as folk music, and the overly exacting demands of a country musician's regional and class background and additional or former occupation in order to be trusted singing a country song—and one less "oblique" ideology of sincerity in country music in which this music could, and should, communicate class and sexuality critique. The first two examples suggest that poor and rural people have special kinds of music, and the third makes a case for this music including a critique of forces of oppression. Yet the ideologies of sincerity and authenticity as they are used both in country music and to ascertain human value are also used as forms of violence against nonnormative people.

The expectations (or demands) of truth and transparency differ for transgender and queer people onstage compared to cisgender and straight country and roots musicians onstage. Straight and cisgender musicians can be exposed for pretending to be from "the country" when they are from an area not presumed to be a region or socioeconomic class trusted for playing country or roots music. (For example, critics have scrutinized early twenty-first-century straight cisgender Americana star Gillian Welch's upbringing. While the singer-songwriter and instrumentalist's musical and sartorial style often recall the working-class, Depression era image and sound of the Carter Family, Welch, who was adopted, was raised in relative privilege in Los Angeles and was introduced to bluegrass while attending college at the University of California, Santa Cruz.) But that sort of exposure of presumed trespassing, appropriation, or even hillbilly-face is not nearly as dangerous as queer and trans people being outed against their wishes or made to feel unwelcome or unsafe by people who work in or are consumers of their profession. Yet queer and trans people are expected to out themselves regularly lest they appear to be hiding something. This presumption of a simple and unchanging descriptor as a key to someone's "real" identity suggests some of the essentialism at play in discussion of gender and sexuality. One older etymological use of "queer" was to describe counterfeit currency, as though one was trying to pass off something deemed "false" as being of equal value. There may be some overlap with use of the term to describe sexuality and gender. For example, we might consider in this light the "bad copy" theory of homosexuality, a common and derogatory misunderstanding that same-gender couples are trying but failing to copy heterosexual gender roles. This definition, which philosopher Judith Butler has persuasively argued against in her famous work, suggests that a queer person is not only somehow "untrustworthy" or "forged" but also "worthless."[47]

The formulation of sincerity traditionally depends on a notion of inner truth (or "authenticity") expressed outward. Thus, not only authenticity but also sincerity appear to be essentialized and in this way conflict with postmodern understanding of identity in which divisions between types of people seem to be products of complex ecologies in which we exist, more so than based in essential physical difference. Thus, a sincere performance of country or folk music or a sincere queer or trans person both imply a tension within the meaning of these important, sometimes life-threatening terms. In certain cases, displaying inauthenticity playing country music is depicted as potentially life-threatening, for example, in the movie Deliverance's "Dueling Banjos" (1972), although as literature scholar Anna Creadick discusses, the film's scene of male-male competition replaces the book's moment of homosocial intimacy between Banjo Boy (an Appalachian and possibly disabled character) and the wealthy urban vacationer guitarist.[48] Moments like this and like Patrick Haggerty's description of choosing country as the medium for his message, when debates around authenticity and sincerity collide in queer and transgender performances of country and folk music, prompt consideration of how these terms became woven into our discourse about the central facets of human identity and artistic value.

Sincerity was originally a term used to describe the purity and value of objects. Jane Taylor argues that in the sixteenth-century European Reformation, "Sincerity arises in order to resolve the problem of the forced confession" for a culture that lacked the concept of evidence.[49] Taylor contextualizes a cultural shift regarding people's access to print and theater in which people played roles different from their own societal position, as well as a change allowing multiple interpretations of the Bible and literature. These developments contributed to enormous societal flux. As literary critic Lionel Trilling traced in his 1969 Charles Eliot Norton Lectures on sincerity and authenticity, sixteenth- and seventeenth-century European society became concerned about the seeming dishonesty and influence of theater.[50] Actors could persuade an audience to feel certain emotions without feeling that way themselves. Or the actor might lose sight of himself and become influenced by a role, which was considered risky for honest actors playing villains, a poor person playing nobility, or a Jewish person playing a Catholic. There was deep anxiety about the new societal changes creating possibility for class mobility and religious conversion. Philosophers worried that this role-playing could confuse and "corrupt" the actors. But people began to realize that society requires us all to play roles, as twentieth-century social science scholarship has researched more fully: "Drawing on [Erving] Goffman, Trilling observes how the fascination with theater led to an awareness of role play in life and to the realization that role play compromises sincerity. Yet if the norms of behavior required insincerity, the question arose whether, underneath these demands of civilization, layers of uncorrupted selfhood could be found."[51]

Postmodernist theorists understood that role-playing was not only part of acting but also a daily and often unconscious reality for everyone. Through thinking about social roles in this way, they deconstructed biased essentialist assumptions, reexamining human difference and hierarchy through the histories of language, social norms, religion, medicine, education, art, and the law. This cultural shift in understanding such basic principles of human difference has also witnessed greater attention to gender and sexual ways of being set against normalized expectations. While people have experienced same-sex desire and challenged birth-assigned binary gender roles throughout most cultures and times, recent scholarship situates sexual and gender roles as socially constructed rather than rooted solely in an inherent bodily essence.[52]

The notion of role-playing and interpretation felt dangerous because, as literary scholars Ernst van Alphen and Mieke Bal explain, "Sincerity is considered fundamentally corporeal rather than textual. Within such logic, truth is enacted through the body and imagined as an integrated semiotic field. Beyond the truth that is stated, this field includes the unwittingly emitted signs of the body."[53] Van Alphen and Bal thus note that the concept of sincerity may be unavailable to or used against Othered people. Authenticity and sincerity are wound up in the ways that this culture thinks about sexual coming out and transgender narratives. Transgender and some queer people are regularly asked to account for their gender identification in a way not asked of most people.[54] Demands of truth expect that there is such an inherent, coherent, unchanging, and knowable truth to each person, an assumption challenged by much transgender and intersex studies scholarship, which demonstrates how gender and sexuality categories have been shaped by a range of ideologies and assumptions. Medical bioethicist Katrina Karkazis's work with international sports organizations on the issue of determining competitors' "sex" demonstrates that our understandings of sex are deeply flawed and unable to meet this demand.[55] Sociologist Sonny Nordmarken describes cisgender strangers' demands for transgender people to identify themselves as a "desire" to "possess" the "Truth" about someone else's identity, a pursuit that assumes gender is stationary for all people, that imagines there is some kind of universal truth about gender, and that offers little regard for the feelings of the person whose gender is being questioned.[56] There may be unequal reactions by normative people to revelations from speakers about sexuality versus gender identity. Gay and lesbian people's coming out may suggest to listeners that they have learned something more true about the speaker; given comparable disclosures by transgender people, listeners may conclude that they have been deceived.[57] Mainstream corporatized gay and lesbian rights organizations argue that gay and lesbian people are no different from straight people, except for what they do in the bedroom. (Their focus on marriage marks a major departure from gay liberation movements' calls for dismantling oppressive structures for all humans.) Thus a disclosure of being gay or lesbian might feel like a trusting sharing of private intimate information that may now seem compatible with straight people's understandings of relationships. For example, in an Instagram post 12 January 2017, CMT host Cody Alan said he was "still the same Cody. . . . You just know a little more about me." This sharing may encourage the listener to feel closer to the speaker.[58] In comparison, when a transgender person discloses that he or she is transgender, the listener may get the sense that he or she has been actively and intentionally "deceived," a misinterpretation of transgender experience that rests on an idea of the gender assigned at birth as the "truth" of a person's existence.[59] Jane Taylor writes that "a lingering preoccupation for modernity [is] the desire that the body be an unambiguous signifier for truth."[60] Even in postmodernity, the expectation of this bodily signification of "truth" extends to the perceived gendering of a person's voice. Musicologist Stephan Pennington writes with irony, "At a time when the relationship between bodies and identities is ever more complex, the voice is clung to as the locus of essential, non-alterable gender 'truth.' The eyes may deceive, but the voice never lies."[61] Pennington's work demonstrates the broad overlap between the sounds of cisgender men's and cisgender women's voices, as well as the multiple independent elements working to establish people's perspectives of someone's vocal character. These elements have been of special importance to transgender women, as one may wish to retrain her voice to communicate a persona different from the one she was encouraged to develop as a child.

"The truth" and "realness" are concepts in use by and about many transgender and queer people in both affirming and abusive ways. "Real" is worked into titles of several creative works, notably, famous trans journalist Janet Mock's autobiography, *Redefining Realness: My Path to Womanhood, Identity, Love and So Much More* (2014). Transgender musician Ben Wallace's first album and the subsequent documentary about his transition were both titled *Real Boy* (2013 and 2016). When Americana musician Joe Stevens discusses the subject of the musical theater production he cowrote, he talks about historical figure Albert Cashier's "truth."[62] This is a concept over which queer theory has split with the discourse of some queer and transgender people. For the most part, queer theory has challenged "realness" and "truth" because they are typically wielded against queers by a mainstream that defines these terms through an invented essentialism that upholds the hierarchies that keep oppressed people differentiated. Yet transgender studies has divided here from queer theory in claiming the material experiences that they believe queer theory resists. Andre Cavalcante's ethnography of transgender people and their engagement with media explores the appeal that ordinary life has for them.[63] While some transgender people are also queer (in terms of sexuality and/or in terms of politics) the twentieth century's medicalized dealings with trans existence included only heteronormative options for trans patients (many of whom may have desired those gender options, but others who have been oppressed by those limited options). Gender studies scholar Jack Halberstam's *Trans*: A Quick and Quirky Account of Gender Variability* maintains that transgender existence is in keeping with queer politics of antinormativity. "Realness" is also often used to idealize financially oppressed people, as Roxane Gay explains in a *New York Times* opinion piece about the (subsequently canceled) 2018 reboot of the *Roseanne* TV series: "When a lot of mainstream media talks about working-class people, there is a tendency to romanticize their lives and to idealize them as the most 'authentic' Americans. They are 'real' and their problems are 'real' problems, as if everyone else is dealing with artificial obstacles." Gay goes on to specify that this idealized "realness" only extends to white working-class people.[64]

"DON'T BE FOOLED BY THE BEARD;
IT WAS EXPENSIVE"

Whether a musician or band "comes out" as part of their regular performance routine depends on several factors. For many musicians, there is a financial and safety incentive *not* to disclose a nonheteronormative sexual or gender identification, and, frankly, it is nobody's business. But because of their appearance, their sound, their choice of band mates, their choice of genre, their desire to share their politics, or even their band name, not all of these musicians can or even want to keep this information a secret. For the band My Gay Banjo, based in Philadelphia, the musicians' queerness is a welcomed given and the banjo can "play a song for me and my kind." But the (now disbanded) California-based band Coyote Grace (figure 4) would need to use a combination of stage banter and choice of certain songs in order to discuss their identification and politics with their listeners.

Coyote Grace's singer-songwriter and multi-instrumentalist Joe Stevens has identified as a transgender man since 2004 and transitioned with testosterone and top surgery (gender-affirming breast removal). Among transgender artists in the United States, Stevens is widely known as path-breaking—he was very actively outspoken as a transgender man and artist, looking for mentors and finding very few and so sharing his experience at a time when many people were just learning about this identification and when people, including transgender people looking for community, shared their life experiences extensively via the internet and, eventually, social media. I have worked with these musicians since 2010, traveling to their shows in several states and hosting them in my classes at Stanford and Temple Universities. Stevens explained to me that he constantly disclosed his identity as a transgender and queer musician for political and artistic reasons: because he is often perceived as a straight and cisgender man and because his (now former) band mate Ingrid Elizabeth is femme (a queer identification that can be indiscernible to many straight people), the band could seem cisgender and straight to unknowing audiences. But very importantly for the band, Stevens's and Elizabeth's sense of the cultural heritage of their music was queer: rebelling against heteronormative assumptions about life and happiness is crucial to both musicians, and Stevens's early socialization as female and young adult identification as queer included learning songs by lesbian singer-songwriters such as the Indigo Girls and Melissa Ferrick, with both of whom he would later go on tour. In 2017, reminiscing on Facebook about his first national tour with Coyote Grace, he posted a photo of a reunion with fellow queer singer-songwriter and now rock guitarist friend Courtney Robbins, who was "the Emily to my Amy," referring to their college-era friendship and musicking while imagining that they might grow up to be like their idols, Indigo Girls' Emily Saliers and Amy Ray. Stevens feels a sense of difference with cisgender straight male musicians who typically developed a different repertoire of songs. Stevens explained to me and my students that he might sit in a song circle at a folk festival or hippie gathering with a group of cisgender men and realize that he doesn't know any of the songs they're suggesting.[65] Touring with the Indigo Girls over the course of 2010 was a dream come true for Coyote Grace. Yet it felt somewhat painful to Stevens and Elizabeth that they needed to explain to the audience each night why this experience was so magical to a band that looked like it might be comprised of two straight cisgender people. The band was used to these explanations, though. While Coyote Grace played many "mainstream" (straight) bars, festivals, and other venues, their income often depended on capitalizing on their queerness by being booked by venues such as university LGBT centers, Pride festivals, progressive churches, and community organizations on the assumption that Stevens and Elizabeth would play their more explicitly queer and trans-themed songs and educate the audience, often also offering workshops such as "Trans 101," "Transitioning Together" (they were a couple during Stevens's transition), sexual pleasure, and songwriting.

Stevens's most requested and known song is "A Guy Named Joe," which explores his gender transition in veiled language and rural natural imagery that could protect Stevens while performing in an unfriendly environment. However, Stevens's usual stage banter before the song announced, "This song will probably make more sense if you know that I'm trans. Don't be fooled by the beard; it was expensive."[66] This short introduction of his earned identity as transgender explained that it came at considerable emotional and monetary cost. Stevens had suffered with self-medication with alcohol for trans issues that had become addiction for more than half of his life. He began to see himself as a masculine singer-songwriter when he was sent to a girls' reform boarding school, where he was isolated from society and media and introduced to peers who had developed even more dangerous habits than his. He had access to a guitar, sounded out songs that he remembered, and developed a sense of the enjoyable possibilities of his persona when he attracted the romantic interest of girls at school. But the school punished this positive attention he received for his "gender rebellion" and forced him to adopt a high-maintenance feminine hairstyle in order to require him to spend extra time on heteronormative grooming. While he left the reform schools and attended summer music training, as well as studied music at Cornish College for the Arts in Seattle, he has continued to battle the addiction he developed as a teenager, coping with a gender identity he did not yet have words for or social skills to navigate. Thus it seems important, if challenging, to him to craft stage banter to introduce some of the issues that his autobiographical songs engage. Discussing his life story may offer points of connection for those audience members unfamiliar with trans life experience but familiar with music that explores personal troubles, often about addiction, journey, family, love, and financial trouble, factors that may each impact achievement of North American ideals of manhood and adulthood.

Stevens's word choice in describing his identification, however, risked suggesting that trans people are trying to fool people and risked naturalizing cisgender identity within a system that casts transgender people as false copies. Accusations of deception can lead to violence against trans people. Yet the expectation that one will out oneself, in keeping with mainstream lesbian and gay advocacy campaigns, leaves transgender people with an uncomfortable choice. They may constantly out themselves as trans, in which case they may be celebrated either as queer or, conversely, as upholding the heteronormative gender binary. Finally, a transgender man's disclosure of an earlier period in life identifying as a lesbian may be critiqued as taking advantage. (Because some lesbian feminists view anyone assigned female at birth as always being womyn-born, some transgender men are more accepted in women-only spaces than transgender women, yet at the same time transgender men tend to benefit from male privilege.) Or they may not out themselves, in which case some radical queer people might interpret their identities as harmfully reinforcing the heteronormative gender binary. But if a transgender person incorporates some mixed-gendered references in their identity (whether as a nonbinary person or as an effeminate man or masculine woman) or simply identifies themselves specifically as transgender rather than as a man or woman, they may face criticism from some other transgender people. For example, I was talking with Stevens at Coyote Grace's merchandise table in Newport in 2010, after they opened for the Indigo Girls, when a disgruntled listener questioned Stevens's word choice of "be[ing] fooled" and asked why Stevens calls himself a trans man and not simply a man, as this listener, also transgender, described himself.[67] To this listener, Stevens's way of describing his identity made transgender identity sound, to this listener at least, like Stevens was not a "real" man. While Stevens realizes that he cannot make every listener happy and has omitted this line in more recent stage banter, he also continues to incorporate reference to his youth when he was considered a girl. After transition he had an XX tattooed on his forearm (figure 5), offering a visible signal of his transgender identity, if a coded and ambiguous one, given that this reference to chromosomes could either challenge or support gender essentialism. Because people see and hear Stevens as being a cisgender man, this tattooed reminder of his being assigned female at birth could suggest defiance of gender assignments based on chromosomes; conversely, the tattoo could be understood as a way to share and honor his time lived as female-identified and the ways it has impacted his life and music, a sentiment that has, as I have discussed above, elicited criticism among some listeners. But Stevens has continued to take further steps publicly discussing his past, even when it means describing other people seeing and hearing him as a "girl."

During 2012–13, documentary director Shaleece Haas filmed Stevens interacting with his younger mentee, Ben Wallace, a trans man also in recovery for addiction and interested in writing music. The film includes a scene where Stevens's mother discusses his childhood and even uses his "dead name" in describing that young and then-female-identified person. The practice of using a transgender person's former name is typically deeply discouraged (seeming to "out" them, allowing listeners access to parts of that person's past that they may not want aired, creating potential for traumatic interactions in which someone intentionally harms them by calling them by their old name, etc.). During Coyote Grace's time, new listeners would sometimes approach Stevens after a show and ask what his name used to be, and Ingrid Elizabeth would intervene and say that this information had to be "earned" through getting to know Stevens. But Stevens shared this name publicly before the film's premiere, choosing at that moment to release a remastered recording of his pretransition college senior recital, featuring some songs his fans would recognize from their later iterations in Coyote Grace's repertoire.[68]

Figure 4. Publicity photograph, Coyote Grace.

Figure 5. Joe Stevens's XX tattoo. Photograph by Stevens, 2015,
reproduced with permission.

"MY BIG FEAR WAS THAT IT WOULD BE IRONIC"

Cultural studies and comparative literature scholar Cesare Casarino and German studies scholar Leslie A. Adelson both argue that, given the standard assumption of a stable "truth" to each person, despite decades of postmodern dismantling of notions of enlightenment humanist conceptions of a unified self and of essentialism, subaltern subjects may instead shift away from the concept of sincerity. Subaltern subjects may either not be believed to be capable of sincerity or, due to others' biased reception of them, refuse the concept.[69] Thus some transgender and queer performers' use of irony as an aesthetic challenge to assumptions of essentialism should not be surprising. Irony is often considered a challenge or even threat to sincerity, perhaps particularly for queer and transgender people. For example, Karen Pittelman, lead singer and songwriter of Karen and the Sorrows, a country band originally comprised of queer and trans musicians (membership has since changed), discussed with the website *Vice* about starting a regular queer country night at a Brooklyn bar: "My big fear was that it would be ironic. . . . But everybody was so earnest. People were crying and saying that this was the music they grew up with and that they never thought there would be a place where they could listen to it and feel like themselves."[70] Pittelman finds her audience's tears to be proof of their sincere appreciation for this music and relief at the opportunity to "feel like themselves" while also connecting with a piece of their childhood. Not surprisingly, considering the name of her band, sadness is a mainstay in Karen and the Sorrows' repertoire, with songs about heartbreak, as well as those reflecting on her experiences as a Jewish woman and her grandparents' immigration to the United States. While one doesn't immediately think of Jewish themes in country music, she uses the country themes and sentiments of loneliness, abjection, and displacement to explore immigrant experience and biblical stories—as she introduced, "This is a song I wrote about Moses parting the Red Sea and feeling sad at the Egyptian soldiers who are left to die."[71]

But the somber quality of some of these bands' performances was suspect to one audience member, Emily, who was attending Queer Country Quarterly on November 19, 2016, for the first time after having recently moved to Brooklyn from Oklahoma. While she was busy embracing her partner at the show, she was also excited about my project and kept leaning over to comment to me about features of the performance that stood out to her. She noted confidently that the audience's sad appreciation for the music was out of place with country audiences back home. She thought the tenor of the audience seemed too morose in comparison with the Tumble Weed Café, where Garth Brooks got his start, saying that in rural country venues, when sad music is performed the audience responds with a jovial transcendence (like the blues). Interestingly, when the featured act of that night's performance took the stage, Sam Gleaves and Tyler Hughes, out gay Appalachian musicians (or, as Gleaves sometimes calls himself, "fabulachian"), the tenor of the evening seemed to change from sadness to joy, even though the show was taking place a week after the election of Donald Trump as president and the lives of the everyone in the room were likely about to change for the worse.[72] Pittelman's concern about her concert series appearing ironic is intriguing, given that much queer performance engages with the form of queer irony and aesthetics known as camp.

The term "camp" is defined as "exaggerated in a knowing or playful way" by the *Oxford English Dictionary*.[73] While early uses of the word referred to gay men as "camps," it developed into a term to describe a practice and aesthetic, a gay way of seeing the world. An early reference to this usage of the term is by English American novelist Christopher Isherwood, who in 1954's *The World in the Evening* described camp as not only a homosexual style but also a "sensibility." Anthropologist Esther Newton, in her pioneering 1972 study of drag queens, defined camp by drawing on ethnomusicologist Charles Keil's understanding of "soul" in Black American culture, "a strategy for a situation," and a sensibility that navigated what sociologist Erving Goffman calls the "spoiled identity" of homosexuality in the era of the closet.[74] To Newton, camp taste creates "incongruity, theatricality, and humor," which mark the distinction between straight and gay culture.[75] Camp allowed coded communication between gay people and could also be used to discharge tension through humor and charm in some dangerous scenarios with straight people, including police.[76] During different moments, straight culture has caught on to camp, and some queer people and scholars saw mainstream embrace as emptying camp's radical queer politics. For example, musicologist Raymond Knapp's scholarship analyzing late nineteenth-century operettas by Gilbert and Sullivan and mid- to late twentieth-century films by Roger Vadim and Mel Brooks (works that "bookend" the height of gay camp) identifies straight "mainstreaming" of camp with use of "homophobic humor and a strong predilection toward using music as a signifier of gay 'excess.'"[77]

Pittelman's 2015 concern, voiced after her very first iteration of her Queer Country series, seems to understand irony (perhaps including camp irony) as working at cross-purposes with country music's, and perhaps also queer people's, expressions of sincerity. Yet popular country music television show *Hee Haw* and the style of avowedly heterosexual cisgender star Dolly Parton can certainly be described as camp.[78] Further, it's possible to imagine that camp may not always be working in opposition to sincerity. Camp values subjects, practices, and styles discarded by current mainstream culture by using heightened emotion and coded humor. This appreciation may be sincere, although sincerity is not typically included in discussion of camp. Innovative nineteenth-century camp artist, poet, and playwright Oscar Wilde argued that masks allow people to reveal the truth.[79] Isherwood writes, "You can't camp about something you don't take seriously. You're not making fun of it; you're making fun *out* of it. You're expressing what's basically serious to you in terms of fun and artifice and elegance."[80] While American critical theorist Susan Sontag encouraged a sense of opposition between sincerity and camp by writing that "one is drawn to Camp when one realizes that 'sincerity' is not enough," queer theorist Ann Pellegrini explores a concept she calls "camp sincerity" in a persuasive essay that rethinks the personal, affective, and political elements of Susan Sontag's famous and criticized essays on camp, which featured changing impressions and cryptically autobiographical theorizing.[81] Pellegrini finds that Sontag, in order to disguise personal feelings of vulnerability she felt as a closeted queer Jewish writer, drew an unnecessary line between gay male aesthetic camp and Jewish, as well as lesbian, moral seriousness. Pellegrini argues that camp sincerity is "a precious form of queer resilience, imagination, and . . . 'moral seriousness' in the face of vulnerability."[82] Pellegrini's examples include (straight and lesbian) Jewish women's humor, but examples do not extend to gay men or transgender figures' "camp sincerity." We might add Patrick Haggerty's Marxist queer country performances, which are playful, joyful, and imaginative yet urgently resilient, rebellious, and serious.

The concepts of sincerity and authenticity have continued to be embraced in North American culture, despite the challenges by postmodernism. The possibly increasing importance of authenticity may be a sign of deep yearning, as folklorist Regina Bendix writes: "Invocations of authenticity are admissions of vulnerability, filtering the self's longings into the shaping of the subject." She continues that we can "deconstruct authenticity as a discursive formation, but such a project cannot simply invalidate the search for authenticity. This search arises out of a profound human longing, be it religious-spiritual or existential, and declaring the object of such longing nonexistent may violate the very core around which people build meaningful lives."[83] Bendix argues that "the crucial questions to be answered are not 'what is authenticity?' but 'who needs authenticity and why?' and 'how has authenticity been used?'"[84] Need for authenticity, or at least for others' appreciation of their sincerity, may be considerably multiplied for those who have been othered by mainstream society and their authenticity and sincerity challenged. Thus, some people have searched for a way to embrace sincerity in the wake of our existence within postmodernist critiques of essence and authenticity. One possible solution was prompted by late twentieth-century and early twenty-first-century literature and theater. Siân Adiseshiah notes that "the *new* sincerity" emerges as an "aesthetic mode," attempting to rethink sincerity in light of "poststructuralist irony, cynicism, and fatigue" without rehabilitating an "essentialist self" or "expressive subjectivity."[85] She writes that "sincerity [is] 'not an integrated consequence and qualification of subjectivity' but ... 'an indispensable *affective* (hence, social) process between subjects.'"[86] Here Adiseshiah draws from art historian and curator Jill Bennett's argument that we find sincerity not "through the perfect confluence of words and emotion, but by revealing a struggle with the feeling or experience of something we might call insincerity."[87] Adiseshiah calls this "critical sincerity" and elaborates: "By this I mean the performance of a genuine, communicative encounter, where trusted and trusting, inter-connected spectators are interpellated as part of a conversation about things that matter in the world, but where residues of an ironic affect continue to trouble the encounter, ironic moments exist within the space of sincerity, and the authentic is always in question."[88] Adiseshiah identifies a mode of performance that acknowledges the predicaments of desiring sincerity in postmodernity: addressing sincerity's ties to the troubling essentialism of authenticity, yet calling forth spectators to join a community of trust during (and perhaps after) the performance in which issues of meaning for the community arise, and the humor and anxiety in meaning that arise with irony are engaged as a crucial part of a "critically sincere" performance in this time. Marginalized by just about every cultural milieu they find themselves in, facing the dual conundrums of sincerity in the face of antiessentialism and the demand for authenticity from a genre that was forged around a crisis of authenticity, queer and trans country musicians' engagements with sincerity bridge the postmodern critical awareness Adiseshiah identifies with the specifically queer camp understanding Pellegrini suggests, producing what we might call "queer sincerity."

"TO RESPECT AND LOVE SOMETHING IS ALSO TO UNDERSTAND THE HUMOR AND ABSURDITY IN IT"

We might consider Canadian popular music star k.d. lang's foray into country music as a performance of "queer sincerity" in which she engaged meaningfully with her audience, challenged gender essentialism, and also felt that she needed (or wanted) to embrace irony at key moments in order to successfully deliver these other two facets of her performance aesthetic. lang's early career in country music offers a telling example of journalists' misunderstanding, hearing queer performance of country as an anomaly or spoof, despite lang's claims of honest love for the genre. lang is typically interpreted as having taken a camp or performance art stance toward country, because before country music, lang studied performance art.[89] While listeners worldwide, whether originally fans of country or not, adored lang's country music, her performances were frequently viewed with suspicion by country music journalists and other industry insiders. Country music journalist Rich Kienzle wrote, "Honesty is what country music has always been about, and in [lang's] case, I don't hear much."[90] Yet lang made repeated claims of honest appreciation for country music and her view that loving a genre could include having a sense of humor about it. As journalist Dave Jennings wrote about criticism of lang's country music performances, "To be completely fair to those hostile country conservatives, lang's visual imagery has, at times, seemed like an elaborate parody of cowboy culture. She's appeared in publicity pictures striking the corniest Lone Ranger poses imaginable. 'Sure,' she concedes, 'but to respect and love something is also to understand the humor and absurdity in it. It is important to have fun with what you do.'"[91] Yet embedded in Jennings's critique lies the already humorous material lang was working with—the corny Lone Ranger poses ready for recirculation (figures 6 and 7). lang wasn't inventing jokes about country, she was embodying the humor that was already present in the genre. Or at least the humor that used to be present in the genre.

Figures 6–7. Figure 6 is the cover of k.d. lang's third album, *Absolute Torch and Twang*.
Photographs from the album depict her serious facial expression (perhaps partly deadpan)
while embodying iconic symbols of country music history, including a farmer or cowboy
alone in a dry field with the ruins of a barn in the distance and a cowboy alone by a campfire.
Figure 7's sepia-toned image from the back of the liner notes may be the photo that Jennings
felt was one of "the corniest Lone Ranger poses imaginable." While lang appears cool and serious in her body language, close inspection reveals that while smoke is emerging from the fire,
none of the logs have burned, and the range of trees in the distance are clearly a backdrop.

lang's humor was seen as criticism of the genre rather than as consistent with
country humor or as evidence of her affection for it. lang alludes to an ongoing
debate in country music around tradition/authenticity versus commercialism/
expansion to explain why her country industry critics seem to be misunderstanding her sense of humor: "I think that there has been a continual phase in
the urbanization of country music. It started with countrypolitan, which happens to be the music I really like. But in the development of country music, I
think it went through a period of urbanization which closeted, or ignored, the

real humor or twang of it. You know, the early, early stuff—the stuff that created rockabilly. They got embarrassed about it and it has never been able to come out of the closet totally. It became a parody of itself."[92] In this statement, lang comments on a pivotal (and still-debated) moment in the history of country music: in the 1950s and 1960s the Nashville sound is understood to have replaced honky-tonk music as the central country style, attracting an enormous new market of coastal and suburban listeners. Honky-tonk is the name for a bar in urban outskirts where men formerly from rural areas who had immigrated to the city for factory jobs would seek community, as well as the name for the music typically heard there. This "situation-specific" music is typically narrated from a man's point of view, and if it includes women, they are typically "fallen angels, corrupted by city life." Songs often center on a man's "struggle to maintain his self-respect in a world that is full of hardship, pain, and temptation" and are set to "pedal steel and shuffling dance beat."[93] The Nashville sound developed uniform and popular music–style production values that attracted a flood of new listeners and turned country music into a multimillion-dollar industry centered in Nashville. As communication scholar Joli Jensen writes, honky-tonk was heard as embodying the "twang" of country, the identifying facets of the music, which also happened to be the features that made it and the people associated with it vulnerable to humiliation. While insiders appreciated these features (like pedal steel, fiddle, strained voices, songs about abjection, and an "us versus them" mentality) as signs of musical authenticity and regional/class identity, outsiders heard the same features as corny and overwrought. As Jensen notes, this pivotal moment is often perceived as a "selling out" of the facets that defined country music in order to garner broader appeal, but as she elaborates, this interpretation incorrectly assumes that there was a prior authentic wave of country music that was noncommercial.

In her statement, lang (perhaps carefully) supports both the Nashville sound and honky-tonk. She says that she is most influenced by the sound of countrypolitan, a portmanteau of country and metropolitan and another term for the Nashville sound. lang's band the Reclines was named after an icon of this style, Patsy Cline, a working-class Virginian who sought fame as a country singer and initially disliked executives' pop aims for her career. She eventually relented as her career trajectory ran parallel to country music's shift from honky-tonk to countrypolitan. As Jensen illustrates, in the years of Cline's rise from fronting a live band in honky-tonks to becoming a pop star, she initially fought anyone who made suggestions for her music that seemed too "pop," even though her voice seemed particularly suited to the slower melodic (pop) music that she eventually became famous for. She insisted on wearing the cowgirl costumes her mother made, shouting the endings of songs as she had in the live bar setting, and yodeling, and she advertised her country repertoire over her more "pop" repertoire, even when the pop songs were getting her more hits. As Jensen argues, Cline eventually found some balance between these seemingly juxtaposed musical (and class and regional) identifications, celebrating her pop hits, becoming a member of the Grand Ole Opry, and yet going onstage in cocktail dresses.

lang explains that despite being a countrypolitan-influenced singer, she loves the hillbilly humor of "the stuff that created rockabilly"—in other words, honky-tonk.[94] Given Cline's ambivalence about seeming too "uptown" and lang's dedication to Cline's legacy, lang's own embrace of hillbilly humor seems appropriate. But lang's interest in both countrypolitan and honky-tonk humor may have seemed awkward to a mainstream country music culture that had long since shed the hillbilly humor it considered embarrassing, in favor of mainstream sales and new coastal and suburban listeners. Some critics, seemingly including lang, argue that this move emptied the semiotics and humor from the genre, leaving the shell of the Nashville sound without the core of "country." Musician, songwriter, and producer Chet Atkins said regretfully in 1976, "I hate to see country going uptown because it's the wrong uptown. We're about to lose our identity and get all mixed up with other music. We were always a little half-assed anyway, but a music dies when it becomes a parody of itself, which has happened to some extent with rock. Of course, I had a lot to do with changing country, and I do apologize. We did it to broaden the appeal, and to keep making records different, to surprise the public."[95] However, Jensen argues that country had always been an urban music about rural living and had always been a commercial music attempting to hide this, so it has always provoked anxiety about its authenticity. For queer and trans musicians and listeners, that has a familiar ring to it—there's a closeted queerness to country, which is pretending to be something it's not.[96]

Perhaps it was lang's obvious queerness that gave country insiders anxiety. Her performances from that period, such as the *Austin City Limits* show from 1988, included on her twenty-fifth-anniversary rerelease of *A Truly Western Experience*, demonstrate her mixed-gender signifiers with butch haircut and preference not to wear makeup, a fringed denim western shirt paired with a floral skirt. Her body language while singing, dancing, and signaling to her band and the audience suggests joy, comfort onstage, and little attempt to appear heteronormatively feminine. She dances like a "hillbilly" and does not signal middle-class femininity in any way.

Her 1984 music video for her satirical song about (a real) Albertan white bread, "Pollyann," draws on 1950s housewife femininity to proclaim her love and devotion to this brand of white bread over all other forms of baked products. Her gestures are exaggerated so that her feminine enthusiasm seems over the top and ridiculous. Of course, the female-associated name of the bread gives the song an alternate queer meaning. And in case any viewer missed the clues that lang does not really identify with this narrator character, she removes her wig at the end of the song.

lang's brilliance in the statement above, as music scholar Martha Mockus points out, is to use "the language of queer liberation to describe her view of urbanized country music"—it "closeted, or ignored, the real humor or twang of it."[97] Closeting, in this formulation, seems to be refusing to allow the truth of what the humor stands for, in this case, that there are ways that rural and working-class people are, as Nadine Hubbs has also argued, "queer." They are never normative, whether straight, cisgender, or not, because gender and sexuality norms are crafted around middle-class and (sub)urban existence. lang could be heard to be, in a way, resolving the honky-tonk versus countrypolitan divide, liberating the twang/queerness of country music and combining it with the polished/mainstream sounds of countrypolitan, all while appearing to be the biggest gay star ever to perform country music.

Communications scholar John Sloop offers persuasive evidence that in reviews of lang's country music performances, journalists rhetorically disciplined her for ambiguity of gender and sexuality, as well as for her supposed lack of genre commitment. While she intentionally played with gender and sexuality, which read to some of her audience as queer camp humor, for the whole of her time as a country musician from 1984 to 1991, she did not come out publicly.[98] At times she would tease her audiences as if she were about to come out, saying, "As you know, I'm a l . . . Lyle Lovett fan." The joke demonstrated her silent understanding that many of her audience knew she was a lesbian. It also allowed a laugh about admiration for another country musician deemed "problematic," if not inauthentic. As Mockus discusses, while some of lang's listeners were understandably disappointed that a seemingly lesbian star of this caliber would not come out and hopefully thus make queerness more visible and accepted, many fans seemed happy that her shows at least offered many clues directed to their queer viewing/listening pleasure.

It seems clear that the particular sort of humor lang infused into her blend of countrypolitan and honky-tonk was not only hillbilly but also lesbian humor. As Hubbs argues, all working-class people are considered nonnormative by middle-class gender and sexuality standards, and so there is already overlap between these categories. (I'd also argue further that many lesbians have been discriminated against such that without family support or protections against employment and housing discrimination, they may end up living a working-class existence regardless of their birth status.) Author and journalist Mikaella Clements coined the term "dyke camp" to describe an aesthetic that demonstrates

> love of the ultra-natural, of nature built up and reclaimed, of clothes that could be extensions of the body, of desire made obsessive, of lesbian gestures or mannerisms maximized by a thousand. Rather than drag, which parodies what is real, dyke camp takes the real and magnifies it, so that it becomes absurd or funny or simply attractive in its own right. . . . [D]yke camp takes private lesbian contact and makes it public—for other women. Dyke camp is less about having a hot body, and more about knowing how to use it. It's why dyke camp is so often rooted in swagger, in cockiness.[99]

As Jennings's critique of lang's humor unintentionally reveals, lang was drawing on existing humor in country music, "the corniest Lone Ranger poses imaginable," as well as hillbilly stereotypes that were heard as funny in honky-tonk but threatening to the mainstream success of countrypolitan. A dyke camp performance of these tensions and contradictions in country music performance and reception "takes the real and magnifies it, so that it becomes absurd or funny or simply attractive in its own right" and is especially directed to other women rather than to men.

lang's simultaneous genre shift away from country and coming out as a lesbian seemed to signal to journalists that her music from *Ingenue* onward was more "honest" and showed musical and ideological progression, maturity, and commitment. Sloop notes that although she was now out (and thus open to more direct homophobic slander), her shift from low-cultural-value country music to higher-cultural-value torch singing and easy listening led to approval from journalists. Sloop's stance marks a departure from musicologist Sheila Whiteley's, which suggests that ambiguity allowed lang some safety to navigate popularity without having to officially come out. Vincent Stephens, who has written widely on the post–World War II history of male performers in the United States and the "open secret," argues that ambiguity allows a performer more flexibility, sales, and career longevity.[100] Yet intriguingly, lang experienced a huge surge in popularity after she came out and simultaneously left country music for adult contemporary. She explained her shift in genre without mentioning sexuality, instead referring to her diverse artistic influences and concepts of freedom, diversity, and honesty: "The time has come for me to let go of being a 'country singer.' Country will always be a major influence on me, but I've also been influenced by everything from opera to Ofra Haza; and I'm not prepared to make the kind of compromises that would be necessary for me to be accepted by those people [in Nashville]. At one time I did very much want to prove to them how much I honestly loved country music, but they make their own assessments whether you're honest or not."[101]

"I WANTED YOU TO THINK I WAS A COWBOY"

A decade after lang's shift away from country and around the same time that Stevens started out, another queer Albertan became a transgender country musician. The award-winning Canadian singer-songwriter and author Rae Spoon began making folk music inspired by ani difranco, as well as writing songs that at church were interpreted as religious but actually expressed Spoon's closeted love for their youth group leader.[102] In the 2013 song "Sunday Dress" Spoon looks back on their childhood in an abusive Pentecostal family, singing, "My prairie home / Fits like a Sunday dress."[103] As a child, Spoon found the prospect of growing up to be a woman unthinkable, came out as queer during high school, developed an eating disorder, and eventually moved away from Calgary in order to find queer community and freedom from family trauma. Once in Vancouver, Spoon discovered transgender identification and, unexpectedly, began to develop a career as a country singer:

> Half a year after moving to Vancouver from Alberta, country music started to swirl in my head. I had put all of myself into escaping from Calgary to the more liberal west coast. I had changed my last name a few days before I moved, and I was keen on reinventing myself. I was queer, and that had

been hard in Alberta. I thought that I would put those difficulties behind me and wake up a new person in Vancouver, but the temperate climate and easygoing people there had reaffirmed the sense that I was still quite Albertan on the inside. It's not like the moment I put my foot down in British Columbia, I was wholly inspired to start making surfer music. The music that had surrounded me my entire life started to creep into my own.[104]

Spoon's sense of being "quite Albertan on the inside" could sound essentialist, but it could also be understood as what scholars of class call habitus, embodied ways of being in the world, which remain imprinted despite changes in one's life.[105] We might consider in what ways habitus survives a regional shift, especially when motivated by queer alienation from religion, family, and region, and how those who experience these changes might reincorporate and make new meaning of the habitus they carry with them. Spoon explained to me, "I think I was also kind of trying to figure out who I was, you know? Like you don't really think about where you're from until you've moved."[106] This feeling of recognition in a memory or symbol of home is familiar to straight and cisgender exiles as well. In his autobiography, *Out of Egypt*, and essay collection, *Alibis: Essays on Elsewhere,* Jewish Egyptian writer Andre Aciman explores the experience of his family never feeling entirely at home in Egypt until they were exiled and looking back at memories of their life in Egypt from their new life in Paris. The feeling was also about their relationship to their new home compared to their imagination of what Europe was like: "What we missed was not just Egypt. What we missed was dreaming Europe in Egypt—what we missed was the Egypt where we'd dreamed of Europe. . . . Parallax is not just a disturbance in vision. It's a derealizing and paralyzing disturbance in the soul—cognitive, metaphysical, intellectual, and ultimately aesthetic. It is not just about displacement, or of feeling adrift both in time and space, it is a fundamental misalignment between who we are, might have been, could still be, can't accept we've become, or may never be."[107] In Spoon's experience, this regional move prompted a new embrace of select memories of childhood daydreams of embodying their uncles' masculinity, men who, at times, rescued the family from Spoon's abusive father:

Sometimes, in daydreams, I pictured myself as one of them, out in the middle of the prairies driving alone in my truck, blowing smoke out the window, and sleeping in hotels and temporary trailers. I would listen to Garth Brooks, Willie Nelson, and Randy Travis. My hands would be dirty with crude oil. I wanted to be a cowboy so that I could hold back my tears and protect my family. I used to smoke and drink, but then I quit both. I never learned how to drive, work the oil rigs, or ride a horse, but I did write songs about these things. I was not a cowboy in reality, but my heart always felt lonely enough to sing about it with conviction.[108]

While declining to offer lived experience as proof of musical authenticity, as Hank Williams demands, Spoon instead compares a queer transgender Albertan exile's musical resonance to lonely cowboy life. Spoon's playlist could be heard on country radio, yet it includes musicians who could be sympathetic in their own ways: Garth Brooks, a mainstream Nashville star scorned as "Walmart country" by alternative country culture yet who released a gay-friendly anthem, "We Shall Be Free," in 1992; Willie Nelson, the long-haired outlaw country singer who has (until a recent Democratic political appearance) found favor with both mainstream Nashville and Americana audiences and in 2006 released Latin country musician Ned Sublett's "Cowboys Are Frequently Secretly Fond of Each Other"; and Randy Travis, a white neotraditional gospel singer beloved by many queer and transgender country music fans.[109] Yet it was actually Hank Williams's music that inspired Spoon, who bought one of his records shortly after moving to Vancouver: "He was almost too twangy for my taste, but he sounded as misplaced as I felt."[110] And in fact this feeling of being misplaced is exactly how Williams's music has resonated from the time he was alive: the quintessential honky-tonk star, Williams's music was played in honky-tonk bars on the outskirts of rural migrants' new urban haunts, singing to them of home, longing, and abjection.[111] Like the loneliness of Spoon's oil field worker uncles, Williams's sound of being misplaced resonated with Spoon's feelings after moving alone six hundred miles from home. Spoon makes note of the "twang" of Williams's music and Spoon's difference in taste. As Jensen notes, the "twang" of honky-tonk is not only in the timbre but also in the instrumentation and the images of rural life, values, and humor, which are often misunderstood by middle-class suburban and urban dwellers. As Spoon describes in Gender Failure and elsewhere, their upbringing in Calgary placed them in between rural and urban. Their uncles were the "cowboys," working the oil rigs where they were (unhappily) separated from their families, while Spoon writes with distaste about their own abusive father's office worker costume of button-down shirt and tie and his embrace of a position of power in their church, which seemed hypocritical with his cruel, abusive treatment of his family. Meanwhile, their hometown was the annual organizer of the Calgary Stampede, a rodeo festival hosted in a stadium shaped like a saddle, in which suburban office workers would arrive wearing unblemished (and thus seemingly previously unused) Stetson hats.[112] Spoon spent six years writing and touring country music as a transgender man and eventually developed new insight regarding gender and genre, moving away from country and also no longer identifying as a man. Spoon now identifies as a nonbinary transgender person and uses they/them pronouns.

As Spoon elaborates in the tongue-in-cheek yet also quite vulnerable book, *How to (Hide) Be(hind) Your Songs*, which could be the epitome of queer sincerity in its embrace of both camp humor and stark sincerity and intimacy, they use the "disguise" of metaphors to write songs about these painful experiences without directly revealing everything about themselves: "After I wrote my first batch of country songs I tested them by going back to Alberta where I grew up. I played them in bars to see if they really disguised me. Being transgender in a bar in Red Deer is not really the safest situation to put myself in, but I believed that I could hide behind my songs and I did. Actually I would not recommend testing your songs by putting yourself in direct danger. I'm still unraveling the mental cost of these stunts."[113] While Spoon released several country albums and toured with this music for several years, they have later come to see some of it as "performance art" and have since expanded their range of genre (a topic explored in chapters 2 and 4).[114]

"Cowboy," a sort of postcountry song, was written for the documentary *My Prairie Home* and navigates the experience of writing country music as a queer and transgender exile from Alberta. Director Chelsea McMullen insisted that this film be set in Spoon's childhood home province, even though Spoon was, at that moment, living in Montreal. While Spoon had been writing indie music at the time, their music for the film engages and blends their current and previous styles and suggests their continued willingness to employ the tropes of country music without adhering to its demands for authenticity. "Cowboy" exposes Spoon's desired identification with cowboys as a way to negotiate other people's expectations (perhaps of Spoon as a family member, a lover, a performer, an Albertan, etc.) and Spoon's own sense of self:

> I wanted you to think I was a cowboy
> So I told you where I was from
> But all I ever did was run from trucks

And I never held a gun.

I wanted you to think I was strong
So I showed you my restraint
Far past when I lost control
I never stopped the game.

I wanted you to think I was a fighter
So I showed you all my teeth
And I held them up like a monument
To the fall underneath.

I wanted you to think I was a cowboy
So I told you where I am from
And I walked around like I didn't care
That I lost everyone.[115]

In the documentary, Spoon sings this song in the Blackfoot Diner, a truck stop in Calgary where they eat when they record in Calgary, a prospect that was easier when Spoon was not a vegan, they explained to me: "It's always kind of tense when I go there [the Blackfoot Diner].... It's kind of like a place that, like a lot of people who are there eating remind me more of my relatives than some other places in Calgary. There's a lot of people who come there who are like my uncles and stuff."[116] The film musically illustrates the last couplet of the song (about losing everyone) as Spoon seems to be ignored or gawked at by most customers while staging an impromptu performance, creating moments of tension for the film's viewers, as well as, presumably, those in the diner, where it was recorded live, with signs on the door alerting customers that if they ate there that morning they might be in a documentary. As the camera shows how different people in the diner react to Spoon's performance, the film pieces together impressions we might draw about the people Spoon has tried to impress and has lost in their life. Gendered markers jump out from every shot in the diner's truck- and cowboy-themed décor and menu, which features "trucker's breakfast," "working man's breakfast," and "cowboy breakfast," its anxiously heterobinary color scheme (figure 8), and the shift to how the camera looks at individual diners (figures 9 and 10). Yet Spoon's reception seems mixed, perhaps with some unexpectedly touched listeners (figure 11), and the film's viewers are interpellated as an intimate audience for this performance.

Figure 8. Rae Spoon performs the lines "far past when I lost control, I never stopped the game" from "Cowboy" while making a point to stop to look at the color-coded bathrooms at the Blackfoot Diner, with blue on the left and pink on the right, in Chelsea McMullen, dir., *My Prairie Home*, 2013, film still.

Figure 9. A diner watches the performance and filming in process of *My Prairie Home*.

This chapter's focus on the sincerity politics of queer and transgender country acts reveals pressures these musicians face regarding their relationships with genre: Patrick Haggerty felt that his Marxist gay critique was more powerful as a country album, but this genre also doomed the album and musician to obscurity for forty years; country insiders questioned k.d. lang's honesty regarding her relationship to country, inferring that her Canadianness,

Figure 10. A customer looks as Spoon walks past, singing, "I acted like I didn't care that I lost everyone."

Figure 11. Customers at the Blackfoot Diner interrupt breakfast to watch Spoon sing.

her veganism, her humor, and her implied lesbianism made her unfit to play country in any way but as a parody; and Rae Spoon toured for six years across rural and urban Canadian venues playing country as a queer and trans person who had to hide these identifications for safety. Since 1973 these out gay and transgender country musicians have self-resourced selectively from their life experiences, creating music that is meant to communicate truthfully, and they have found country genres helpful in telling those stories. At times they have been positioned by others as not fitting in with cultural expectations for this music. And the rhetoric of sincerity, with its foundation of essentialist authenticity and its demands for outing oneself, can create challenges for their musicking. But their queer and trans politics appeal to a growing number of listeners and fellow musicians, leading to familiarity with and excitement about the socioaesthetic phenomenon of queer country.

In 2018, thirty years after her initial country debut, k.d. lang received the Americana Trailblazer Award from the Americana Music Association (AMA), an association that didn't exist when she was working as a country musician and that represents a genre/format that she never attempted to participate in. The AMA, which has a more progressive-identified listenership than the Country Music Association (CMA), has something to gain by attention to queer country and folk musicians. Celebrating a musician snubbed by country homophobes would seem like a move in keeping with cisgender straight men courting Patrick Haggerty to demonstrate that they are not Trump voters. Some country musicians have spoken out about the strange experience of simultaneous acceptance by the AMA and rejection by the CMA. Further, the AMA's attention to minority musicians has been limited and, to some musicians, feels more symbolic than demonstrative of a commitment to creating ongoing opportunities for musicians previously discriminated against by this industry. Yet its (limited) acknowledgment of diversity has pushed the CMA some. Musician and activist Karen Pittelman formed a group called Country Music Against White Supremacy (of which I am a member), pushing industry professionals to make more concrete commitments to the diversity of the genre.

Calling queer country a "socioaesthetic phenomenon" is different from approaching it as a (sub)genre. And it has much to do with the musicians' and the country, Americana, and folk industries' relationships to gender and sexuality. In chapter 2 I craft a history of queer and trans country performance and also analyze three trans musicians' simultaneous musical and identity transformations: Spoon's departure from country music and from male identification, singer-songwriter and multi-instrumentalist Namoli Brennet's path to womanhood and folk music, and rock musician Lucas Silveira's move away from folk music and lesbian identification, transitions that all three explain in terms of sincerity and gender politics.

CHAPTER 2

GENRE TROUBLE

When I asked the members of the band Mouths of Babes (figure 12) about the genre of their music, Tylan Greenstein (formerly of the band Girlyman) described the panic that this question induces as "that deer-in-the-headlights reaction." Her bandmate and wife, Ingrid Elizabeth, then chimed in to say how difficult it was for her previous band Coyote Grace (with transgender musician Joe Stevens and straight cisgender musician Michael Connolly) to label their genre, even with the help of a consultant. While most artists dislike labeling or explaining their work, queer and trans musicians often experience what I suggest we think of as "genre trouble."[1] Greenstein elaborated, "I do think that genres are very limiting. We have always had a hard time really saying what genre we are. Because we're not really Americana. We're not really blues. We're not really soul. We're not pop. We're not really folk, even. I mean, there's contemporary folk. But again, it's similar to identity categories, where now we can be fitting into one or two or maybe even three. So you know the struggle."[2]

This chapter explores the ways queer and trans country (and country-adjacent) musicians have navigated the identity politics of genre in their careers. In *Queer Country*'s introduction, I considered how identity categories and genre categories work as ways to define and manage people and practices. In the cases of queer and trans musicians playing country and related musics in the period covered in this book, we might understand identity categories as becoming "intersectional" with musical genre, to think further with law scholar Kimberlé Crenshaw's influential theoretical intervention in identity studies.[3] In other words, a musician's relationship with genre is inseparable from and partially defined by facets of their identity, and these facets of their identity are, in turn, sometimes impacted by genre. The relationship between identity and genre thus can be seen as cogenerative. (These musicians also, of course, experience "regular" identity intersectionality, in which identifications such as gender, sexuality, race, class, region, age, ability, and religion influence and define each other such that no facet could stand alone.) And if identity and genre are intersectional, then genres—perhaps for coherence and self-preservation—may regularly exclude those whose identity seems a mismatch with this genre. Thus, this chapter, and this book, may serve as an example of the limits of genre as a useful analytic, unless scholars also look at the margins of any genre in question.

By centering queer and trans musicians' navigations of country and related musics, this chapter crafts an alternative history of the development of country-related musics through the experiences of musicians who have not typically been historicized in these musics.[4] In doing so, it draws together genres that specialists might typically understand as distinct, such as folk, commercial country, bluegrass, old-time, women's music, and Americana. Yet in order to engage with sexually marginalized and gender-marginalized people playing any of this sort of music, one *must* be willing to consider musicians across (and excluded from) these genres, as these types of music relate to each other in ways for queer and trans participants that are different from those for straight and cisgender participants and in standard country and folk music scholarship.

In addressing relationships between these styles, the chapter navigates ongoing debates defining these genres and joins a web of rich discussion about identity, community, and the policing of boundaries. As musicians' rhetoric and artistic work demonstrate, they have both drawn upon and challenged the discourses and archetypes of these musics. Their relationships to standard country and folk discourse and archetypes are usually defined by their identifications and often result from negotiations of self in conversation with contemporary identity politics and in a difficult dance with the rhetorics of selfhood already crafted by these music industries. Studying musicians whose

Figure 12. Mouths of Babes, Burlap and Bean Coffee Shop, Newtown Square, Pennsylvania, 24 April 2015. Photo by the author.

careers have been impacted by being out queer or trans people in country and folk music helps draw new insights about these genres, including how these types of music have interacted with one another over inclusion and exclusion of different groups and how these genres are holding up in relation to heated struggles around identity, politics, and social justice. As this chapter highlights, some of these musicians have found themselves at the center of debates and projects within these genres to counter embedded oppression within these musics.

Finally, the chapter closes with case studies of three transgender musicians whose identity and genre changes happened simultaneously. Singer, songwriter, and multi-instrumentalist Namoli Brennet found folk music the most honest way to understand herself as a woman. Lucas Silveira reflects on how listeners misunderstood his more angry and aggressive musical affects in his folk music as he was coming to understand himself as a man and how this prompted a shift to rock. And former transgender male country musician turned nonbinary indie pop artist and activist record label owner Rae Spoon discusses how genre changes felt important due to their changing sense of self. All three musicians were drawn to a different genre to better articulate their newfound sense of identity, although in each case, these musical shifts and rearticulation of gender identity have presented new challenges.

"WHAT KIND OF MUSIC DO YOU PLAY?"

"What kind of music do you play?" is a striking way to open a film about transgender musicians.[5] A question about musical style is probably not the first topic most cisgender people would think to ask an out transgender musician. While a growing population accepts transgender experience, many cisgender people's initial interaction with a transgender person is to interpret their gender as difficult to categorize. Sociologist Sonny Nordmarken identifies this process as a "desire" to "possess" the "Truth" about someone else. In an essay exploring gender illegibility and its disruption of the categories many people presume are standard and required of everyone, Nordmarken shares an autobiographical experience:

On the bus, I sit, on my way to work. I look out the window, thinking about the children I will see soon. In the next moment, I feel energy reaching out to me. I sense eyes following me. I am being watched—realization dawns in an instant.

Glancing up, I confront eyes querying me. Eyes wondering. Boy or girl? Man or woman? This is beyond curiosity. It is desire. It is the wanting to possess, the intention to extract, it is the mission to obtain for oneself information—no: Truth. I feel a sense of amusement watching the eyes' confusion, their concentration. I enjoy the chaos my body prompts. These eyes feel and imagine themselves to be legitimate knowers. How dare I, as Other, challenge their abilities to "know"? My very ambiguity challenges their understanding of themselves as omniscient. My ambiguity moves into their space, cornering their minds. They do not know which way to turn. My androgyny fucks with their imagined able-bodiedness: I impair their ability to categorize me. I challenge their conceptions of gender; I shake the foundations of their narrative. I upheave their ideas of Truth and their trusty methods to know it. I am successfully undoing gender (Butler, 2004) by being illegible. I am living the unlivable. Their failure to attribute a gender category to me makes my ambiguous gender performance a form of resistance. I take power in their confusion. I feel a rush of heat and euphoria in this moment of freedom—as I monster, gender-fuck and gender-terrorize.[6]

"Gender-normate" people's gawking and demands on "nonnormative" people's identifications assume gender is stationary for all people, imagine there is some kind of universal truth about gender, and, above all, offer no regard for the feelings of the person whose gender is being questioned. Nordmarken shares both the power and terror in leaning into illegibility rather than feeling aligned with and interested in adapting to binary gender expectations. Nordmarken points out the further injustice that "I am read as sexually deviant because I appear gender-deviant."[7] While in the instance above, Nordmarken feels euphorically free and powerful, in another similar moment discussed in this essay, Nordmarken describes feeling "suffocat[ed]," "cornered," and "attack[ed]."[8] Nordmarken closes this 2013 essay by generously acknowledging that "students share with me how anxious they feel when they see someone they cannot categorize as male or female. They want to interact with them appropriately, but they do not know how. After feeling so much pain when experiencing others' fumbling treatment of me, I soften. Many people are doing their best. They do not mean to be disrespectful. They just do not know how to follow rules of gender attribution when people break rules of gender performance."[9] While many people may be trying their best, others ridicule and view as alien people whose appearances fall outside norms (gender, sexuality, class, ability, race, religion, size, etc.). Even when filmmakers focus a documentary or film on transgender subjects, the gaze of the camera can reify negative stereotypes rather than depicting transgender and nonbinary people as fellow humans.[10]

And so it seems an important lesson that a question about genre, not gender, is how the 2010 documentary *Riot Acts: Flaunting Gender Deviance in Music Performance* opens. Transgender filmmakers and scholars Madsen Minax and Simon Fisher Strikeback began filming *Riot Acts* while on tour as bandmates in the antifolk band Actor Slash Model (active 2006–12). Their documentary features musicians who play a wide variety of genres, all linked by their public "deviance" of gender norms, and thus find their music politicized (most intentionally, some less so). Minax and Strikeback's framework for beginning the film by exploring genre, not gender, reveals their wisdom in revealing to audiences that discussion of musical categories elicits insights about the relationships between music and identity.[11]

GENRE TROUBLE

Telling a history of out queer and trans musician involvement in country and related genres means entering ongoing debates about how this music is categorized, without necessarily holding the typical investments in category difference and meaning often wielded by those who "police" some of these genres (a wide array of actors, from powerful major label producers and the Clear Channel Radio monopoly to local bluegrass jam or folk song circle leaders and/or participants). Instead, I come bearing commentary about how genre categorization affects people—both the listening and playing opportunities people have, but also the way that people are categorized. As musicologist Marcia Citron found in her pathbreaking analysis of the omission of women from the canon of Western art music, simply adding some of the women who had accomplished most in the "standard" categories of production was not the obvious or only solution. For those categories of music had been part of the problem of exclusion, as well as our means of analyzing and appreciating them.[12]

It is not at all unprecedented to discuss folk and country in the same conversation, but in scholarship about country music, the discussion of folk is typically dropped after describing the eighteenth-century origins of the concept of "folk," its import to North America, and the early twentieth-century spread of interest in collecting and eventually in performing this music at home. However, a compelling body of scholarship shows that the story of country-related musics' "genre trouble" goes back at least to the eighteenth-century popularity of *Volk* and *Volkslied* led by philosopher Johann Gottfried von Herder, whose case for the establishment of nation-states rested not on military strength but rather on the culture of a region's people. He argued that the topographical features of the region shaped language, stories, and music and could serve to define "a people."[13] Yet as German studies scholar Vanessa Agnew demonstrates, this system imagined non-European peoples as "behind" in a linear stage of "development" toward European ideals of "civilization," thus providing rhetorical support for colonialization of "primitives."[14] As historian Benjamin Filene has argued, the music called "folk" has never been easy to define because it was invented on myth shaped by cultural middlemen who saw other people as "the people"—agrarian, working class, people of color, and so on. And Cecil Sharp's introduction to *English*

Folk Songs from the Southern Appalachians notes that folk music will provide (white) Americans with their "racial heritage," of value to demonstrating a connection back to England, shaping American education systems by the perceived "racial heritage" of (white) people's home countries, and providing fodder for art music composition that will help develop a (white) national sound.[15] Eventually, folk collectors such as John Lomax and his sons worked with Black populations in the United States, although mostly looking in places they perceived as cut off from modern times and mass entertainment, such as prisons. There, they found Huddie Ledbetter, known also as Leadbelly, a prisoner they would make famous while failing to secure his financial future. Benjamin Filene analyzes this phase of the development of folk music in America as the creation of "outsider populism," in which folk-collecting white, middle-class middlemen Other a group of people, collect their music, and proceed to depict it to audiences as both exotically different and yet also "of the common people."[16] The commercial invention of country music was not so different, as told by Peterson, Filene, and Hagstrom Miller. Yet since then, folk and country have continued to maintain separate identities. The reasons for the distinction are not always clear. While country is often original music or covers of music authored by a known and somewhat recent commercial musician, folk is not limited to anonymously authored, orally transmitted songs from hundreds of years go. As folk music scholar Thomas Gruning's ethnography of the US folk scene since the mid-twentieth-century revival demonstrates, musicians write their own songs now and cite popular music (such as the Beatles) as inspirations, both of which frustrate some traditional revivalists. While folk is no more clear as a category (and probably less clear than ever), it still draws on the notions of "the people," community engagement, and the power of sharing stories through compelling acoustic music.

To Patrick Haggerty, the division of folk and country happened after Woody Guthrie, when country music abandoned class critique. But he noted that "the anticommunist movement of the fifties was so thorough and so complete and so disruptive to art in America, that nobody after 1960, nobody was promoting songs that were overtly about class struggle."[17] Haggerty elaborated:

> While country music did the absurd thing of not being able to sing about the working-class as a class, . . . folk was . . . doing something different but

equally disastrous. It was an emphasis on the petite bourgeoisie peacenik politic. Well, that ain't it either, girlfriend. I sensed that. I knew that that's what I didn't like about that movement. Nobody was coming out and hitting the nail on the head when it came to working-class, class struggle. Woody Guthrie hit that nail on the head, quite adequately and quite properly, in the thirties and forties. But from my point of view, he was sort of the last. The guy who wrote "Take This Job and Shove It," he was always on the outs with Nashville anyway.[18] From where I'm sitting, from what I've heard, which was not a ton. But what filtered down to me is that "Take This Job and Shove It" was the last actually working-class struggle song to come out of Nashville and have popularity. Baez went a ways with dragging "Joe Hill" back out. But as politically sophisticated as Joan Baez was, I never heard her sing about working-class solidarity. My point of view on both Nashville and Baez, from the life that I've led, my perspective now if I was talking to Baez or Garth Brooks, my basic reaction would be, "Oh, come on. You're not stupid. You know better. Don't tell me you never thought about this. How could you not? What is missing in this picture? What's missing in the picture is your lack of clarity, and your own disingenuousness about the issue. What do you mean you're not singing about class struggle? Why not?" I would have to start the conversation . . . with both of them there and say, "This isn't about a personal trash. This is about you answering me honestly and frankly, from the bottom of your heart. With all the intellectual skill that you have, why didn't you? What stopped you?" Another reason that I chose country over folk was for the shock value of just talking about gender.[19]

One explanation for the unwelcome reception out queer and trans musicians have received in country music is its "tradition." Country is a commercial music invented in the 1930s. In an essay demonstrating a dialectical relationship between the two main divergent styles of country music, hard-core and soft-shell country, Richard Peterson challenges the notion of a "traditional" versus a "popular" style, noting the gender and class markers that distinguish how these are discussed: for hard-core, this means originality, tradition, masculinity, rawness, truthfulness, rusticity, and value, and for soft-shell, this means formulaic, diluted meaning, femininity or effeminized presentation, and selling out to draw a wider audience. Instead, Peterson shows how the soft-shell style preceded the hard-core style and so could be called "originary" and that the two types have shifted in and out of popularity over the entire history of recorded country music, with hard-core benefiting from waves of soft-shell popularity.[20]

Even if there were a clearly "traditional" form of country music, some queer and trans people would love it. Mainstream culture tends to assume that all queer and trans people identify against social norms and traditions. Some do, given that many American norms tend to overtly or silently support heteropatriarchy and white supremacy. But as media studies scholar Andre Cavalcante's ethnography of transgender Americans' media engagement at the turn of the millennium shows, most participants sought an "ordinary" life, and their media usage demonstrated this.[21] In chapter 1 I discussed media scholar Vincent Stephens's argument that some queer musicians have preferred to live with the "open secret" in which they maintain plausible deniability about their queerness.[22]

Some of what the relationships between gender and genre generate is trouble—not just what philosopher Judith Butler famously called "gender trouble" but also what I'd call "genre trouble." Or maybe, most specifically, the "gender trouble" that causes "genre trouble." Many of these queer and trans musicians have trouble choosing which genre label to use for their music, as Greenstein and Elizabeth's discussion and artists later in this chapter reveal. Musical genres are built around particular expectations for credible identity performance, message, and use value. As I discussed in chapter 1, problems in a musician's fit with genre can prompt doubts of the performer's authenticity that place the ability to book shows and sell music at stake. As I have argued elsewhere, since an othered identity in relation to genre norms typically keeps a musician from being seen as belonging fully in any one genre, atypical performances of gender, sexuality, or race can damage a musician's perceived integrity and ability to draw an audience.[23] Genres also set up different norms and expectations. For example, Simon Frith notes that rule-breaking is a built-in expectation in rock—rock musicians are supposed to break certain rules onstage. When this rule-breaking extends to gender and sexuality, I would argue that they may feel safer doing so because they are presumed to have a normative identity to fall back on. As philosopher Robin James argues, it is only white straight and cisgender musicians who claim to be "post-genre," a classification that implies that they may also claim to be "post-identity."[24]

Instead of feeling any accessibility to being "post-identity" or "post-genre," queer and trans musicians I studied might feel that their genre is also "trans." Reflecting on reviews of their recent album, trans singer-songwriter and performance studies scholar Elena Elias Krell, who has performed at several Queer Country Quarterly events, posted on Facebook:

> Reviewers seem to be having trouble with the wildly trans-genre nature of my most recent album. Gender and genre are linked for me: it's never made any bit of sense to belong to one and not another, or to even see them as separate. Music is music, expression is expression. It's always a bummer to read critical reviews (which I guess is why everyone says not to read your reviews) but it feels especially personal when people don't get my transgenre-ness because it resonates on the same frequency as people not getting your gender. . . . "Why don't you fit into X box" or "If you don't fit into Y box, you better make it worth my while." I'm trans in my transness, and I'm trans in my musicianness, and I'm not planning on stopping anytime soon :) #transgender #transgenre #queerpop #queermusic.[25]

"Transgenre" is not a commonly used musical term, but its use makes sense, particularly, as Krell notes, in relation to transgender musicians whose music also crosses categories. Krell's second sentence could indicate that assigning people to gender and genre categories has never made sense; rather, it makes more sense to them to embrace multiple genders and multiple genres. While Krell tags this post with pride in these terms, trans roots artist Eli Conley explained to country music journalist Rachel Cholst that "I don't want to be billed as like, Eli Conley, the transgender singer songwriter. I feel like often people who aren't in the [LGBTQ] community don't know how to see anything other than like, 'oh, this person's trans.' Like trying to look at me and see if they could imagine me as a woman—which is thankfully changing over time."[26] Yet Conley also notes in the same interview that the auspices of the Queer Country Quarterly and Queer Country West (which Conley hosts) have been a much-needed home for queer and trans musicians, including himself, who find themselves without as many fully welcoming venues for their performances because they are out queer and trans country musicians.

So given these complications surrounding identity and genre intersections, it can be difficult to find a name for this music. One factor of importance is whether the artist/band in question is trying to make a living from this music or not. Professionals usually want or need to draw a straight and cisgender audience in addition to attracting queer and trans listeners. More amateur bands (meaning those playing for the love of it without trying to support themselves on it) are often happy to play mainly to queer and trans people. My Gay Banjo even titled their band to frame genre through sexuality and attract queer and trans listeners.

Queer country musicians' creative work distinguishes itself by queer and trans genre politics, as well as trans, queer, feminist, and interracial musical collaboration. Queer country musicians thoughtfully perform aspects of genre in order to communicate successfully with fellow musicians and audience, using facets of country, folk, old-time, bluegrass, Americana, pop, and rock music as it suits them. Artists may more quietly adopt some of the identity assumptions attending one genre music or another while bringing attention to others (at some times with camp rhetoric, at other times with deep earnestness). Some musicians, such as Karen Pittelman of Karen and the Sorrows, promote taking the description "country" back as a political gesture and not capitulating to the country music industry's preference that queer musicians participate in Americana instead of country.[27] In identifying queer country as both a musical and an identity phenomenon, this chapter explores the cogenerative relationship between specific gender and sexuality politics and genre identifications.

The next section crafts a history of key developments in music (and discourse about it) by and about out queer and trans people that sounds like or has been categorized as country, bluegrass, old-time, folk, or Americana music in order to consider some of the relationships that queer and trans musicians have drawn between these genres.

A SELECT HISTORY OF OUT QUEER AND TRANS COUNTRY AND RELATED MUSIC

Country and related music such as folk, old-time, Americana, and roots music have almost definitely always had same-gender-loving and gender nonnormative people involved. No historical narrative is ever complete, as it would be impossible to include all actors. But this account of queer and trans musicians' engagement in country and related music is also incomplete, because many have not been fully "out" in these communities and industries, and I would not out anyone for the sake of my research.

Before there were out queer musicians in country, there were country songs about queerness, often treating it negatively. In its early days as a commercial music, country occasionally referenced gender nonnormativity that seemed to indicate same-sex desire, typically to send a homophobic message. For example, the song "Lavender Cowboy" derides its effeminate main character, who has just "two hairs on his chest" but "wished to follow the heroes / And fight like the he-men do." "Lavender Cowboy" originated as a poem by Harold Hersey in 1923. Ewen Hail wrote the music and released the first recording in 1927. The song appeared in the movie western *Oklahoma Cyclone* in 1930 and has been recorded by many country and folk musicians, including Burl Ives in 1950. In 1939 Vernon Dalhart's version was banned from the radio. A 25 March 1940 *Time* article about the past week's 147 blacklisted songs declares that 137 of these, including "Lavender Cowboy," were not even allowed to be played instrumentally due to their "suggestive" titles.[28] Paddy Roberts's 1959 version of "Lavender Cowboy" added new lyrics detailing the cowboy's effeminacy and having other cowboys shoot him at the end of the song. Intriguingly, queer musician Tom Robinson released a cover of Roberts's version of the song in 2000, which Queer Music Heritage deejay, archivist, and author J. D. Doyle suggests is due to Roberts and Robinson being from the UK, where Robinson would have more readily heard Roberts's version. There is one campy recording, from 1980 by Newfoundland group the Sons of Erin, in whose version the lavender cowboy rides "the sexiest horse in the West" and avoids being shot by blowing the sheriff a kiss.[29]

There are a number of homophobic country songs that were released over these decades. In 1951 Imperial Records released Billy Briggs's "The Sissy Song," which lists qualities attributed to gay men, concluding that "when I get sissy enough to . . ., I'll go out behind the old red barn and let a gray mule kick my brains out." In 1976 Rod Hart released an album titled *Breakeroo*, which included two trucker country songs featuring the lisping, lilting voice of a gay character. His disco country song "It's My Dog" uses a dog story to hide a gay sexual scenario. Hart's "CB Savage" (an answer song to C. W. McCall's "Convoy") was a trucker song featuring a character whose same sex CB radio come-on turns out to be a police trap. "CB Savage" reached number

23 on *Billboard*. Moe Bandy and Joe Stamply released "Honky Tonk Queen" about a drag queen on their self-titled 1981 album. In 1984 Columbia released their "Hee Haw satire aesthetic" trucker song, which complains about Boy George's gender performance, called "Where's the Dress?," in which they joke that "if it'd make some money, where's the dress?"[30]

Yet there were also sympathetic songs about queerness, including the Sweet Violet Boys' "I Love My Fruit," released by OKEH in 1939. The band the Prairie Ramblers took a pseudonym to record this song. They begin by singing "I am wild about all kinds of fairies," a gendered term regarding gay male sexuality roles that listeners would recognize. In 1978 David Allan Coe's "Fuck Aneta Briant" (an intentional misspelling of antigay activist Anita Bryant's name) claimed the importance of sexual freedom for gay men and Coe's identification with them, as Nadine Hubbs has demonstrated.[31] In 1991 Pirates of the Mississippi had their biggest hit (number 15 on *Billboard*'s Hot Country) with Danny Mayo's "Feed Jake," a poignant song in the tradition of country songs dedicated to dogs, in this case about a protagonist dying of AIDS whose last wish is for his friend/lover to feed his dog. And in 1992 Garth Brooks recorded Stephanie Davis's "We Shall Be Free," a song that offers several indirect messages about freedom but whose subtle line suggesting support for same-sex relationships caused an enormous stir in mainstream country audiences.

LAVENDER HEROES

Among the most influential folk singers of the twentieth century there have been several bisexual or lesbian musicians. Possibly the earliest was Ronnie Gilbert (1926–2015), raised by Jewish Marxist immigrant parents in New York. Gilbert got her start in the late 1940s as a teenage activist singer in Washington, DC, with the Priority Ramblers, wartime temps in government jobs who sang Carter Family and Coon Creek Girls' country songs and befriended Alan Lomax and Woody Guthrie.[32] Gilbert participated in Pete Seeger's traveling musical accompaniment of third-party progressive candidate Henry Agard Wallace's 1948 presidential campaign, and soon after Seeger and Gilbert, with friends Fred Hellerman and Lee Hays, formed the Weavers, the singing group that brought international commercial attention to the US folk revival. The Weavers' broad repertoire tended not to include what would be described as country music and instead focused on music the band considered as "folk revival." Later in life, Gilbert befriended folk and women's music artist Holly Near, who dedicated a record to her. This friendship led to Gilbert's more firm adoption of feminism and many tours together as HARP (featuring Near, Arlo Guthrie, Gilbert, and Seeger). On one tour, Gilbert met her future wife, Diane.

The first out lesbian country singer I know of was Florida-born Wilma Burgess (1939–2003). While she was originally a fan of popular music, Eddy Arnold's music drew her to country.[33] Burgess studied physical education at Stetson University and only pursued country singing at a friend's encouragement. She moved to Nashville in 1960 and worked as a demo singer and then released her first recording as a vocalist with United Artists.[34] In 1964 she signed to Decca Records with the famous Nashville sound producer Owen Bradley, who was looking for a singer after the untimely death of country star Patsy Cline, whom Bradley had worked with.[35] Burgess even bought Cline's home. Within the industry, Burgess was known as an out lesbian, yet it is not clear how many listeners knew. Like other musicians who employed the "open secret," Burgess made a point of recording love songs that did not specify the gender of the object of affection.[36] One exception was "Ain't Got No Man," a song with mournful lyrics about the narrator's sadness and loneliness for lack of a male partner (though set to a perky tempo and accompanied by upbeat instrumentals), which Burgess only agreed to record if Bradley would allow her to record another song that he otherwise would not have.[37] Between 1965 and 1975, Burgess had fifteen *Billboard*-charting country records, first with Decca, then with Shannon Records. Shannon was owned by Jim Reeves Enterprises, and Burgess befriended Reeves's widow, Mary, whom she helped run the Jim Reeves Museum. Her final album, *Could I Have This Dance*, was released with 51West, owned by Columbia. In the late 1980s, Burgess opened Nashville's first lesbian bar, the Hitching Post, where she performed every weekend. As Mary Reeves developed Alzheimer's, her second husband allegedly had her sign everything over to him, which he then sold. Mary died in 1999. The new owner of the estate did not allow Burgess to collect her belongings from a storage unit Mary owned.[38] Burgess died unexpectedly of a heart attack in 2003.

While Burgess was surprisingly open about her sexuality in this industry, she did not address sexuality directly in her music or publicity, and thus the title of the "first out gay country musician" is more typically bestowed on

Patrick Haggerty, born in Washington state. While Haggerty is credited with this title because he released the first out gay country album, he stresses in conversation that the period around the 1969 Stonewall Rebellion was a time when young people were desperate for change and many of the people he knew were working to make similar radical and creative statements about, contributions to, and interventions in society.[39] He describes whole communities of terrified people working creatively and intersectionally on issues such as gay rights, women's rights, antiracism, anti–Vietnam War, and Marxism, among others. When he chose in the early seventies to write and record a Marxist gay country album, he worked with other gay activists and allies, but he had no other gay country musicians to connect with and, as chapter 1 explored, no gay role models. In his now-iconic 1973 release, Patrick Haggerty's album invoked genre, sexuality, and place in its name, *Lavender Country* (which was also the name of the band and an imagined place referred to in one of their songs). While making an impact with isolated gay listeners across the country, Haggerty was not welcome in Nashville until 2017. After a few years of performances at pride events and elsewhere, the original Lavender Country band dissolved, and its members developed other careers and lives.

Given Haggerty's and others' testimonies about the activism and creative fervor of the early 1970s, it should be no surprise to learn that in 1973, when Haggerty and his friends released the first out gay country album in a pressing of just one thousand records, which were advertised in gay bookstores and magazines, the newly lesbian-identified folk singer-songwriter Alix Dobkin, who had been active in folk music since 1962, released her now-iconic first album of the women's music movement, *Lavender Jane Loves Women*. Dobkin stopped performing for men and gave lectures, as well as toured, with her music, working to arm women with feminist knowledge. Like Lavender Country, Dobkin pressed one thousand albums and sold them via ads in *Ms.* and *Off Our Backs*. The album included the existing folk song "Beware Young Ladies" (also known as "Beware, Oh Take Care"), warning young women about nefarious men. The folk song took on a new meaning as an invitation to join the lesbian feminist movement and avoid such men, as Dobkin, in her song "View from Gay Head," proclaims, "Any woman can be a lesbian!"

Meanwhile, also in 1973, Moses Asch's Folkways Records released three gay and lesbian folk albums: Michael Cohen's *What Did You Expect? . . . Songs about the Experience of Being Gay*, Kathy Fire's *Songs of Fire: Songs of a Lesbian*

Anarchist, and producer Ginni Clemmons's compilation *Gay and Straight To-gether.* As ethnomusicologist Cindy Boucher richly details, these albums were part of Folkways' turn to embrace lesbians and gay men as "newly imagined audiences," or what seem to me to be newly valuable groups of "the folk" whose activism and stories became viewed by straight allies (as well as, probably, not-yet-out folk industry insiders) as worth collecting and disseminating.[40]

The following year, self-described "outside psychedelic country experimen-tal" musician Peter Grudzien (1941–2013) released a five-hundred-copy press-ing of his entirely self-created album *The Unicorn,* featuring the song "White Trash Hillbilly Trick" and a song about his lover Mark from Kentucky, "Ken-tucky Candy." Grudzien's later life was documented by filmmakers Isabelle Dupuis and Tim Geraghty in a 2017 film titled after Grudzien's first album. Unfortunately, Grudzien suffered from severe mental health issues and never developed financial security, likely affecting the circulation of his music.

Also in 1974, well-known folk musician, activist, and author Si Kahn re-leased *New Wood,* featuring a gay song, "Curtains of Old Joe's House." And successful all-women country rock band the Deadly Nightshade came to-gether with three members of 1967's band Ariel (a five-piece alt-rock band who met while students at Smith College and Mount Holyoke College), reuniting in 1974 to play a women's music festival. Unlike the other lesbian and gay country and folk musicians of this moment, they were signed to a major label, RCA, which released their self-titled album in 1975, followed by *Funky & Western* in 1976. At the height of their popularity they toured as an opener for Billy Joel's "New York State of Mind" tour in 1976, played the Philadelphia Folk Song Festival, and appeared on PBS's *Sesame Street.* While the band was perceived as being comprised of out lesbians, Pamela Brandt, the band's lesbian member, told Chris Dickinson that she was not out dur-ing the band's first run, which spanned 1974 to 1977 (the band reunited from 2008 until Brandt's death in 2015, releasing their third album in 2012).[41]

Trans lesbian singer-songwriter Beth Elliott, a member of her local chapter of the lesbian activist group Daughters of Bilitis, wrote and recorded *Kid, Have You Rehabilitated Yourself?* in 1976, which features, among several earnest folk songs, a humorous anticountry lesbian-feminist folk song, "The Oklahoma Women's Liberation Front." This album was only first released in 2005 with the new title *Buried Treasure,* as Elliott was bullied out of the women's movement by a stalker who has followed her for most of her adult life.[42] Elliott went on to independently record a "dykeabilly" album, *The Bucktooth Varmints*, with San Francisco drag king and transgender male musician Anderson Toone in the 1990s.

The all-women old-time group Reel World String Band formed in 1978 and has been active since, featuring lesbian musician Sue Massek, who has mentored many queer Appalachian musicians during her career.[43] While Massek is lesbian and the group consists of women, their repertoire focuses on the topic of labor, especially coal mining, which is of central urgency in Appalachia, where big industry has ravaged the environment and community. Massek's work mentoring later generations of out queer Appalachian musicians (discussed below) has, however, contributed to a new body of work that continues to address labor rights, as well as making space for (other) queer Appalachian concerns.

In 1984 world-famous singer and songwriter k.d. lang got her start as a country musician with *A Truly Western Experience*, followed by 1987's *Angel with a Lariat* and 1988's *Shadowland*, with famous Nashville sound producer Owen Bradley. While lang did not officially come out to her audience until 1992, when she had shifted genre to adult contemporary, to many early fans it was clear all along who she was. Her 1984 debut, *A Truly Western Experience*, begins with a cover of rockabilly song "Bopalena," in which she repeats, "Bopalena, she's my gal!"[44] lang realized after her 1989 Grammy win for *Absolute Torch and Twang* that if she was still not getting played on country radio, she never would be.[45] She switched genre with 1992's *Ingenue*, which went double platinum in the United States and earned her a Grammy Award. Her final country album was a soundtrack for the 1993 film *Even Cowgirls Get the Blues*. Yet she was never fully embraced by the country music industry, which, as I discussed in chapter 1, could not decide if she was sincere in her performance in the genre. Whether it was her dashing butch looks, her genderqueer hijinks, her songs that seemed pretty clearly lesbian, her veganism, or her Canadianness, country radio refused to play her music. Yet in 2018, Americana claimed her as a trailblazer.

GAY RODEO AND THE AIDS ERA

The International Gay Rodeo Association was founded in 1985 and hosted some gay country musicians who appeared in few other venues. Sid Spencer was one of the most successful gay country singers on the rodeo circuit, active in the late 1980s and releasing the album *Out-n-About, Again* in 1995, as well as *Lovin' Strangers*, the posthumous album, in 1996 after he died from AIDS-related causes.[46] "The Castro Cowboy," Charlie Pacheo, started listening to country to find solace due to his partner's death from AIDS-related illness in 1996. He released *Here Comes the Blues* in 1999.[47]

In 1992, Teresa McLaughlin (maiden name Stevens) from rural Mississippi and based in New York, was known as a gay male-identified baroque counter-tenor. Stevens was diagnosed as HIV-positive. Stevens' partner left and Stevens fell into despair. While Stevens had been "trying forever not to be a country person," the diagnosis and breakup led to an unexpected embrace of country music, forming the Out Band, which recorded *Out in the Country* in 1993, *When Love Is Right* in 1995, and *From Christopher to Castro* in 2000.[48] In 1998 Stevens founded the Lesbian and Gay Country Music Association, which supported and created networking opportunities for lesbian and gay musicians in country music until 2007. Chris Dickinson's 1999 article about gay country musicians for the *Journal of Country Music* led to Stevens connecting with Patrick Haggerty.[49] They toured together between 2001 and 2003 but could not attract enough interest to sustain their musical work together. Stevens retired from musical performance in 2007 and transitioned gender in 2009. She married and works in cyber security, publishes science fiction, and lives in a suburb of Portland, Oregon.[50]

While the International Gay Rodeo Circuit continues to flourish, this community has not produced out country musicians who have recorded and worked to create community in the way Stevens and the others did. And even Stevens's and Haggerty's efforts to promote lesbian and gay country music were an enormous challenge and went largely unrewarded until straight white cisgender male music producers discovered Haggerty's music in 2014.

LESBIAN AND GAY MAINSTREAM COUNTRY ARTISTS?

Richell Renee Wright, known professionally as Chely Wright, was a mainstream country star for fifteen years before coming out in 2010 and having her sales cut in half. In 2017 her website featured prominently a *Rolling Stone* article that explained her genre trouble:

The former mainstream country star and current New York resident Chely Wright, making a rare Music City appearance to debut material from her just-released *I Am the Rain* album, who had the lion's share to win or lose [at the 2016 AmericanaFest]—and win she did. The startling production [by Americana producer Joe Henry] and lyrical heft to the material on Wright's exceptional LP (think *Interiors*-era Roseanne Cash) is tailor-made for Nashville's preeminent listening room. . . . *I Am the Rain* was funded in part by a record-breaking Kickstarter campaign. When all was said and done, the LP was the number one most-funded country music Kickstarter project to date. It also ranks as the 11th most successful music campaign in the global benefit corporation's history.[51]

In *Rolling Stone* writer Stephen Betts's passage above, Wright is no longer identified as a country artist; instead, she is now a "New York resident," as though coming out and moving to New York City entirely shifted her identity and genre. The references all clearly point the album toward Americana rather than country music, including comparison to Roseanne Cash and mention of her appearance at the AmericanaFest. Perhaps most startling is the enormous Kickstarter campaign, which demonstrates the continued interest of listeners, as well as the fact that Wright no longer had the support of any executives in the country music industry.

While Wright has continued to make music, she has been forced to shift genre affiliation to Americana, a change that she does not seem happy about. In a 2014 *Guardian* interview celebrating Paradise of Bachelors' reissue of Patrick Haggerty's 1973 out gay country album, Wright said that she doubted that either the world or Nashville was ready for the lyrics in Haggerty's album or for an artist to come out at age nineteen, which she said would be "idiotic." She explained, "People in the industry—studios, labels, radio programmers—are generally open and understanding . . . but the fanbase is a different thing. . . . I wouldn't call the industry homophobic, but they're afraid of the fear lots of fans have about gay people. So they package us as straight, and we let them." Why? "Because we all want to be part of the big game."[52] As a closeted commercial artist signed with MCA Nashville Records, Wright played stadium shows, but as an out independent artist, she more recently booked the 490-seat Freight and Salvage in Berkeley, California, which also hosted Girlyman and Coyote Grace. Yet at least Wright was able to pivot to appealing to an Americana audience. Her fellow out gay mainstream country musician peer Ty Herndon's style is firmly pop country, and although he was outed by arrest in 1995, he had three number 1 country songs between 1995 and 2000. He didn't reach the stardom Wright had (with a certified gold record, tours with then-boyfriend and mainstream country star Brad Paisley, and multiple award nominations, including a win for the Academy of Country Music's Top New Female Vocalist). Coming out in 2014 brought Herndon more attention than he had received in over a decade. Afterward, he became involved in activism, a move Wright has also made.

Wright was already active in charity before she came out, and after coming out she developed an identity as an activist, donning a rainbow flag for the cover of the DVD release of the documentary *Wish Me Away* (figure 13) and identifying herself as "artist, activist, author" on her website and on Instagram. Coinciding with the release of her autobiography, *Like Me*, she launched "a non-profit organization, dedicated to providing education, assistance, and resources to LGBT teens and their family and friends."[53] She announced in March 2021 that after "more than a decade" of "work in a multitude of corporate spaces to advance Diversity, Equity & Inclusion," she had accepted a position at real estate corporation "Unispace as their Chief Diversity, Equity and Inclusion Officer," crediting "the practice and craft of storytelling [for] open[ing] up yet another portal of opportunity and fulfillment for me."[54]

Since 2015 Ty Herndon has been organizing an annual Concert for Love and Acceptance through sponsorship with Country Music Television, a benefit for his Foundation for Love and Acceptance. His concert features out musicians as well as allies. While the concert happens in June (Pride month in the United States), the 2020 iteration referenced nonnormative gender and sexuality mostly obliquely through rainbow imagery, without direct reference in stage banter or most songs. Herndon sang several songs meant to signal his identification, such as "So Small," performed with the Rainbow Squad, a support group for LGBTQ youth in Nashville, and "Some Lies I Told Myself," which he said he was glad he didn't believe. Out gay country artist and award-winning songwriter Shane McAnally was most frank, sharing the sort of stage banter that's entirely typical of other queer and trans country musicians at other shows but that was surprisingly rare in this concert. It seemed clear that participants were being careful to focus the concert on a more generalized "love and acceptance." Yet this concert revealed the complicated politics of advocating for LGBT acceptance among some country listeners. Brett

Young participated, singing his number 1 gold single "Lady": "I remember when I heard your heartbeat / It was only eight weeks," a line that references the scientifically inaccurate notion of embryonic heartbeat seemingly as an antichoice dog whistle. The cover art for the single features an embroidered electrocardiogram (presumably the embryo's). The song continues with heteronormative lines about how the expected child, gendered female, will "learn how to be a lady" by following her mother's example and how as a father the narrator will help when the daughter "get[s] [her] heart broke by the wrong guy [*sic*]." But Herndon's 2020 concert also included the Indigo Girls, whose antiracist, feminist, trans-allied, and indigenous sovereignty politics are well known as part of their public personae.

Chely Wright has appeared in Herndon's annual concert multiple times. While she lives in New York, she has yet to attend or perform at the Queer Country Quarterly events in Brooklyn, run by Karen Pittelman, who is less famous and operates in a different circle (although Pittelman has expressed

Figure 13. Promotional poster and DVD cover for Bobbi Birleffi, dir., *Chely Wright: Wish Me Away.*

interest in hosting Wright at Queer Country Quarterly). Wright's activism and social media presence demonstrate her focus on equality and assimilation rather than the radical politics Pittelman's collaborators and audience participate in (discussed further below).

Mary Gauthier (pronounced Go-shay) was born in New Orleans and adopted into a Catholic family in Thibodeaux, Louisiana. Gauthier describes how adoption and her awareness of being a lesbian led to having a difficult childhood, developing drug and alcohol addiction as a teen, and spending time in rehabilitation, halfway houses, and jail. She enrolled briefly in college but dropped out, moving to Boston and eventually enrolling in the Cambridge School of Culinary Arts. Gauthier opened a successful Cajun restaurant, Dixie Kitchen, which she cooked in and ran for eleven years. When she was arrested for drunk driving in 1990, she became sober and also began, at age thirty-five, to write songs.

Her first album was named after her restaurant, and her second album, 1998's *Drag Queens and Limousines*, was financed by selling her share of her restaurant. This album led to major attention, including an invitation to play at the Newport Folk Festival and a Gay and Lesbian Music Award for Best Country Artist of the Year. From the very first song, she tells a queer life story—as a teenager who did not fit in with the "jocks and their girls" at a private high school, she stole her adoptive mother's car and ran away to live with friends (and in the chorus of the song, she describes these friends as "drag queens in limousines, nuns in blue jeans, dreamers with big dreams," "poets and AWOL marines, actors and bar flys [sic], writers with dark eyes, drunks that philosophize"). Songs on the album explore the lives of other outsiders, including a drug addict who finds love and faith and an erotic dancer the narrator is attracted to. Her now-well-known fictionalized song "I Drink" first appeared on this album, using her moving speech-song vocalization to trace the narrator's childhood memory of family discord due to her father's drinking to her later alcoholism.

Gauthier moved to Nashville in 2001 and signed with Harlan Howard Songs. Howard died in 2002, and Gauthier ended up helping Howard's widow, Jan, also a famous country artist, complete some of his final work. In 2005 Gauthier told *The Advocate* that her audience is comprised "mostly of straight guys who have had an inordinate amount of trouble with women. Just like me! They can relate."[55] She was the first public out lesbian to play the Grand

Ole Opry and appears there regularly. Her 2014 song "When a Woman Goes Cold" is perhaps her most obviously lesbian song, although her songs often feature a female lover. Her songs have been recorded by artists from different genre backgrounds, including Jimmy Buffett, Bettye Lavette, Mike Farris, Tim McGraw, and Blake Shelton (the latter of whom, interestingly, does not encourage the queer contestants on his reality TV show, *The Voice*, to try to be country artists).[56] Gauthier's songs have been featured in the country music industry–themed HBO drama *Nashville*, although her music, including her most recent album, *Rifles and Rosary Beads*, cowritten with US war veterans, is more often nominated for awards in folk (where it won the 2018 Album of the Year at the International Folk Music Awards) and Americana music (where it was nominated for 2018 Album of the Year by the Americana Music Association) than country (the Gay and Lesbian American Music Awards, in awarding her a prize in 1998, recognized her as "country"). With fellow songwriters Eliza Gilkyson and Gretchen Peters, Gauthier tours as Three Women and the Truth, a play on Harlan Howard's saying. While Val Denn agency describes them as folk singers and songwriters, bookings describe the variety of genres they might be called, including as a "supergroup of country/ Americana" and "alternative folk."[57] During the Covid-19 pandemic, Gauthier was active playing in virtual queer-themed country and folk shows hosted by Country Queer and Queer Folk Fest and especially her own weekly live-streamed shows from the home she shares in Nashville with girlfriend and fellow country musician Jaimee Harris, featuring a prominent rainbow flag in the background.

Brandi Carlile has been out as a lesbian since her career began. While her band takes her name, she shares the stage with two (straight and cisgender) twin brothers, Tim and Phil Hanseroth, who have been in the band from the beginning and share songwriting credit. Carlile is often described as a rock, folk, or Americana artist and has said, "I've gone through all sorts of vocal phases, from pop to blues to R&B, but no matter what I do, I just can't get the country and western out of my voice."[58] She signed with Columbia Records in 2004. Like many queer country/folk musicians, Carlile was mentored early on by the Indigo Girls, who invited her to tour with them. The song "The Story" led to a breakthrough in fame and sales for Carlile after it was used in GM commercials during the 2008 Summer Olympics. It became a gold record in 2017. In 2019 she was the most nominated woman at the Grammy Awards and won three of the six awards possible, all for music in the Americana genre. Carlile featured two senior women musicians, Mavis Staples and Tanya Tucker, during many shows of her 2019 tour. In her September 2019 performance in Philadelphia, Carlile asked audience members to support female country musicians by buying their music. She also featured sixty-year-old outlaw country star Tanya Tucker as a surprise guest, supporting that artist's first new album of original material in seventeen years, which Carlile produced and cowrote. In 2020 the Americana Music Association nominated Carlile as artist of the year.

Carlile's music has not centered on activist themes the way that a band like Lavender Country or My Gay Banjo has. Perhaps this is one of many reasons her band was able to attract a much larger audience before releasing a political song like "The Joke" in 2017, which empathetically depicted boys fearing bullying over gender, sexuality, and ability; girls facing sexism; and immigrants facing danger at the southern border of the United States.[59] Indeed, I've noticed some instances of listeners objecting to anti-Trump messages in her music, shows, or social media feed. At the outdoor show in Philadelphia I attended in 2019, two audience members sitting next to me shook their head when Mavis Staples suggested she'd run for president to oust Donald Trump, yet they appeared to enjoy both Staples's set and Carlile's.

These artists' success and yet ambiguity in genre suggest that while out lesbians and gay men can reach relative stardom in the early twenty-first century, their ability to register their country-like music *as country* is still limited.

"QUEER AND FUCKED"

Lesbians' participation in folk music during this same time period was limited, and they often depended on women-focused music scenes for loyal audiences. The discourse of and about the twentieth-century folk revival did not figure prominent musicians Joan Baez's and Ronnie Gilbert's bisexuality into the conception of folk. Ongoing oppression of women and lesbian musicians made creating a separate women's music scene a necessity, as Amy Ray argues in response to a *New York Times* article by David Hajdu on queer people in folk music:

> Women always have to ruin everything. Now we are strangling the life and diversity out of folk music. You would think lesbian folk musicians are sailing

up the radio charts and selling millions of records; instead we're fighting the same battles we've fought for years. In fact, the world of singer/songwriters is still dominated by men. . . . Sure there is a queer folk scene out there and luckily, it's thriving, but only in the most marginal way. It's never really a good time in the mainstream music industry to be a queer girl with a guitar. I can look at the trajectory of my own career and see that the more political the Indigo Girls have become, the less radio play and press we have received.[60]

The women's music scene developed out of necessity—women have never been treated fairly by the music industry or generally by society, so if they wanted to make music on their own terms, they *had* to create a women's music industry to support the many musicians who simply were not regarded as the musically skilled, poetically insightful humans they were. Ray educates readers about the role marketing demographics have in making a certain facet of identity a major part of a band's publicity and that, if successful, this information is then used to sell something else to this demographic. But as Ray points out,

as far as the mainstream media is concerned, our image is our handicap. Gay musicians aren't marketed to the mainstream as, "Hurray! Here's a new lesbian band, aren't they cool?" Instead, we are the subject of painstaking scrutiny and strategizing to figure out how to overcome our image. Being gay is not considered an asset at most record labels, indie or major. When the record label finally takes advantage of the gay press, its [sic] because the mainstream press won't touch the band. Gay press coverage is the last resort for most publicist [sic]. In the Indigo Girls' case, it took Epic Records years to catch up. Epic simply preferred not to respect or cater to the gay press, but when the mainstream media stopped paying attention to us, Epic starting returning gay media's phone calls.

So while Epic might have seen the band playing a woman-themed event as a limitation, Ray notes in another entry from the band's blog that their experience performing in all four years of the Lilith Fair tour (1997–99, 2010) exposed their music to a broader audience. These events were also extremely important, given that their experience was that all-woman bands were not as likely to receive the invitations and support they need to thrive. Yet one problem within the women's music circuit was that the Michigan Womyn's Music Festival, the major festival from 1976 until its final gathering in 2015, excluded women of trans experience. In 1991 Nancy Jean Burkholder circulated a survey of participants about their willingness to allow trans women. But organizer Lisa Vogel reaffirmed her "intention" that the festival was for "womyn-born-womyn." Beginning in 1995 this policy was protested by Camp Trans, a direct-action campsite just outside the boundaries of Michfest. The Indigo Girls, who had raised the issue publicly with the festival organizer at least as early as 2005, eventually told the festival that they would not play again until the festival allowed trans women entry.[61] Hajdu was correct that a growing number of lesbians were finding some success within folk music, but their achievement was often limited to the opportunities they were creating for themselves and one another through collaboration, discussed in the next section, as well as in the final chapter of the book.

"ANOTHER COUNTRY"

Some of the queer and trans musicians active in the first twenty years of the twenty-first century have spoken out with alternative understandings of the history of country music, rethinking genre boundaries, explaining exclusions of people and styles from existing genres and forming coalitions to include them, reclaiming genres from which they have been excluded, and inventing new musical and identity labels. Karen Pittelman's Another Country festival on 2 July 2017 was named after gay Black author James Baldwin's 1962 novel of that name, which is set in 1950s New York City and, in its title, imagines an alternative nation in which people are not oppressed into self-hatred and suicide due to racism, interracial relationships, and queer love.[62] Pittelman's festival was a fundraiser for the Trans Justice Funding Project, which she cofounded, and highlighted coalitional embrace of straight and cisgender Black country and folk musicians as kindred members of her regular queer and trans country lineup.[63]

"OLD-TIME MUSIC IS ACTUALLY VERY QUEER"

White old-time musician and American studies scholar A. J. Lewis began his September 2016 Queer Country Quarterly set at Branded Saloon in Brooklyn with the song "Darling Corey," about a woman who was a "rounder" (figure 14). This word has been used since the mid-nineteenth century in North America to describe "a habitual criminal, idler, or drunkard," someone

Figure 14. A. J. Lewis plays the Another Country festival, 2 July 2017, Brooklyn. Photo by the author.

who seems to exploit charity, and also sometimes an itinerant rail worker. In terms of its resonance to Lewis's queer analysis, a rounder is someone who is excluded from her community, impoverished, thus roaming, perhaps using substances for comfort, and generally seeming to fail to behave according to community expectations.[64] After the song, while noodling on his banjo, Lewis explained his queer theory of old-time music to the audience:

> For any of you who haven't heard me play before, I have this view that the old-time genre is actually a very queer cultural tradition. The songs I'm doing this evening have a theme: death, destruction, and decline. Death in its literal and metaphorical incarnations: biological death, the wearing away of the body. But also forms of social and psychic death: the deteriora-

tion of social ties, the undoing of normative social orders, the unraveling of the self. There's actually a lot of this in old-time music. Don't worry, a lot of these songs will also be pretty chipper! In fact, I think death and destruction is a cool lens through which to explore the queerness of the old-time genre, because these are all songs by and for misfits, social outcasts, social outsiders, people who lived their lives outside of heterosexual kinship structures, who refused dominant norms of capital accumulation, health, longevity, happiness.[65]

Lewis's interpretation brilliantly reveals resonances for queer and trans listeners in the song characters' "queered" social positions and life experiences, for even if these characters and songwriters were attracted to people of the "opposite sex," the way they lived their lives was outside of the middle-class norms presumed when many people think of heterosexuality and cisgender experience. Lewis's narrative thus aligns with Nadine Hubbs's assessment of the "queerness" of the working class, in which straight men may be feminized by poverty and rural life and straight women may be masculinized by it. Hubbs's argument also squares with Lewis's discussion of the rural working class's differing ability to or prioritization of accumulation of capital, health, longevity, and happiness.[66]

Lewis went on to play a medley of morphine songs before bringing queer fiddler Nell Geiser onstage and introducing the "omnipresent" old-time song, "The Cuckoo." Lewis built on rock critic Greil Marcus's point that the cuckoo is

a paradigmatically American bird.[67] The cuckoo in [Marcus's] view is a sort of outsider bird. It's a brood parasite that lays its eggs in other birds' nests and doesn't have a home. And in Griel Marcus's view, America is a kind of outsider nation. There's a tacit American exceptionalism in this reading that I do not endorse. Also a kind of amnesia around settler colonialism that allows him to romanticize his America as an outsider nation. But I do like to think of the cuckoo as a queer bird in the sense that its primary allegiances are not those of biological kinship. It refuses the cult of child-rearing. And as a transsexual I have a special affinity for the cuckoo, because, as we all know, when that cuckoo egg hatches, it flouts whatever biologized expectations that the rest of us have projected onto it and ends up being something else entirely.

Hearing old-time music through Lewis's interpretation takes Marcus's "old, weird America" to reveal a queerness and transness that was there all along. Yet his analysis of Marcus's book does not allow for his celebration of the song's queerness to forgive Marcus's interpretation of America as exceptional nor to forget its settler colonialism.

Lewis's intersectional analysis of this well-known song and the famous rock journalist's interpretation resonates with Black gay fiddler Jake Blount's unraveling of genre around the concept of old-time. Blount describes his music as "genrequeer," a musical play on "genderqueer," a term used in the first decade of the twenty-first century to describe gender performances tied to queerness, often those not exclusively masculine or feminine, an identification now more often described as nonbinary. As Blount explained to journalist Rachel Cholst when asked about his music's genre, "I play fiddle and banjo music from black and Native American musicians, mostly in the Southeastern United States, which is not a genre, but a sentence."[68] Cholst continued:

> You'll see that Blount uses the term old-time throughout our conversation, but he cautions that it erases the most fundamental history of country, bluegrass, and roots music. "It references these kinds of genre divisions that were put in place at the outset of the recording industry in the South, which were partially based on the race of the performers and the race of the target demographics for those records. So what they called 'hillbilly records' at the time, we now call that stuff old time. That was by white musicians and for white people. A lot of black people who were playing the music, the folks that I'm now spending so much time studying and basing my career around, they were written out of the story because they weren't considered marketable." Which, in turn, has consequences for the artists who originated the form. "For me, the term 'old time,' and really any synonymous term, is this racist fabrication of what the musical landscape of the South really was. And I don't view old-time and blues and gospel and bluegrass as being these neatly separable categories. For me, it's really about different ways of voicing some of the same musical themes and same lyrical themes that you find throughout all of those genres."[69]

As Blount describes genre, so too is he describing the problems with identity categories, which intersect and define one another by their intersections. Blount's understanding is one that a number of musicians and scholars share, but it has not yet gained traction with most bluegrass and old-time players.

"AMERICANA'S IDENTITY CRISIS"

One solution to shedding trappings of other related genres is to invent a new name, which is what happened with "Americana." Americana, also called "alternative country," started to gain attention in the late 1980s. The fans of the band Uncle Tupelo are often credited with naming and propelling this genre through an early online community, alt.country. In describing this genre, Richard Peterson and Bruce Beal posit that musical genre is not always dependent on style, instrumentation, record label, or radio format but rather may be shaped by image, listeners' rhetoric, canonical lyric topics, and distribution techniques. However, musicologist Jason Kirby argues that alternative country actually has more in common with rock than with country.[70] Its stylistic elements include a blend of country and punk rock (previously called "cowpunk") that draws on elements of the honky-tonk era, what Peterson calls "hard-core" country (versus "soft-shell").[71] Perhaps demonstrating this genre's disputed relationship to country, the Americana Music Association has used the term "Americana" since 1999 to describe a radio format featuring a variety of roots and country musicians, including some old-timers who have been repackaged as precursors to and members of this genre. This process of rock-based genres identifying and redefining certain kinds of music or musicians as "roots" is, as Benjamin Filene and Elijah Wald argue, the basic premise of the category of "roots" music.[72]

As Fabian Holt notes, the turn of the millennium, especially the 2000 Coen Brothers' hit film *O Brother, Where Art Thou?*, exponentially increased the already growing interest in this music. The issue of the name of this music became a problem: Where were record stores shelving the nine-million-record-selling *O Brother* soundtrack, the 2001 follow-up release of a Ryman Hall performance on film and CD, and copycat compilations such as Rounder's *O Sister! The Women's Bluegrass Collection*? "Country" signified "mainstream country," and marketers did not want to turn away those middle-class customers who liked *O Brother* after having always claimed to like "anything but country."[73] Holt observed that as the classification debate extended to existing specialist music communities, those experienced participants interpreted the new interest generated by *O Brother* as more sweeping and general and thus not drawing in new practitioners of bluegrass or old-time. He notes that New York City's Tower Records employees created a "roots" room, tying *O Brother* to PBS's 2001 *American Roots Music* series. But the question remains as to why "folk" was not employed. Holt muses that perhaps using a different term deployed a novelty effect and that "roots" sounds as if it covers more styles, concluding that "the term [roots] could also signal that the distinctions between folk and popular have collapsed" and that folk's perceived ties to socialism were not as widely appealing in that historical moment.[74] Indeed, the politics of "alt.country," "Americana," or "roots" did not seem readily apparent, other than to distinguish itself from mainstream country.

And this ambiguity may explain why, in the second decade of the twenty-first century, some participants and critics were more vocal about "the Americana genre's identity crisis," as *Rolling Stone* writer Jonathan Bernstein's 2017 article about the lack of Black musicians and musicians of color in Americana stated.[75] But what does it mean for a *genre* to have an identity crisis? Alynda Segarra's 2015 op-ed in the *Bluegrass Situation* suggests the stakes for folk music at the core of this "identity crisis."

"WHAT DOES FOLK MEAN TO YOU?"

In a (now removed) 19 May 2015 op-ed in the *Bluegrass Situation* titled "Alynda Segarra's Call to Folk Singers: Fall in Love with Justice," Segarra urges fellow folk singers to engage with the Black Lives Matter movement.[76] She claims that addressing this issue is a defining facet of being a folk singer in the contemporary moment: "If you are too afraid to stand up for people who are marching in the streets saying 'STOP KILLING US' then you, my friend, are not a folk singer." She goes on to ask, "What does folk mean to you?" This question is crucial, although it's not clear that there's an agreed-upon answer among musicians. Segarra argues that folk music is an alternative to corporate media. She looks back to those musicians from folk's history now idolized and repositions them as "fragile and real" people "who felt they needed to be free. They fought and they sang and they spoke out." Since at least the 1940s, folk groups such as the Almanac Singers and the Weavers had characterized the folk revival as powered by social justice imperatives. The Weavers began as a

Figure 15. Hurray for the Riff Raff, World Café Live, Philadelphia, 21 April 2017. Photo by the author.

group that organized for a candidate, and throughout their lives, its members organized around issues of justice. Yet both then and now, there have been folk musicians and listeners who were *not* using music to participate in justice work. In his documentary *Festival!* about the Newport Folk Festival in the early 1960s, director Murray Lerner included interviews with folk listeners who did not subscribe to social justice politics. Sometimes the genre has simply been romanticized as a remnant of a simpler agrarian past.

Segarra draws insights from the ways that she has been tokenized as a bisexual Puerto Rican woman playing folk music with her band, Hurray for the Riff Raff (figure 15):

As a folksinger, I have met with much appreciated critical acclaim this year. As a young Puerto Rican female, I have also been besieged by interviews questioning every part of my identity in the context of folk music. I have been asked again and again how it feels to represent "the voiceless."

This term "the voiceless" is a blanket phrase used for anyone who strays from the white heterosexual normative. It is a term used for the people I come from, and not many know how frustrating it can be. People who experience oppression are not voiceless; their voices are simply not being heard. I'd like to offer a new term for "the voiceless": "the unheard."

What does it mean when we ignore people and then label them "voiceless"? What does it do to our collective psyche? I believe it conditions us not to listen to them. I believe it creates an environment where anyone who is an "other" is tokenized. When people of color are "allowed" into the world of modern folk music we are held up as spokespeople. We are thought to be special, unlike the "voiceless" others of our background. Though I am proud of my people and enjoy speaking about where I came from, perhaps some context and education is in order. No one enjoys to be treated as a token.[77]

That she felt the need to write this op-ed and then felt pressure to take it down suggest that Segarra's definition of folk music was quite different from her fellow musicians' in the Americana Music Association at the time. She did, however, receive accolades from peers and reviewers even as her sound dramatically shifted to incorporate less Appalachian sound and more musical inspiration and activism around her Puerto Rican roots. (The fact that this focus should make her seem less like an Americana musician is a problem in itself and something that she and Rhiannon Giddens, the mixed-race straight cisgender multi-instrumentalist and singer songwriter of the Carolina Chocolate Drops, Our Native Daughters, and MacArthur Award fame, spoke about in her 2017 International Bluegrass Music Association keynote address.)

As the Americana movement and the International Bluegrass Music Association (IBMA) worked to navigate the politics of their music in the BLM era, tokenization seemed to be a step in the process, developing a "diversity showcase" in which gay and lesbian musicians played alongside musicians of color. (Although queer fiddler Tatiana Hargreaves noted to me that she and other participants of the Shout and Shine Showcase at the IBMA conference felt grateful that there was a stage/tent available throughout the entire conference for minoritized participants to jam with, socialize with, listen to, and dance with like-minded participants.)[78] Yet as Giddens reminded her audience in her 2017 keynote address to the IBMA, musicians of color were crucial to the historical development of bluegrass and thus should not be invited to feel (newly) welcome but rather credited as originators and, if they wish, be embraced back into the fold.[79]

Alternately, some Black queer musicians seem happy to have forged a career that engages with country elements and isn't concerned with how country music defines their music or career. Grammy Award–winning singer-songwriter Brittany Howard was famous first as the then not publicly out singer, guitarist, and songwriter of the southern rock band Alabama Shakes, active since 2009, with a 2012 debut album and a follow-up album that was number 1 on release in 2014. Howard became aware that she was a lesbian around age twenty-five, although she didn't discuss her sexuality with the press until releasing her solo album *Jaime* in 2019. Howard has pursued multiple projects apart from her original band, seemingly as a way to navigate some of the constraints she feels around creativity and identity. She's lead singer and guitarist of a rock band named Thunderbitch, started in 2012 in Nashville, with a surprise album in 2015. In Thunderbitch, which makes few live appearances but has a music video, Howard performs in whiteface and often appears on a motorcycle and wearing a black leather jacket, about which she wrote a telling song, "Leather Jacket," which explores rock myths about coolness. She has been changed for the better by this article of clothing, with the lyrics "they said it would change me and it does," "is gonna hold my soul in," and "I would look so real, / Now I do what I wanna." In 2017 she, Becca Mancari, and Jesse Lafser (her future wife) formed a queer Nashville-based band called Bermuda Triangle.[80] She released her solo debut in 2019 to critical acclaim and public discussion of her sexuality, which was a topic of songs for the first time. Her Instagram handle, "Blackfootwhitefoot," refers to being interracial but also seems to point to her feet standing in different places, perhaps in different genres. In 2021 the array of genres in which she was nominated for Grammy Awards was truly remarkable: Best Rock Song, Best Alternative Music Album, Best R&B Performance, Best American Roots Performance.

British country soul singer-songwriter Yola was invited to join the Highwomen in 2021, signaling an embrace by this activist women's super group to change the experiences of women in country music. In media, both artists seemed to describe their approach to country music's racist exclusion as simply having one foot planted in country and not fighting about genre categorization. This strategy seems beneficial yet unfortunate, since country music has so often been defined *against* Blackness, from Cecil Sharp's song collection to the musically unwarranted invention of "race records" as separate from "hillbilly."

"FABULACHIAN" MUSICIANS
AND "COUNTRY [FOLX] IN THE CITY"

Appalachian lesbian and gay musicians make choices around what parts of
their identities they reveal and how, as well as what political issues are at the
forefront of their musical work—often these are labor and, specifically, coal
workers' union politics. They are working within a network of established
folk and traditional professional musicians and activists of the baby boomer
generation, some of whom, like the Reel World String Band and duo Cathy
Fink and Marcy Marxer, are lesbian but not loudly so (for a variety of reasons,
one being that they have been active as children's music artists).[81] Meanwhile,
the musicians of Generations X and Y who are based on the East and West
Coasts often operate in the indie singer-songwriter scene, and their gigs tend
to connect with their queer and trans activism and education. While My Gay
Banjo, a queer country band whose members play their own songs, as well as
an occasional mashup of a popular song with their own material, come out
simply in the name of their band, they do not attempt to draw an audience
large enough to make their living from their music. Both musicians also earn a
living doing other work. For My Gay Banjo, queerness is front and center for
nearly their entire set. But for other musicians who have played Queer Country Quarterly, country, or other related musical genres, music and other concerns typically take center stage, while their sexual and gender identifications
may or may not be directly discussed onstage or in their standard publicity.

These two worlds have collided some, for example when Pittelman (figure
16) invited Appalachian musicians Sam Gleaves and Tyler Hughes (figure 18)
and welcomed the return of Philadelphia-based My Gay Banjo (figure 17) to
perform at Queer Country Quarterly on 19 November 2016. Their performances and interactions with other musicians and the audience on those
nights made clear that their musical worlds are each somewhat different. One
moment I witnessed demonstrates the ways that different musical traditions
come together in this scene in ways that might offend "the bluegrass police."
The members of My Gay Banjo are from the Northeast, where Owen Taylor
grew up on a farm in Connecticut before moving to New York City and then
Philadelphia. Professionally he's an urban farmer, and he wrote about this
queer migration in his song "Country Boys in the City" (and the album of the
same name). After the show, I was chatting with Julia Allen and Owen Taylor

Figure 16. Karen and the Sorrows, Brooklyn, 22 September 2017. Photo by the author.

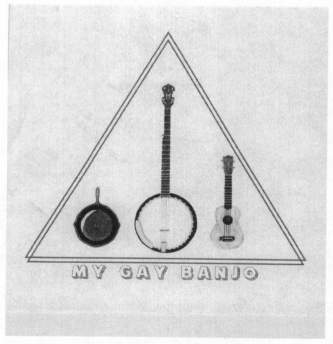

Figure 17. My Gay Banjo image for their album *Country Boys in the City*, 2014.

Figure 18. Sam Gleaves's and Tyler Hughes's debut at Queer Country Quarterly, 19 November 2016. Photo by the author.

from My Gay Banjo when we met Gleaves and Hughes for the first time. Two things happened that confirmed my sense that this series had brought together people from very different musical backgrounds who don't call their music the same thing or even play similar music. First, Taylor said how impressed he was with Gleaves's banjo playing and that he felt embarrassed to be playing in front of him. Gleaves replied that Taylor's playing worked well for his music, which was friendly and also showed that he understood a distinction between the two bands' music. Gleaves and Hughes both have Appalachian musical training with famous mentors (in Hughes's case, a college major in bluegrass, old-time, and country music studies at East Tennessee State University, and in Gleaves's case, a major in Appalachian studies at Berea College). They play multiple instruments, including banjo, guitar, and fiddle, and they sing. They can jam in bluegrass, a musically virtuosic genre related to both jazz and country that features showy improvisational solos. My Gay Banjo's music seems designed for a queer and trans audience to feel supported, recognize their community's history, and feel activated to participate in social justice. Their musical lines are simple and require no instrumental or vocal virtuosity to perform. Yet their songs are moving and their performances compelling to their intended audience. The second interaction that stood out was that Steele Allen told Gleaves and Hughes how she hadn't seen anyone hold a violin on their armpit. This style of holding the fiddle is standard in old-time music, but Steele Allen comes from a singer-songwriter and activist tradition in which players might not have been exposed to the traditional ways of playing. Pittelman's consistent efforts to create the Queer Country Quarterly phenomenon brought these musicians together for the Brooklyn audience.

At my kitchen table thirteen months later, Gleaves, Hughes, and their Nashville-based white lesbian country and bluegrass bassist friend, Hasse Cacciolo, discussed how they typically describe their music and how queerness fits in with that. It was clear that Queer Country Quarterly had been a fun and unusual gig for them and that they typically don't play shows to a majority queer audience or under the description of country. Gleaves appears via folk societies and traditional music festivals. On the Google music profile for Gleaves he's described as folk, but on his own website he describes himself as an "Appalachian singer—multi-instrumentalist—songwriter." He studied with Sheila Kay Adams and has been mentored by and appeared on tour with lesbian folk singer duo Cathy Fink and Marcy Marxer (figure 19). With the help of Fink, he recorded a debut album featuring a host of famous straight guests, mostly from the bluegrass world, but also Janis Ian, a well-known lesbian folk musician. Gleaves and Hughes attend the IBMA, where they appeared in a new "diversity showcase" (the Shout and Shine Showcase), but as they clarified to me, they do not identify their genre as bluegrass. Hughes instead prefers the term "Appalachian." Gleaves and his friends' invented term for their identities is "fabulachian."[82]

Amythyst Kiah (figure 20), from East Tennessee, earned a master's degree in bluegrass, old-time, and country music studies from East Tennessee State University and is Black and queer. Simply being a Black country artist is enough difference for Kiah to maintain on a regular basis, and while she appeared in Pittelman's Queer Country Quarterly, she did not "come out" regularly during her shows until 2020. At the shows I observed remotely at

Figure 19. Marcy Marxer, Cathy Fink, and Sam Gleaves play a Philadelphia Folk Song Society show on 22 October 2017. Photo by the author.

Figure 20. Amythyst Kiah's New York debut, Queer Country Quarterly, Branded Saloon, Brooklyn, 2 September 2016. Photo by the author.

Figure 21. The very white-appearing audience for Rhiannon Giddens's and Amythyst Kiah's concert at Longwood Gardens near Philadelphia in Pennsylvania, 13 June 2018. Photo by the author.

Colgate University, in person at Longwood Gardens in Pennsylvania (figure 21), and in person at Queer Country Quarterly, Kiah did not mention sexuality. However, in her latest work with the Black female quartet of banjo-playing singer-songwriters and solo album debut includes her openly lesbian song "Black Myself." At the 2020 virtual Philadelphia Folk Festival, Kiah shared with the live-streaming audience that writing music for and with Our Native Daughters had emboldened her to make music that would have seemed too political earlier in her career.

"HOW DO YOU BECOME A
TRANSGENDER COUNTRY SINGER?"

In *Gender Failure*, an autobiographical performance piece and book about queer "gender failure" and how the gender binary fails everyone at some point, Canadian artist Rae Spoon poses a question about their own career path and answers partly in jest with a list of best practices for becoming a transgender country singer: "How do you become a transgender country singer? For some, it's easier to be transgender from the start and then work towards becoming a singer. For others, it's better to play music first, and then come out as transgender. About ten years ago, I managed to do both in the space of a few months."[83] While likely realizing that audiences might be surprised to learn of the existence of a transgender country singer, let alone imagine this combination as a career path, Spoon does not invest in concerns about gender and genre fit in this statement. Instead, with a combination of both deadpan humor and earnestness, an approach I outlined in chapter 1 as "queer sincerity," they reframe a question that may have been (intrusively) asked of them in the past and instead make it rhetorical, considering the people in their audience who might want to become transgender country singers and offering a list of options for those interested in this path. As is typical of camp aesthetics, Spoon's live performances and writing use humor to engage issues that audience members might have a hard time understanding. The humor in this advice stems from the opposing essentialism presumed in both of these identifications, gender and musicianship, which makes "transgender country singer" seem impossible. Yet Spoon's statement doesn't even acknowledge this impossibility, instead offering three different approaches to develop this gender and genre identification: "For some, it's easier to be transgender from the start," Spoon says, knowing that some transgender people recognized something important about their gender at an early age, although until recently in North American culture, there has been little recognition of a path to honor this understanding of self.[84] For others, becoming a musician first allowed a pathway to coming to understand themselves as transgender later. Some singers have described the benefits that their sophisticated knowledge of their voices and bodies has offered to their transitions. But as Spoon illustrates in the third option, they unintentionally became identified as transgender and a country singer during the same period.

Spoon's semijoke does raise questions. Is country a welcoming genre for transgender singers? Is singing a hospitable profession for transgender musicians? What do these questions assume about transgender people and about country music, and, more generally, what do they assume about the relationships between people and types of music? What sorts of narratives about identity and genre fuel the assumption that transgender singers would have a hard time in country music?

Country music and its audiences connote tradition and patriotism, while queer and trans North Americans are thought to be untraditional, suspicious of patriotism, and active in social justice work and to consume music that reflects these values. Yet both halves of this narrative rely on assumptions. Nadine Hubbs and others have argued that the working class was framed as unusually bigoted in order to benefit the (newly culturally omnivorous) middle class.[85] Country music in particular is typically thought to enforce "traditional" images of North American identity, a misleading assumption both about culture and music. In fact, there have always been queer and trans people in North America, although they did not and may still not use the same terms as contemporary middle-class urban and coastal people to describe themselves. Further, as Hubbs demonstrates, country music has actually drawn on the perceived nonnormativity of gender and sexuality in the working class in ways that created both quiet and announced alliances with queer participants. Meanwhile, not all queer and trans people fit the antinormative queer stereotype or even the progressive stereotype that is assumed of them.[86] Queer and trans people live in all parts of the country, despite the mainstream narrative that in order to be happy as a queer person, one must differentiate oneself from one's community of origin and flee to a city (preferably on the coast) to live with other queer-identified people. As ethnographer Mary Gray's research with queer and trans teenagers in Appalachia argues and as oral historian Rae Garringer's work demonstrates, queer and trans people from rural areas may decide to stay and may be happy about that.[87]

White transgender musician Mya Byrne writes in "The Case of the Missing Trans Country Artists" for *Country Queer* that the history of trans country and folk musicians would have been much different if "one of the most respected folk/Americana songwriters of the modern era," Dave Carter, had not died suddenly and unexpectedly in 2002 at age forty-nine, a few months after starting hormones.[88] Carter had come out to musical and (sometimes) romantic partner Tracy Grammar in 2000, shared a new name with friends, and planned a new name for their band (the Butterfly Conservatory, a name that suggests a beautiful and natural identity metamorphosis).[89] Instead, Byrne reflects,

Navigating the early 21st Century without any trans women folk, Americana, or country stars as mentors, has been difficult because as a butch-leaning trans dyke in country/Americana, I honestly don't know many others like me. I don't really have any "possibility models," to use Laverne Cox's term. I mean, I'd love to be hanging with and opening for artists like Mary Gauthier and Lucinda Williams. Our music fits together; we're on playlists together. But it seems, and I've been told as much, that the industry isn't prepared for someone like me. . . . New York periodicals that used to routinely cover me pre-transition—I'd even been named one of New York's most promising artists by *The Aquarian* two months before I came out—didn't respond to any of my requests for press after I came out, and didn't list a single show from that point on.[90]

Byrne points out that the few better-known trans folk, Americana, and country musicians are all white trans men.

SINGING AND (TRANS) IDENTITY

Vocal music has been particularly compelling as a locus of identity performance because, as musicologist Suzanne Cusick observes, while many have assumed that "voices stand for the bodily imperative of biological sex, . . . we know, when we think about it, that voices are culturally constructed."[91] Stephan Pennington challenges the assumption that while appearances may "lie," voices reveal the "truth" about gender; he illustrates the technical workings of vocality that allow most people to "pass" in artificially distinct identity categories.[92] That the material sounds of the interiorly emanating voice are products of social conditioning and can be interpreted and used by listeners in multiple and changing ways makes study of musical performance and reception an enticing subject for better understanding identity. Sung performances of self matter not only for singers but also for all involved in "musicking."[93] Simon Frith argues,

> The issue is not how a particular piece of music or a performance reflects the people, but how it produces them, how it creates and constructs an experience—a musical experience, an aesthetic experience—that we can only make sense of by *taking on* both a subjective and collective identity. The aesthetic, to put this another way, describes the quality of an experience (not the quality of an object); it means experiencing *ourselves* (not

just the world) in a different way. . . . Music making and music listening [are] best understood as an experience of this *self-in-progress*.[94]

Singing can thus be studied as a stylized and (often more) conscious version of identity performance: singing is understood by both musicians and listeners as an articulation of individual agency (having a voice) and an enactment of community (through group singing, as well as a singer's representation of a larger group). (Examples of musicians representing a larger group include Mary Gauthier's award-winning 2018 album of songs "co-written with US veterans and their families," *Rifles and Rosary Beads*, and Joe Stevens's Songs of the People project, in which listeners share a story that becomes a song about their life.)[95] Listeners expect a voice to convey information about a singer's identity and to confirm assumptions based on a singer's visual appearance; popular song genres come with expectations about who is suitable to perform them, how the music is made, and for whom it is intended; and listeners think about their own identities in relation to song characters and singers. Vocal song performance also has special import for publicly expressing and exploring feelings that listeners may express only selectively and privately.[96] Cusick suggests that the pleasure, self-discovery, and communal intimacy of musicking approach—and in identity terms may even surpass—sexuality itself (especially in its limited definition based on gendered object choice).[97] While these insights gesture to the rich potential of transgender musicality, they also suggest the risks it entails.

Given the power and pleasure of voice in popular song, one can imagine some transgender musicians' simultaneous desire to sing and reluctance to be scrutinized on the basis of voice. While not all transgender people transition or make the same choices around transition, staging a professional musical career draws attention to these choices.[98] Why build a career around singing when, for trans men, hormone therapy (if they choose it) may impair their ability to sing or when, for trans women, they may feel the need to significantly alter their vocal range and style? While there are some physiological differences between many men's and women's vocal apparatuses, these do not account for the larger gender disparity in much speech and song. Thus, Pennington recommends analysis of learned gendered tendencies around "pitch, resonance and formants, intonation, timbre, articulation, emphasis, volume/intensity, flow, language usage, and non-verbal communication."[99] For reasons of preference, safety, privacy, and coherence, some transgender people work to change their speaking voices. Some trans people prize this coherence, but others consider vocal adaptation part of the medical establishment's enforcement of an overall gender presentation that reads as heterosexual and otherwise normative.[100] The timing and amount of testosterone used in hormone therapy is thought to be crucial for transgender men who elect this treatment. As musicologist and singer Alexandros N. Constansis has found, for transgender men who abruptly supplement their bodies' testosterone levels later in life than cisgender males' typical adolescence, hormone therapy may thicken the vocal folds without the accompanying cartilage lengthening that cisgender men usually experience. Testosterone ossifies the cartilage in both cisgender and transgender men and, with menopause, cisgender women. For transgender men adding additional testosterone to their bodies, this abrupt ossification can cause hoarseness, can limit control and color, and can reduce the ability to project.[101] Even if a singer supplementing his body's testosterone avoids significant ossification, he can expect other changes that destabilize his vocal range and affect the muscle memory that tells him where to find a particular pitch and where his vocal break is; moreover, he may now be expected to harmonize differently (if there exist, and he wishes to follow, gendered expectations for harmonizing in his preferred genre), and he faces a potential problem with brand recognition if his old voice was his musical signature.[102] Some trans male singers have observed that transgender identification alone (without or prior to hormone usage) has prompted a shift in their vocal gender performance, but others who have chosen not to use hormones face challenges to their gender identification based on the sound of their voice.[103] For example, historian and queer and trans folk musician Simon Fisher Strikeback (previously of Actor Slash Model and currently Mac and Strikeback) performs profoundly intimate music with a slight smirk, singing through the side of his mouth, thus seeming masculine in his demeanor, yet singing vulnerably and with a high vocal register that blends with his cisgender female singing partner (figure 22). While the use of hormone blockers can prevent vocal deepening in adolescents who were assigned male at birth but identify otherwise, transgender women who transition as adults cannot rely on hormones to alter their voices, and so, if they wish to adapt them, they make careful study of the qualities that gender voices.[104]

Despite these complexities, queer and trans country singers are deeply invested in and grateful for their musical careers. The opportunity to write and

Figure 22. Mac and Strikeback performance, house concert, West Philly, 8 June 2017. Photo by the author. Strikeback, on the right, is singing out of the corner of his mouth.

sing about their experiences, to harmonize with others, and to get positive feedback from listeners is worth the risk of opening themselves to additional scrutiny. For some, it feels imperative. In his song "Man in the Moon," Joe Stevens writes, "I'm selling songs for a dollar / . . . / It's all I can do with my life."[105] Stevens has inspired many young listeners who attend his shows and workshops and correspond with him. He has mentored several young trans and queer singer-songwriters, helping two of them write, record, and release their first albums (a process featured in Shaleece Haas's 2016 documentary *Real Boy*).[106]

"SO I GUESS I MOSTLY IDENTIFY AS A SONGWRITER"

"After five years of constant touring" as a transgender male country singer who did not take testosterone (a decision partly intended to prevent vocal changes but also to resist the gender binary), Spoon stopped identifying as a country musician and a transgender man. Spoon's musician friend had asked for a list of queer-friendly and nonsexist prairie venues, and Spoon could barely come up with any suggestions. "I realized that I had been very unkind to myself" by continuing to play there and censoring their songwriting.[107] Spoon lived briefly in Germany, where "I was really inspired by the folk music in Germany—which is techno."[108] This humorous challenge to the mythology of folk music's purity (which Spoon said they had previously believed in) illustrates Spoon's moment of becoming open to incorporating the sounds of nonacoustic grassroots music (perhaps especially given electronic dance music's importance to some queer communities) and camping the presumed authenticity of acoustic folk music.[109]

During this time Spoon returned to Canada and also experienced a sense of change in gender. Spoon "retired" from gender altogether, taking up the pronoun "they."[110] Spoon may have invented the "retired from gender" description. The wording lends an air of camp to gender (non)identification—to retire from gender compares years of gender identification to saving to take a hard-earned rest from a job after a long career.[111] Spoon's phrasing cleverly reveals the labor that goes into all of our maintenance of the gender binary, but especially some nonbinary people's efforts to exist in a world policed by sex-category policies.[112] We could contextualize this nonidentification with Spoon's collaboration with Ivan Coyote and Clyde Peterson, *Gender Failure*, which is also campy in joking about "failures" at gender rather than expressing abjection or hopelessness. Spoon notes that the binary system is the problem, not Spoon's identification. It's interesting to note that while Spoon's terminology campily suggests a sense of ease and relaxation of being nonbinary, they consider being retired from gender as a difficult identification and something that they may not always choose to do.[113]

At the point of retiring from gender, Spoon also began incorporating some of the electronic music techniques they learned in Germany into their country/folk aesthetic and moved to Montreal, where the indie rock movement was taking off, both of which led to their music being identified as "indie." While this shift led to important invitations to perform at big-name music festivals, Spoon encountered similar issues of gender phobia and male privilege in indie music: "Fleeing the construct of genre turned out not to include freedom from the constructs of gender. I started to see the same patterns in the indie rock scene that I saw in country music."[114] These patterns included noticing that little space is allowed for people of color or women in either genre and that sound techs and all-male bands were disrespectful of Spoon, incorrectly gendered Spoon, and did not extend the courtesies afforded male musicians. Spoon notes feeling estranged by cisgender male indie musicians' abuse of male and middle-class privilege when performing at the same high-profile festival.[115] Spoon says, "I feel about the same amount of comfort in any performing space. I have spent my career playing in lots of different types of venues. It's as likely for me to be gendered in a queer space as in a mainstream one." They decided, "I am done trying to find a genre of commercial music that will accept my gender. Instead, I have been focusing on the spaces that are accepting of me and trying to find ways to extend that as much as possible to others in the same position."[116] Despite this stance, Spoon did not claim to be postgenre and spoke critically of journalists trying to describe their genre as "in-between."[117] Spoon's experiences with musical genre's policing of gender expression led them to prioritize gender-retired identification and shape their music for performance in relation to community. Spoon still travels back to the prairies, making a sort of blended genre of indie pop and country music, but they now think of some of their country music as "performance art."[118] In December 2015 they explained to me when I asked about the wide range of venues they play, including queer anarchist squats in Europe, as well as the only music venue in a rural place:

> I've always tried to make music that I could play in a little hall in a small town and mostly everyone like aunts, uncles, and gender-neutral relatives of that name we haven't come up with. The kind of thing you could sneak out of a club, something I could play in a club in Berlin at midnight but also play in the Yukon for a bunch of folks who have only heard about my country music. And so I think I rely a lot on my vocals and songwriting skills to do that. So I guess I mostly identify as a songwriter. I don't think I've gotten much into the electronic scene in Canada or Germany. I think I'm more in the songwriter scene.[119]

Although they find the material practices and audience expectations of country and indie too restrictive, Spoon interestingly retains musical influences from these genres in a musical setting that allows for their gender-retired expression to fully flourish. Spoon elaborated to me six months later, in May 2016, about their primary musical identification as a songwriter: "I guess that one thing that kind of tied all that stuff together [genre changes over fifteen years as a professional musician] is songwriting. I love a song [*laughs*]. You know, I love old country songs, and I think that still kind of shows sometimes when I write dance music. Yeah, I listen to a lot of Willie Nelson and Dolly Parton now. I like the country song. The archetype of a country song is very much like what I do."[120] We can see here how both the cogenerative possibilities and limitations of the relationship between gender and genre make these identifications vividly important in queer country and trans Americana.

Spoon was unable to get the support of other more famous country musicians. And with the discrimination Spoon faced, requiring being closeted and sometimes afraid while touring, they made a choice to shift away from that scene. Spoon relates, "I used to play banjo for the Boomers [a cisgender male middle-aged Canadian rock band], but it wasn't safe as a trans person. So now I play for the younger crowds, and I don't have to hide it. I find that younger hipsters accept it all."[121] Whereas adhering to a strict genre code did not safely allow for transgender identification, incorporating country sounds into music played for a "younger hipster" audience, accompanied by rhetoric of inclusion, has led to relative artistic stability (further supported by governmental arts funding). Yet to note that Spoon's hipster audience may be Hubbs's middle-class "cultural omnivores" raises further questions. Does acceptance by this audience come at the expense of understanding the traditional country audience as open-minded or even queer? Or does an indie transgender artist's incorporation of country elements challenge the biased middle-class "anything but country" stance? Spoon may offer an answer: identifying as transgender automatically entailed breaking rules in country music and requiring listeners to break the rules as well: "The gender and genre rules of the country music industry had been strict, but luckily by already breaking one set of rules, the audiences who came to my shows seemed ready to let me break others."[122]

"GETTING BACK TO WHO I WAS CREATIVELY"

For Namoli Brennet, coming to identify as a transgender woman who is a folk singer-songwriter offered a sense of artistic and personal honesty unavailable to her when she identified as a man who played Top 40, rock, and jazz, as she explained in an interview with trans woman journalist Liz LaVenture for a Midwest LGBT magazine and website:

LAVENTURE: Did you perform professionally before you transitioned?

BRENNET: I did, yes. I did Top 40 and played with Rock Bands, Jazz Trios—so the decision to transition was also about getting back to who I was creatively. I had gotten lost in this other persona. . . .

LAVENTURE: Your first CD *Boy in a Dress* came out in 2002. How long did it take to go from being a male musician, to transitionaing [*sic*] enough to be able to express that journey in your music?

BRENNET: It was a fluid process. I did release a CD in 1999 before transition, but I was still lost in that other persona. I thought at the time that if only I could be a big success as a male musician, the need to transition would fade.[123]

In this conversation, Brennet disrupts cisgender readers' likely expectations that she desired coherence between her body and her gender. Bodily and identity cohesion is important to many trans people, and there is nothing wrong with that. However, this one feature of trans experience is often the first (and sometimes only) thing that cisgender people ask transgender people about. So it is striking that Brennet shifted the conversation to consider how musical genre can be an important path to gender identification. Brennet's focus was on creating coherence between her gender identification and her musical genre identification. She revealed a former hope that musical success would lead to affirmation of the gender she was assigned at birth, which is a lot to expect of genre! In my conversations with Brennet, I gathered that a sense of professional success was important to her. She discussed her time in graduate school for choral conducting, which she once saw as a pathway to professional success. Brennet grew up in an Irish Catholic family who moved several times. While she described herself to my students as "middle class," through her newsletters with fans she told us that her parents lived in a trailer park, and Brennet has written an autobiographical song about being called "trash." The relationship between womanhood, lesbian identity, and folk singing can be read between the lines in Brennet's search for a musical path that would lead her to (re-)claim the persona that she felt had been "lost" in the quest to play rock, jazz, and Top 40 and to conduct choral music.

The interviewer's second question assumes that the musician would transition first before writing songs about it; however, Brennet reveals that her 2002 album, *Boy in a Dress* (with a title song exploring gender liminality), was written during her early transition. The song is based on Brennet's experience wearing her sister's Girl Scout uniform for Halloween when she was nine. Writing the song was "a growth process of figuring out what sound felt good to make" as she transitioned and an "attempt to process my experience," including the "binary and not really identifying with it."[124] The song begins with a gentle $^6/_8$ with a light pendulum sense as the bass swings back and forth, outlining the tonic chord on beats 1 and 4 of the first two measures as though striking bells, while Brennet's voice takes the lilt of a children's song as she explains her childhood moments, "when I was a little girl, free as a bird, painting my world, filled it with colors like birthday balloons."[125] The song goes through emotional shifts with heightened moments of crisis ("I never saw no picture like me") emphasized harmonically and through vocal strain, but these resolve through the return to the song's gentle and reassuring chorus. Yet Brennet's chorus constructs reassurance in a singsong play with gendered words that disrupts the taken-for-granted gender binary. The words repeat over a scalar melody that arrives on the tonic on "girl" and moves, so that "girl or a boy in a dress or a girl or a boy in a dress" rolls across the measures without the sense of horror or division that would typically be used for gender ambiguity.

Brennet's description of the process as "fluid" challenges the establishment of a fixed arrival point for gender or genre identification and articulates the performance of both as mutually informative rather than separate. LaVenture's question also suggests that expressing transition would be crucial to Brennet's music, and while she has written songs about this process and how gender informs her sense of self, actually many of her songs are not pointedly about her gender: many explore relationships with friends, family, and lovers; others engage her dreams; many make a political case for ending oppression; some draw literary inspiration from famous works such as *The Grapes of Wrath*; and many explore the experiences and imagery of rural life and migration. Still, this interview does show that her identification as a folk singer is intimately tied to and makes space for her gender identification.

Brennet invented her name, Namoli, to signal that she is an anomaly.[126] While there are a few other trans women Americana singer-songwriters, Brennet, more than other musicians in this study, is pursuing her career without much contact or collaboration with other transgender and queer folk musicians. I first met Brennet in 2010 at a concert she shared with transgender singer-songwriter Joe Stevens at El Rio in San Francisco. In 2014 at a private house concert at a (then) recently out transgender woman's house in Rhode Island, I reintroduced myself to Brennet as a scholar interested in transgender folk singers. She responded with humor, "Well, you've come to the right place," before continuing in earnest, "Are there others besides me and Joe [Stevens]?"[127] Other musicians discussed in this book arrange concerts or tours together and have recommended additional musicians for me to include in the study. But Brennet typically tours solo in the United States, performing without an opening act. In Germany she formed a trio with trans woman bassist and vocalist Amy Zapf, who approached her to ask for singing advice, and drummer Micha Maass. They released a live album in 2016, and Brennet has toured Germany with them at least once a year until 2020. Brennet's otherwise seeming isolation points to a tension in trans Americana's musical and political ancestry around gender and sexuality politics: transgender women are not always included as part of lesbian feminist organizing, which means that the small but dedicated women's music audience is not fully open to

Figure 23. Namoli Brennet performs in the author's Queer Country seminar at Temple University, 2 November 2018. Photo by the author.

Brennet. In 2018 Brennet described to my Queer Country seminar students an experience playing at a women's music festival where she had been invited to play and explaining to the audience how significant this felt to her as a transgender woman (figure 23). When some festival listeners reacted with surprise and left the audience, Brennet's fear was confirmed, that her hosts had not known she was transgender.[128]

"I FOUND MYSELF FREER TO EXPLORE
THAT DARKER . . . SIDE"

The intersectionality between gender and genre—their cogenerative effects—may lead musicians away from their "original" genre as they transition gender or as they come out as sexually nonnormative. Chapter 1 included analysis of mainstream country journalists' distrust of k.d. lang's sincerity in performing country music and her subsequent transition away from country and into adult contemporary as she came out as lesbian. This chapter has discussed country singer Chely Wright's reluctant shift from closeted mainstream country star to out lesbian occasional Americana participant. More so than any other musician in this study, Wright was forced from her genre due to coming out as gay. But other musicians' departures from country and folk music may feel more celebratory. Portuguese Canadian artist Lucas Silveira spent the first thirteen years of his career identified as a lesbian and folk singer-songwriter before coming out as transgender to "himself, his friends, and his family" in 2004 and starting his rock band, the Cliks (a portmanteau of "clits" and "cocks").[129] Silveira's discussion of a shift in his musical affect and gender identification seems strikingly intersectional in the following statement from a journalistic interview:

> When I was identifying as female and as a lesbian, people had this perception of me [as] being a lot softer. I used to play a lot of folkie music, and I remember when I picked my electric guitar up and started heading more into what was really my roots, rock 'n' roll, I found a lot of people going, "Why are you so angry?" I think I was trying so hard [via folk music] to identify with what I thought was feminine that I was pushing away this other part of myself. When I finally came out as being trans, I found myself freer to

explore that darker, more hard-core side, and my songwriting started getting heavier and heavier. So it really changed the intensity of my music.[130]

Silveira uses the language of "roots" to bridge music and self, implying that he was playing a music ("folkie music") that involved "trying so hard" at femininity that it felt like "pushing away this other part of myself." He describes shifting to a music ("rock 'n' roll") that was "really my roots" and that also allowed him a sense of freedom to explore different musical expressions (ones that are typically coded as masculine—"dark," "hard-core," and "heav[y]"), which he felt that listeners misinterpreted. Performance studies scholar and singer-songwriter Elena Elias Krell analyzes this passage in discussing Silveira's use of cover songs in the process of transition:

> The "softness" that playing folk music granted [Silveira] was a practice by which he enacted femininity. As his identity shifted, he started writing and performing "harder" rock, one of his as-yet untapped musical roots. While the songs he wrote both before and after coming out as trans were vehicles for navigating feminine and masculine genders, these were not necessarily read by others in the ways he intended. Because of expectations around affects he should (not) perform, based on his (perceived) sexed morphology, his "softness" remained unremarked upon when he was playing folk, and yet his performance of rock was interpreted as angry. The reception of his music was thus disjointed from his own experience and intention, where he understood himself as exploring the rock and roll genre more than emoting a particularly gendered affect.[131]

Krell notes that while Silveira identified as trans and shifted to a harder rock style, listeners continued to perceive him as female and thus felt that his performances were "angry" in a disconcerting way. They did not understand that he had come to identify as male and was shifting to play rock. What they mostly remarked upon was Silveira's anger. This reaction speaks to the perceived gendered differences in emotional expression and types of genre, which Krell discusses and sociologist Anna Feigenbaum also found in music from the turn of the twenty-first century. Feigenbaum's study is of presumably cisgender musicians and focuses specifically on folk musician ani difranco, whose music was often considered "angry." Feigenbaum notes that when artists who are perceived as women express anger within their emotional musical palette, this anger is misinterpreted as all-encompassing, in that it overwhelms listeners' and critics' reception of any other emotion from them, and they become "angry women." Meanwhile, Feigenbaum argues that musicians who are perceived as men may express anger among a range of emotions.[132]

Silveira's statement draws on a gendered musical binary in which folk is associated with softness (connoting femininity) and rock is associated with darkness, hard-core, and heaviness (implying masculinity). Lesbian women's and folk musician Tret Fure also draws on this perceived gender binary–influenced musical genre dynamic in the context of fitting in with a women's music audience: "I started out playing harder music, rock 'n' roll.... I found that that just didn't work very well with the women's music audience, and I softened my presentation to more of a folk-rock kind of thing. There's something about the folk format, maybe the intimacy, that makes it a very effective way for women to connect with other women."[133] While Fure, who describes herself as a "tomboy girl," could have expressed a sense of unease at the women's music audience expecting a more "intimate" folk sound, she expresses no regrets about shifting to a folk sound, instead demonstrating the benefits of folk intimacy. Silveira recalled "trying hard" at folk and femininity in a way that eventually felt like suppressing a side of himself. Thus, while Silveira's audiences seemed to maintain a sense that Silveira was "really" a woman and that Silveira's newer music thus seemed strangely "angry," Fure does not mention a problem with how audiences perceive her gender. Silveira's account of genre transition in the moment of gender transition as getting back to personal "roots" recalls Namoli Brennet's sense of folk and womanhood as feeling like a more "true" version of herself, a throwing off of artistic personae that had obscured sense of self.

This chapter has illustrated the potential resonances for queer and trans musicians with country and folk genres, as well as some of the ways that these genres can feel too limiting. For some, identity and musical genre feel cogenerative. But the most common experience musicians have described over these eight decades is an ongoing genre trouble—queer and trans musicians are perceived as not "fitting" with their desired genre of country or folk music. Musician Jake Blount describes the experience as being "genrequeer." But rather than be stopped by "genre police," queer and trans musicians fully explore the appeal of rural and journey narratives in country and folk musics, as chapter 3 explores.

CHAPTER 3

RURALITY AND JOURNEY AS QUEER AND TRANS MUSICAL NARRATIVES

In her semiautobiographical country soul song "Sure Feels Good Anyway," released on *Holler* (2018), Amy Ray of the Indigo Girls sings with her country band about some of the tensions of being a touring queer musician and an antiracism activist from the South:

> I'll get your text about three a.m., when I cross back over the border
> again
> Bye-bye Canada Hello USA
> Those lefties sure make a lot of sense, and sometimes it's nice to feel
> good in my skin
> But I'd trade it all for some Southern hospitality
>
> I know that you don't like me
> But it sure feels good anyway[1]

In many of her songs, including this one, Ray examines how she and others negotiate boundaries: traveling between these distinct geographic zones results in delayed communication between lovers, allows opportunities for political discussion over shared understandings, as well as heated debate, and makes for varying degrees of comfort "in [one's] own skin." Yet the narrator prioritizes "Southern hospitality" over "feel[ing] good in my skin," an issue of enormous importance to queer and trans people, who are more likely to experience discrimination, poverty, homelessness, disordered eating, and barriers to receiving medical care.[2] The song creates a sense of feeling unsettled, with relentless motion in the fiddle repeating slurs between neighbor notes without any sense of arrival or rest. The fiddle's movement is set against a slower, soulful, electric guitar melody that takes turns with Ray's singing until the final verse, when they sweetly join forces.

After the narrator reveals a willingness not to feel comfortable in her own skin, the next verse is striking, with a backing brass ensemble and stop time as the narrator asks in punctuated silence, "Ain't you tired of fightin' 'bout the damned ol' flag? / It's not Southern pride, it's just Southern hate." The fiddle's relentless motion returns as we learn that this comment is framed from an insider's perspective, one that "know[s] from your mamas that you're better than that, every time I call, well, you have my back." Here Ray illustrates a seemingly contradictory situation of neighborly support even in the face of political disagreement. Sociologist Mary Gray argues that this type of scenario doesn't destroy the fabric of rural communities, because people living in these areas need one another's help to survive.[3]

The band continues to build tension that is only briefly relieved by a sunny bridge, in which the narrator is asked what makes her want to live in "the backwards south": the narrator revels in its gravel roads, intense heat, lingering kiss from a lover, and regionally special flora and fauna. She reaches the song's climax, explaining that she lives there "'cause it feels fine," holding her note on "fine" for several bars. The tension and stop-time return as she explains that its "rebel yell . . . and Whip-poor-will . . . [t]hey haunt me and they hold me just the same / But it's an ounce of comfort for a pound of grief." The melody hovers around her vocal break such that she strains intentionally on the word "haunts," a technique that E. Glasberg identified as part of Ray's "butch throat" "polyvocality," shifting audibly between chest voice and falsetto in a melody as a means of emphasizing physical and metaphorical borders.[4] After the narrator explains, "I just wanna sit on the porch with you and hear the tall pines creak," the song ends without resolving the tension.

"Sure Feels Good Anyway" reveals the problems of being a queer activist southerner and then embraces the pain and joy of living with them in this song and others from Ray's solo repertoire with her country band (figure 24). Its seductive assortment of eclectic country influences, from traditional fiddle to electric guitar, pedal steel, Wurlitzer, and horns, refuses to let the conflicted narrator out of its grasp. Songs like this demonstrate that there is no easy solution to resolve these tensions that seem central for this southern butch lesbian singer-songwriter and social justice activist. But being part of a rural community in northern Georgia for nearly her whole life while traveling for a living has offered her opportunities to sing insightfully about real problems that her listeners may relate to. And sharing these feelings about what's good and how a queer, southern, antiracist activist deals with Republican neighbors offers listeners a way in to better understand what many people in the country experience.

Queer rurality and tension over life's metaphorical and literal journeys are important musical themes for queer and trans country and folk musicians. Many but not all queer country musicians were born in or currently live in rural areas, although almost all travel through such places in order to perform, and the imagery and political tensions that country and folk music have embodied in those spaces serve as useful settings for negotiating contemporary life as queer and trans people. Country and folk music often depict rurality and stories of journey. These topics contextualize and authenticate the music within genre norms and also offer artistic and interpretive metaphors for musicians and listeners. Rural imagery might connote feelings associated with home and (seemingly) simple lives tied to the land, as well as a sense of the tight community that rural areas are known for. Stories of journeys over vast open spaces conjure a history (and romanticized colonialist accounts) of settling "wild" territories, the human will to survive, independence, and ingenuity. Familiar narrators or characters in folk and country songs included travelers who might be immigrants, homesteaders, runaways, outlaws, cowboys, truckers, hobos, or musicians, most of whom experience long, arduous, solitary journeys across wild and rural spaces and perhaps also cities. The traveler is often depicted as a "stranger"—a social outsider. They are also typically working class or poor. These stories not only involve change of scenery but also show personal growth and sometimes mobility of identity provided through the liminality of the adventure. These journey stories often also develop an interaction with notions of "home," idealistic or critical, and employment of related feelings of safety, arrival, longing, and/or stasis that the idea of home can represent. Thus, the tropes of journey and rural spaces are rich for interpretation. When engaged

Figure 24. The Amy Ray Band, World Café Live, Philadelphia, 24 May 2019. Photo by the author.

by trans and queer musicians or used to represent trans or queer characters in films, these tropes take on resonances as metaphors for trans and queer characters' literal and figurative journeys, symbols of authenticity and belonging, and are used in countering the invisibility, misunderstanding, and stereotypes often perpetuated about queer and trans people.

For several filmmakers and musicians around the turn of the twenty-first century, country and folk depictions of rurality and journey have allowed opportunities to shape how audiences would interpret queer and trans characters, as well as in some cases how the audiences might reimagine rural spaces and the idea of journey. This chapter examines the use of rurality and journey depicting transgender and queer life and politics in music by Amy Ray, Joe Stevens, Actor Slash Model, and Rae Spoon and in the early twenty-first-century film *Transamerica*.

"KEEP THE ENGINE RUNNING"?

For transgender and queer country and folk musicians, the use of rural settings and journey narratives may seem unexpected to some, given that the rural is typically represented in the media as a space of death for queer and trans people (if not also for straight and cisgender city slickers, as controversially depicted in *Deliverance,* James Dickey's 1970 book, adapted as a film in 1972 by John Boorman).[5] Travel, too, especially traversing rural spaces, is sometimes expected to be dangerous for queer and trans people rather than the exciting or transformative experience depicted for straight and cisgender characters in books, films, and music. Yet gender and sexually "nonnormative" people have always existed in and traveled across rural spaces, cocreating them with a variety of people not typically credited with defining this space.[6] Further, Nadine Hubbs argues that the working class is already queered in terms of gender. Thus, straight and cisgender working-class rural people often fail to measure up to the nation's (middle-class, urban) standards of heteronormativity. The labor and living conditions of rural areas render working-class men feminized by their lack of autonomy and failure to accumulate wealth from their abusive employers. And working-class women are seen as masculinized by the work and lifestyles left to them, by their lack of health and wealth to maintain middle-class norms of femininity, and by any perceived abnormalities about their romantic and domestic lives, such as out-of-wedlock births, young parenthood, and so on. (These are effects of structural inequity, of course, although outsiders may see these as personal failings.) In the case of queer country musicians, rural and working-class symbols may in some cases even help articulate queerness. For example, in "Oyster and Pearl" from *Goodnight Tender,* about being an aging rural southern butch, Amy Ray compares herself to several marine animals: "I'm just a southern gar with no spar left to be had.... I been so long in this world / All I got left is all I need now. You want me to be the oyster that has the pearl.... But there ain't nothing like that in this girl." She compares herself to a southern "treasured trash" fish that was formerly valued for sport and eating (except for its toxic eggs) but that is no longer widely valued due to refrigeration and shipping making edible fish from other regions widely available.[7] But the narrator is trying to convey that she's a product of her environment, and by this age, she has what she needs to live in this world. The person she's speaking to hopes for Ray's oyster-like narrator to contain, inside her protective rough shell, a feminine, expensive jewel. But Ray's narrator challenges this idea by using the working-class, southern dialect, "There ain't nothing like that in this girl."[8]

There are, of course, dangers in rural settings, but they often affect *most* people who live there, as Elizabeth Catte and other rural studies scholars explain: rural residents lack the kinds of resources provided in cities. Further, some rural communities were owned by the extractive industries of the region, and the local government is often biased in favor of protecting these industries rather than their workers. Thus, these areas are often polluted or irrevocably damaged, and labor and any protest movements are violently suppressed.[9]

The danger for queer and trans people in the idea of the rural is one centered on an image of rural residents as being ignorant, violent, and bigoted. These impressions have been supported by media representation, focusing on the murders of Matthew Shepard and Brandon Teena while sometimes paying less attention to the murders of queer and trans people in cities (especially queer and trans people of color). Rural and working-class studies scholars challenge these depictions. As Hubbs argues, rural communities are not necessarily the national center of bigotry imagined by mainstream media.[10]

One of the problems with recognizing that same-gender-loving and gender nonnormative people have always lived in rural places is, as Mary Gray argues, that the modern "out and proud" discourse of contemporary queer and trans activism demands visibility, differentiation, and migration.[11] Gray notes that rural areas seem from the outside to be bad places for queer and trans people to live because turn-of-the-millennium expectations of queer and trans life assumed that a queer person is patently different from their straight and cisgender family and community members, must be outspoken about this difference, and will have to form a new queer and trans community, preferably in a city. This is an oversimplification that hides multiple debates both within "the LGBT community" and between queer and trans people and straight and cisgender people. While some queer and trans people embrace nonnormativity and encourage revolution to free all humans from categories that they argue are oppressive and hierarchical, other queer and trans people advocate for assimilation into existing society, which might include embracing norms. And as Hubbs argues, working-class people's identities are seen as "queered" in comparison to middle-class people's identities in terms of gender and sexual nonnormativity. Further, as we'll see, a director might position the "normality" of their queer and trans characters in relation to the "nonnormality" of straight and cisgender characters whose intersecting identifications, such as race, class, and region, Other them.

Transgender Canadian artist Rae Spoon has explored different understandings of whether or not rural spaces are safe to queer and trans people in their music. Their song "Keep the Engine Running" is about crossing the US-Canada border by car to tour the Midwest of the United States.[12] Spoon discussed with me the added stress to touring of being nonbinary and yet having to show documentation of gender to cross the border into the United States, as well as paying for a visa to play professionally and needing connections to make good on the investment of the trip to participate in this country's more specialized musical markets and vast territory, compared to the fewer Canadian venues that welcome musicians of all genres. Finally, Spoon notes in this song the threat of gender-based violence as a gender-ambiguous person who does not know how safe each stop will be throughout the trip. The song features a strategy of keeping the car running at rest stops in case they're threatened, delivered musically with both solemnity and humor. Spoon's delicate voice against a spare banjo part is poignantly vulnerable, and yet their lyrics and enunciation poke fun: Spoon sings that people at the station are so impressed with their "Sunday best" that they "want to know all about us." (As a former white Pentecostal church member, now atheist, Spoon is not dressed for church. They're using humor about the people's curiosity perhaps to diffuse what could be a discriminatory or dangerous situation.) Spoon's yodeling melisma on the phrase "gas station" makes it sound like "gay station."[13]

In historian, musician, and filmmaker Simon Fisher Strikeback's song "TN Tranny Two-Step," the now disbanded antifolk group Actor Slash Model explores a US northerner's dating experience in Tennessee. The song cleverly surprises any potential expectations that rural Tennessee would be unappealing to a trans person and also sets up expectation for and then disrupts a trans coming-out narrative. The song begins by positioning the narrator as different from and often thwarted by most residents of a Tennessee town. He has, however, found a girlfriend who works as a waitress. Having set the listener up for an "admission" presumably about gender, the song instead tells a cross-regional love story that displaces the otherness of queer gender onto regional difference:

I admit that I'm a transport [*sic*] from the North,
And she was born right here in town.
But like she told me on the first night we met
That she'd never turn a Yankee tranny down.[14]

Strikeback, who grew up in Chicago, told me that this song was semiauto-biographical and written when he was living on a radical faerie commune in Tennessee.[15] It was there that he learned folk music through his friend Spider John Dubeck (whom I heard play a show with Strikeback and My Gay Banjo in Philadelphia on 8 June 2017). While Strikeback did date a local woman, he said that he did not, in fact, work at the lumber yard. Still, he did feel a sense of difference between the radical faeries and the "Baptists lined up for church on Saturdays," as the song depicts.[16] Strikeback's song doesn't, however, depict his "Yankee tranny" narrator as fully out of place, though. Later in the song, the narrator compares transgender people's hormone therapy disapprov-ingly to growth hormone usage on farms. In the historical moment when the song was written (prior to the 2007 release), some transgender activists were critiquing the medicalized and universalized "transgender narrative." Thus, their version of trans masculinity is compared to organic farming (which has a high rate of lesbian and gay participation).[17] But where "organicism" might be used against a trans person, Strikeback's narrator has no shame about displaying his packer while skinny dipping and thus challenges genital-based exclusions of trans men from masculinity and male identification.[18] Finally, the song cheerfully employs the term "tranny," which, by this historical moment, middle-class queer and trans people determined to be derogatory, despite its continuing use by trans women of color sex workers, as L. H. Stallings notes.[19] And indeed, Actor Slash Model's community includes sex workers. As Strikeback recalled to me, "Me and Madsen's first show was an opening of a porno that some local community friend had made. . . . You know, it's like, that's our context—It was not a show at a country night or something, you know?—All of our friends are, like, dom[inatrixes], and porn stars, and musicians, and accountants to porn stars and doms. . . . So that's who loves us. . . . I mean that, in Chicago, that was our home scene, right? Because, like, there was not very much. There was no trans music."[20]

Journey- and rurality-themed songs like these hold compelling trans and queer possibilities, but as these and the examples below show, the risks not only of medical coercion and media exploitation but also of critique from listeners have obliged queer country musicians to take care to make space for different modalities of transgender and queer living in crafting their music and professional narrative.

"A DESTINATION ON A MAP STILL BEING WRITTEN"

Queer country music often invokes a sense of journey across North America and also within oneself. Musicians' literal travel as touring musicians and their figurative gender (and sometimes sexuality) transit are juxtaposed in their work—on the one hand, they create thematic musical connections to rurality, "roots," and groundedness, and on the other hand, they craft narratives of multiple, ongoing journeys both literal and figurative. Coyote Grace and Namoli Brennet regularly mention miles traveled in their professional presentation. Brennet's email updates to fans sometimes count how many miles she has toured. Coyote Grace's record label was called Mile After Mile (figure 25), a phrase Stevens came up with both to capture the sense of endless touring and to allude to the twelve-step measurement of sobriety and progress taught by Alcoholics Anonymous. Stevens's vagabond lifestyle is part of his professional image, and he tags himself on social media as a #RoadDog, traveling the country in his live-in van. Coyote Grace's song "Runaround," for several years their captivating a cappella show opener, conjures the metaphorical and literal homelessness arising when one is cut adrift from societal expectations (whether due to identity or becoming a professional musician) or excommunicated from family. The final lines, "Put your ear to the ground, / and you will find your sound," suggest that a person's relationship with the earth is the solution to feeling a sense of rootlessness, as well as to the problem of finding the musical style that speaks best.[21] As Sylvia Sukop wrote about Coyote Grace, "There's a yearning, freight-train-hopping, propulsive energy to many of their songs that suggests not only an indie-band road tour, but the road to one's true identity, a destination on a map still being written. These youthful travelers depend on the kindness of strangers and of lovers, and on their journey they've experienced enough joy and heartbreak to last a lifetime."[22] Sukop's reference to "true self" found on a "journey" across an unfinished map references several different tropes about trans people's lives that are used in the media. She invokes the power of authenticity, with its links to essence and sincerity, employed in the phrase "true self." Her use of the literal and metaphorical journeys the band undertook makes the notion of a transgender professional traveling folk singer a very compelling proposition, conveying the wisdom Stevens has gained from life on the road and a young adulthood in gender transit. Members of Coyote Grace never hopped trains (although among the queer and trans country musicians, Alynda Segarra told a 2015 Philadelphia audience I was part of that she used to), yet Coyote Grace's liner note images for their first album look as though they are about to (figure 26). These two band members often toured so much that they had no permanent address and instead lived in their van or RV. The train could serve as a symbol of the work of touring, or it could help align them with the folk personae of the (maligned and romanticized) Okie and the hobo. Stevens's grandfather was, in fact, a farmer who migrated from Missouri to California during the Dust Bowl (figure 27). The subdued, almost sepia-toned color lends the image the look of an old photograph and also draws connections with the palette (as well as plot and musical material) of *O Brother, Where Art Thou?* (2000), the Coen brothers' enormously successful film and one that Stevens said influenced his interest in playing folk music. Sukop's depiction of "true identity, a destination on a map still being written" captures the moment in 2004 when Stevens transitioned, casting him in the role of an explorer who is drawing a map as he journeys through this new territory. While Stevens had few transgender role models visible in the mainstream media when he transitioned, it was his chance encounter with transgender author Loren Cameron's 1996 book *Body Alchemy: Transsexual Portraits*, documenting his own and others' transitions, a book that Stevens noticed while he was opting out of a sexual bondage and flogging tutorial at a sex shop in Seattle, that exposed him to trans identity and gave him a profound sense of connection.[23]

> And so I sat down right next to the bookshelf, and it was like chaos going on around me. There's people rolling, people around all tied up on the floor, and somebody was full on flogging somebody in like five, six feet of space. You know? And some people were totally into it, which embarrassed me, and so all this commotion was flap, flap, and flapping, laughing and stuff around me. And I was sitting there, and I looked over on the counter on the bookshelf, and *Body Alchemy* was right there. I had kind of seen it out of the corner of my eye and avoided it on purpose. And for whatever rea-

son, I picked it up, even though there were people around. But they were busy, and I must have been more open than I [had been when I noticed the book previously].

I picked it up, and I didn't even open it, I didn't look at it. And I remember everything around me got quiet, and I just—I was in my own world with this book. And I was just in a zone. And just the picture on the cover made it clear to me that this was a thing, and oh my God, that's what I am. And I kind of leafed through it a little bit, ignored the junk surgery pictures, because that freaked me out—but I just, and as I leafed through that book—and it couldn't have been more than like ten minutes, you know? But I was just—it was like time stopped, and everything else fell away. And it made sense in that moment in a way that it had never made sense before. And I was like, "Oh, God. Oh my gosh."

And the workshop kind of wrapped up, and Ingrid and my friend Hammer came over, and they were like, "Did you have fun?" And I was like—you know? It was like a—and I was like—I sort of put the book back on the shelf, and I had kind of like—I didn't know what else to do, so I played it off like nothing was going on, and I was like, "Uh, yeah, it was good. Are we going to go to the Rose?" That's what, I'm sure, that's what our plan was. And I kind of didn't say anything for the rest of the evening. And I think I stole away like I do, and I went and drove around and drank beers and smoked weed and a million cigarettes and cried and punched my steering wheel and wrote all over everything in my car. And it just totally came flooding out. And I think I did that for three days.

Of the many striking points of Stevens's story, one is that his moment of discomfort with the kink instruction and desire to remove himself from that activity was also a moment in which he allowed himself to return his gaze to Cameron's book, which felt more risky in some ways than participating in the group activity. (While this may be an obvious reminder to some readers, it's important to note that this story shows how not all queer and trans people are interested in the same types of sexual practices, identifications, communities, or politics. At different moments, a person's relationship to certain activities, identifications, or groups may be more or less of a priority.) Stevens's experience of this moment of recognition describes a liminal space in which he became out of synch with the activity in the immediate space around him, felt a sense of time stopping, and had a crucial realization

Figure 25. Coyote Grace's business card (ca. 2010) depicted, from the view of the traveler, a road running through the American desert. Stevens takes the same routes through his favorite parts of the country every year.

Figure 26. Coyote Grace, *Boxes & Bags*, back cover.

Joe Stevens is with **Chris Stevens** and **2 others** at **First Christian Church of Nevada Missouri**.
February 17, 2016 · 👥

My great grandfather, a farmer and mechanic, left this little #missouri town during the #dustbowl, took his son, moved to California. He set up a mercantile, raised a son who loved to sing, who raised a son who loved to sing, who raised a son who loves to sing. #joestevens #immigrantamerica #ilovetosing

👍 You, Joe Stevens, Ingrid Elizabeth and 220 others   16 Comments

Figure 27. While traveling to research for his work on the musical theater production *The Civility of Albert Cashier*, about a trans Civil War soldier from Illinois, Joe Stevens posted to his Facebook friends about the Dust Bowl migration in his family history.

Figure 28. Stevens with his new (to him) "dream vehicle," a Sprinter van, which he converted into a traveling home. Photo by the author on 6 March 2016.

about his identity. In the days (and years) after this realization, Stevens took to his car, a space where he could be alone and a vehicle for local and cross-country travel (figures 28 and 29).

Mainstream narratives of trans existence have changed over the last century from widespread derogatory depictions to characterizations of courageous difference and struggle for inclusion. In order to better explain trans experience, the notion developed of a "trans narrative," in which a person realizes that they identify as the "opposite" gender, takes steps to transition into this self, and then feels a sense of arrival and completeness. Historian Joanne Meyerowitz has traced the path of transsexual people's stories from letters written to doctors, twentieth-century journalism, and biographies of early

Figure 29. Scene depicting Joe Stevens driving in the desert, from the end of *Real Boy*, dir. Shaleece Haas, 2016.

transsexuals to the medical textbook on transsexuality by transsexual medicine pioneer Dr. Harry Benjamin, in which these stories were used as part of what would become standards of "diagnosis" and treatment. As Meyerowitz outlines, certain early autobiographical accounts of transitions shaped what doctors came to expect, and so patients learned to tell their own life stories in the form of these narratives because they hoped that doing so would assure the medical outcomes they desired.[24] For many decades, this narrative included the imperative of heterosexual identification and heteronormative gender presentation after transition, use of hormones and surgeries, silencing gendered aspects of one's personal history, and passing as cisgender. Controversial rhetoric of "being trapped in the wrong body" may or may not accompany this depiction.

Some trans people find the description "trapped in the wrong body" a useful shorthand to describe their experiences. Ben Wallace uses this phrase in director Shaleece Haas's 2016 documentary *Real Boy*, which featured Joe Stevens as mentor to the then-teenage protagonist. Wallace uses this phrase while fighting with his mother about his identification. Other trans people find that this phrase sets them at odds with their embodied experience. For example, sound engineer turned anthropologist Sandy Stone offered a different theorization of a satisfying transgender narrative in her landmark autobiographical essay "The Empire Strikes Back: A Posttranssexual Manifesto," written in response to Janice Raymond's transphobic 1979 book, *The Transsexual Empire*. Stone writes about the pressure of narrative coherence to trans people's life stories and the expectation for a turning point from which there's no looking back. She notes the expectation of a name change and the inability to mention earlier life experiences that are marked by gender (e.g., participation in the Boy Scouts, attending a women's college, singing in a boys' choir, playing Little League or softball). One of her striking examples is the expectation by doctors and regular people that trans people "shouldn't" enjoy their existing configuration of genitals if they want to. Stone argues that these narrative expectations annihilate the person that one was in the past, a narrative death that not all trans people may desire. Rather than inventing a new life story that would hide these features, Stone proposes a story that includes these moments and offers a narrative that feels more sincere to her.

Joe Stevens's song "Daughterson" engages some of the points of Stone's model. The song's title is a portmanteau that combines daughter and son, a rhetorical gesture that seems directed at listeners who are parents of trans kids and also to communicate to trans people about their experiences with their parents. This made-up word does not seem to be meant as acquiescence to anyone's expectations (e.g., a parent's refusal to acknowledge their child's gender identification); instead, it is a gesture to avoid obliterating anyone's sense of the family's past. In their home, Stevens's parents have prominently displayed a painted portrait of him as a toddler wearing a dress alongside portraits by the same artist of his brothers. To Stevens and his family, his girlhood is part of their family story. "Daughterson" also reaches out to gay people—"the kids won't leave me and my queeny brother alone." In it Stevens looks back on his experiences in high school and wishes he'd realized that his masculinity (then interpreted as butchness) was attractive to the girls he thought were excluding him (as a peer). He also addresses Christian accusations that trans people are going to hell for doing something "unnatural" to themselves, reversing the question to those cisgender Christians who have had cosmetic surgery, take erectile medication, and support the pillaging of the earth's natural resources. He thanks the famous doctor who performed his chest surgery but also says that transition may not be necessary for everyone.[25] In this way he is making space for different listeners to find themselves in this song, particularly those people who have sought or desire to utilize medical transition, as well as those listeners who may identify as nonbinary. The song is uplifting, funny, and anthemic. In conversations when we first got to know one another in 2010, Stevens and band mate Ingrid Elizabeth made a point of saying that the style of this song is influenced by "bluegrass" music (with Stevens on banjo and Elizabeth on upright bass and, later, their added band member, Michael Connolly on fiddle, mandolin, and accordion). "Daughterson" does not include full bluegrass instrumentation, song structure, or trading of virtuosic instrumental solos. It does, however, borrow the fast-paced and cheerful affect of some bluegrass music, and this down-home rootsy sound encourages audiences to hear the musicians as wholesome and earnest. Six years later I learned that Coyote Grace had been struggling to define their genre during this time and may have been trying to make their "roots" performance seem more "authentic" by referring to bluegrass, which has a reputation for seeming traditional (despite its "beginnings" in the 1940s as a commercial and thus "popular" music).[26]

Law scholar Dean Spade takes Stone's proposal a step farther by challenging transnormative narratives at the doctor's office.[27] Spade, who is transgender, shares moments from a doctor's visit when the physician prompted him to share evidence of "gender dysphoria" in order to qualify for treatment. Spade resists these prompts, sharing stories of enjoying childhood, embracing the toys and clothing he was given, and appreciating his body. Such efforts can be said to "resist the trans narrative" and help teach medical and emotional health care providers to welcome many different narratives of trans experience. However, as one of my trans students pointed out in 2010 during my Gender Transgression class at Stanford University, doctors who treat transgender patients with respect and appropriate care are rare, and he greatly appreciates their professional care. He also pointed out that Spade's essay seems to delight in disrupting a well-intentioned doctor's care during a period when few doctors were providing respectful care to trans patients. This issue identifies a point of debate among trans people: while Spade was making a point that he did not desire conformity to the heterosexually defined gender binary, there are many trans people who do wish for this identification.

The categories of gender and sexuality have also been debated in terms of both linkage and usefulness in describing different people's understandings of their identifications. Anthropologist Gayle Rubin has been a central theorist in arguments around the division of gender and sexuality, which profoundly affect the navigation of those who might identify as "gay" and present as "women" but not identify as "transgender." Rubin originally argued for the separation of gender and sexuality because feminism and the growing women's studies movement within academia was not adequately addressing nonheteronormative sexuality.[28] Anthropologist David Valentine found in his fieldwork at the turn of the millennium in New York City that whether a community identified as "transgender" or not was partly predicated on racial and socioeconomic factors. While a growing number of white middle-class people were self-identifying as transgender during this period, the people of color Valentine got to know for his study only appeared under the title of transgender in order to access needed services from an LGBT community center. Assigned male at birth, many of these people identified as "gay" and "women," and many participated in sex work in order to support themselves.[29]

More recent debates about the transgender narrative include discord over the gender binary and interpretations of different people's relationship to politics of assimilation versus revolution. There is a growing population of people who identify as nonbinary, challenging the hegemony of the heterosexually defined gender binary. Sometimes incorporated in this stance is an implied or explicit critique of trans people who are perceived to adhere more closely to the gender binary, including those who identify as men or women. As Stephan Pennington has noted, this critique of some trans people's relationship to "normative" gender categories overlooks the vast differences in safety and privilege between white people who identify as nonbinary and trans women of color especially, who are most at risk for experiencing violence against them.[30] For some people, appearing not to trouble the gender binary is a matter of life and death. And as Pennington pointed out, one may identify as transgender and as a man but also have a long-standing critical relationship to the gender binary.

A (CAUTIONARY) SONG FOR "TOURISTS IN THE QUEER COMMUNITY"

Spoon counters the notion of the rural as a potential space of death for queers in songs about queer and trans people of the Canadian prairies, like

"A Message from the Queer Trans Prairie Tourism Co.," which seems to use "queer sincerity" to counter audiences' "outsider populism."

At the 2016 joint meeting of the US and Canadian chapters of the International Association for the Study of Popular Music, fellow music and queer studies scholar Craig Jennex and I arranged for Rae Spoon to be a guest speaker and performer at the conference, playing a concert and engaging in an onstage interview. During this song, Spoon cheerfully reassured our audience, "Don't worry, this isn't a 'tourism Alberta' song. It's for tourists in the queer community" and explained that the song is "a tuneful sing-along and a good way to test a room."[31] In revealing to their audience that they're testing the room with a song about tourism in the queer community, Spoon is both joking and putting audience members on the spot to behave properly with trans and queer solidarity and allyship, as well as with singing skills and general friendliness. The last line of the chorus stands out from the rhythm of the rest of that verse, partially for making an ideological point of including both "queer" and "trans" in the tourism company name (which seems like an unlikely and thus funny name for a company), as well as squeezing in more words than the rest of the lines (which is also more awkward and less easy to anticipate for the audience's sing-along). Yet how audience members react to this experience could "test the room" for willingness to experience discomfort, laugh, or consider the idea of perhaps being "tourists in the queer community" simply by being straight or cisgender and in the audience at that moment.

Lesbian, gay, bisexual,
Transgender and transsexual
It's better to ask if you don't know
A message from the Queer Trans Prairie Tourism Co.

Moustaches, cowboys, and the stampede
You might not think there's a queer trans scene
But Brokeback Mountain filmed some scenes
Fifteen miles from Calgary.[32]

The song's chorus advises straight and cisgender "tourists in the queer community" to "ask if you don't know" a person's identifications and pronouns. The other verse I've included describes the Calgary Stampede, an annual rodeo event held at the saddle-shaped stadium, which Spoon has discussed critically in their autobiographies as drawing office workers to wear unused Stetson hats and boots to play at being cowboys for one weekend each year. Spoon's song anticipates that many listeners would not imagine Calgary having a "queer trans scene" but comedically uses the fact that director Ang Lee's 2005 romantic film *Brokeback Mountain*, adapted from the short story by Annie Proulx about two cowboys in love with each other, filmed some scenes outside of Calgary as evidence to the contrary.

The song's lilting, simple melody in a relatively high register delivers the list of often-derided identities usually named in an acronym (in which some speakers express irritation with the added letters) as a beautiful list of possibilities. The song's cheerful announcement of these identifications could hark back for some listeners to lesbian feminist folk singer Alix Dobkin's classic track "View from Gay Head," from her historic 1973 folk album, *Lavender Jane Loves Women*. In this much earlier "tuneful sing-along," Dobkin sings, "They agree that it's a pleasure to be a lesbian," and a chorus seemingly consisting of all the women working behind the scenes at the studio, whether trained singers or not, joins her enthusiastically midline to sing, "Lesbian, / Let's be in no man's land. / Lesbian, lesbian, / Any woman can be a lesbian!"

> I heard Cheryl and Mary say
> There are two kinds of people in the world today
> One or the other, a person must be
> The men are them, the women are we
> And they agree it's a pleasure to be
> A lesbian, lesbian,
> Let's be in no man's land.
> Lesbian, lesbian,
> Any woman can be a lesbian!

In fact, the humorous final line of Spoon's chorus causes some Albertan listeners to realize that this song is a parody of "Tourism Alberta" messages, offering "a message from the Queer Trans Prairie Tourism Co.," a carefully named imaginary business whose intentional inclusiveness takes priority over the song's rhythm, making those of us joining the "tuneful sing-along" deliver words in double-time to keep up. In a way, this feature also resembles Dobkin's song, which seems deceptively simple but includes enjambment, in which her lyrics spill over lines, and the chorus enters midline, except for after one verse, when a bridge surprisingly stops the flow of verse to chorus. Both songs are joyous examples of queer country's signature queer sincerity, demonstrating both extreme earnestness and humor.

"I'M JUST TRAVELIN' THRU"

Director Duncan Tucker's 2005 debut film, *Transamerica*, a road trip film about a white trans woman who forges a relationship with the young adult son she never knew she had, attracted an unexpectedly large audience.[33] *Transamerica*'s main character, Bree Osbourne, was played in a Golden Globe Award–winning performance by cisgender actor Felicity Huffman, known by then for her role on *Desperate Housewives*.[34] Bree is rendered as likable. Perhaps unexpectedly, she is somewhat conservative, dressing modestly and in the most feminine coded colors. She describes herself as "stealth," not wanting people to know about her transition to womanhood. She's horrified by the radical queer trans people she meets in the film, whom she refers to as "ersatz." In the first scene we see that Bree, who we later learn was an anthropology major, collects indigenous objects and images from around the world and listens to legendary South African singer and activist Miriam Makeba. Throughout the film we learn that she is culturally middle class yet lives frugally due to employment discrimination and family estrangement. She has no friends except her therapist and seems somewhat socially timid. She is eagerly awaiting her gender-confirmation surgery, which she discusses as a pivotal final event that will allow her to simply be a woman.

The title of the film cleverly invokes the cross-country journey theme, as well as, in a huge departure from previous derogatory film characterizations of transgender women, an intent to depict its main characters solely as Americans. This depiction is significant not only because of its inclusion of a transgender character but also because Bree's long-lost son is a runaway teenager doing sex work and hoping to star in pornographic films. Tucker went so far as to say that this was not a film about a transgender woman but a road trip adventure narrative about an American family (figure 30): "It was really important for me to show that they're just two more Americans. I really wanted to ground them in the music of America. It was also important for me to get the range of American music—from mountain music, roots music,

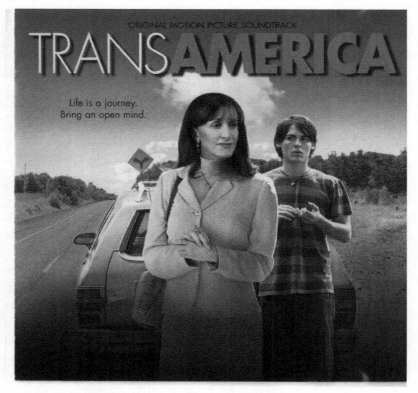

Figure 30. The official poster for *Transamerica* depicts Bree and Toby as a family on a road trip. This poster and soundtrack cover represent a change from an earlier promotional poster that inappropriately depicted Bree standing indecisively between men's and women's restroom entrances, as if she were confused, as media scholar Andre Cavalcante has discussed.

bluegrass music, to Nashville pop, Western music, Texas cowboy music, to American Indian."[35] This "American music" soundtrack frames the narrative as a typical road trip in which uniquely atypical characters connect with the cultures of the places they are passing through and, in the process, learn about one another and themselves. Musicologist Susanna Välimäki asserts that a "mainstream audience . . . can identify and sympathize with the protagonist thanks to the appealing, demystifying music."[36] *Transamerica* was created in the wake of the enormous success of *O Brother, Where Art Thou?*'s employment of country and folk music in a modern, clever, and ironic film that

allowed progressive middle-class, coastal audience members a sense of freedom to listen to country music. The use of country and folk music as an invitation for cisgender audience members to think humanely about a transgender
character and a sex worker character may result in challenging middle-class
viewers' assumption that country listeners form a "bigot culture," as well as
persuading these viewers to think more openly about transgender people's
and sex workers' lives.[37] Yet while the country and folk music may serve in the
film to connect cisgender viewers to one representation of transgender life,
the audience may continue to hear this music as natural and unperformed,
with the complexities of its background perpetuating myths about identity
that are inaudible as it plays this "demystifying" role for understanding a
transgender character.

The naturalized positioning of music is awkwardly evident, for example,
when Calvin Many Goats, the Native American rancher who helps Bree after
she is robbed, sings Stephen Foster's song "Beautiful Dreamer" while courting her. While this scene shows that transgender people, like anyone else, may
experience romance, it does not address the complicated web of blackface minstrelsy and patriotism in which Foster's well-known songs circulated or the
tension in the film between allying Bree's transgender identity with people of
color and maintaining a separation between them, which affords her character an extended story even as characters of color quickly disappear.[38] "Beautiful Dreamer" was a parlor song, not one of Foster's blackface minstrel songs.
However, musicologist Susan Key illustrates shared musical, lyrical, and thematic material between the parlor and the minstrel songs and notes a debate
about whether both types of Foster's songs may have functioned akin to Harriet
Beecher Stowe's *Uncle Tom's Cabin* in humanizing slaves and serving an artistic
role in the abolition movement or whether they romanticized the Old South
and slavery. Musicologist Deane Root notes that Foster attempted to reform
his contemporaries' comedic depictions of Black Americans and that his widely
popular songs have been interpreted differently as social politics change. Historian Brian Roberts notes that the common understanding that

> blackface represented working-class exuberance versus middle-class re-
> pression does not match the cultural fluidity of the genre. It fails, that is, to
> take into account the changes the genre underwent through the nineteenth
> century. In the 1830s and 1840s, blackface audiences had several major

clashes with middle-class reformers. By the 1850s, the American middle class embraced blackface. The embrace, in turn, added another layer to the genre's style. Along with the older, vibrant, and consciously vulgar style of numbers like "Jim Crow" and "Old Dan Tucker," there appeared the deeply emotional and sentimental [blackface] songs of Stephen Foster. Along with the effervescent, free Northern black of many early acts there emerged the happy and loyal slave. . . . By embracing blackface, middle-class audiences valorized a version of common-culture democracy. As a result, they were able to contain the threat of working-class culture, consuming its style of rebellious anger, softening it with sentiment.[39]

Contemporary nonacademic discourse on Foster's music, however, seems marked by the absence of discussion about blackface minstrelsy, for example, in journalist Robin Young's conversation with Americana star Roseanne Cash about her contribution (singing "Beautiful Dreamer" and two minstrel songs) to an album of Foster's songs by the Cincinnati Pops Orchestra.[40] While contemporary listeners may have little knowledge of the fictitious identities created in blackface minstrelsy, folk, and country music, the film's use of this "natural-sounding" music to demystify trans experience may contribute to forgetfulness about the unequal power relationships encapsulated in these musical histories.

Interestingly, while the music of white, working-class, rural, cisgender male characters is used to naturalize Bree and Toby, the film does not offer the same support of such characters. In its work encouraging the audience to embrace Bree, *Transamerica* uses white, working-class, rural, cisgender male characters as unappealing foils. For example, when Bree tries to return Toby to his hometown in Kentucky, we learn that Toby's stepfather abused and molested him. In the scene in which Toby confronts him, his stepfather responds by physically assaulting him in front of Bree and their kind Black woman neighbor, who serves as a sort of "mammy" figure for Toby (whose own mother, we learn, died by suicide). This kindly neighbor yet again rescues him by knocking the violent and drunk stepfather unconscious. And in the scene in which Bree meets Calvin Many Goats, the editing work of the film compares him to a white male trucker who pays to have sex with Toby. Since a hitchhiker has just stolen everything they have, Toby tells Bree that he'll try to sell his remaining drugs to raise money for them but instead goes to the bathroom to pick up a trucker for paid sex. Scenes of old-fashioned

Bree and Calvin politely conversing with one another from a distance cut back and forth with the sweaty and cramped, anonymous, paid, gay, underage sex Toby is having in the truck cab. In this way, the film maintains a "white trash" stereotype about white men in rural areas—they're sexually selfish and happy to take advantage of Toby. Meanwhile, *Transamerica* develops Calvin's character along the lines of Bree's—in place of the worst stereotypes of Indians in American film, Calvin is instead gentle, generous, and honest. Just like Bree, he's no radical, but scenes like this are meant to privilege Bree and Calvin as "normal," discreet, harmless, and likeable while using the white, working-class, cisgender male characters, including Toby, and their nonheteronormative sexual activities as foils.

The plot device of a (usually male) character's geographic journey as a metaphor for inner exploration is as old as literature itself. This journey is forced on Bree by her therapist, who holds Bree's genital surgery hostage until she helps the newly discovered son, who is an unsettling reminder of Bree's ("male") past. Thus Bree's journey across America may have appeared to audiences as a metaphor for gender transition, with the idea that the surgery at the end of the trip is an arrival that finalizes transition. While some people agree with this interpretation of transition, it risks assuming that genitals equal gender, an equation that others have criticized for its reinforcement of medical pathology and "correction," for singling out genitals over self-identification and presentation, and for the idea that transition must follow a unidirectional and medical path from one sex to "the opposite." By the time Bree begins the trip to help her newly discovered son, she has long considered herself a woman. Her planned vaginoplasty is but one of several modifications she has made at the expense of friendships, family relationships, and more gainful employment. In contrast, some transgender people, including Joe Stevens, Ben Wallace, and Anohni, describe being transgender as a lifelong journey or spirituality that may or may not include transition or identification as a man or a woman.[41]

Tucker honors the many understandings of trans narratives by challenging the anticipated happy ending. The film illustrates that Bree's surgery, while a positive occasion, is not a magic bullet and that her journey is not over but has only become more rich: she has developed what literary scholar Rebecca Scherr argues is a queer parental relationship in that "*she* is Toby's *father*," thus disrupting her dream of attaining unadulterated womanhood." The film closes by cutting the camera from inside Bree's house to outside, viewing this queer family at home in their complex but rewarding new relationship.[42] While the film begins with Bree using vocal coaching tapes to practice changing the gendered performance of her speaking voice, Bree is marked by her choice not to join others in song in social scenarios.[43] Her compliment to Calvin, "You can sing!" may serve as a poignant cue to cisgender viewers that singing can be difficult territory for some transgender people.[44] Instead, at the close, when Bree realizes a new arc to her life's journey, we hear a representation of her inner voice over the credits sung by country star Dolly Parton. As the crowning piece of *Transamerica*'s Americana soundtrack, Parton's song "Travelin' Thru" articulates in music a compelling first-person narrative of the film's trans themes, which explore both "the transgender narrative" and challenges to it.[45]

Tucker commissioned the song from Parton in clear terms: "It should be a song that has to do with traveling. It should be a song that has to do with redemption. It should be a song that you could sing in churches and you could sing in dancehalls."[46] Parton's persona in the song is not explicitly identified as transgender—her main identity is as a traveler: "I can't tell you where I'm going, I'm not sure of where I've been." The rousing chorus Parton cheerfully sings—"I'm just travelin', travelin', travelin', I'm just travelin' thru"—situates her as unthreateningly on her way elsewhere without much intent. These lyrics might be taken to confirm the inaccurate but ever popular assumption that transgender people are confused about their gender identities.[47] Yet Parton counters such an interpretation. The journey in her song is lifelong; moreover, the song expressly echoes lyrics and imagery from two Christian American folk songs, "Wayfaring Stranger" and "I Am a Pilgrim," the latter of which also appears in the film's soundtrack.[48] These songs' resonance tends to universalize the transgender character's quest for meaning. Parton explained that she was stuck when writing the song until she realized it could be a gospel song. She cleverly positions the transgender character and, crucially, herself as outsiders. Much beloved as a "backwoods Barbie" queer ally, Parton explained in an interview about "Travelin' Thru," "I've always been a weird, out-there freak myself. . . . My grandfather was a Pentecostal preacher. It was a sin to even pluck your eyebrows, and they thought it was a sin for me to be there looking like Jezebel."[49] This statement frames Parton as sympathetic to the transgender heroine of the film, but it also stigmatizes them both. Furthermore, Parton's portrayal of a sympathetic outcast enlists strong cultural support: she compares her persona's suffering to Jesus's in a secular setting that exemplifies "hillbilly humanism," where religiosity in a song communicates the rural characters' secular humanist values more than any religious beliefs.[50] American studies scholar Robert Cantwell characterizes bluegrass musicians' use of secular gospel song as eliciting a public and social sanctioning of conventional values, and so it is here too.[51] This song by a nationally treasured country music icon, a song that is appropriate for either a dance hall or a church, epitomizes, in closing, the film's depiction of its transgender heroine as a nuanced and relatable human being. This ending allows multiple interpretations of the relationships between transgender people and the concept of "normal," potentially expanding it to include a trans character, or instead illustrating that "normality" is an unappealing goal that Bree discards by the end of the film.

These stories of queer and trans journey and rurality have all covered physical and emotional distance using characters' relationships to changing scenery to demonstrate personal growth and understanding and depicting rootedness to the earth and to rurality as demonstrations of trans and queer characters' humanity, sincerity, and politics. Journeys reveal boundaries and draw connections between places and people. For Amy Ray, the political geography of the northern and southern United States reveals a tension in what feels like home versus where she feels "good in [her] skin" as a butch lesbian antiracist activist musician. Actor Slash Model's "TN Tranny Two-Step" suggests that these geographic boundaries may feel more important to some than the difference between cisgender and transgender, as well as the value of different configurations of trans existence. Joe Stevens also sings of different trans narratives, forging a new word for himself, his parents, and his listeners to make space for the person he once was and the person he is now to both exist rather than crafting a life history that hides his transition. Stevens's priority to live in a motor vehicle and to travel the same routes across the country each year parallels his framing of his life's journey, his gender identity, and his relationship to addiction. *Transamerica*'s road trip, with its Americana soundtrack, created a family between a transgender woman and the son she never knew for a mainstream audience not that familiar with "normal" transgender lives. Yet the journey also set the stage for Bree's letting go of the ideal of total normality. While Bree may have abandoned normality for more realistic and interesting company, *Transamerica*'s use of Otherness in plot, soundtrack, and the casting of a cisgender actress raises questions of representation of disenfranchised people and cultural and artistic ownership. As chapter 4 explores, queer country musicians are interested in how oppressed subjects are represented, what creative work may constitute appropriation, and whether folk and country music can recover from the misuse of Othered people that has plagued its history.

CHAPTER 4

(MIS)REPRESENTATION, OWNERSHIP, AND APPROPRIATION

In a song from the 2016 album *Armour*, white, Canadian, and transgender musician Rae Spoon sings that it's understandable that those from "a nothing town where they sing the same song in every house" would "try on" other people's sounds in order "to be someone new in the big city." But, as Spoon sings, "you can take it off and that's why it doesn't belong to you. It's a stolen song." In the online article that premiered "Stolen Song" as a single, Spoon explained:

> A couple of years ago, a band put out a music video with a gender variant protagonist. I felt like the portrayal only perpetuated stereotypes about trans/gender-diverse people. It really upset me because no one in the band or the actor was gender-variant/transgender. It felt like my identity was being treated like a costume to make the band appear more interesting. Then I realized that there are a lot of these examples in the music/arts industry. I have also mistakenly appropriated culture from other people. "Stolen Song" is a call to folks, including myself, to stop using identities that don't belong to us in our art. Musically, the song is upbeat and has some great drum programming by Berlin artist Alexandre Decoupigny. I wanted it to sound optimistic and positive.[1]

This issue of representation of marginalized people in art is urgently important, as examples in this book have shown, yet it can be fraught in terms of the political work done by the representation. Spoon, who identifies as nonbinary, raises what seems to be a reasonable critique in response to a representation of their identity group that replicated stereotypes and, as they explained to me, felt insufficiently researched.[2] But this critique prompts some complicated questions: Whom do identity categories "belong" to? What does it mean for an artist to "stop using identities that don't belong to [them] in [their] art"? And if an artist refuses this call, what responsibilities should that artist have in representing people who are different from them, especially those from an oppressed group? This chapter examines "Stolen Song" to consider the friction created between appropriation and essentialism in the context of theories of identity and musical genre. The question of appropriation is most often discussed around race, and while "Stolen Song" was prompted by another group's appropriation of transgender representation, as we will see, that appropriation conflated and confused race, gender, and sexuality.

"YOU CAN TAKE IT OFF"

Identity appropriation seems particularly common, as "Stolen Song" notes, for white middle-class people from the suburbs, who often think that they come from a "nothing town" where tastes seem uniform and boring. The suburbs were invented as a racially and socioeconomically segregated space for white people to flee the poverty and violence caused by structural inequality and capitalism. In this homogeneous space, their dominant culture, like others before and since, is so normalized that it's often imagined to be contentless. Members of such cultures often participate in the manufacture, consumption, and performance of Otherness. There's a continuum of awareness about why—as Spoon notes, some find their own community "boring" and hope to seem different or cosmopolitan. Some realize that they've been raised in an artificially homogeneous society—and with this realization may come focus on Otherness as more "authentic" (and a way for the white middle-class person to seem more "real"). This interest may lead some to engage with Othered culture with the aim of healing societal divides and working toward social justice for those who have been Othered and oppressed. For example, American studies scholar Barry Shank notes that in the case of the mid-twentieth-century folk revival, members of the New Left aimed to advocate for civil rights through their consumption of Black musicians' "folk" music and also believed that they'd "find themselves" in the process.[3]

Musicologist Olivia Bloechl traces theories of race and racial impersonation in music to at least the sixteenth century.[4] So the ideas of societal divisions, mimicry of stereotypes, and borrowing from an oppressed group that seems to have more "content" than one's own culture is part of a long tradition. Due to the increasing awareness of and desire to address social inequity, as well as a lack of equal representation in art and media, the issue of cultural theft has become increasingly important. As arts, fashion, advertising, sports, journalism, and other mediums depict different identifications and draw inspiration, fierce debates have arisen over how marginalized people are represented—who may create these representations, for whom, and how may they be consumed.

Avoiding cultural appropriation is important to Rae Spoon's politics and to their listeners. Instead of calling out the band, Spoon acknowledges that as an artist they too have "appropriated."[5] Further, Spoon's "optimistic and positive" response song follows their overarching artistic aim of drawing listeners into this political artwork in order to be open to consider its messages (e.g., of critiquing racism and colonialism—including their own). Yet the song's politics, and the politics against appropriation in general, are in tension with a prevalent theory of identity—that identity is socially constructed. "Stolen Song" and Spoon's discussion of it seem to depict identity as inherent. The Othered people in "Stolen Song" are marked by not being able to "take it off," where "it" is presumably the "song." This phrase implies an enticing *musical* object or practice that marks its owner as different. While this song can be imitated, for the Othered person it seems to be something that helps define or support their relationship to an identity category, and it cannot be disconnected from society's view of them whether they want it to be or not. "Stolen Song" sets up identity difference as both *musical* and *essentialist*.

Marginalized and oppressed people should have the right to self-definition and protection against the misuse of identifiable cultural markers of self or group, which could take the form of putting on another identity as a costume or stealing music. But how might those invested in the well-being of oppressed musical subjects reconcile the notion of the ownership of sound or song as a self that cannot be "taken off" with the last several decades of scholarship on identity in music, which draws from social constructionist understandings of identity? After all, taking off a costume sounds like what Judith Butler calls the "bad reading" of her foundational 1990 book *Gender Trouble*, in which the reader thinks her theory of performativity means there is a conscious, stable "self" that decides to put on gendered outfits in the morning.

A helpful example of thinking about music in relation to identity as a social construct is sociologist and rock critic Simon Frith's 1987 point:

> The question we should be asking is not what does popular music reveal about the people who play and use it but how does it create them as a people, as a web of identities. If we start from the assumption that pop is expressive, then we get bogged down in the search for the "real" artist or emotion or belief lying behind it. . . . What we should be examining, in other words, is not how true a piece of music is to something else, but how it sets up the idea of "truth" in the first place.[6]

In 2002 music scholar Keith Negus and sociologist and communication scholar Patria Román Velázquez took this idea a step further, reminding scholars not to jump to conclusions: "Too often 'identity' is the end of a road well travelled, when it should really be the beginning of a journey, a point of departure. Too often identity seems to be a conclusion to be illustrated through a case study rather than an idea to be interrogated, explored and then expanded, or perhaps even abandoned. We are arguing here for a need to move beyond a particular approach that is most apparent when identity is imputed from that which is visibly enacted, displayed, performed, outwardly embodied, gestured, and 're-flected.'"[7] In other words, even social constructionist scholarship on identity representations reveals essentialist underpinnings.

Further, while social construction theory attempted to dismantle essentialist understandings of identity categories, not all people embraced this way of understanding identity, including some members of the marginalized people whom scholars had directed their dismantling of inherent categories for. While Butler was concerned about a "bad reading" of performativity, some people understood that reading as explaining their relationship to gender. It is not always beneficial for people to argue that a person's (already misunderstood and endangered) existence is socially constructed, especially when social construction is typically discussed by dismantling marginalized people's identities, as Stephan Pennington argues.[8]

No one seems to understand this journey of identity and music better than Spoon themselves, who describes their path to understanding who they are in relation to moving to different places, finding role models, and even asking hard questions about their sense of fit with different categories. In the trailer for director Chelsea McMullan's documentary about Spoon, *My Prairie Home*, Spoon is depicted summarizing their experience:

> Music was the first way I learned how to bridge the gap with people. I realized that I could, like, communicate better through music. Initially I thought I was a lesbian. I was like, "Oh that's why I don't fit in. I'm gay," you know? But then I moved to Vancouver and met the first transgender people I'd ever met. It was very soon after that that I decided to switch. When you don't fit into the gender system people tell you that you shouldn't exist, and you don't exist. I'm here to tell ya, "I exist!"

In this short introduction, Spoon shares three important themes in their life and work: they use music to communicate with people—a crucial tool after realizing that they didn't fit into "normal" society; they realize that moving to a different place revealed new possibilities of existence; and they address the existence of people who do not fit into purportedly crucial categories.

Spoon developed a country career playing banjo in a band and writing solo songs and duets with a friend. Yet after six years of touring as a country musician across Canada, the United States, and Europe, Spoon retired from being transgender and shifted from country music to open themselves to electronic music and indie rock. This happened when they met a new friend in Germany, Alexandre Decoupigny, the person who would go on to program the beats for "Stolen Song." When they first met, he asked Spoon what sort of music they played, and Spoon replied, folk music. Decoupigny asked what folk music was, and after Spoon explained, Decoupigny joked that by Spoon's definition, the folk music of Germany was electronic music. Through this new friendship, Spoon learned how to make music with computers and rethink their musical genre boundaries. The album that resulted, *Superioryouareinferior*, became their break-out success and includes Spoon's first upbeat dance song about colonialist appropriation, "Come On Forest Fire, Burn the Disco Down."

Like "Stolen Song," "Come On Forest Fire" brings awareness to how young people, often from the suburbs, are "looking for a new song" because they are trying to individuate in a homogeneous-seeming culture, and Otherness is appealing to them. Spoon sings, "Ask the colonial ghosts if they live in your home / ask the colonial ghosts if they live in your bones / ask the colonial ghosts what they took." As we dance to the appealing song, Spoon replies, "You're dancing on it!" In dancing along, we may realize that the point is to be reminded that we are the descendants of colonialists, building our dance clubs on stolen land and dancing to sounds created in (but not necessarily credited to) oppressed communities.

Yet Spoon's command to "burn the disco down" for dancing on stolen indigenous land sends an additional and unintended somber message for queer and trans listeners.[9] Dance clubs are often spaces in which marginalized people can feel some joy and release from the everyday structures that torture them. My Gay Banjo addresses the importance of dance clubs for queer and trans people in their song "Bombs Away," about the 2016 mass shooting at the Pulse nightclub. The song is devastating in its narration from the perspective of a gay person bleeding from bullet wounds and crying on the floor of the bathroom that night in the club. Every time I've heard the band perform this song, listeners' eyes well up, and band member Julia Allen's voice catches as she sings, "Bullets spray [in the club today]."[10] The shooting and the band's discussion of it raised conversation about the location of gay clubs in neighborhoods of color, as well as the existence of gay Latinx people and straight and cisgender Latinx friends of LGBTQ clubbers and the rush to essentialize the shooter's actions: "When I heard the news of the mass shooting in Orlando at the Latin Night at the Pulse (a gay club in a Latinx neighborhood), I lay in bed crying and wrote this song as a way to work through my sadness and anger—including at many folks responding with Islamophobia and warmongering. This was an attack against LGBTQ people in a place of joy, and it is also part of a legacy of mass killings of black and brown and indigenous people in this land and across the world."[11]

In 2017 Spoon followed up their earlier discussion of appropriation with a tongue-in-cheek, yet serious, recommendation about ethical songwriting in a short instructional book for songwriters called *How to (Hide) Be(hind) Your Songs*:

> I am cautious with the word authenticity because it is mostly employed to lie to music audiences. . . . I like to think . . . the people who are listening to and buying these false songs [are] ke[pt] . . . up at night, even if only for a minute. . . . If you see a bunch of people in squeaky clean clothes with perfect

straight teeth singing about working on the railroad you have to wonder to yourself, "When did they find the time to work on the railroad in between their bachelors' and masters' degrees?" Are you worried this is you? A good authenticity test is to close your eyes and try to remember if you, your family, your friends, anyone you know, anyone you've ever met has ever worked on the railroad. If not, try to divert your songwriting to relate to things that have actually happened to you. . . . What in your past makes you feel like throwing up? That's where the gold is. . . . If you are being your song you will be able to access these feelings over and over on command.[12]

Spoon's implied example ("I've Been Working on the Railroad") is particularly prescient (if unintentionally) for being a blackface minstrel song first published by Princeton University students and alumni. Yet this general artistic instruction is a far cry from the Rae Spoon of chapter 1, who "never learned how to drive, work the oil rigs, or ride a horse, but I did write songs about these things. I was not a cowboy in reality, but my heart always felt lonely enough to sing about it with conviction."[13] While Hank Williams spoke to Spoon's queer exile and inspired them to write songs about being a cowboy (an experience Hank Williams also did not have), by 2017 this did not seem like a valid artistic pathway for Spoon.

The very notion of "appropriation" seems to fix and essentialize identity. Sociologist Beverley Skeggs theorizes gender and sexuality as resources one may (or may not) have the ability to deploy in order to realize value in the self. Her ethnography of white working-class British women explores how class, race, gender, and sexuality intersect to either fix or allow people's social mobility. Skeggs argues that "some people use the classifications and characteristics of race, sexuality, class, and gender as resources even as others are denied their use because they are positioned *as* those classifications and are fixed by them. The 'self' then becomes a metaphoric space in which to store and display resources."[14]

An example is the trucker hat, a baseball cap with a foam front and a mesh back, historically worn by truckers and farmers. In early twenty-first-century North America, trucker hats were adopted ironically by middle-class teenagers in several subcultures (including hip hop, pop punk, and skaters). Previously giveaways from rural feed stores or farm equipment manufacturer John Deere, these hats became available from both middle-class and luxury brands.[15] Repurposed as fashion accessories, trucker hats allow more privileged wearers momentary costuming of working-class aesthetic without the wearer being marked by any of the cultural devaluing that this clothing often signals when worn by a working-class person. Applying Skeggs's theory, a trucker wearing a trucker hat would be understood as a person fixed by low status, with the hat offering no "resources" for the self. Meanwhile, a wealthy white person who wears a trucker hat is able to draw on a clothing signifier of the working class to make a fashion statement without loss of their dominant culture status.

While fashion seems an easy target for appropriation, the idea of a song or voice being appropriated and thus being originally fixed in a (type of) person seems more complex. Philosopher Steven Connor, theorizing claims of "appropriation or silencing" of voices in recent cultural theory, argues that this line of thinking results from "a concept of self related to itself in terms of ownership and possession" developed in seventeenth- and eighteenth-century Europe: "The politics of voice is inseparable from this phonographic hunger. The ethical injunction against the reduction of others to the condition of objects suggests the injunction against the theft or misuse of the attributes of the other, and especially of their voice. But it is only as a result of having been thus construed as a possessable and therefore alienable kind of object, that the voice can appear vulnerable to such illegitimate appropriation."[16] As Connor argues, the idea that someone could steal another person's voice reduces the victim of theft to an object that can be possessed. It invests in a sense of Otherness that then seems to be vulnerable to appropriation. Thus, Connor seems to be making a case against charges of appropriation, which are used to objectify Othered people in the name of protecting them.

Folk music makes an ideal subject for considering this issue of appropriation and the questions surrounding whether voices, songs, identities, or genres can be possessable and alienable. Folklorist Regina Bendix demonstrates this in her critique of the concept of authenticity, arguing that there is no authentic, original culture—culture has always been hybrid.[17] "Folk," as I explored in chapter 2, was invented as a concept to support Herder's idea of the nation-state, a place defined by its people, who were distinct because of geographical difference, language, stories, and music. Yet, Herder's model was based on a Eurocentric linear progress narrative in which all (Othered) nations might hope to achieve the development of German society but until then seemed trapped in the past. "Folklore" arose as a category during a period of enormous societal change from agrarian to industrialized production and mass migration of workers to urban centers. The urban middle class felt that this societal transformation prompted loss of pure, simple, and authentic culture and sought to preserve these qualities, seeking songs, stories, and crafts from those people who they imagined were less impacted by these changes and thus appeared to live in a less modern time than their own— rural, working-class, racially othered, and seemingly isolated people. Spoon's notion of folk and country music replicates myths. As scholars like Benjamin Filene and Richard Peterson have demonstrated, folk and country music are inventions thought up by middle-class white men. Musicians who had shown up for recording sessions in neat suits were instructed by producers to dress as "hillbillies" and then later as cowboys. They may have been neither, but the music sold, and audiences were happy. While some identified with aspects of these categories, they could never fully satisfy them because they were never based in reality.[18]

Documentary filmmaker Murray Lerner captures this tension in *Festival!*, filmed at the Newport Folk Festival in the early 1960s. In a scene that could have prompted Skeggs's theory, blues musician Mike Bloomfield identifies himself as a white wealthy Jewish blues musician and implies that while he can *play* the blues, Black southern musician Son House *is* the blues. Playing the blues made Bloomfield cool (by learning a perceived feature of American Blackness that had cultural value), but it did not fix him with the other features of Blackness that are devalued and pathologized when attached to a Black person. And in fact, the folk revival, which indeed rescued Son House from obscurity, giving him a national platform to share his exceptional musicianship, also attempted to fix him in the past, asking him to play like he used to.

These fixed selves and appropriated voices make money for the music industry, but the musicians are caught embodying an impossible identity. Filene identifies this as "outsider populism," in which Othered people are positioned, usually by the middle class, as exemplary "common people," a process that both solidifies a sense of otherness and draws audience identification with othered people's "grit and character."[19] Artists who are framed through "outsider populism" are expected to seem inherently different from their audiences and yet somehow also universally the same as their audience (or embodying some inherent humanity that the middle-class listeners feel that they've lost and hope to return to).

If, as Bendix argues, all culture is hybrid, then the quest for authenticity is problematic and sometimes dangerous—it ignores this hybridity and attempts to argue for essentialism in its place. In an essay entitled no less than "Rhiannon Giddens and What Folk Music Means," folk musician Rhiannon Giddens argues, "Nobody owns an instrument. No culture gets to put the lockdown on anything."[20] She notes that instruments have hybrid histories and explains, "It's not who owns the instrument, it's who owns the narrative."[21] Yet as the article's title demonstrates, the very meaning of folk music seems to be at stake, and Giddens does feel that some people are appropriating. Her judgment about appropriation focuses on material gain, individual connection, aims for communication, and the difference between authenticity and faking:

> The question is, who is materially gaining? . . . [W]hen you start bringing in money, commercialization, mass commodification, that's when it becomes really problematic. . . . Race is nonexistent—it's all culture and language. . . . I ask people, "Why are you singing it?" and "how are you singing it?" Are you singing it because it touches you? Because something in that song speaks to you, and that's something you want to communicate? Are you singing it because you want to pretend to sing like an eighty-six-year-old Black man from Mississippi? Because please don't. It's how you approach it. It's why you're doing it. It's the authenticity with which you are approaching the music, and I think it's a different question for everybody, but you *know* when you're doing something authentic and when you're faking something. And my job is to—I never fake it. If it doesn't feel right to me, I never do it, even if it's from my own tradition.[22]

Giddens's statement seems to challenge essentialist stereotypes (claiming instead that both culture and identity are hybrid), yet it argues against "faking" and in favor of authenticity, which then causes her to invest in essentialism and the possibility of appropriation. And that seems to be the case for Spoon, Giddens, and many others participating in this debate. In her interview for Ken Burns's country documentary (PBS, 2019), Giddens describes the hybridity of country music as a defining and positive feature of American music. Interspersed with her commentary are stories lauding the Carter family and Jimmie Rodgers's use of Black gospel, blackface minstrel music, Hawaiian music, and existing and invented lyrics, all serving producer Ralph Peer's desire to record old-sounding new music that could be copyrighted (and thus make him and the musicians more money).

Bendix acknowledges that the quest for authenticity may be inspired by the sort of yearning for meaning that is understandable and important to people.

As she and others have demonstrated, the invention of folk and folklore is one such moment of yearning for meaning and experiencing a sense of fear and loss around cultural changes. But we also know that this quest for authenticity invests in essentialized notions of Otherness against a foil of white middle-class suburban or urban "normalcy" and creates havoc for Othered people in agreeing on cultural definitions. Performance studies scholar E. Patrick Johnson theorizes that Blackness is *always* appropriated, even by Black people, and that notions of Blackness are in fact *defined by* debates over these different embodiments. Johnson notes at the same time, however, that the concept of authenticity remains important to oppressed groups in countering harmful stereotypes:

> Often, it is during times of crisis (social, cultural, or political) when the authenticity of older versions of blackness is called into question. These crises set the stage for "acting out" identity politics, occasions when those excluded from the parameters of blackness invent their own. ... [T]he mutual constructing/deconstructing, avowing/disavowing, and expanding/delimiting dynamic that occurs in the production of blackness is the very thing that constitutes "black" culture. ..." [B]lackness" does not belong to any one individual or group. Rather, individuals or groups *appropriate* this complex and nuanced racial signifier in order to circumscribe its boundaries or to exclude other individuals or groups. When blackness is appropriated to the exclusion of others, identity becomes political. ... When black Americans have employed the rhetoric of black authenticity, the outcome has often been a political agenda that has excluded more than it has included.[23]

Johnson's argument reminds us to ask how and why someone might be defining a category that they are associated with and what the repercussions might be for others who identify with the same term. If the category of Blackness was invented in order for some people to own other people, then use of this category to police authenticity, as Johnson mentions, seems not only to exclude but even perhaps to risk reinvesting in the same essentialism that enslaved people.

WE EXIST

From my research, I have inferred that the video that prompted Spoon's "Stolen Song" was *We Exist*, created for a 2014 song by the American and Canadian indie rock band Arcade Fire. Spoon has not named the band or song in these conversations with journalists or with me or in "Stolen Song," but I have come to believe that it is important to discuss how both songs and surrounding discourse engage comparisons of race in thinking about the (mis-)representation of gender.

The phrase "we exist" seems to imply that it would be helpful for a band made up of cisgender and/or straight people to use their privilege to remind listeners of queer and trans people's existence. Spoon and the members of Arcade Fire were living in the same neighborhood of Montreal at the time Arcade Fire wrote the song. Spoon mentioned that the musicians never approached them to ask about what life was like as a gender-variant person. Spoon said to me that this made them want to say to the band, "Hey, I'm here, I'm alive," or, to use the language of the song (which Spoon might have been attempting to omit from our conversation), "I exist."[24] Spoon's statement "I'm alive" also implies a critique of Arcade Fire's presentation of gender-variant people's lives, since the trans character in the music video is beaten, perhaps to death.

The lyrics of the alternative rock song "We Exist" begin as a narration from the point of view of a member of an unspecified oppressed minority, saying that people seem to be pretending that these othered people don't exist. Later verses are directed at the narrator's father, who seems to be considering abandoning his child over this identification. According to lead singer Win Butler, the premise is that the narrator is a gay Jamaican boy coming out to his father. The band did not use any Jamaican musical elements in the song, but Butler says the song was inspired by talking to gay Jamaican kids about homophobic violence while writing the album *Reflektor* in Jamaica:

> There is a very kind of homophobic undercurrent, even in a lot of popular music and dancehall music, where there is a lot of violence against gay people. . . . And we were in Kingston, and we went to this kind of film event and met some gay Jamaican kids and just kind of talked to them and realized that they were constantly under the threat of violence. For me, I get kind of used to being in this sort of extremely liberal bubble—where we have Whole Foods and people are tolerant. And you can kind of trick yourself into thinking that the world is that way. For me, it was really eye-opening to hang out with these kids who, if they were going to dress differently or express who they were, there was this real tension.[25]

Butler's trip to Jamaica seemed to reveal more homophobia than he under-stood as happening in the United States and its popular music. Yet a dispro-portionate number of queer and trans youth in the United States experience homelessness.[26] Butler's linking of luxury grocery stores in cities and affluent suburbs with tolerance for homosexuality and transgender identification is overly simplistic, trusting the middle-class cultural omnivore stance of con-suming culture by queer and trans people as evidence of "tolerance" for their existence. While Whole Foods may seem friendly to its shoppers, until 2016 it benefited, like many large corporations, from un(der)paid labor by prisoners, who are often people of color, poor people, and queer and trans people, and since Amazon's 2017 purchase of Whole Foods, its in-store labor practices have also suffered. But the main problem is that video and surrounding discourse create confusion about whether the narrative follows a gay or transgender character. Butler seemed to think the song was about a gay character and uses "he" to describe the protagonist, but the video seems to figure a transgender character, who the director, David Wilson, who is gay, calls "she" and "Sandy." Given that Butler mentions that the Jamaican gay kids may want to dress dif-ferently to express themselves, he may have felt that the main character of the music video was doing the same. But critics felt that this discussion revealed ignorance about both gay and transgender people's lives.

When the music video was cast in rural North America featuring cisgender straight actor Andrew Garfield playing the narrator, the band was criticized for not casting a trans actor and for replicating stereotypes, in that their point was to feature a trans character who is punished for being trans (a common trope) rather than creating a trans character who has any number of other life experiences, like real trans people do.[27] Butler responded, seemingly with anger and hurt over the critique: "For a gay kid in Jamaica to see the actor who played Spider-Man in that role is pretty damn powerful, in my opinion. . . . There was just so much thought and love that went into the video I don't personally see it as negative, . . . [but] I can totally see the sensitivity of the issue."[28] Butler's most prominent critic was Laura Jane Grace, transgender lead singer of the punk band Against Me! Grace took to Twitter, suggesting that they should have cast a transgender actress in the video and been clear distinguishing between gay and transgender identification in describing it.[29] She "compare[d] the phenomenon to 'white actors in black face [*sic*].'"[30] Her reference to blackface minstrelsy is compounded when one realizes that the song was written by white Canadian musicians about young gay Black Jamaican boys, who are depicted in the video by a British American cisgender male actor playing a rural North American transgender woman, and that Win Butler introduced the song at Coachella (where a scene from the music video was filmed live) by discussing same-gender marriage rights.[31] We have come so far from the original premise that it is unlikely that any unhoused gay Jamaican boy is going to see the video and realize Spider-Man is there for him. So what work is going on here, and for whose benefit?

The video begins by showing Sandy alone at home, visibly upset. She seems to feel drawn to present herself in more feminine clothing and hair than her character wears at the outset, yet she seems afraid and weeps. After getting dressed in a cropped feminine Western shirt, short cutoff denim shorts, cowboy boots, and a wig and consoling herself in the mirror that she looks good, she walks on her own along the highway through farmland to go out to a rural bar. Entering the bar alone, Sandy seems to have no support network, and people stare at her as if she's a stranger. Her body language is anxious, protective, and uncertain. She looks longingly at a seemingly straight cisgender couple who are slow-dancing. When a man asks her to dance and she hesitantly allows him to take her onto the dance floor, she experiences a brief moment of pleasure before other men burst in to taunt and assault them. The video seems to demonstrate this abusive experience as standard, when in reality, of course, many transgender people have friends and do not necessarily get beat up each night for dancing at a bar or having a relationship. The video instead shows an *imaginary* support network of gay friends who are dressed like Sandy, encourage her in a line dance using gay-coded "heels technique" dance moves (figure 31), and then open a secret portal for her to escape the violence of the rural and gain acceptance at the Coachella music festival (figure 32).[32] At no point does the video include the sounds of country music. Rather, viewers may surmise that Sandy's acceptance is predicated on leaving the country and country music for the more "progressive" audience and music of Coachella.

The music video's closing scene was filmed live onstage at Coachella in 2013 (figures 33 and 34). Sandy is cheered by the predominantly young middle-class white audience, and she is welcomed onstage. The audience happily sings along, "we exist" and the members of Arcade Fire share Sandy's new

Figure 31. Sandy's imaginary gay friends dance for her during a dream sequence of *We Exist*, dir. David Wilson, music by Arcade Fire.

Figure 32. Sandy's imaginary gay friends magically transport her from a rural bar to Coachella. Still from *We Exist*, dir. David Wilson, music by Arcade Fire.

makeup, which depicts her in a pink mask. Video director Wilson says that the Coachella audience "accept her just the way that she feels and just the way that she is." But if Sandy were a working-class rural queer or trans person, she might feel a sense of class and regional disconnect from the Coachella audience that might make this "accept[ance]" feel hollow.

Figure 33. Sandy wanders onstage at Coachella and exchanges a gaze with lead singer and songwriter, Win Butler. *We Exist*, dir. David Wilson, music by Arcade Fire.

Figure 34. Sandy is overwhelmed and happy to be accepted by Arcade Fire and the 2013 Coachella audience. *We Exist*, dir. David Wilson, music by Arcade Fire.

In her early twenty-first-century study of queer and trans youth in Kentucky, ethnographer Mary Gray argues that while the country has been set up by queer visibility politics as a huge closet to an urban queer utopia, rural spaces have, for a long time, allowed queerness to exist (if not flourish). The key is that being queer and trans must not affect the person's commitment to the tenets that hold rural life together: family and community.[33] As Gray shows, familiarity is crucial in rural communities, and the politics of "out and proud" visibility/difference makes it difficult if not impossible for rural queers to follow previous generations' open secret. In an article about the video and Laura Jane Grace's critical response, *Advocate* author Lucas Grindley writes, "There is something powerful in what both Butler and Grace are trying to say, though from seemingly opposing sides of debate about the video. Whether trans or gay, it's important to be visible, for a lot of reasons."[34] But who is visible in this video? Not the gay Jamaican boys. For whom is it important that gay and trans people be visible, given Gray's argument that rural queer and trans existence is predicated on not creating strong divisions between straight and gay, cis and trans? And what sort of visibility or audibility counts? What if this insistence on visibility and differentiation worsens conditions for rural queer and trans people? To return to Filene's notion of "outsider populism," it seems clear that this concept is most valuable to the unmarked, seemingly normal people consuming a marked other who they have decided is a hero and yet different from them (perhaps in ways that they can consume and emulate, e.g., in Arcade Fire's wearing the same makeup as Sandy onstage at Coachella or Mike Bloomfield wanting Son House to actually be or be possessed by the blues). In *We Exist*, the trans character is created to show "grit and character" surviving the scenes of abuse that the cisgender director placed her in so that her urban, coastal, middle-class saviors can welcome her onstage.

One striking point is that Garfield received praise for trying something new in playing a transgender character and in performing a dance scene. He received minimal training for these new tasks.[35] Sandy's fantasmatic gay friends wear costumes in homage to hers, yet they all appear to be cisgender gay men. Is the point to represent solidarity and friendship between gay and trans people? Or perhaps a continuation of the song and video creators' conflation between gay and transgender people? Anthropologist David Valentine was one of the early scholars to point out that not all queer people distinguish between being gay men and trans women and that transgender was, in the case of the working-class people of color in his study, a category applied by aid workers. Yet in 2013, white middle-class gay men and trans women typically saw themselves as very distinct. Sandy's friends mix gay bear masculinity and stripper moves, seductively offering the beaten-up Sandy a chance to loosen up, follow their moves, and begin to feel more comfortable.

Her body language changes in these scenes. In her dance solo, she is clearly meant to demonstrate "freedom" with her more flowing moves and taking up of space. The choreographer, Ryan Heffington, has worked on RuPaul's popular television show, *RuPaul's Drag Race,* and is drawing on the movement vocabulary developed from queer of color vogueing in 1980s Harlem and used in contemporary "heels technique" classes in cities.[36] Indeed, these imaginary friends seem to be showing Sandy the ropes the way that David Halperin discusses the mentoring that goes on for newly out gay men.[37] But what can we draw from their mentorship? They open a magic door for Sandy to escape the rural bar to end up at Coachella rather than helping her draw on her rural community in the way that Gray writes that her rural queer and trans subjects do? What might we make of the ominous sound of "We Exist" versus the upbeat and danceable sound of "Stolen Song"?

In his scholarship on Bob Dylan, appropriation, and the failure of the New Left, American studies scholar Barry Shank argues that we are all wearing "masks" and that while the New Left attempted to use music to create solidarity between white suburban kids and people of color, it did so through appropriation that Shank equates to blackface minstrelsy. Yet Shank argues that Bob Dylan made these "inauthentic" masks visible and audible so that we would be forced to reconcile with our own acts of appropriation and masking. But it may be difficult for trans artists to embrace the notion that all identity is socially constructed and that we are all wearing masks, especially for those in country music, where the expectation is that this music is "three chords and the truth."

In *We Exist,* Sandy and the members of Arcade Fire are wearing masks as they share a moment together onstage, perhaps to show that we are all wearing masks. Yet they hid behind the mask of normative saviors when critiqued about their representation of transgender women in rural areas. Meanwhile, in "Stolen Song" and "Come on Forest Fire," Rae Spoon warns listeners, and themselves, that many white people's cultural environment has set them up to consider themselves empty and needing to appropriate in order to "be someone else" or to understand themselves. In case listeners think this song is about someone else, Spoon gets us to dance along to these upbeat songs to make us all feel complicit in colonialism and appropriation. But Spoon's songwriting standards demand that musical inspiration must be drawn from one's own life. Meanwhile, the very genres and materials that musicians are working with are inventions. It may not help matters of misrepresentation for everyone to adopt the standards of essentialism that led curious white people of many eras to try on what they understood as the authenticity of Blackness. Setting firm standards around representation does not seem to help trans people in arguing for the variety of transgender existence in the world now. Instead, trans and queer musicians and musicians of color may benefit more from acknowledgment of their status as skilled professional artists who create a range of fictionally and autobiographically inspired work that at times can't help but expose the wishful, if not fraudulent or harmful, creation myths of their associated genres, as my analysis of three gay male hit country artists of 2017–20 reveals.

CHAPTER 5

MASKS, SINCERITY, AND (RE)CLAIMING COUNTRY MUSIC

Queer country has been having a moment. New musicians are earning un-precedented success, and older musicians are finally being recognized for their pioneering contributions and activism. As this book has explored, this com-pelling music highlights the appeal of this genre for queer and trans people through themes of rurality and journey that not only help them tell their stories but also reveal the deep tensions about authenticity and sincerity at the heart of country and folk music. These debates show the lasting impact of white supremacist patriarchy on this genre and reveal the long struggles not only for queer and trans musicians but also for women and nonwhite people in forging country music careers.

In the summer of 2019 a majority of competition winners at the Clifftop Bluegrass Festival were gay, celebrated by participants as a "Gay Sweep," and a number were also Black. And in February 2021, T. J. Osborne became the only artist signed to a major country label to come out. Thanks in part to the visibility of and mentoring by pioneers like Haggerty, the Indigo Girls, k.d. lang, the Reel World String Band, Si Kahn, Cathy Fink and Marcy Marxer, Doug Stephens and the Outband, Chely Wright, and Ty Herndon, as well as support from straight allies, continued thoughtful coverage from publications like the *Bluegrass Situation* and *Country Queer*, community-building and vis-ibility from organizations like Bluegrass Pride, and concert series like Queer

Country Quarterly and the Concert for Love and Acceptance, there were many more queer and trans country musicians and listeners in 2021 than at any prior time, and they had more access to meeting one another than ever before. There is also far greater interest in queer country among straight and cisgender listeners, such that several newer acts have been able to quickly build large followings.

Between 2017 and 2021 three unrelated cisgender gay male country musicians created international intrigue and, at times, controversy over their music. In addition to attracting millions of listeners, their unique acts attracted different audiences and contributed to the ongoing debates this book has explored about how country music is defined, how the stories it tells relate to the performers' and listeners' lives and politics, and how the expectation of sincerity continues to bear on who is understood as a country musician, as well as a human being. The earnest traditional country albums by Trixie Mattel, the 2018 winner of *RuPaul's Drag Race All Stars*, earned praise from country and folk critics, as well as attention from fans of drag queens who may have had no prior interest in country music. The mysterious gay crooner Orville Peck, whose signature look is a fringed "Lone Ranger" mask that disguises his identity while allowing him to create deeply moving musical performances in a homophobic world, released his self-produced debut album, *Pony*, in 2019 with Sub Pop Records (famous for signing Nirvana and other grunge bands in the 1980s) and launched an international tour that led to top festival invitations. One of the most important musical phenomena of 2019 was then-unknown teenage musician Lil Nas X's self-released single "Old Town Road," which went viral and set a *Billboard* record amid critiques that his song was not country. What these very distinct-sounding musicians have in common is their artistic use of personae, their communication of sincerity, and the divergent reactions their music raises about whether or not they belong in country music.

"NOBODY WANTS TO HEAR ANOTHER WHITE GUY WITH A GUITAR"

Trixie Mattel is the Barbie-inspired drag queen persona created by Milwaukee-born mixed-race (white and Ojibwe) gay cisgender male comedian and musician Brian Firkus. Firkus included country music in Mattel's performances

Figure 35. The cover of Trixie Mattel's debut country album, *Two Birds*, 2017, depicting Brian Firkus costumed as both a male-identified country musician and in female drag as Trixie Mattel.

on the seventh season of *RuPaul's Drag Race* and when she returned to win season 3 of *Drag Race All Stars.* Firkus's three folk/country albums have been released as a subset of Mattel's international fame as a drag queen.

Firkus's original country music features his own autoharp and acoustic guitar playing and vocals. His excellent vocals are recorded and engineered to sound natural and uncomplicated.[1] The albums sold well (especially on iTunes, where *Two Birds* immediately shot to number 1 in sales after Firkus's *All Stars* victory) and attracted attention from some country music journalists. The debut album cover (figure 35) offers a sense of Firkus's humor and yet sincere attention to country music history. The image depicts an impossible scene of Firkus in costume as Mattel alongside himself in costume as a male-identified country musician. Firkus as Mattel rests her hand on the male-identified musician's shoulder, giving the impression that they are bandmates and perhaps also romantic partners or siblings, as is sometimes the case in country music. The image draws on a standard depiction of country music authenticity, a wooden fence and wagon wheel in a rural field with a family band holding acoustic instruments, the autoharp representing "traditional country" (and also no longer popular instruments, as one of the only famous commercial country musicians who still regularly plays it is Dolly Parton), and thus signifies both as authentic country music and as gay camp love of outmoded things. The cover depicts 1950s country music fashion, a faded color scheme that makes the photo appear to be old, and a faux ring of "wear" on the album cover where the "record" would have rubbed (had this album been several decades old and played frequently). For those who own the compact disc version of the album, this feature has an extra element of camp humor, as compact discs stored in plastic jewel cases don't create this pattern of wear. Mattel's album packaging reminds us of the preciousness of albums for record collectors in an age when most people listen to music online.

Being able to sing as well as write and perform original music sets Trixie Mattel apart from most drag queens, for whom lip syncing is the standard. While Firkus knows that he has found a unique niche, he doesn't think a drag country act is entirely alien. He pointed out to my Queer Country class during a live video conversation in 2018 that cisgender women's country performances can also be considered "drag" in terms of being heightened, sometimes comedic, and even intentionally unrealistic performances of femininity.[2] But Firkus thinks that for his drag audience, his choice to perform country and folk styles is particularly powerful when combined with the exaggerated appearance of his drag persona. He said to my class, "I honestly think it's interesting, because in drag, you're inauthentic. You're a fabricated, produced, painted picture. But then when you're doing music, specifically folk music, you're doing something very authentic. So it's that crossroads that makes it interesting, I think." This statement suggests multiple interpretations of Firkus's beliefs about the relative "realness" of drag and country music, as well as what might be happening when he combines them. In highlighting the juxtaposition between his "inauthentic" drag persona and his "authentic" musical genre, Firkus draws on the perception (which authors like Benjamin Filene and Richard Peterson have challenged) that folk and country music are more "authentic" than other styles of music, presumably because of their agrarian roots, working-class players, grassroots participation, and the social justice politics of revival. His unshowy, earnest vocals and acoustic instrumentation, especially the autoharp, which he reminded us was the instrument that "Mother" Maybelle Carter played, adds to the sense of "tradition" and "authenticity," showing preference for the Carter Family and other older acts favored by the Americana industry in authenticating its version of country music history and suggesting in interviews that he didn't listen to contemporary mainstream country music or popular music.[3] As I noted in chapter 2, sociologist Richard Peterson challenges the notion of a "traditional" country music, especially one that is based on acoustic instruments, given that the first country music was in the more pop, soft-shell style, and waves of this style have resuscitated the popularity of country music between waves of the "rustic," acoustic, hard-core style. At the same time, Firkus frames drag as highlighting the performative nature of all gender, particularly the way that some female country stars intentionally play with the fabrication of femininity in their stage appearances. He said in our conversation that country music performances include elements of drag for *all* participants: "We're all in costumes and shit. If you think of Loretta Lynn or old videos of Dolly Parton, they're in a corset and wigs. They're *in drag*. There's no difference other than their genitals. And if that's what you're thinking about when someone's playing music, then you have some other issues."[4] His examples absolutely have merit—literary scholar Leigh Edwards notes the juxtaposition of authenticity and fakeness at the heart of Dolly Parton's persona, a tension that is also true of country music in general, but why not mention male performers in their brightly colored, fringed, rhinestone-studded suits from Nudie's?[5] Firkus's solely female examples of drag in country music performance might suggest a perceived distinction between the masculine "realness" of country and folk music and the feminine "fabrication" of drag (as well as pop-oriented styles of country, as Peterson analyzes). Yet Firkus also discussed with my class creating male personae for (then) future albums, so he may feel that his performances of masculinity are also opportunities for drag.

What is clear is that the combination of drag and country/folk music is profitable for Firkus in professions crowded with talented artists. Country music lends authenticity to Trixie Mattel. And drag allows Firkus to perform country music in a competitive market where, as he told us, "nobody wants to hear another white guy with a guitar."[6] He elaborated, "I was actually interesting, and I'm the white guy with a guitar, which isn't interesting. Being in drag and playing the [auto]harp is a lot more like, 'What is going on?'"

What's going on is a disarming musical display of earnestness coming from an unbelievable-looking source. And the image of Trixie Mattel, rather than damaging the sense of sincerity listeners might feel, instead imbues Firkus's music with a glimpse into the very real suffering of gay men that is at the heart of drag and that also aligns with this book's examination of a musical affect that could be called queer sincerity. One country reviewer noticed this sincerity in the midst of Firkus's performance of gay camp and was taken by surprise. Journalist Kyle "The Triggerman" Coroneos, the creator and editor of the website *Saving Country Music*, expressed his inability to have predicted that ten years after the website started, he'd be enthusiastically reviewing a drag queen's country album: "As strange as it might sound, there is an authenticity to Trixie Mattel's music that many of today's country performers just can't emulate, because they're just too well-adjusted." Here, "Trigger" (as he's known on the site) invests in the notion of country "realness," the contradiction at the heart of this music—that we are all supposed to believe that all country artists grew up in rural Appalachia and/or the South in a family of farmers or as a cowboy, that their songs are entirely autobiographical, and/or that this music is not a business but a window into their souls. Importantly, Trigger implies that the suffering Firkus experienced growing up in a homophobic world earned him the requisite country "authenticity" of not being "too well-adjusted," which, by inference, his comparison draws to some (presumably straight, cisgender) mainstream country stars.[7]

Firkus clearly loves country/folk music and finds it important for expressing his story in a much different way from the stand-up comedic aspect of his Trixie Mattel role. In some respects, a man who experienced the stigma of homosexuality from a young age sees an opportunity for queer performance in emulating its beautiful female stars, even as he sees the tension of fabrication with authenticity at the core. He explains that playing this music in drag allows him to take an intellectual stance that connects with everyone and to address relevant political issues in ways that people will listen to without seeming to preach:

> In drag playing folk music, you're taking something that's traditional and conservative, and you're taking maybe the most treasonous gender act

there is, cross-dressing, and you're marrying the two. If you can marry it with a sense of humor, you're not getting political. You just accidentally are importantly political. You're not preaching, you're just existing as a violation of natural law. . . . I've always been interested in that, especially since folk and country and Americana music, to me, it's always been, maybe not music for intellectuals, but it's emotionally intellectual, I think. It's obvious that people cover loving God or cheating or drinking too much. It's also universal. It's also honest in all walks of life, I think. Some people were like, "I didn't like country music until I heard your album." To me, I can get up there, and the sense of humor that I do, the comedy that I do, with this actual developed musical gift, it really doesn't leave a lot of room for anybody in the audience to criticize it, because it has a large sense of, "I know this is a joke because I'm dressed like a joke." . . . [A]s a white man, you can't really go there. Whereas in drag, I get to be the butt of the joke and make the jokes at the same time. It's like your permission slip. I've noticed that I can make school shooting jokes not because it's okay but because, from my point of view, making jokes about that stuff makes it easier to digest. Sometimes joking about it is the only way to digest.[8]

Firkus's point seems to be that drag allows him to include intellectual and political discourse in his acts with less risk than saying those same things while out of drag and without humor. His statement about drag being "treasonous" discounts the long history of straight, cisgender men cross-dressing for comedy and consolidating patriarchal power through bonding over misogyny. (Mattel's humor is not very sexist as far as drag queens go.) What *is* still a "treasonous gender act" in the (biased) view of some straight cisgender people in North American society is being a trans woman. Interestingly, Firkus shared with my class that he hadn't realized that trans listeners heard his song "Mama Don't Make Me Put On the Dress Again" as offering resonance to their own gender battles with parents. For Firkus, the song is about the exhaustion of working hard (and in a very elaborate costume) for a living as a person raised working class. He was happy about this unintended interpretation, but his aim with the song (and with his career) seems to be more pragmatic by appealing to a (larger) cisgender audience.[9]

The issue of his sincerity in playing folk/country was put to the test at the 2020 Philadelphia Folk Festival (which was virtual, due to the coronavirus pandemic). Festival director Justin Nordell came onscreen to introduce Mattel but also to teach the audience what drag was, asserting that drag is an "art form" (for "telling stories, just like folk music") and that "Trixie Mattel is a *folk artist*." Seeming to imagine audience members' questions about why gay sexuality or drag would be relevant to discuss in relation to folk music, Nordell connected Mattel's performance to his own relationship to folk music and to the Folk Song Society for fostering his identity as an out gay man happy in his own skin. Meanwhile, Mattel seemed uncharacteristically flummoxed by the situation, not only because, as she explained, the performance was virtual and she couldn't feed off the audience's energy but also because Firkus largely removed or altered the comedic elements of the act to avoid offending the folk festival audience. These strategies seemed to work, as, according to Nordell's remarks after Mattel's performance, several longtime audience members texted him during the show to let him know how much they enjoyed Mattel's performance. The question was how much meaning remained.

Firkus does seem serious about some of the politics of what he as a working-class gay male artist has been able to accomplish and why. With 2020's *Barbara*, Firkus took the opportunity to pay tribute to Patrick Haggerty. He and Haggerty duet on Lavender Country's "(I Can't Shake the)

Figure 36. Brian Firkus (*left*) and Patrick Haggerty (*right*) in the recording studio for Trixie Mattel's cover of "Stranger" for the album *Barbara* (2020).

Figure 37. Brian Firkus and Patrick Haggerty embrace after the session depicted in figure 36.

Figure 38. Trixie Mattel in concert at Temple University, pairing drag and country sincerity, 29 February 2020. Photo by the author.

Stranger (out of You)," a song that brilliantly calls upon the rural character of "the stranger" to discuss the drawbacks of anonymous gay sex for those who desire sustained intimacy and relationships (figures 36 and 37). Rather than shaming gay men for this sexual practice, though, Haggerty's 1973 song is part of his structural and intersectional critique, in which this practice is considered an effect of societal oppression. Mattel and Haggerty's earnest collaborative effort performing it in 2020 frames the song as one of poignance and sincere intergenerational gay solidarity. A video filmed of their studio work together sets this tone, as well as the recording's melancholy and ethereal harmony by Firkus on the last word of "I can't shake the stranger out of you." *Now This News* produced a story on "Cryin' These Cocksucking Tears," interviewing Mattel, who was absolutely serious (unlike any moment in either of the live shows I attended in October 2018 and February 2020 (figure 38) or in her drag comedy videos) in conveying the message of that song, the song narrator's reclaiming of the searing words of a homophobe to demonstrate how little straight men care about the pain they cause gay men.[10]

While Brian Firkus's success is a triumph, it's difficult to assess the state of queer and trans country musicians' chances by discussing his career. He doesn't need mainstream country's acceptance. Firkus's brand is Trixie Mattel, the drag queen, who, in addition to releasing three successful country albums, has an enormous following as a comedian, solo and with fellow *Drag Race* contestant Katya Zamolodchikova, with whom he has a show and a best-selling book.[11] He is also the creator of a cosmetic line. There's a practical reason for his aims. My students and I had the impression, after speaking with him in 2018 and reading published interviews with him, that Firkus, who grew up working class, was being careful to aim for financial success (or "monetizing," as he sings in the unreleased song "Goner").[12] He explained to us that while mainstream country's acceptance would be welcome, his career does not hinge on it: "One of my initiatives this year [2018] is to play all the charts the same and sell the same as all these other folk and country artists. But I'll never be at the festivals. I'll never be on all the locations. The magazines [covered the albums] because I just think it's still too weird. But, at the same time, being a little odd or being the Other is also what makes people interested in it. The part of drag that makes it fun to do, in some ways, is to be the thing that's out of place."

"IT'S MY AGENDA TO BE AS SINCERE AS POSSIBLE"

Brian Firkus pairs drag with earnest acoustic country music to address his suspicion that he might not be trusted or noticed if he appeared simply as a white-looking, male-identified, gay entertainer. Likewise, masking seems to allow cisgender gay country crooner Orville Peck a route to a sincere, intense, and unmistakably gay connection with his audience. "Orville Peck" is a pseudonym for this musician whose name is locatable online but who has requested listeners to not reveal his birth name.[13] His desire for anonymity is not driven by fear of homophobia, as was likely the case for the 1939 pseudonymous release of the obviously homoerotic song "I Love My Fruit," released by the Sweet Violet Boys (who we now know typically recorded under the name the Prairie Ramblers). Rather, Peck's mystery persona is part of an artistic agenda to use masking as an expressive opportunity for his obviously gay country music.

Like many gay artists, characters, and images before him, Peck has drawn his stage persona from the long-standing homoeroticism of cowboys: their displacement from domestic scenarios (which are typically coded as feminine and heterosexual) and replacement with homosociality and/or solitary living, their strong and resilient physique from outdoor labor and living, as well as the aestheticized Western and rodeo wear, and their poetic musical embrace of longing. Peck's costume combines elements of butchness and femininity, drawing on gay leather culture while referencing the 1933 radio (and later television, comic, and film) character the Lone Ranger's eye mask and cowboy hat (figure 39). The masculinity of his leather mask is paired with long, feminine fringe, which is more typically found on a Western shirt. The fringe disguises the lower half of his face and hangs from his mask almost like hair. Peck's singing style and song topics also pair a range of gender performance, as he uses a baritone voice in a crooning style, and his songs traverse common country types and themes like murder ballads (this one gay), buffalo stampedes, field hollers, and hokum. He also depicts the "torturous nostalgia" of unrequited love of a hustler, being a "drifter," his drag queen friend "chasing what [she] love[s] in the face of adversity," and "the struggle I've had feeling like an outsider and an outlaw my whole life and not letting that turn into resentment."[14] His crooning combines seductive, plaintive, and sinister elements, which journalist Ian Crouch describes as "a voice with the

Figure 39. The masked crooner Orville Peck using one of his dramatic gestures in performance at Union Stage, Washington, DC, 22 September 2019. Photograph by Jeff Henry, reproduced with permission.

sexy, menacing melodrama of Roy Orbison, run through the filters of New Wave and the opening theme of 'Rawhide.'"[15] Crooning, as literary scholar Allison McCracken writes, emerged from a moment in the early twentieth century of sensitive masculinity enabled by early microphone technology and personified by Rudy Vallee. His singing style appealed to housewives but threatened heteronormative masculinity and was replaced by the more domineering, heteronormative style performed by Bing Crosby.

Peck explains that his childhood pain forged a connection to the cowboy image and country music: "I grew up fairly lonely, feeling pretty outcast and alienated, . . . [s]o my translation of that into a country and western star was to be this lone cowboy figure."[16] Peck's discussion of his childhood draws on the loneliness many musicians hear in country, particularly in the figure of Hank Williams. At his November 2019 Philadelphia show, he acknowledged the audience members who attended the show alone (the first time this often-solo concertgoer has heard such a message, especially framed as a *queer* message), and he also reminded listeners that his music was about embracing everyone in society. In discussing the perhaps surprising career choice of being a queer country singer, Peck explains that country narrates a sense of otherness, rejection, and loneliness that resonates with his experience as a queer person:

> I'm surprised more gay people don't feel connected to country music. And that's mostly because of the stigma that country music as an establishment has kind of pushed. . . . The thing that I connected with country music when I was a kid is it's about isolation, heartbreak, disappointment. That's the gay experience for everyone at some point. I feel like that music is written for people who feel like the minority or feel somehow alienated. Somehow the stigma got twisted around where it's like, oh this music is for well-adjusted, straight white men or whatever. And I actually disagree. I think that it's meant to be for people who feel like freaks.[17]

Here Peck identifies the element of country music that Nadine Hubbs has explained was always queer in its relation to middle-class North American culture.[18] He also refers to those privileged country listeners (according to Hubbs, its more recent middle-class suburban and city audience) who have embraced the element of stigma in country music (which follows the Republican agenda to urge white, straight voters to feel threatened by anyone else).

In an interview for the *Gay Times*, journalist Sam Demshenas asked Peck how being gay figures in his artistic agenda. "'I've never felt like I've had to come out as a gay artist,' he says, acknowledging *Pony*'s overtly queer overtones. 'I've never felt like that was a point of contention for me. Those songs, those experiences happened to me from the perspective of a gay man. It's a huge part of what I do and it's a huge part of who I am, but it isn't an agenda for me to be visible because I'm a gay man. It's my agenda to be as sincere as possible.'"[19] It might at first seem counterintuitive to some for a masked performer (who might be seen to be practicing a form of in-visibility) to claim sincerity as his artistic agenda. Yet for his listeners, Peck's sincerity seems more convincing because of his masking. The mask allows him to create personal, dramatic, and intensely emotional songs that seem more universal because his anonymity makes us think these songs could also be about anyone—maybe ourselves. The elements that we learn about him through these songs seem to suggest that, like him, we are all carrying deep, exciting stories beneath our exteriors. Masking seems to be a way Peck artistically represents and perhaps also counters his prior lack of expression and engagement, which he describes in his first album's liner notes: "I didn't realize how closed I was emotionally for a very long time."[20] By eliminating some of the possibilities of facial expression, Peck can instead focus on the drama of bodily gesture. He extends his long arms in wide, slow, and frozen poses that might seem strange, exaggerated, and fake if he were not masked. Audience members seem to relate very personally to these expressive gestures, taking photos and discussing them in the "Iron Hoof Outlaws: Orville Peck Fan Club" on Facebook. Fans' devotion to his look and his message seems evidenced by the popularity of fan art featuring his image (which he uses with their permission on his merchandise) and fans' sharing of their Orville Peck tattoos.

In May 2021 Mattel and Peck released a delightfully queer cover of folk and country singer-songwriter, musical theater composer, and author Billy Edd Wheeler and pop songwriter Jerry Leiber's 1963 song "Jackson," known to country listeners by the Grammy-winning single released in 1967 by Johnny Cash and June Carter Cash.[21] The duet is narrated by a couple who "got married in a fever" and whose desire for one another is fading. They anticipate that moving to the city of Jackson (state not specified) will provide them with a more exciting nightlife—this hope becomes competitive between the two singers. In Mattel and Peck's performance, the implication that this masked pseudonymous gay singer and drag queen singer are a married couple plays with delightful camp on the original cisgender, heterosexual, married couple narrative. That they are fighting to win over the nightlife in a new city sets these two contemporary queer stars in a friendly fictional competition akin to their real-life dual stardom.

Both Peck and Mattel have reinforced understanding of the sincerity of their queer country politics through public gestures with septuagenarian queer country predecessor Patrick Haggerty. Peck featured Haggerty as a surprise guest in a 2019 show (figure 40) and invited him to tour again in 2021. Recalling bisexual, Puerto Rican American artist Alynda Segarra's impassioned 2015 plea, one of the most potent postrevival purposes of folk music is its stand against injustice. By associating themselves with Haggerty, Peck and Mattel demonstrate that while they may simultaneously be white men in an era in which white men's authority and trustworthiness are in question and enormously successful commercial musicians, they are queer, sincere, and fighting the good fight.

Figure 40. Lavender Country's Patrick Haggerty as surprise guest during Orville Peck's May 2019 show at Barboza in Seattle. Photograph by Megan Rainwater, reproduced with permission.

Peck's response to interviewer Demshenas's question about his artistic agenda demonstrates the centrality of queerness to his life and music but with a sense of ease about this queerness. He doesn't gesture toward visibility politics the way that Chely Wright and Ty Herndon have been positioned to do as formerly closeted mainstream country musicians who were excluded by the industry after coming out. Instead, Peck responds that his agenda is sincerity. Meanwhile, Wright and Herndon had to ask for forgiveness of their audience regarding truthfulness after they came out—Wright especially, who had publicly dated straight cisgender male mainstream country star Brad Paisley. In a way, Peck's situation reveals a minor advantage as someone who doesn't need the mainstream country music industry's approval to have a successful career. Releasing his first country album on Sub Pop, the indie rock label on which, in the 1990s, Kurt Cobain sang "everyone is gay" to great acclaim, Peck's queerness and persona could be delivering exactly the amount of rule-breaking Simon Frith argued was expected and even required to be successful in a more rock-oriented arena. The success of his first album then attracted Columbia Records. Perhaps Peck, whose earlier career (under his birth name) explored punk/grunge and musical theater, could be benefiting from the "post-identity"/"post-genre" opportunity that philosopher Robin James identifies as possible for some white musicians (who can claim to be "post-identity" and thus freed from popular music genres' constraining ties to identity categories) but not possible for nonwhite musicians. Yet Peck's queerness makes "post-identity" movement between genres seem less attainable, especially given that he makes queer, antiracist, working-class politics clear in his work, including through his public statements, song topics and lyrics, and musical collaboration.[22] In June 2020 he announced on Instagram that he was postponing release of his EP, *Show Pony*, to maintain international focus on the Black Lives Matter protests over George Floyd's murder:

> Hey gang, I know it's only two days away but I've decided to push the release of my new EP 'Show Pony' to July. We're undergoing a huge overdue worldwide transformation thanks to the Black Lives Matter movement and that is mainly what I want to put my focus on at the moment. The momentum is currently so strong, and it needs to keep going in order to dismantle the injustices of oppression, so if your voice hasn't been heard yet just use it, or walk out and hear the protesters, and if you're scared, tell them Orville sent you! Last week, thanks to the help of some lovely people we raised close to $37k, and this week I'll be performing a little surprise from the EP at @wynwoodpride where we're hoping to raise $100k. Lots of great performers, so if you guys like what you see, remember to tip—and y'all, even if you can't tip, watching to actively educate yourself is also a win for everyone. Love you all for being kind people and I can't wait for you to hear the album—but lets use this month to get our shit in order because this is only the start of the marathon for equality[.][23]

When the EP came out in August, it debuted at number 9 on iTunes' All-American chart. One of its most striking songs is a cover of Bobbie Gentry's feminist 1969 country soul song "Fancy" (a crossover pop hit). In it, a girl named Fancy is born into abject poverty and is urged into prostitution by her desperately poor and sick mother as Fancy's "one chance" to save herself. The song is narrated from Fancy's adult perspective, in which her sex work made her a wealthy "lady" who owns multiple homes. While the lyrics reveal a struggle, Gentry's performance is upbeat, with a rhythmically driving, singable chorus. Reba McIntire, an internationally beloved country star and icon for her gay male fans, made a country pop cover in 1990 that became her most requested song and reached eight on *Billboard*'s Hot Country list. With her accompanying music video, Gentry's lines "And though I ain't had to worry 'bout nothin' for nigh on fifteen years / I can still hear the desperation in my poor mama's voice ringing in my ears" are made literal with memories of her long-dead mother's voice echoing as viewers see into the narrator's memory of that day. In Peck's revisioning, "Fancy" is sung by a narrator who is a transgender woman. The narrator dons the fitted red dress, makeup, and a locket that says "to thine own self be true" that her mother bought her and transforms from a "half-grown boy" (replacing Gentry and McIntire's "kid") into a woman in the mirror. When Peck's narrator sings about making a vow to "be a lady someday, though it didn't matter when or how," and knowing what to do in that moment but refusing to live in shame for doing it, she refuses not only the presumed essentialism of class that the song challenges but also that of assigned gender. Fancy's reflection on "self-righteous hypocrites that call [her] bad" takes on an additional meaning, criticizing transphobia. Peck opens the song at the very bottom of his vocal range, straining to stay in tune on the record and in a virtual live performance, in keeping with a punk aesthetic. His bleak atmospheric electric bass drone throughout the song anchors the opening melody, preventing harmonic development, and seems to challenge the interpretation that Fancy has earned a happy life free from her early suffering. While eventually the band joins with sparse drums, electric guitar, and limited bass movement, the song is still grim.

Show Pony's pop country–sounding celebratory duet, "Legends Never Die," with "fellow Canadian crossover country artist" Shania Twain left some fans worrying where he was headed as an artist and whether they'd still enjoy his music if it didn't have that dark, melancholy, David Lynch feeling. Thus, they seem to be adding a contemporary iteration of Peterson's hard-core/soft-shell authenticity dialectic, in that they like that Peck's music seems more like "indie" music (or Americana) than like mainstream country. These fans also expressed concern that he not end up like Lil Nas X, an intriguing comment, considering his enormous following.[24]

"CAN'T NOBODY TELL ME NOTHIN'"

While audiences and critics agree that Trixie Mattel's Barbie-like drag persona and Orville Peck's mysterious queer Lone Ranger persona connect sincerely

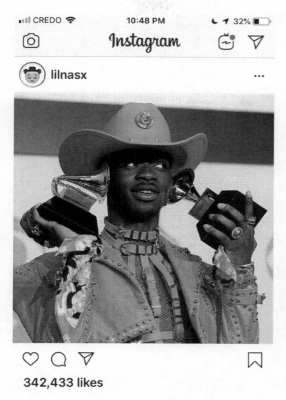

.ıll CREDO 📶   10:48 PM   🌙 ↑ 32% 🔋

📷   *Instagram*   📺 ✈

🙂 **lilnasx**   ...

♡ ◯ ✈   🔖

342,433 likes

Figure 41. Lil Nas X's Instagram post after winning two Grammy Awards in 2020. His costume combines multiple gay fashion symbols, including bondage straps, a mesh strapped/collared clubbing shirt, a hot pink studded biker jacket, a cowboy hat, and designer scarves tied around each wrist.

with audiences through their country music, Lil Nas X's cowboy persona (figure 41) and song were met with dramatically disparate reactions—viral fame, on the one hand, and unprecedented removal from the *Billboard* country chart, on the other. The major difference is that while Mattel and Peck are white-appearing (Firkus is part Ojibwe), Lil Nas X is Black and combined country with trap music in his December 2018 hit song "Old Town Road." Drawing on the country-associated images of escape on long, open roads and a lonely journey, critique of nihilistic consumption, and pursuit of a goal against all odds, Lil Nas X's "Old Town Road" was one of the most important—yet also, crucially, disputed—songs of 2019.

Montero Lamar Hill of Lithia Springs, Georgia, known by his stage name, Lil Nas X, rose from obscurity to fame in just a few months when, in December 2018, he shared his song, through his already substantial Twitter and Instagram following, on SoundCloud and iTunes. He categorized the song as country partly because he thought that it might have less competition with country songs than with hip hop, according to his manager, Danny Kang.[25] A rapper and singer, he created the original just-under-two-minute track by following his interest in a then-popular cowboy theme, which was known on the internet at the time as "the yeehaw agenda."[26] He bought a beat online for thirty dollars from producer YoungKio that samples a mandolin and banjo melody that Lil Nas X didn't realize was from "34 Ghosts IV" by Nine Inch Nails. He added animation from the Wild West video game *Red Dead Redemption 2,* and the track took off on the then-new video-sharing platform TikTok. In December 2018, when he released the song, he also posted to Twitter asking his followers to help him get Billy Ray Cyrus to make a guest appearance on a remix. The song went viral and appeared in the nineteenth position of *Billboard*'s Hot Country chart on 11 March 2019. But behind the scenes at *Billboard*, someone decided it wasn't a country song and removed it from the following week's Hot Country chart. It next appeared on the 23 March Hot Rap Songs chart at number 24 with the label "new," as if it was its first week charting.[27]

Rolling Stone published an article about the removal, claiming an anonymous insider take on the controversy:

> *Billboard* quietly removed "Old Town Road" from Hot Country Songs and informed Lil Nas X's label, Columbia Records, that his inclusion on the ranking was a mistake, according to an insider with knowledge of the matter who spoke on the condition of anonymity. *Billboard* did not publicly announce the change, but in a statement released to *Rolling Stone*, the publication said that "upon further review, it was determined that 'Old Town Road' by Lil Nas X does not currently merit inclusion on *Billboard*'s country charts. When determining genres, a few factors are examined, but first and foremost is musical composition. While 'Old Town Road' incorporates references to country and cowboy imagery, it does not embrace enough elements of today's country music to chart in its current version." ... "What do we do with artists that blur genre lines when they're [artists] of color?" the [anonymous *Billboard*] insider wonders. "No one else has that problem."[28]

The anonymous insider is right to wonder about the judgment that this song was not country music, given that since country's inception as "hillbilly" music in the early twentieth century, it has been defined through racial seg-regation. A sixteen-tweet post that was written by Shane Morris, who claimed to be a "former country music label person," and that shared information about racism in the country industry and Black cowboys (part of which was inaccurate) went viral.[29] *Saving Country Music* initially posted an article in approval of the removal of the song from the country chart, even going so far as to question whether "Old Town Road" was a song: "The debate about what is country music and what isn't is an eternal one, and can turn nauseat-ing and redundant very quickly in the way different factions fight back and forth about the definition and boundaries of the genre. That debate won't be resolved here or anywhere else. But a 1:53-long viral 'song' that is really nothing more than an internet meme entitled 'Old Town Road' by rapper 'Lil Nas X' has rekindled the debate anew, with critical implications behind it."[30]

This book has explored how queer and trans country musicians and their music may be musically marginalized for reasons of "fit" with genre. Their difficulties have helped expose how genres like country are predicated on identity stereotypes, often assumed to be essential. Lil Nas X's "Old Town Road" and its path to fame present challenges to interpreting this song's and this musician's genre. Trigger's statement might be interpreted as racist, given that it resembles a common critical reaction to hip hop—that it's not really "music." However, Trigger is also correct that Lil Nas X is an expert in internet memes and was more focused on virality than acceptance from the country music industry. When "Old Town Road" was first shared, several elements of the song and its appearance understandably raised questions about what it was and why it was so famous: it was a very short track by an unknown artist that merged trap music and country with video game visuals, and it went viral on a social media platform that, at that time, was unfamiliar to most adults in the United States, although children and young adults were using it. One of the reasons that country music journalists like Trigger might be frustrated with the song's categorization and enormous success is that Lil Nas X com-pletely skirted the country industry's process for signing artists, songwriting, recording, releasing, and promoting music. Power brokers in the country music industry have a heavy hand in the activity of making country music. Musicians sign with certain labels, cowrite songs with country songwriters, record and perform with country musicians and producers, are marketed as country, and are pitched to country radio and booked at country venues.

Many of them live in Nashville in order to make this process easier. Lil Nas X and "Old Town Road" side-stepped all of that.

The *Rolling Stone* article generated a lot of media outcry and attention to "Old Town Road," as Trigger noted in a chronological report on the events (partly written to correct inaccurate reports that his 23 March article had impossibly prompted the 18 March song removal).[31] On 3 April 2019 Billy Ray Cyrus used Twitter to write publicly to Lil Nas X: "Been watching everything going on with OTR. When I got thrown off the charts, Waylon Jennings said to me 'Take this as a compliment' means you're doing something great! Only Outlaws are outlawed. Welcome to the club!" With this statement and his choice to join Lil Nas X on the remix, Cyrus cleverly authenticated Lil Nas X as an outlaw country musician for being thrown off the charts by the mainstream country industry, quoting one of the original outlaw country stars, Waylon Jennings, authenticating Cyrus's outlaw status.[32]

Lil Nas X released four very popular official remixes that included musicians such as Cyrus, Diplo, Young Thug (the originator of country trap), and ten-year-old Mason Ramsey. (Ramsey's 2018 video singing Hank Williams's "Lovesick Blues" on YouTube went viral. Interestingly, Ramsey wasn't asked to yodel on the remix despite his lyrics "yippee-yo kay-eh" on the track.) Another remix features RM, the leader of the worldwide sensation Korean boy band BTS. With each of these collaborations, Lil Nas X expanded the genres his song was relevant to and gained thousands of fans of these famous musicians as his own. The popularity of these remixes, the viral memes, and the enormous media attention propelled "Old Town Road" to the top of *Billboard*'s Hot 100 chart, where it remained for a record nineteen weeks.

During this moment of enormous popularity, Lil Nas X also came out to listeners as gay in an Instagram post. He assumed his followers might have already figured it out, given very subtle rainbow shading on a small picture of a high-rise building on the cover of a forthcoming release. But on "Old Town Road" he sings, "Cheated on my baby / you can go ask and her," and he even took the time to annotate this line on the lyrics website Genius. It was there that he also added the backstory about writing this song. He describes dropping out of college after a year to pursue music, resulting in his parents' and eventually also his sister's strong disapproval, a reaction that left him worried about where he'd live. Like Peck, Lil Nas X felt that he was like "a loner cowboy," as he explained:

Okay, so the real story behind "Old Town Road." I dropped out of school and I started to do music. I started to live with my sister because I didn't want to go back home because my parents was not gonna be having that. For one, they feel like music is not a realistic future for anybody. I was living with my sister, and she was ready for me to go, basically. It started off as this loner cowboy kind of vibe. It's like running away from everything, basically. I found the beat in late October on YouTube and released the song early December. It was gonna be a serious kind of song with country influence, of course. A lot of my music before "Old Town Road," I was just trying to make music I thought everybody wanted. I changed the meaning of it later on down the road from a runaways type of story to Old Town Road being a symbol for a path of success, where you're just staying on it. The horse, me not having too much to work with, but getting to where you're trying to go. . . . In the chorus, the, "Can't nobody tell me nothin," it was like a jab to my parents in a way. Wanting me to not really stop doing music, but to get back into school. It's like, "Can't nobody tell me nothin.'"[33]

His story resembles that of many queer young people: family disapproval, even being thrown out of the house because of his queerness, and (perhaps also against family wishes) pursuing a music career, a choice that, in some circumstances, is marked for its queerness.[34] His story also finds a way to authenticate his use of country themes after criticism that he wasn't truly a country musician.

Just a few months after Lil Nas X wrote the initial version of the song, he transformed "can't nobody tell me nothin'" from a teenager's reproach to his parents into a celebration of his genre-confounding musical success and, via his star-studded, five-minute, "official movie" version of his video, a statement corroborating the long-standing existence of Black cowboys. Playing a bank robber from 1889, Lil Nas X falls through a hole that transports him to 2019 Los Angeles, where contemporary urban Black residents stare at him, seemingly not only for his very old-fashioned clothing but also because they've never seen a Black cowboy. He claims success by bringing new listeners to country, saying, "Honestly, it makes me feel great that I was able to put completely different worlds together and make a song that so many people like. Almost everybody who I've shown this song to, even people commenting comments like, 'Hey, I hate this genre and that genre, but I like this song.'"[35] This response echoes Hubbs's development of sociologist Bethany Bryson's study of the relationship of musical taste to socioeconomic status and politics: some middle-class Democrat listeners at the turn of the millennium said that they "like everything but country" in order to demonstrate their cultural omnivorism, meant to display their identification with the tolerance of difference (if not also more progressive stances on social justice) and their perceived understanding that country music represents bigotry.[36] Lil Nas X, who follows internet trends carefully, knew that cowboy imagery was trending and developing an identity apart from its perceived ties to white rural bigotry.[37] For middle-class viewers excited by celebrations of multicultural collaboration, as well as for attention paid to musicians of color, his Grammy Awards performance was welcome, especially given the previous years' critiques of racism at the Grammys. This was also an interesting spectacle that brought together several genres that raise critique: anxieties about boy band inauthenticity, fear of country music being bigoted, racist distaste for hip hop, and homophobic discomfort with out gay musicians. Lil Nas X sang, rapped, and danced on the Grammy stage in a shiny silver cowboy costume. Just days later he appeared internationally again, this time in a Super Bowl commercial as a cowboy in a duel against noted cowboy movie star Sam Elliott. In a story line drawing on Lil Nas X's by-then-famous queerness against the white straight cisgender male cultural anxiety about dancing, he uses his dance moves rather than a pistol against Elliott, who, surprisingly, responds in kind. After winner Lil Nas X invites the next challenger, a white male guitarist observer, played by Billy Ray Cyrus, reinforces the message about straight masculinity and dancing by commenting, "I ain't dancing."[38] Cyrus may not be dancing, but his career benefited from his collaboration with Lil Nas X. And as this book has demonstrated, he may not be the only progressive straight and cisgender country musician to gain from collaboration with a queer country artist and international interest in queer country music.

In November 2019 Lil Nas X became the first out gay male musician to win an award from the Country Music Association. In 2020 he won two Grammy Awards. That year he and Orville Peck were each booked to perform at the popular music festival Coachella and the country festival Stagecoach (operated by the same parent company and held at the same California location on different dates). However, both festivals were canceled in 2020 due to the global coronavirus pandemic. Trixie Mattel has not sought festival opportunities (although she did appear at the 2020 Philadelphia Folk Festival), instead focusing on her solo tour (with a backing band), her successful collaborations with fellow *Drag Race* alum Katya, a film, and the launch of her own cosmetic line.

One might wonder if masking, pseudonyms, drag, and elaborate costuming could work against queer country's aims of honest storytelling conveying the life journeys of queer and trans North Americans' sincerity. While these three gay male country acts engaged in elaborate costuming and masking in order to explore their sincerity and relationship to country themes, three collaborative female and lesbian acts released personal, simple, and uncostumed accounts of their queer relationships to country music.

For Black queer musician Amythyst Kiah, it took a supergroup collaboration about the transatlantic slave trade with three other Black women banjo playing singer-songwriters to feel safe enough to write a song that courageously demonstrates how Black Americans have faced the legacies of enslavement, as well as how her race and sexuality intersect, sometimes problematically, with her instrument and genre. In stage banter and interviews, Kiah has explained that she has always been careful to make her song narratives seem universal and that writing about her identity seemed too specific and sharing her politics too dangerous: "A lot of my fear came from reading history books when people spoke out and got blacklisted, they'd have letters sent to their house. That stuff would terrify me. I'm done being terrified now. We can't be silent if we want to see things change."[39] On a Smithsonian-released album of songs performed by Kiah, Rhiannon Giddens, Leyla McCalla, and Allison Russell, Kiah's was the track nominated for a Grammy Award. And it was one that was right for the summer 2020 moment of international reckoning with antiblack racism. As she shares:

> There had to have been 300 white English people under that tent and they were all singing "Black Myself" back to us. It was such a beautiful moment because even though you're not a Black person, but if you can understand being othered or if you can understand what it would feel like to be othered, it's so amazing that people are able to see beyond that. The song was able to reach across in spite of it being so confrontational and being so specific. I've prided myself on writing songs which anybody can relate to. It was really eye-opening and very empowering to know that.[40]

While her original Grammy-nominated track was in an acoustic roots style, the track was reimagined for her 2021 solo album, *Wary + Strange*. The genre of this album proved to be a point of tension and revision. She changed course over style and sound of the album multiple times, as journalist Rachel Cholst discusses: "Wary and Strange has been a long time coming. Kiah began work on the album in January of 2018, but as she worked on more songs she realized she needed to overhaul the album's sound—twice. She did record a version of the album in September, but since she was in the middle of touring at the time she wasn't happy with the sound and moved on to a third producer."[41] These changes are evidence of the importance of genre and the pressure for musicians marginalized from genre to figure out the best possible solution to prevent "genre trouble." While Kiah's main musical experience is in country music, with a master's degree in bluegrass, old-time, and country music from East Tennessee State University, her Rounder Records debut album reflects a mix of rock and country, seemingly pitching her through Americana rather than mainstream country. Meanwhile, her other popular 2021 release provided an example of the strange commercial and ideology-driven journeys that songs take. In live shows over the last several years, Kiah has been introducing her cover of Black mid-twentieth-century domestic worker and musician Vera Hall's "Trouble So Hard" by saying that she had first learned the tune through electronic dance musician Moby's 1999 track "Natural Blues." (When I first heard her say this at her New York debut in 2016, I thought it was an embarrassing admission for a country/folk musician, but I immediately decided it was a perfect demonstration of the problematic categorization of music and resulting unrealistic expectations regarding transmission and authenticity.) Moby's popular album *Play* drew extensively from Alan Lomax and other folklorists' field recordings of southern African Americans from the early to middle twentieth century, these recordings meant to preserve the "natural" music of America. On *Play*, phrases from these folkloric recordings of Black Americans are sampled seemingly to lend a problematically racialized sense of "naturalness" and authenticity to an otherwise electronic sounding and thus potentially "lifeless" track by a white artist.[42] In Kiah's solo shows, her powerful voice, driving guitar playing, and earnest commentary seemed to wrench "Trouble So Hard" from its twenty-first-century identity as an electronic dance music sample. Yet in 2021, reckoning with a newly vocal antiracist audience, Moby seemed to be attempting to redeem the album from accusations of appropriation by rerecording it with contemporary singers, including Kiah on this track. The trouble is that these

Black guest artists may seem to set up an expectation that they simply replace the ghostly sampled voices, continuing in a tradition of pigeon-holing artists of color as samples of "naturalness" in American vernacular music rather than allowing them the same creativity and flexibility of white cisgender artists. Kiah and her team's navigations of genre in releasing her Rounder Records debut is demonstrative of the appalling lack of opportunities in every facet of the industry for BIPOC and Black queer country musicians that country music scholar Jada Watson's statistical research exposes.[43] Yet "Black Myself" performs triumph over the anxieties it confesses—the final verse shifts from the song's earlier discussion of slavery and its legacies, revealing the positive effects of being "Black myself": "I stand proud and free," "I'm surrounded by many lovin' arms," and "I'll stand my ground and smile in your face."[44]

Similarly to Kiah's "Black Myself" addressing the vulnerability marginalized people regularly face in moments designed around normative culture, the Indigo Girls' 2020 song "Country Radio" tells the story of a gay teenager who longingly listens to country radio, wishing they could experience the simple, socially rewarded love described in heterosexual country lyrics. The song takes on a road trip journey as the narrator speeds, with country radio playing, away from a church sign threatening passersby to "repent now." Both songs depict the narratives of a queer person excluded from something they love as well as from basic things they need to survive. There are no masks or aliases; the narrators are deadly serious and deeply vulnerable in relaying their characters' simple wishes, suffering, and courage. And neither could have been made without the solidarity the songwriters received from female bandmates. But both also manage to invite a wide variety of listeners to embrace these song narrators.

In 2016 when straight country musician Amanda Shires was touring, she listened to country radio and made note of how few female artists are played in comparison to male artists.[45] When she raised the issue, her producer, Dave Cobb, recommended she contact lesbian Americana star Brandi Carlile, whom she didn't know. They joined forces with Maren Morris and Natalie Hemby to launch an all-woman country supergroup called the Highwomen, a name that plays on the Highwaymen, a famous all-male country supergroup featuring Johnny Cash, Waylon Jennings, Kris Kristofferson, and Willie Nelson, active from 1985 to 1995.

As its only out queer member during its first two years, Carlile performed a lesbian love song, "If She Ever Leaves Me," written by country star Jason Isbell with his wife and Highwomen member Amanda Shires and their friend Chris

Tompkins. Isbell at first incorrectly referred to the song as the first gay country song, demonstrating that straight mainstream country musicians, even those with lesbian country musician friends, are not aware of the existence of queer country. The release of the song did, however, lead to some press around the history of queer country music.[46] The Highwomen debuted at Loretta Lynn's birthday party and included guest appearances by a host of women in country and Americana. In 2021 the Highwomen announced new members, including Black queer British country soul musician Yola and Black queer country musician Brittney Spencer, adding that they had never intended the group to be only the four original members.

The Highwomen were nominated for a Grammy award as group of the year, for album of the year, and song of the year with "Crowded Table," cowritten by Carlile, Natalie Hemby, and Lori McKenna. The song expresses its narrator's wish for "a house with a crowded table," a desire sometimes poignantly difficult for queer and trans people, whose families may reject them. Yet Carlile has crafted just that for herself, with a queer kinship structure in which she shares a large property with her bandmates Tim and Phil Hanseroth and their spouses (one of whom is Carlile's sister) and children.

"Black Myself," "Country Radio," and "Crowded Table," as well as "Mama Don't Make Me Put On the Dress Again," "Stranger," "Fancy," and "Old Town Road," share a sense of otherness and a desire to experience some parts of being considered normal, as well as have their difference—and suffering for it—respected. In *Romancing the Folk*, historian Benjamin Filene theorizes that folk music is built on valuing "outsider populism"—embracing folk musicians as representatives of people outside of the mainstream yet who come to represent what Americans want to think about themselves.

> There is, of course, an oxymoronic quality inherent to "outsider populism": how can one build populism around those outside "the people"? The outsiders appealed, though, because they reminded Americans of themselves—or of how they wanted to see themselves: independent, proud in the face of hardship, straightforward, beholden to no special interests. Images of the folk attracted Americans because they suggested sources of purity and character outside the seemingly weakened and corrupt mainstream of society. Ironically, then, to highlight a person's marginality in relation to the mainstream helped authenticate him or her as an exemplar of American grit and character.[47]

The strategies of these three currently successful gay male country musicians actually help them develop a queer sincerity in their performance of self as gay men, their business playing country music, and queer country's appeal for both new and seasoned listeners. Meanwhile, these three lesbian musicians navigated country's tensions by performing in a way that seemed to use country narratives to lower masks in the empowering company of supportive straight female collaborators. The wave of success now meeting the socioaesthetic phenomenon of queer country has shown an increased interest in a range of queer artistry and storytelling about trans characters, as well as a need for doors to be opened for trans artists and BIPOC artists, especially after the Covid-19 pandemic ravaged the music community and further marginalized already vulnerable musicians.[48] Queer and trans country and Americana musicians draw on and simultaneously attempt to rectify folk and country musics' projections and appropriations of Otherness, complicating connections across imagined and real differences yet rejecting a fully assimilationist path that would supposedly leave queer and trans country musicians with nothing "interesting" to sing about. As the Brothers Osborne sang in 2021, "I'm Not For Everyone," seeming to suggest that they know not everyone will listen to them now that T. J. is out. Their video makes this difference vivid, starring out gay actor and gospel musician Leslie Jordan walking peacefully and happily through a honky tonk while the (presumably straight, cisgender) men around him fight violently with one another. But it may be too soon to tell how many more country listeners will embrace queer and trans singers. As lesbian country musician Mary Gauthier explains, the success of songwriting is finding "empathy through vulnerability . . . [which] capture[s] a room with truth."[49]

Using the name Lavender Country for the band, the album, and the song that invited listeners to "come out to Lavender Country," both to "come out" sexually and to visit the place, created what communication scholar Josh Kun calls "audiotopia"—"small, momentary, lived utopias built, imagined, and sustained through sound, noise, and music."[50] Queer Country shares that capacity for creating a radical shared space amid continued misunderstanding and exclusion, summoning useful, inspiring elements of a long history of music while creatively changing or omitting others, navigating the inner tensions between authenticity and invention with both the urgent need to be understood as human and share humor with kin, engaging its central themes to tell their own stories of self and belonging.

NOTES

Introduction

1. Karen Pittelman, https://www.gayoleopry.com/.

2. Stephen L. Betts, "Why Chely Wright Had to Wait 10 Years to Play the Opry after Coming Out," *Rolling Stone,* 20 August 2019, https://www.rollingstone.com/music/music-country/chely-wright-coming-out-opry-873928/.

3. Elias Leight, "Lil Nas X's 'Old Town Road' Was a Country Hit. Then Country Changed Its Mind," *Rolling Stone,* 26 March 2019, https://www.rollingstone.com/music/music-features/lil-nas-x-old-town-road-810844/; and Kimberly Richards, "Twitter Cheers Lil Nas X and Billy Ray Cyrus Remix amid Country Chart Controversy," *Huffpost,* 5 April 2019, https://www.huffpost.com/entry/lil-nas-x-billy-ray-cyrus-country-music_n_5ca76b20e4b0dca033009007.

4. "Musicking" is a term coined by ethnomusicologist Christopher Small in *Musicking* to consider the entire context of music-making.

5. Karen Pittelman interviewed in Neville Elder, "A Gay Old Opry," *No Depression,* 10 October 2011, http://www.nodepression.com/a-gay-old-opry.

6. Rachel Cholst, "The Gay Ole Opry: Building a Queer Country Community," 2018, https://www.wideopencountry.com/the-gay-ole-opry-building-a-queer-country-community/. She repeated the story to Cholst: "I remember feeling really happy. It was very stressful, but I remember feeling a deeper joy connecting to everyone because I was also worried that people were going to come ironically. But they came with their true hearts on their sleeves. That felt like the place I'd been longing to play."

7. This lack of industry backing means that out queer and trans country musicians are particularly reliant upon the support of listeners (and, whenever possible, my readers),

through purchasing music rather than streaming for free and buying merchandise and concert tickets. Most of these musicians sell directly from their websites and their music can also be found on https://bandcamp.com/ which endeavors to share a higher percentage of each transaction than many other venues.

8. Thankfully readers can now draw upon two terrific directories of this ever-growing field: https://directory.countryqueer.com/ and https://www.gayoleopry.com/queer-country-bands/.

9. Patrick Haggerty, interview with the author, September 22, 2017.

10. Tony Russell, "Obituary: Harlan Howard: Prolific Writer of Country Music Hits," *The Guardian,* 5 March 2002, https://www.theguardian.com/news/2002/mar/06/guardianobituaries.

11. Interview with Dave Jennings, "The Twang's the Thang: k.d. lang," *Melody Maker,* 26 May 1990, 41, quoted in Mockus, "Queer Thoughts," 260, 264; and Rich Kienzel, "Review: *Absolute Torch and Twang,*" *Country Music,* September/October 1989, 59, quoted in Mockus, "Queer Thoughts," 271n24.

12. Peterson, *Creating Country Music.*

13. For example, Janice Raymond's 1979 book *The Transsexual Empire* implausibly and insultingly claimed that trans women were actually cisgender men posing as trans to invade women's spaces in order to dismantle the feminist movement. More recently, many US states have considered "bathroom bills" reasoned to protect cisgender women and children from the supposed threat posed by sharing public restrooms with trans women. In actuality, there are no documented cases of harm caused by trans people toward cis people in restrooms; rather, trans people in public bathrooms have most often been the victims of unprovoked abuse or assault by cis people. Carlos Maza and Luke Brinker, "15 Experts Debunk Right-Wing Transgender Bathroom Myth," *Media Matters for America,* 19 March 2014, https://www.mediamatters.org/sexual-harassment-sexual-assault/15-experts-debunk-right-wing-transgender-bathroom-myth; Marcie Bianco, "Statistics Show Exactly How Many Times Trans People Have Attacked You in Bathrooms," *Mic,* 2 April 2015, https://www.mic.com/articles/114066/statistics-show-exactly-how-many-times-trans-people-have-attacked-you-in-bathrooms.

14. In fact, Toby Beauchamp, *Going Stealth,* demonstrates the centrality of surveillance to transgender experience, arguing that the United States polices nonconformity out of perceived security concerns.

15. Jenny Boylan, *Queer/ish,* 18 February 2017, www.thisisqueerish.com.

16. Gray, *Out in the Country.* Some of the growing body of scholarship on queer and trans rural life includes Howard, *Men Like That*; and Herring, *Another Country.* One recent collection and bibliography of rural queer studies is Gray, Johnson, and Gilley, *Queering the Countryside.*

17. Sam Gleaves, *Ain't We Brothers,* Community Music 2015 CMCD301, http://www.samgleaves.com/buy-a-cd.php.

18. Observation by the author, Queer Country Quarterly, 2 September 2016, Branded Saloon, Brooklyn, NY.

19. Butler, *Gender Trouble.*

20. The combined efforts of feminist, queer, and transsexual and transgender activism and scholarship have led to increased public understanding of gender as a social construction rather than an inherent category. The category of sex has also faced serious challenges.

21. "gender, n.," in *OED Online*, March 2019, Oxford University Press.

22. "genre, n.," in *OED Online*, March 2019, Oxford University Press.

23. Halberstam, *Trans*.*

24. Foucault, *The History of Sexuality Volume 1*, 43.

25. D'Emilio, "Capitalism and Gay Identity"; Chauncey, *Gay New York*; Rubin, *Deviations.*

26. Butler, "Imitation"; Halberstam, *Trans*.*

27. Halberstam, *Trans*.*

28. Jim Samson, "Genre," in *Grove Dictionary of Music.*

29. Ibid.; and Tracy McMullen, "Gender and American Music," in *Grove Dictionary of American Music*, 2nd ed.

30. Samson, "Genre."

31. Cecil Sharp discusses avoiding Black Americans in his introduction to Campbell and Sharp, *English Folk Songs.*

32. Citron, *Gender and the Musical Canon.*

33. As MacArthur Award–winning Black old-time musician Rhiannon Giddens explained in her keynote address to the International Bluegrass Music Association (IBMA), when she first learned to play the banjo, she thought that she was an interloper to a white musical scene because the important Black American contributions to this genre, including enslaved people's music for plantation dances and Black string bands, had been all but erased to the point that the IBMA was working to showcase its diversity and welcoming atmosphere to musicians from oppressed identifications. "Rhiannon Giddens' Keynote Address at IBMA Conference: Community and Connection," 3 October 2017, nonesuch.com.

34. Pecknold, *Hidden in the Mix*, 7.

35. Toynbee, *Making Popular Music*, 110.

36. Peterson, *Creating Country Music*. Benjamin Filene centered *Romancing the Folk* on American roots music around the powerful middlemen that shaped these genres. See also Miller, *Segregating Sound*; Rosenberg, *Transforming Tradition*; Cantwell, *Bluegrass Breakdown*; Cantwell, *When We Were Good*; Wald, *Escaping the Delta.*

37. James, "Is the Post- in Post-identity."

38. Peraino, *Listening to the Sirens*; Dyer, "In Defense of Disco"; Hughes, "In the Empire"; Morris, *Eden Built by Eves*; Kehrer, "Goldenrod Distribution"; Lawrence, *Love Saves the Day*; Brad Rogers, "The Queer Pleasures of Musicals," in *The Oxford Handbook of Music and Queerness*, ed. Fred E. Maus and Sheila Whiteley (Oxford: Oxford University Press, 2021); Hubbs, *The Queer Composition.*

39. Frith, *Performing Rites*, 40. For example, ethnomusicologist and folk musician Thomas Gruning's book *Millennium Folk*, on folk music since the 1960s, opens with an

example of how he misunderstood the rules in some folk jam circles, resulting in his join-ing into the music-making when he was unwelcome. Conversation about this faux pas was not part of folk music convention, but it became clear to him that he had broken an unspoken rule when the members of the circle shunned him.

40. Ethnomusicologist and performance theorist Michelle Kisliuk describes "socioaes-thetic" as "an implied musical awareness that reveals social concerns and a social aware-ness that supports musical concerns—the social and the aesthetic fused experientially into what I now call socioesthetics" (*Seize the Dance!*, 11).

41. Country music's record company executives, Country Music Association leaders, major venue owners, radio station managers, and journalists wield considerable authority and tend to act in concert to maintain norms much more so than those of other genres. With the deregulation of radio after the Telecommunications Act of 1996, the radio mo-nopoly Clear Channel Communications could and did effectively censor artists and particular songs from a major portion of the national audience of radio listeners. Musi-cologist Reebee Garafalo, in "Pop Goes to War," addresses the country music industry's multiyear blacklisting of the Chicks (formerly known as the Dixie Chicks), as of March 2020 the best-selling all-women band and top-selling country band in the United States since 1991 (the Neilsen SoundScan Era). At their 10 March 2003 London concert, lead singer Nathalie Maines said, "Just so you know, we're on the good side with y'all. We do not want this war, this violence, and we're ashamed that the President of the United States is from Texas." (The United States invaded Iraq nine days later.) Clear Channel and other country stations blacklisted the hit band, whose then number-ten-ranking record dropped to forty-three before falling from the *Billboard* chart the next week. Band member Martie Maguire went so far as to say to *Der Spiegel* in 2003, "We don't feel a part of the country scene any longer. It can't be our home anymore."

42. Despite looking, I have not yet found this ad in *The Hook*'s archives.

43. Eve Kosofsky Sedgwick, "You're So Paranoid, You Probably Think This Essay Is about You," in *Touching Feeling*, 149–50.

Chapter 1. Queer Country and Sincerity

1. *Lavender Country*, 2014 liner notes, 19.

2. Haggerty explains that tenant dairy farmers are "essentially sharecroppers for the dairy industry" (ibid., 2).

3. In addition to discussing this experience several times with me between 2017 and 2020, he described this story in the liner notes to the 2014 reissue (ibid., 3–4, 8–10). On 13 June 2018, during a car ride with me and Anne Balay, Haggerty elaborated most fully, "I had a sort of angelic experience in the hospital. In that a woman who wasn't on my ward, worked at the hospital, who worked at a completely different ward, who I had never met. Who I had no idea even knew my name. Walked up to me, and she pulled me aside in the hallway. She said, 'You're not sick, you're gay. They're not the same thing. Being mentally ill is not the same thing as being gay. There's nothing wrong with your brain.

You're gay, you're not sick, and nobody here can help you. You need to get out of here, and you need to get out of here as fast as you can. Because there's nothing here for you. Trust me, I know these things.' Then she walked away. It was like, 'Wow. Where did that come from?' I said, 'But, but, but . . .' She said, 'I know. I know. You have no idea what to do. I'm telling you, nobody here can help you. You're a clever fellow. You can figure this out.' That was in 1967 in a public mental hospital. The same one that gave Francis Farmer shock treatments. The very same hospital."

4. Queer country music often continues to be made and sold via personal and some-times nonstandard means, including Chely Wright's Kickstarter fundraising, Rae Spoon's arts grants from the Canadian government, and several artists mailing compact discs from home. Even one of the most successful of these artists, Nashville singer-songwriter Mary Gauthier, mails albums herself with a handwritten thank-you note.

5. Haggerty, *Lavender Country*, 2014 liner notes, 18.

6. "'Faygele' is Yiddish for 'little bird' or 'faggot'" (Eli Sanders, "Gay Marriage's Jewish Pioneer: Faygele ben Miriam," *Tablet*, 6 June 2012, https://www.tabletmag.com/jewish -news-and-politics/101628/gay-marriages-jewish-pioneer).

7. Patrick Haggerty and Anne Balay, conversation with the author, 13 June 2018.

8. Haggerty, *Lavender Country*, 2014 liner notes, 8.

9. Ibid., 7.

10. One could compare Haggerty and friends' "coming up with information, out of whole cloth, by ourselves . . . about what it means to be gay" with Joanne Meyerowitz's account of how in the twentieth century word traveled between trans people via au-tobiographies, newspaper articles, and medical texts about favorable experiences with sympathetic doctors. Meyerowitz notes the importance of these documents and their circulation but also discusses the limitations—doctors used these accounts as the standard by which to assess future patients' descriptions of gender identity, and so when speaking with doctors, transgender people learned to repeat "acceptable" stories whether they were representative of their own experiences or not. See Meyerowitz, *How Sex Changed*, as well as a challenge to the effects of these constrained and medicalized transgender narratives in Spade, "Mutilating Gender."

11. Haggerty, *Lavender Country*, 1973, back cover.

12. Ibid.

13. Pitchfork writer Jayson Greene was interviewed in director Dan Taberski's 2016 documentary.

14. "When Seattle DJ Shan Ottey played the album's single, 'Cryin' these Cocksuck-ing Tears,' on station KRAB in 1973, she lost her job for it" (Genevieve Trainor, "'Don't Hold Anything Back'—the World Finally Catches Up to Lavender Country," 30 April 2018, https://littlevillagemag.com/dont-hold-anything-back-the-world-finally-catches-up-to-lavender-country/). And while "Blowin' in the Wind" was radical enough to excite a generation of young people determined to rethink the world, in just a few short years the song was deemed suitable to be sung by my mother's graduating high school class of 1968 to their families in the audience. Haggerty believes that contemporary audiences

are accustomed enough to "naughty words" that they can appreciate the actual meaning of the song. Patrick Haggerty, conversation with the author, 8 June 2018.

15. "How Patrick Haggerty Put Queer Country on the Map," *Now This News*, 29 June 2020, https://nowthisnews.com/videos/news/how-patrick-haggerty-put-queer-country-on-the-map.

16. FCC v. Pacifica Foundation, 438 U.S. 726 (1978), https://supreme.justia.com/cases/federal/us/438/726/case.html. In 1966 comedian Lenny Bruce was arrested for saying "cocksucker," among nine seemingly indecent words, in a performance. George Carlin, "Seven Words You Can Never Say on Television," *Class Clown*, 1972 Little David / Atlantic LP.

17. Dan Taberski, dir., *These C*cksucking Tears*, 2016, 15:50, http://www.thesec-cksucking tears.com/; "How Patrick Haggerty Put."

18. Patrick Haggerty, conversation with the author, 22 September 2017.

19. Patrick Haggerty, phone conversation with author's Queer Country seminar, Temple University, 2 October 2018. Haggerty and Morris fell out of contact over the years, and I was unable to locate her to discuss her experience.

20. Rodnitzky, *Feminist Phoenix*, 138. Also Barbara Hoffman, "Joan Baez's List of Ex-lovers Is Better Than Yours," *New York Post*, 22 January 2016, https://nypost.com/2016/01/22/joan-baezs-list-of-ex-lovers-is-better-than-yours/.

21. There are a few moments when Baez has focused on gay and lesbian rights. Baez's 1977 song "Altar Boy and the Thief" is dedicated to her gay listeners. In 1978 Baez was active in several concerts opposing California's Briggs Initiative, which attempted to bar openly gay and lesbian teachers from teaching in public schools. That year she also marched for assassinated San Francisco city supervisor Harvey Milk. In the nineties she appeared with her friend, out lesbian folk musician Janis Ian, for benefits for the National Gay and Lesbian Taskforce and performed in San Francisco's Pride celebration.

22. Filene, *Romancing the Folk*; Miller, *Segregating Sound*; Peterson, *Creating Country Music*.

23. Patrick Haggerty, conversation with the author, 22 September 2017.

24. Ibid.

25. "Patrick Haggerty and Robin Bolland," *Story Corps*, aired on NPR, 27 June 2014, and animated as Julie Zammarchi, dir., *The Saint of Dry Creek*, Corporation for Public Broadcasting, Point of View, and It Gets Better Project, https://storycorps.org/animation/the-saint-of-dry-creek/. See also Taberski, *These C*cksucking Tears*, 2016, 15:50, http://www.thesec-cksuckingtears.com/.

26. I initially approached him via Facebook messenger.

27. Patrick Haggerty, conversation with the author, 22 September 2017. Haggerty seems to be talking about specific kinds of country music, for example, the changes in the mainstream country music industry because there are artists who are glamorous and sequined but who are also beloved for their perceived honesty. One interesting case of an artist who embraces "glitz and glamour" and yet is embraced as both "real" (not phony) and

iconic for queer and trans audiences is Dolly Parton, as Leigh Edwards discusses in *Dolly Parton, Gender, and Country Music*.

28. He also said that he thinks contemporary audiences are less offended by the term "cocksucking."

29. Thanks to Susan Fraiman for discussing this point and for courageously fighting the good fight herself. Conversation with the author, 20 October 2017.

30. Patrick Haggerty, conversation with the author, 9 June 2018.

31. Ibid.

32. Ibid.; Lavender Country and Other Artists, *Blackberry Rose*.

33. Patrick Haggerty and Anne Balay, conversation with the author, 13 June 2018.

34. Owen Taylor, email conversation with the author, March and April 2018.

35. He used the terms "icon" and "elder" critically in our June 2018 conversations.

36. Patrick Haggerty, phone conversation, 14 June 2021.

37. Patrick Haggerty, interview with the author, September 2017.

38. Haggerty, *Lavender Country*, 2014 liner notes, 19.

39. Tony Russell, "Obituary: Harlan Howard: Prolific Writer of Country Music Hits," *The Guardian,* 5 March 2002, https://www.theguardian.com/news/2002/mar/06/guardianobituaries; Andrew Dansby, "Country Scribe Harlan Howard Dies," *Rolling Stone,* 5 March 2002, https://www.rollingstone.com/music/music-news/country-scribe-harlan-howard-dies-197596/. Howard was such an influential songwriter that "he enjoyed 15 of his own songs in the country Top 40 simultaneously, a feat never equaled, before or since," according to the Songwriters Hall of Fame, https://www.songhall.org/profile/Harlan_Howard/.

40. Jimmie N. Rogers, quoted in Stimeling, "Narrative."

41. "Country Music Goes to Town," *Nation's Business* 41 (February 1953), reprinted in Huber, Goodson, and Anderson, *The Hank Williams Reader*, 35–38. See also Peterson, *Creating Country Music*, 217.

42. Being a professional musician requires absolute precision in repeated physical performance at exact moments onstage and in the recording studio. Musicians must understand and condition their bodies in order to attempt to prevent repetitive stress injury to the body parts doing this precise physical work. This profession also typically requires heavy manual labor, including repeatedly carrying, setting up, and repacking heavy and awkwardly shaped and fragile instruments and equipment. Many of these musicians take turns driving long hours on tour. Touring also interrupts their sleep, eating, and exercise habits, which puts their bodies at further risk of injury. Finally, professional musicians are often expected to play in settings with alcohol and drug use and are sometimes paid in alcohol instead of money, which can lead to or exacerbate risk of addiction.

43. As Miller discusses in *Segregating Sound*.

44. Peterson, *Creating Country Music*: on rustic imagery, see 55–80, 95–97; on Rodgers, see 42–58; on Williams, see 173–84.

45. Jensen, *The Nashville Sound*, 83.

46. Taylor, "'Why Do You Tear,'" 22.

47. "queer, adj.2 and n.1," *OED Online*, June 2018, Oxford University Press, http://www
.oed.com.libproxy.temple.edu/view/Entry/156237; Butler, "Imitation."

48. Creadick, "Banjo Boy."

49. Taylor, "'Why Do You Tear,'" 25.

50. Trilling, *Sincerity and Authenticity*, 2.

51. Bendix, *In Search of Authenticity*, 16.

52. For example, Butler, *Gender Trouble*; and Fausto-Sterling, *Sexing the Body*. Both
the essentialist and the socially constructed views of gender and sexuality can lead to
affirmative or dehumanizing reactions by others. "Born this way" may be understood
to describe natural variation that is impossible for a person to change, which could still
be dismissed as "freakish." Social construction understandings could seem to allow for
(widely criticized and violent) "gay conversion therapy."

53. Van Alphen and Bal, introduction, 1.

54. Analyses about identity formation and how music contributes to sense of self are
fraught and have often relied on discussion *about* (and not *with*) transgender people as
examples, as Stephan Pennington argues in "Transgender Passing Guides."

55. Karkazis, *Fixing Sex*; Karkazis et al., "Out of Bounds?"

56. Nordmarken, "Becoming Ever More Monstrous," 40.

57. Marcus Desmond Harmon, conversation with the author, 8 November 2014.

58. This limited definition of queerness, however, puts other queer people who are
more perceptibly different and their sexual encounters more public (whether by choice
or by necessity). Those who have different priorities are at a disadvantage if they don't
have access to normative gender identification, able bodies, and private spaces.

59. I intentionally used female pronouns for the trans person and male pronouns for the
listener because so often this scenario ends in violence against the trans woman. Transgender men, on the other hand, are more often rewarded for having transitioned, even if
the listener knows the person is transgender, as sociologist Kristen Schilt has shown in
Just One of the Guys.

60. Taylor, "'Why Do You Tear,'" 26.

61. Pennington, "Transgender Passing Guides," 2.

62. Author observation of audience talk-back after performance of *The Civility of Albert
Cashier*, Chicago, October 2017.

63. Cavalcante, *Struggling for Ordinary*. Medical maintenance of heteronormativity is
certainly not limited to transgender people. And as medical anthropologist S. Lochlann
Jain writes in "Cancer Butch" and *Malignant*, breast cancer patients assigned female at
birth have been limited in terms of choices regarding breast surgery over concerns about
gender queerness. For example, if only one breast is cancerous, double mastectomy has
sometimes not been covered by insurance, which has deemed this as an elective and potentially gender-confirming surgery rather than a preventative measure or a choice about
bodily symmetry. Insurance does cover reconstructive surgery involving silicone implants,

which do not last a lifetime and may leak chemicals into one's body. The reconstructed breast maintains heteronormativity, whereas the double mastectomy is seen to require psychiatric approval and transgender diagnosis.

64. Gay, "The 'Roseanne' Reboot."

65. Artists in conversation with the author's Gender Transgression class, Stanford University, 27 October 2010.

66. Coyote Grace, "A Guy Named Joe," *Boxes & Bags*, and *Buck Naked*. Song introduction observed by the author during concerts between 2010 and 2018 in San Francisco, Stanford, Sebastopol, Newport, Pittsburgh, Newtown Square, Philadelphia, and Chicago.

67. Observation by the author, 29 July 2010.

68. Caitlin Stevens, *The Waterclock: Caitlin Stevens 2004 @ Cornish College of the Arts*, Joe Stevens BMI 2015.

69. Casarino, "Can the Subaltern Confess?"; and Adelson, "When Sincerity Fails."

70. Alice Newell-Hanson, "Brooklyn's Radical Queer Country Music Scene," *Vice*, 22 October 2015, https://i-d.vice.com/en_us/article/xwx7e7/brooklyns-radical-queer-country-music-scene. It's striking that Pittelman says her audience was surprised and happy to have a *place* to listen and yet be themselves, given that film scholar Ruby Rich notes that lesbians socialized in country bars in the 1970s. It's possible that this practice fell out of fashion and had to be invented (or reinvented) by a younger generation, given that the majority of Pittelman's QCQ audience are millennials. B. Ruby Rich, "On Standing by Your Girl," *Artforum* 30 (Summer 1992): 19.

71. Branded Saloon, Brooklyn, 19 November 2016.

72. Garringer, "'Well, We're Fabulous.'"

73. "camp, adj. and n.5," *OED Online*, Oxford University Press, June 2020, www.oed.com/view/Entry/26746.

74. Newton, *Mother Camp*, 105, citing Keil, *Urban Blues*, 164–90; and Goffman, *Stigma*.

75. Newton, *Mother Camp*, 106.

76. Kennedy and Davis, "'They Was No One,'" 76.

77. Editors Christopher Moore and Philip Purvis summarizing Knapp, "The Straight Bookends," xiii–xiv.

78. Edwards, *Dolly Parton*.

79. Wilde, "The Truth of Masks."

80. Isherwood, *The World in the Evening*, 110.

81. Pellegrini, "After Sontag," 181; Sontag, "Notes on 'Camp.'"

82. Pellegrini, "After Sontag," 174.

83. Bendix, *In Search of Authenticity*, 17.

84. Ibid., 21.

85. Adiseshiah, "Spectatorship," 186.

86. Ibid., 188.

87. Bennett, "A Feeling of Insincerity," 199.

88. Ibid., 189.

89. lang's country music achievements include two Grammy Awards, the Entertainer of the Year Award by the Canadian Country Music Association, and an appearance singing at the Winter Olympics. lang won the Grammy Award for Best Country Collaboration with Vocals in 1989 for her duet with Roy Orbison on his standard "Crying" and the Grammy Award for Best Female Country Vocal Performance for her 1989 album *Absolute Torch and Twang*. Scholarship about gender and sexuality in lang's country music includes Negus, "Country"; Bruzzi, "Mannish Girl"; Mockus, "Queer Thoughts"; Whiteley, "k.d. lang"; and Sloop, "So Long."

90. Rich Kienzle, "Review: *Absolute Torch and Twang*," *Country Music Magazine*, September/October 1989, 59, quoted in Mockus, "Queer Thoughts," 271n24.

91. Jennings, "The Twang's the Thang," 41.

92. De Savia, "k.d. lang's Truly Western Experience," 7.

93. Jensen, *The Nashville Sound*, 35, 27–28, and 23, respectively.

94. Rockabilly, a portmanteau of "rock 'n roll" and "hillbilly," began in the 1950s and was made famous by Johnny Cash and Elvis Presley.

95. Jensen, *The Nashville Sound*, 119, quoting Patrick Carr, *The Illustrated History of Country Music* (New York: Times Books / Random House, 1995), 276.

96. Thanks to one of my anonymous readers for their comments on this point.

97. Mockus, "Queer Thoughts," 265.

98. Perhaps the country journalists' reaction assumed that her seeming lack of "commitment" to gender and sexuality suggested a lack of commitment to country?

99. Mikaella Clements, "Notes on Dyke Camp," *The Outline*, 17 May 2018, https//the outline.com/post/4556/notes-on-dyke-camp.

100. Sloop, *Disciplining Gender*; Whiteley, *Women and Popular Music*; and Stephens, *Rocking the Closet*.

101. Jennings, "The Twang's the Thang," 41, quoted in Mockus, "Queer Thoughts," 260, 264.

102. Spoon, *How to (Hide)*, 33.

103. Chelsea McMullen, dir., *My Prairie Home* (Ottawa: National Film Board of Canada, 2013), C9913425; Rae Spoon, *My Prairie Home* (SOCAN 2013).

104. Spoon and Coyote, *Gender Failure*, 129.

105. Hubbs, *Rednecks*, 16–19, citing Pierre Bourdieu, *Distinction: A Social Critique of the Judgment of Taste*, trans. Richard Nice (Cambridge, MA: Harvard University Press, 1984), as well as responses to his theory based in ethnography.

106. Rae Spoon, interview with the author, 19 December 2015.

107. Aciman, *Out of Egypt*; and Aciman, "Afterword: Parallax," 189.

108. Spoon and Coyote, *Gender Failure*, 62.

109. David Berman, quoted in Heather Nelson, "A New Shine: Silver Jews Tunesmith/Poet Moves to Town," *Nashville Scene*, 13 January 2000, www.nashvillescene.com/nashville/a-new-shine/Content?oid=1183887, cited in Hubbs, *Rednecks*, 165n17. Willie Nelson drew some negative reactions among the few mainstream country listeners who

had not figured out his politics when he made an announcement that he would headline Democratic candidate Beto O'Rourke's 29 September 2018 campaign rally. (O'Rourke unsuccessfully challenged Republican Ted Cruz's Texas seat.) Timothy Bella, "Willie Nelson Is Playing a Political Concert for Beto O'Rourke. Some Fans Are Abandoning Him," *Washington Post,* 14 September 2018, https://www.washingtonpost.com/news/morning-mix/wp/2018/09/14/willie-nelson-is-playing-his-first-ever-political-concert-for-beto-orourke-some-fans-are-abandoning-him/?utm_term=.d09e343f161e.

110. Spoon and Coyote, *Gender Failure,* 130.

111. Jensen, *The Nashville Sound.*

112. Spoon and Coyote, *Gender Failure*; and Spoon, *First Spring Grass Fire.*

113. Spoon, *How to (Hide),* 44.

114. Rae Spoon, interview with the author, 19 December 2015.

115. Rae Spoon, "Cowboy," *My Prairie Home* (SOCAN 2013). Lyrics reproduced with permission.

116. Rae Spoon, interview with the author, 19 December 2015.

Chapter 2. Genre Trouble

1. "Genre trouble" is a musical play on Judith Butler's foundational book *Gender Trouble.* The trouble that gender nonnormative musicians face in defining genre is also a topic I have discussed in print before in "The World Has Made Me."

2. Tylan Greenstein and Ingrid Elizabeth, interview with the author at Temple University after their visit to my Music in American Society course, 16 November 2016.

3. Crenshaw, "Mapping the Margins."

4. Yet this history demonstrates that queerness and trans existence have indeed been depicted in country-related musics, and, as Nadine Hubbs argues, country and working-class identities have long been shaped by their relationships with queerness. See Hubbs, *Rednecks.*

5. Or so viewers may surmise, given that the first thing we experience is a collage of interview clips with members of twenty-one acts describing what sort of music they make. Madsen Minax, dir., *Riot Acts: Flaunting Gender Deviance in Music Performance,* 2010.

6. Nordmarken, "Becoming Ever More Monstrous," 40.

7. Ibid., 41.

8. Ibid.

9. Ibid., 45.

10. Sam Feder and Amy Scholder's documentary film *Disclosure* (2020) analyzes a century of stereotypes in depicting transgender subjects (http://www.disclosurethemovie.com/about/).

11. Minax and Strikeback's collaborator on the film, Jules Rosskam, was known at this time for directing a film called *Against a Trans Narrative* (2008), which sought to tell multiple stories without a linear narrative, thus countering a medicalized, often heterosexual path known as "the trans narrative."

12. Citron, *Gender*.

13. For a discussion of the racism in Herder's theory, see Agnew, "Songs from the Edge." For discussion of how Herder's theory of folk spread to the United States, see Filene, *Romancing the Folk*; and Gruning, *Millennium Folk*.

14. Agnew, "Songs from the Edge."

15. Cecil Sharp, introduction to Campbell and Sharp, *English Folk Songs*, xxx–xxxiii.

16. Filene, *Romancing the Folk*.

17. Patrick Haggerty, conversation with the author in the car on the way to hear Amythyst Kiah and Rhiannon Giddens perform at Longwood Gardens, Pennsylvania, 13 June 2018.

18. Outlaw country singer-songwriter David Allan Coe (whom Nadine Hubbs has analyzed as an example of the queerness of country music) wrote "Take This Job and Shove It" in 1977, and outlaw country musician Johnny Paycheck popularized it as his only number 1 hit.

19. Haggerty, conversation with the author, 13 June 2018.

20. Peterson, *Creating Country Music*, 137–60. He notes that until Roy Acuff shifted focus onto himself as singer of the band and brought a sense of "sincerity" to singing styles through vulnerable performances in which he "often cr[ied] openly," country was dominated by pop-sounding songs with focus on instrumentals performed by clean-cut musicians in collegiate costumes (145–46). Peterson also shows that throughout country's history since Acuff, the style most popular with listeners has shifted between something considered more commercial and something considered traditional but that these categorizations are inaccurate.

21. Cavalcante, *Struggling for Ordinary*.

22. Stephens, *Rocking the Closet*.

23. Goldin-Perschbacher, "The World Has Made Me."

24. James, "Is the Post- in Post-identity."

25. Elena Elias Krell, Facebook post, 24 March 2019. Reproduced with permission.

26. Cholst, "The Gay Ole Opry."

27. Pittelman, "Another Country."

28. J. D. Doyle, "Lavender Cowboy, a Song History," *Queer Music Heritage*, March 2005, https://www.queermusicheritage.com/mar2005lavender.html.

29. My understanding of this song's history benefited from J. D. Doyle's important *Queer Music Heritage* radio show and archive.

30. Thom Jurek, "AllMusic Review: The Ultimate Moe and Joe," https://www.allmusic.com/album/the-ultimate-moe-joe-mw0000031062; Dickinson, "Country Undetectable," 31. J. D. Doyle devoted an episode of his radio show, *Queer Music Heritage*, to the topic of homophobia in country music: https://www.queermusicheritage.com/apr2005a.html.

31. Hubbs, *Rednecks*.

32. Gilbert, *Ronnie Gilbert*, 43.

33. "Burgess Wilma," in *Encyclopedia of Popular Music*, ed. Colin Larkin (Oxford: Oxford University Press, 2006), https://www-oxfordreference-com.libproxy.temple.edu/view/10.1093/acref/9780195313734.001.0001/acref-9780195313734-e-3697.

34. Jim Bagley, "Obituaries: Wilma Burgess, Country Singer," *Goldmine*, 28 November 2003, 49, http://libproxy.temple.edu/login?url=https://search-proquest-com.libproxy.temple.edu/docview/1499106?accountid=14270.

35. Incidentally, Bradley was lured out of retirement to produce a country album with lesbian country artist k.d. lang. It would be interesting to learn more about the unmarried star producer's support for lesbian artists.

36. Readers interested in the "open secret" would benefit from Vincent Stephens's brilliant book *Rocking the Closet*.

37. Riese, "6 More Out Lesbian and Bisexual Country Musicians for Your Collection," *Autostraddle*, 4 May 2010, https://www.autostraddle.com/7-lesbian-country-musicians-whove-been-out-44213/.

38. Public post by Bruce A. McGuire, 2008, https://www.facebook.com/remembering wilmaburgess/.

39. Conversation with the author, June 2018.

40. Boucher, "Newly Imagined Audiences."

41. Dickinson, "Country Undetectable," 34; https://www.thedeadlynightshade.net/Home.html; and https://en.wikipedia.org/wiki/The_Deadly_Nightshade.

42. See her autobiography, Nettick, *Mirrors*. While trans women have faced discrimination from some members of the women's movement, several authors have pointed out that characterizing the entire second wave of feminism as trans exclusionary is inaccurate. See Williams, "Radical Inclusion"; and Heaney, "Women-Identified Women."

43. Sam Gleaves, Tyler Hughes, and Haselden Ciaccio, conversation with the author, 3 December 2018.

44. "Bopalena," written by Mel Tillis and Webb Pierce, was originally released in 1958 by Ronnie Self.

45. lang, quoted (without source citation) in Ainley and Cooper, "She Thinks I Still Care," 51.

46. Dickinson, "Country Undetectable," 36.

47. Ibid., 38.

48. Michael Rubiner, "Country Person," *New Yorker*, 23 August 1992, https://www.newyorker.com/magazine/1992/08/31/country-person.

49. Dickinson, "Country Undetectable."

50. Email conversation with the author, 5 November 2017.

51. Betts, "Chely Wright."

52. Graeme Thomson, "Country Music's Gay Stars: 'We're Still Kicking Down the Closet Door,'" *The Guardian*, 10 April 2014, https://www.theguardian.com/music/2014/apr/10/country-music-gay-stars-kicking-closet-door-lavender-country.

53. Chely Wright Scholarship, Like Me Organization, http://likeme.org/chely-wright-scholarship/.

54. Chelywright, Instagram, 30 March 2021, https://www.instagram.com/p/CNDdO08jIo6/?utm_source=ig_web_copy_link.

55. Kurt B. Reighley, "Singing Her Stories," *Advocate*, 29 March 2005.

56. Kameron Ross, a 2020 contestant on another reality competition television program,

America's Got Talent, introduced himself as a gay country singer from the outset of the season and was lauded by judge and music producer Simon Cowell. Heather Kansteiner, "Country Singer Kameron Ross Talks about His Journey to 'America's Got Talent,'" *Click 2 Houston*, 6 August 2020, https://www.click2houston.com/houston-life/2020/08/06/country-singer-kameron-ross-talks-about-his-journey-to-americas-got-talent/.

57. https://littlevillagemag.com/just-announced-three-women-and-the-truth-at-the-mill-nov-18/ and https://chocolatechurcharts.org/2018–2019-calendar-data/2019/5/17/three-women-the-truth-folk-rock.

58. https://xpn.org/artist-to-watch-m/item/53-brandi-carlile-wxpns-november-2005-artist-to-watch.

59. Ann Powers, "Songs We Love: Brandi Carlile, 'The Joke,'" *NPR*, 13 November 2017, https://www.npr.org/2017/11/13/563358018/songs-we-love-brandi-carlile-the-joke. Intriguingly, it's not clear if the political intent was the main drive to writing this song, however. Powers notes that Carlile explains in this interview that "The Joke" came about because cowriter and coproducer Dave Cobb encouraged her to write an epic "vocal moment" follow-up to her 2008 hit "The Story" and that while the earlier song had been intensely personal, the newer song was, as Powers notes, "directed outward."

60. Amy Ray, "Queer and Fucked," correspondence, IndigoGirls.com, 12 September 2002, http://indigogirls.com/?p=1571.

61. Interview between Amy Ray and Lisa Vogel, Michigan Womyn's Music Festival, 13 June 2005, https://web.archive.org/web/20060319145443/http://www.indigogirls.com/correspondence/2005/2005–06–13-a/interview03.html.

62. James Baldwin, *Another Country* (New York: Dial Press, 1962).

63. Another coalitional effort is the Country Soul Songbook site and community, highlighting "(BIPOC/LGBTQIA) [people] in Country and Americana." www.countrysoulsongbook.com.

64. "rounder, n.2," *OED Online*, June 2020, Oxford University Press, https://www-oed-com.libproxy.temple.edu/view/Entry/167958.

65. Observation by the author, Queer Country Quarterly, 2 September 2016, Branded Saloon, Brooklyn.

66. Hubbs, *Rednecks*.

67. Greil Marcus, *The Old, Weird America: The World of Bob Dylan's Basement Tapes* (New York: Picador, 1997).

68. Rachel Cholst, "Jake Blount's 'Genrequeer' Vision," *Country Queer*, July 2020, https://countryqueer.com/interview/jake-blounts-genrequeer-vision/.

69. Ibid.

70. Peterson and Beal, "Alternative Country." The Americana Music Association's homepage is http://americanamusic.org/. Barbara Ching explores the gendered rhetoric of alt.country's central text, the magazine *No Depression*, in "Going Back." The genre is explored in Fox and Ching, *Old Routes*; Kirby, "Antimodernism."

71. Richard Peterson, "Soft Shell vs. Hard Core: The Vagabonds vs. Roy Acuff," in Peterson, *Creating Country Music*, 137–58.

72. Filene, *Romancing the Folk*; and Wald, *Escaping the Delta*.

73. Nadine Hubbs examines the assumptions about class and bigotry in the phrase "anything but country" in chapter 1, *Rednecks*.

74. Holt, *Genre*, 40.

75. Bernstein, "Inside."

76. Alynda Segarra, "Alynda Segarra's Call to Folk Singers: Fall in Love with Justice (Op-Ed)," *Bluegrass Situation*, 19 May 2015, https://web.archive.org/web/20150701215915/http:/www.thebluegrasssituation.com/read/alynda-lee-segarras-call-folk-singers-fall-love-justice-op-ed.

77. Ibid.

78. Video conversation with the author in the context of a String Band Antiracism Collective conversation, 12 July 2020.

79. Rhiannon Giddens, "Keynote Address at IBMA Conference: Community and Connection," 3 October 2017, https://www.nonesuch.com/journal/rhiannon-giddens-keynote-address-ibma-conference-community-connection-2017-10-03.

80. Jillian Mapes asked Howard, "Do you see your solo career changing things with the Alabama Shakes moving forward?" and Howard replied, "I can't possibly know that, really. I just go where creativity wants to take me. I was trying to write with the Shakes, and it wasn't working. For a whole year we tried rehearsing, getting together. Nothing was happening. It was really torturous, because we're usually really good at that. I thought, Whoa, I got to take some time from this. We all sat and talked about it for a few hours, then came out the other side. It wasn't bitter or anything, just like, 'I'm going to go my own way'" (Mapes, "Brittany Howard"). In Smith, "Brittany Howard," she explained, "Walking away from something that works is never advisable but I did it and I didn't think I could, didn't think I would, but then I did and that's very rewarding because I'm finally taking my power and being empowered."

81. Sam Gleaves suggested this to me.

82. Garringer, "'Well, We're Fabulous.'"

83. Spoon and Coyote, *Gender Failure*, 129. While this book is coauthored, chapters are credited to Spoon or Coyote.

84. In the twenty-first century there have been at least thirty different ongoing annual conferences that families of transgender, nonbinary, and gender-questioning children of all ages can attend together and seek camaraderie with other families and a variety of professional advice.

85. Hubbs, *Rednecks*.

86. See, for example, Warner, *The Trouble with Normal*; Spade, *Normal Life*.

87. Gray, *Out in the Country*; Garringer, "'Well, We're Fabulous.'"

88. Mya Byrne, "The Case of the Missing Trans Country Artists: Country and Ameri-

cana: Y'all Got a Trans Problem," *Country Queer,* https://countryqueer.com/stories/article/the-case-of-the-missing-trans-country-artists/.

89. Bill Kohlhaase, "Road Yet Taken: Singer Tracy Grammer Forges Her Own Path," *Santa Fe New Mexican,* 12 April 2013, https://www.santafenewmexican.com/pasatiempo/music/in_concert/article_0ff77864-a2e5-11e2-bd08-0019bb30f31a.html. Trans scholar Elizabeth Sandifer's 2019 self-published essay, "The Wasted Daughter of the Moon: The Trans Genius of Dave Carter," analyzes the Dave Carter and Tracy Grammer Duo's music, as well as music that the musicians were planning to release as the Butterfly Conservatory, for posthumous understanding of Carter's trans identification. As Sandifer argues, "Carter's music, with its mythologies that are at once rooted in the ancient material and constructed out of a tapestry of wondrous multiplicity, is constantly capturing sentiments akin to the truth that is at the heart of transition—the absolute and stony certainty that I am not the person I am being." Sandifer's essay also explores the "vexed" situation regarding referring to Carter with female pronouns, given Grammer's wishes that Carter be referred to in death as "he," explaining, "Trans lives are always contingent, made of ghosts and stories about people who were not there for the events described. The use of she/her pronouns is not the whole story. As we've seen, nothing is ever the whole story. They're just the kindest option." http://www.eruditorumpress.com/blog/the-wasted-daughter-of-the-moon-the-trans-genius-of-dave-carter/.

90. Byrne, "The Case of the Missing."

91. Cusick, "On Musical Performances." Cusick's immediate examples are two female art music singers whose voices change when performing folk styles.

92. Pennington, "Transgender Passing Guides."

93. Christopher Small's term in *Musicking* for all involvement in a musical scenario challenges the active/passive dichotomy between performers and everyone else.

94. Frith, "Music and Identity," 109.

95. *Rifles and Rosary Beads* won best album at the International Folk Music Awards. See https://www.marygauthier.com/store/rifles-rosary-beads and http://joestevensmusic.com/songs-of-the-people.

96. Frith, "Towards an Aesthetic," 142.

97. Cusick, "On a Lesbian Relationship."

98. The risks involved in transgender identification vary widely by gender, race, and class. While some trans men who previously found community with lesbians may, in some cases, retain ties with a queer community yet also gain acceptance in cisgender society through male privilege (predominantly when viewed as white and straight), trans women (especially of color) experience disproportionately high rates of homelessness, unemployment, incarceration, and violence. See Schilt, *Just One of the Guys.* Statistics may be found in the National Transgender Discrimination Survey, National Center for Transgender Equality, 2012, http://transequality.org/issues/national-transgender-discrimination-survey.

99. Pennington, "Transgender Passing Guides."

100. See ibid. on vocal adaptation. For analysis of expectations that transgender individuals shape their gender along the heterosexual binary and pathologize their personal history, see Stone, "The Empire Strikes Back"; and Spade, "Mutilating Gender."

101. Constansis, "The Changing Female-to-Male (FTM) Voice." Constansis, whose essay prioritizes art music vocal technique, calls the "'entrapped FTM voice' . . . utterly unconvincing for transmen" without considering the range of transgender men's gendered and sexual, as well as musical, identifications (e.g., some trans men may be happy with an ambiguously gendered or effeminate-sounding voice because it identifies them as gay men, and some transgender male singers of popular music styles may welcome the "husky" sound of this entrapment). However, the limits on projection or timbral variation that accompany this "entrapment" are likely unwelcome. Constansis's study and Lucas Silveira's and other singers' anecdotal evidence suggest that slower titration of testosterone and careful, regular singing practice during the early months of transition may prevent "entrapment." Silveira, "To Trans Men Starting T[estosterone] Who Are Singers," 10 January 2012, https://www.facebook.com/notes/ Silveira-silveira/to-trans -men-starting-t-who-are-singers/10150519956654771.

102. Many of these changes are explored in Minax, *Riot Acts*; and Krell, "Contours through Covers." Geo Wyeth discusses the problem of hormonal transition for vocal brand recognition in *Riot Acts*.

103. Krell's "Contours through Covers" analyzes their own experience of voice change, as well as Silveira's, first without and then later with hormone therapy. Spoon's masculine identification was policed by some listeners and music industry employees. Spoon notes, "It kind of became absurd to me at one point fighting for, for a pronoun. Because there were certain things like the higher voice or certain things that would make people convinced that I wasn't allowed to be called the male pronoun. I think I basically just wanted to take the authority out of other people's hands to decide" (Anne Strainchamps's interview with Spoon, "Retiring from Gender," *To the Best of Our Knowledge*, 29 August 2013, http://www.ttbook.org/book/transcript/transcript-retiring-gender.com/2004/06/ namoli-brennet/). Brennet uses the country technique of the yodel to shift to a higher register: Liz LaVenture, "Interview: Namoli Brennet," *The Vital Voice*, 25 October 2012, http://www.thevitalvoice.com/interview-namoli-brennet/.

104. Olson, "Medical Intervention," 443. In "Transgender Passing Guides," Pennington argues that insights about the vocal performance of gender are useful for developing more nuanced socioaesthetic tools to analyze all voices. Pennington draws insight about not only gender but also sexuality, class, and emotional expression in his study. In 2004 Brennet said that she occasionally sang as a baritone in the privacy of her car and felt that this was proof that her vocal changes were not the result of hormones but rather of conscious effort. Doug Rule, "Namoli Brennet: Gender Variant," *Metro Weekly: Washington's LGBT Magazine*, 19 June 2004, http://www.metroweekly.com.

105. "Man in the Moon," *Ear to the Ground*, Mile after Mile Records, 2009, MAM003.

106. Ben Wallace, *Real Boy Vol. 1*, produced by Joe Stevens, Bennett Wallace, 2013, http://

www.cdbaby.com/cd/benwallace. Wallace and his mentee relationship with Stevens are the subject of the documentary *Real Boy*, directed by Shaleece Haas, copyright Shaleece Haas (2016) in coproduction with Independent Television Service. Amy Matarazzo, *Older*, produced by Joe Stevens, Holy Depth Records, 2014, http:// www.cdbaby.com/ cd/amymatarazzo.

107. Spoon, *How to (Hide)*.

108. Spoon and Coyote, *Gender Failure*, 135, 136.

109. Conversation with the author, 19 December 2015. See, for example, Dyer, "In Defense of Disco"; Hughes, "In the Empire of the Beat"; Hubbs, "'I Will Survive'"; and Rogers, "The Queer Pleasures."

110. Spoon and Coyote, *Gender Failure*, 249–52.

111. In a 2012 interview with Elisha Lim, Spoon said, "I'm going by 'they' now. I'm gender retired. I'm no good at gender." This was most likely wry humor and in keeping with the humor and poignance of *Gender Failure*, and it was also during Spoon's earlier days of identifying in this way. I have not read or heard Spoon describe their gender this way recently; instead, they identify as nonbinary and point out how the gender paradigm is the problem, not any one individual. Elisha Lim, "Elisha Lim and Rae Spoon: Talking Shop," *NoMorePotlucks*, January 2012, http://nomorepotlucks.org/site/elisha-lim-and -rae-spoon-talking-shop/.

112. Davis, *Beyond Trans*.

113. For example, in May 2016, during Spoon's onstage interview Craig Jennex and I organized at IASPM, they mentioned "someday being an old woman."

114. "An Interview with Rae Spoon," *Beyond the Binary UK*, 11 March 2015, https:// beyondthebinaryuk.wordpress.com/tag/interview/.

115. Spoon and Coyote, *Gender Failure*, 165, 166.

116. Ibid., 166.

117. Rae Spoon, phone conversation with the author, 19 December 2015.

118. Ibid.

119. Ibid.

120. Spoon, conversation with the author, Blackfoot Truck Stop, 29 May 2016.

121. Spoon conversation, 19 December 2015.

122. Spoon and Coyote, *Gender Failure*, 164.

123. Liz E. LaVenture, "Interview: Namoli Brennet," *Vital Voice*, 25 October 2012, http:// www.thevitalvoice.com/interview-namoli-brennet/.

124. Namoli Brennet discussion with the author and Queer Country seminar at Temple University, 2 November 2018.

125. Namoli Brennet, "Boy in a Dress," *Boy in a Dress*, Flaming Dame Records, 2002.

126. Doug Rule, "Namoli Brennet: Gender Variant," *Metro Weekly: Washington's LGBT Magazine*, 19 June 2004, http://www.metroweekly.com.

127. Brennet, conversation with the author, 12 October 2014. There are a number of transgender folk singers, as this chapter explores.

128. Brennet, conversation with the author and class, 2 November 2018.

129. Krell, "Contours through Covers," 478.

130. Brandon Voss, "Trans Rock: Lucas Silveira Front Man of the Burgeoning Canadian Rock Band the Cliks, Was Born to Rock and Roll—He Was Also Born a She," *Free Library*, 24 April 2007.

131. Krell, "Contours through Covers," 479.

132. Feigenbaum, "Some Guy."

133. Hajdu, "Queer as Folk."

Chapter 3. Rurality and Journey as Queer and Trans Musical Narratives

1. Ray, "Sure Feels Good Anyway," *Holler*, Daemon Records 2018 DAM-19061-2. For an explanation of the song being semiautobiographical, see Jackson, "Brandi Carlile Interviews."

2. https://www.nationaleatingdisorders.org/learn/general-information/lgbtq.

3. Gray, *Out in the Country*.

4. Glasberg, "'Fine with the Dark,'" 77.

5. Anna Creadick critiques *Deliverance*'s depictions of rural Georgian residents as ignorant, inherently inferior, and violent. Creadick notes the implied homophobia especially in the filmic treatment of the difference between the city men and rural men. The inaccurate depiction of rural people, Creadick discusses from personal experience, has been cause for Appalachian people's shame. See "Banjo Boy."

6. Sears, *Rebels*; Howard, *Men Like That*; Johnson, *Sweet Tea*; Herring, *Another Country*; Gray, *Out in the Country*.

7. Deane, "Gar: Treasured Trash Fish," http://www.eattheweeds.com/gar-treasured-trash-fish/.

8. Amy Ray, "Oyster and Pearl," *Goodnight Tender*, Daemon Records 2014, DAM-19059-2.

9. Catte, *What You Are Getting Wrong*.

10. Hubbs, *Rednecks*.

11. Gray, *Out in the Country*.

12. Rae Spoon, "Keep the Engine Running," *Your Trailer Door*, 2005, Washboard Records 621365082120, https://store.cdbaby.com/cd/raespoon1. Lyrics reproduced with the artist's permission.

13. Gas stations are not always unpleasant or dangerous places for queer or trans people on the road, though. As queer studies and working-class studies scholar Anne Balay discusses, queer and trans people (and the diverse array of people attracted to them) regularly have consensual sex at truck stops. See Balay, *Semi Queer*.

14. Actor Slash Model, "TN Tranny Two-Step," *Cheap Date* (Actor Slash Model, 2007). Strikeback uses "transport" rather than "transplant" in this verse. In this song the two trans-identified musicians of Actor Slash Model reclaim a term often understood as disparaging to trans people.

15. The radical faerie communes in Tennessee have served as important locations for

rural queerness, as well as tourism for urban middle-class gay men, as Scott Herring explores in *Another Country*.

16. Phone interview with the author, 4 March 2018.

17. Some band members' stance toward hormone usage have since changed, but this song offers the opportunity for listeners to consider different options. Their songs also resist interpretation as strictly autobiographical, as Actor Slash Model called their genre "antifolk" in a camp gesture that queerly disidentified with the narratives of authenticity and sincerity expected of folk singers. For a discussion of "disidentification" as queer strategy, see Muñoz, *Disidentifications*.

18. A "packer" or "soft pack" is a flaccid rubber cock that can be worn in one's underpants.

19. Stallings, *Funk the Erotic*.

20. Interview with Strikeback, 4 March 2018.

21. Coyote Grace, "Runaround," *Ear to the Ground*, Mile After Mile, 2009, http://www.coyotegrace.com/albums.

22. Sylvia Sukop, "Transamericana: From Folk Roots Up and Out," *Huffington Post*, 18 March 2010, http://www.huffingtonpost.com/sylvia-sukop/transamericana-from-folk_b_424035.html.

23. Conversation with the author, Philadelphia, 6 March 2016.

24. Meyerowitz, "A 'Fierce and Demanding' Drive," chap. 4 in *How Sex Changed*.

25. Chest or "top" surgery is an elective double mastectomy to address gender dysphoria.

26. The heated debate about whether bluegrass is a folk or popular music and thus when and with whom its beginnings lie is beyond the scope of this project. See Bidgood and Přibylová, "Bluegrass as Global Folk Music."

27. Spade, "Mutilating Gender."

28. Rubin, "Thinking Sex," in *Deviations*.

29. Valentine, *Imagining Transgender*.

30. Conversation about research in progress, September 2019.

31. Rae Spoon in concert and conversation, International Association for the Study of Popular Music United States and Canadian chapters' joint meeting, 28 May 2016, Calgary, Alberta.

32. Rae Spoon, "A Message from the Queer Trans Prairie Tourism Co." (unpublished). Lyrics reproduced with the artist's consent.

33. *Transamerica*, written and directed by Duncan Tucker, original music by David Mansfield, music supervisor Doug Bernheim, supervising sound editor Louis Bertini (Belladonna Productions, 2005; Weinstein Company, 2006).

34. Trans actors and viewers criticized the choice of Huffman to portray Bree, although they noted that the choice of a cisgender woman actor was preferable to a cisgender male actor (such as was the case in the 2014–19 series *Transparent*, which featured cisgender actor Jeffrey Tambor in the role of Maura, a trans woman).

35. Tucker quoted in Craig Shelburne, "Gender Identity and Country Music Merge

in Transamerica," cmt.com, 3 March 2006, http://www.cmt.com/news/1525363/gender
-identity-and-country-music-merge-in-transamerica/. *Original Motion Picture Soundtrack:
Transamerica*, executive soundtrack producers Tucker, Sebastian Dungan, and Bernheim,
soundtrack album producer Maria Alonte McCoy, Nettwerk Productions, 2006, Nettwerk 5 037703 047525.

36. Välimäki, "The Audiovisual Construction," 382.

37. Hubbs challenges this construction of the working class as a bigot class in *Rednecks*,
especially the introduction and part 1.

38. The problematic racial politics in the context of queer and trans politics in *Transamerica* are addressed in Scherr, "(Not) Queering 'White Vision.'"

39. Roberts, *Blackface Nation*, 18, 184.

40. Graham Greene, "Beautiful Dreamer," *Transamerica Original Motion Picture
Soundtrack*; Stephen Foster, "Beautiful Dreamer" (composed ca. 1862, published 1864;
New York: Wm. A. Pond & Co.); Cincinnati Pops Orchestra, *American Originals, Fanfare
Cincinnati*, 2015, B00ZSXIMHC; Robin Young, "Singing The Songs Of Stephen Foster,"
Here & Now, September 21, 2015, http://hereandnow.wbur.org/2015/09/21/stephen
-foster; Key, "Sound and Sentimentality"; Root, "Foster, Stephen C."

41. Joe Stevens explores these many trans journeys as equally valid and challenges cisgender notions of "naturalness" in his song "Daughterson" (*Buck Naked*, Mile After Mile Music,
2010). Välimäki's otherwise nuanced investigation of *Transamerica*'s musical landscape
could be understood as limited by her use of controversial phrases to describe transgender
experience ("being trapped in the wrong body" and surgery as "complet[ing] [Bree's] arrival 'home' in her body" ["The Audiovisual Construction," 376, 377]). Anohni similarly
challenged Fresh Air host Terry Gross on her question about whether she had had "the
surgery," explaining that being transgender was a spirituality and lifelong journey for her.
See "Antony Hegarty's Otherworldly Sound," *Fresh Air with Terry Gross*, WHYY, 3 February
2009, https://freshairarchive.org/segments/antony-hegartys-otherworldly-sound.

42. Scherr, "(Not) Queering 'White Vision.'" Other stories, such as the television series
Transparent (2014–19), use the nongendered term "parent."

43. Välimäki argues that Bree's vocal agency is represented via the soundtrack ("The
Audiovisual Construction," 383–85).

44. Bree does sing to herself while taking a pill, "You'll take some hormones and I'll
take some hormones," to the theme of the 1841 Scottish folk song "Loch Lomond" ("You'll
take the high road and I'll take the low road").

45. Dolly Parton, "Travelin' Thru," Blue Eye Records, 2005. "Travelin' Thru" was nominated for an Academy Award, a Golden Globe, and a Grammy.

46. Tucker, quoted in Shelburne, "Gender Identity."

47. A point that Andre Cavalcante addresses in his reading of the official posters for
the film, "Centering Transgender Identity."

48. Parton released a recording of "Wayfaring Stranger" on *Heartsongs: Live from Home*,

Columbia Nashville / Blue Eye Records, 1994. "I Am a Pilgrim" appears in *Transamerica*'s soundtrack as performed by Duncan Sheik.

49. Parton, quoted in Peter Cooper, "Parton's Plea for Tolerance," *USA Today*, 23 February 2006, http://usatoday30.usatoday.com/life/people/2006-02-22-parton_x.htm; Parton, *Backwoods Barbie*, Dolly Records, 2008, DP 925.

50. Steve Goodson, "Hillbilly Humanist: Hank Williams and the Southern White Working Class," *Alabama Review* 46 (April 1993): 104–36, discussed in Fillingim, *Redneck Liberation*, 48–54.

51. Robert Cantwell, "The High, Lonesome Sound: Ritual, Icon, and Image," in *Bluegrass Breakdown*, 200–225.

Chapter 4. (Mis)representation, Ownership, and Appropriation

1. Sarah Kitteringham, "Rae Spoon Constructs Their Armour, Piece by Peace + 'Stolen Song' Track Premiere," *Beatroute*, 1 February 2016, http://beatroute.ca/2016/02/01/rae-spoon-constructs-their-armour-piece-by-peace-stolen-song-track-premiere/.

2. Interview with the author, May 2016, Blackfoot Diner, Calgary.

3. Shank, "'That Wild Mercury Sound.'"

4. Bloechl, "Race, Empire."

5. This stance aligns with racial justice work, such as Robin DiAngelo's *White Fragility*, that rejects the idea of "racists" and "nonracists," instead urging people to acknowledge that we all live in a structurally racist society as a first step toward dismantling these institutions and discourse.

6. Frith, "Towards an Aesthetic."

7. Negus and Román Velázquez, "Belonging and Detachment."

8. Pennington, "Transgender Passing Guides."

9. I asked Spoon about whether discos as a space of refuge for queer and trans people figured into their colonialist critique, and they said no—the term "disco" was meant more broadly to reference any dance club, and this lyric was not a critique of queer and trans people. Conversation with the author, 28 May 2016.

10. My Gay Banjo, "Bombs Away," *To the Wolves*, 2017.

11. My Gay Banjo, "Bombs Away by My Gay Banjo," YouTube, 15 June 2017, https://youtu.be/olJdC6TukEE.

12. Spoon, *How to (Hide)*, 28–29.

13. Spoon and Coyote, *Gender Failure*, 62.

14. Skeggs, "Uneasy Alignments," 292.

15. Moore, *Fashion Fads*.

16. Connor, "The Ethics of Voice," 220, 221, 226.

17. Bendix, *In Search of Authenticity*, 9.

18. Filene, *Romancing the Folk*; Peterson, *Creating Country Music*.

19. Filene, *Romancing the Folk*, 65.

20. Sullivan, "Rhiannon Giddens."

21. Giddens in response to a question about points she made in her interview with Sullivan in the *New Yorker* during an interview with Meghna Chakrabarti, *On Point*, 31 July 2019.

22. My transcription of ibid.

23. Johnson, *Appropriating Blackness*, 2–3.

24. Spoon used that last phrase in the 2013 documentary about their life, *My Prairie Home*, released before "We Exist."

25. Lucas Grindley, "Arcade Fire Interview: 'We Exist' Sends Message to the Mainstream," *Advocate*, 24 May 2014, http://www.advocate.com/arts-entertainment/music/2014/05/24/arcade-fire-interview-we-exist-sends-message-mainstream.

26. The Trevor Project suggests that as many as 40 percent of unhoused youth are LGBTQ (https://www.thetrevorproject.org/get-involved/trevor-advocacy/homelessness/). Bianca D. M. Wilson, Soon Kyu Choi, Gary W. Harper, Marguerita Lightfoot, Stephen Russell, and Ilan H. Meyer analyzed data from the Generations Study and the U.S. Transgender Population Health Survey and wrote for the Williams Institute that "the study findings support concerns that homelessness is experienced at disproportional rates among sexual and gender minority people." Their report notes that "17% of sexual minority adults have experienced homelessness in their lives, while 6% of cisgender straight people have" and that "20% of sexual minorities experienced homelessness before age 18. 71% of sexual minorities experienced homelessness for the first time as an adult" (https://williamsinstitute.law.ucla.edu/publications/lgbt-homelessness-us/). Reports analyzing data from the U.S. Transgender Survey are available from the National Center for Transgender Equality, http://transequality.org/issues/national-transgender-discrimination-survey.

27. In 2018 Garfield found himself in hot water again around questions of his suitability for a role, this time as the gay lead character in *Angels in America*. R. Kurt Osenlund, "Andrew Garfield on Stage Fright, Spirituality & His Role in Broadway's *Angels in America*," Out.com, 8 February 2018, https://www.out.com/out-exclusives/2018/2/08/andrew-garfield-stage-fright-spirituality-his-role-broadways-angels-america.

28. Butler in Grindley, "Arcade Fire Interview."

29. @LauraJaneGrace, 22 May 2014, https://twitter.com/LauraJaneGrace/status/469510201511387137, and 25 May 2014, https://twitter.com/LauraJaneGrace/status/470413951583670273.

30. @LauraJaneGrace, 22 May 2014, https://twitter.com/LauraJaneGrace/status/469553731369840640.

31. Grow, "Laura Jane Grace."

32. Coachella has been criticized on multiple issues recently, including for allowing sexual assault and rape and for its no longer so "local" or "independent" artistic atmosphere.

33. Gray, *Out in the Country*.

34. Grindley, "Arcade Fire Interview."

35. Transgender musician and writer Our Lady J coached Garfield, and Ryan Heffington choreographed the dance scene. Heffington was nominated for two Grammy Awards for his work on this video and has worked with Sia and on *RuPaul's Drag Race*. The video features dancers Hani Abaza, Tom Pardoe, Logan Schyvynck, and Austin Westbay.

36. Thanks to Elizabeth Bergman for her insight about this video, Heffington, and heels technique classes.

37. Halperin, *How to Be Gay*.

Chapter 5. Masks, Sincerity, and (Re)claiming Country Music

1. All recording involves engineering, but what I mean is that these albums don't employ recognizable autotune or other effects audible to the lay consumer like some of the processing that contemporary mainstream country uses.

2. Brian Firkus, Facetime interview with the author's Queer Country seminar, 22 October 2018. Thanks to Christina Colanduoni for helping me to arrange this interview.

3. Fox and Ching, *Old Routes, New Routes*. Although in 2019 and 2020 interviews, Firkus did mention contemporary popular music he likes.

4. Firkus, interview with the author, 2018.

5. Edwards, *Dolly Parton*.

6. Firkus, interview with the author, 2018.

7. Trigger, "Album Review—Trixie Mattel's 'One Stone,'" SavingCountryMusic.com, 26 March 2018, https://www.savingcountrymusic.com/album-review-trixie-mattels-one -stone/. Similarly, songwriter Shane McAnally describes coming out as "finally [having] something to write about," in Parker, "Country Hitmaker."

8. Firkus, interview with the author, 2018.

9. Although in her show at Temple University on 29 February 2020, Mattel included in her act discussion of how many more lesbians like the act than gay men and asked us to look around the audience as proof. Mattel also told us that a lesbian couple got engaged at the VIP meet and greet before the show that night.

10. Now This, "How Patrick Haggerty Put Queer Country on the Map," 29 June 2020, https://nowthisnews.com/videos/news/how-patrick-haggerty-put-queer-country-on- the-map.

11. The Trixie and Katya Show on Viceland, "UNHhhh" on YouTube, and Mattel and Zamolodchikova, *Trixie and Katya's Guide*.

12. My student Christina Colanduoni wrote a conference paper on this topic titled "'Moving Parts': Trixie Mattel's Country Performance and Gender Subversion," presented at "Balancing the Mix: A Conference on Popular Music and Social Justice," Memphis, Tennessee, March 2019.

13. Music critic Brooklyn Vegan revealed Peck's identity in a March 2019 prerelease review of *Pony*.

14. Orville Peck, *Pony*, iTunes, https://music.apple.com/us/album/pony/1446363542.

15. Ian Crouch, "Orville Peck: The Masked Man Our Yee-Haw Moment Deserves," *New Yorker*, 9 August 2019, https://www.newyorker.com/recommends/listen/orville -peck-the-masked-man-our-yee-haw-moment-deserves.

16. Leonie Cooper, "Orville Peck: 'I Grew Up Feeling Alienated—So I Became a Cow- boy,'" *The Guardian*, 19 November 2019, https://www.theguardian.com/culture/2019/ nov/19/orville-peck-i-grew-up-feeling-alienated-so-i-became-a-lone-cowboy.

17. "Orville Peck and Diplo on Why Country Music Is Inherently Queer," *Attitude*, 27 March 2020, https://attitude.co.uk/article/orville-peck-and-diplo-on-why-country -music-is-inherently-queer-1/23102/.

18. Hubbs, *Rednecks, Queers, and Country Music*.

19. Sam Demshenas, "Orville Peck Is the Queer Cowboy Taking the Campness of Country Music to the Next Level," *Gay Times*, 6 August 2019, https://www.gaytimes .co.uk/culture/125547/orville-peck-is-the-queer-cowboy-taking-the-campness-of-country -music-to-the-next-level-amplify-by-gay-times/?fbclid=IwAR3kCKnE7ORlfWEtQqPd mgodSaq7zlAiBuiO8rUUA2FuCIneZ_GRttZv4O8.

20. These notes are only available in the LP and Apple Music formats.

21. Leiber used his wife Gaby Rogers's name as a pseudonym in this collaboration. Wheeler and Rogers, "Jackson," *A New Bag of Songs*, 1963 Kapp Records KL 1351.

22. James, "Is the Post- in Post-identity." Peck invited the queer nonbinary Black artist known professionally as Evil to open some 2019 concerts to share a mixture of coun- try, pop, and hip hop. Peck has also collaborated with EDM artist Diplo, whom James discusses in her essay as a white musician who seems to be able to shed genre. (While Diplo has been partnered with two women, he has also made comments suggesting that he may be "half gay.") Diplo shifted to bounce music before in 2020 releasing a country album that features a remix of Lil Nas X's "Old Town Road." He debuted this remix at the 2019 Stagecoach Festival, where he took to the microphone to assert, "Let me tell you, this is a country song!" in reference to controversy I discuss at the end of this chap- ter (Coachella Valley Solar Expert, "Lil Nas X & Billy Ray Cyrus—Old Town Road at Diplo—Stagecoach 2019," YouTube, https://youtu.be/Mj6ZcofRAxA, a YouTube post seemingly confirmed in the comments by Lil Nas X himself). Diplo prominently used (part of) his birth name, Thomas Wesley in releasing the country album. He claimed on Twitter, "My kind of country will unite us all. / Diplo Presents Thomas Wesley / Chapter 1: Snake Oil" (April 20, 2020, https://twitter.com/diplo/status/12662198749 02106113?s=20). His statement about unifying the country came during a moment of intense political animosity. Yet his unexplained titular reference to "snake oil," a fraudu- lent product sold as part of nineteenth- and twentieth-century traveling medicine shows often accompanied by blackface minstrel music, suggests that something is not what it claims to be. In New Musical Express, Leonie Cooper claimed that "at its heart, this isn't a country album at all; rather it's an excuse for Diplo to wear some razzle-dazzle Nudie Cohn–style suits and fancy cowboy hats" ("Diplo—'Diplo Presents Thomas Wesley Chapter 1: Snake Oil' review: super-producer falls off the saddle," 28 May 2020, https://

www.nme.com/reviews/diplo-diplo-presents-thomas-wesley-chapter-1-snake-oil-album -review-2677727). The album includes collaborations with a number of country-related musicians with marginalized identities, including Peck and Lil Nas X, as well as country musician and diversity and inclusion advocate Cam but also country musician Morgan Wallen, a supporter of Donald Trump and figure whose public behavior since 2020 has met with controversy, including arrest for disorderly conduct at Kid Rock's steakhouse and suspension from his record label after being caught using a racial slur. Diplo doesn't explain the album's titular reference. His advocacy for unity may not find fans with all feminists, though, as "Do Si Do" from this album, a collaboration with country trap artist Blanco, features a narrator acting like a sexualized line dance caller to just one person, "baby girl," who in the video is depicted anonymously in seemingly nude silhouette while dancing provocatively.

23. Orvillepeck, Instagram, 10 June 2020, https://www.instagram.com/p/CBQoLKU gaS-/?utm_source=ig_embed&utm_campaign=loading.

24. Conversation in August 2020 about *Show Pony* on "Iron Hoof Outlaws: Orville Peck Fan Group," Facebook.

25. Elias Leight, "Lil Nas X's 'Old Town Road' Was a Country Hit. Then Country Changed Its Mind," *Rolling Stone*, 26 March 2019, https://www.rollingstone.com/music/ music-features/lil-nas-x-old-town-road-810844/.

26. Brittany Spanos, "Giddy Up! Here's What You Need to Know about the Yeehaw Agenda," *Rolling Stone*, 8 March 2019, https://www.rollingstone.com/music/music-features/ welcome-to-the-yee-yee-club-bitch-805169/.

27. Trigger, "Billboard Must Remove Lil Nas X's 'Old Town Road' from Country Chart," *Saving Country Music*, 23 March 2019, https://www.savingcountrymusic.com/billboard -must-remove-lil-nas-xs-old-town-road-from-country-chart/.

28. Leight, "Lil Nas X's 'Old Town Road.'"

29. Trigger argues that Morris is not an industry insider: "Lil Nas X, the Media Echo Chamber, & Shane Morris's Vile Past," *Saving Country Music*, 12 April 2019, https://www .savingcountrymusic.com/lil-nas-x-the-media-echo-chamber-shane-morriss-vile-past/.

30. Trigger, "Billboard Must Remove."

31. Trigger, "Lil Nas X, the Media Echo Chamber, & Shane Morris's Vile Past," *Saving Country Music*, 12 April 2019, https://www.savingcountrymusic.com/lil-nas-x-the-media -echo-chamber-shane-morriss-vile-past/.

32. Of course, outlaw is itself what Peterson would call "creat[ed]" and not the music of actual criminals but an aesthetic and marketing category. See Stimeling, "Narrative"; and Ching, *Wrong's What I Do Best*.

33. https://genius.com/16899512.

34. See, for example, Brett, "Musicality, Essentialism."

35. https://genius.com/16899512.

36. Hubbs, *Rednecks*; Bryson, "'Anything but Heavy Metal.'"

37. Spanos, "Giddy Up!"

38. "The Cool Ranch featuring Lil Nas X and Sam Elliott," Doritos commercial, debuted 29 January 2020 ahead of the Super Bowl, https://youtu.be/9OpuHa2vwdk.

39. Cholst, "Amythyst Kiah Is Done Hiding."

40. Ibid.

41. Ibid.

42. For discussion of the relative humanness of voices on this album and roboticized voices in other music, see Auner, "Sing It for Me."

43. Jada E. Watson, "Redlining in Country Music: Representation in the Country Music Industry (2000–2020)," SongData Reports, 12 March 2021, https://songdata.ca/2021/03/12/redlining-in-country-music/.

44. Amythyst Kiah, "Black Myself," *Wary + Strange*, Rounder Records 2021, compact disc 116101236.

45. For a statistical study of the inequity of gender representation on country radio, see Watson, "Gender Representation."

46. Blake Taylor, "Watch the Highwomen's Debut Live Performance of 'If She Ever Leaves Me,'" iHeart Radio, 28 July 2019, https://www.iheart.com/content/2019-07-28-watch-the-highwomens-debut-live-performance-of-if-she-ever-leaves-me/.

47. Filene, *Romancing*, 65.

48. As Jake Blount discussed in a virtual group conversation with Lee Bidgood's class, the author, and several musicians from marginalized identity groups, Eastern Tennessee State University, 10 November 2020.

49. "Mary Gauthier in Conversation with Brandi Carlile—Saved by a Song," Third Place Books Livestream Event, 12 July 2021, attended virtually.

50. Kun, *Audiotopia*, 21.

DISCOGRAPHY

Actor Slash Model. *Cheap Date*. DIY, 2007, compact disc.

———. *Hardly*. Actor Slash Model ASM 003, 2011, compact disc.

Actor Slash Model and Brenna Sahatjian. *"Things You Can't Keep."* 2009, compact disc.

Alabama Shakes. *Boys & Girls*. ATO Records, 2012, ATO0142, 88088217871.

———. *Sound & Color*. ATO Records, 2015, ATO0269.

Amythyst Kiah & Her Chest of Glass. *Amythyst Kiah & Her Chest of Glass*. 2016, compact disc.

Blount, Jake. *Spider Tales*. Free Dirt Records, 2020, DIRT-CD-0097, compact disc.

Brennet, Namoli. *Alive*. Namoli Brennet, 2006, NB5432, compact disc.

———. *Black Crow*. Flaming Dame Records, 2010, compact disc.

———. *Boy in a Dress*. Namoli Brennet, 2002, NB5428, mp3.

———. *Chrysanthemum*. Namoli Brennet, 2006, NB5431, compact disc.

———. *Ditch Lilies*. Flaming Dame Records / Tucan Records, 2015, compact disc.

———. *The Brighter Side of Me*. Namoli Brennet, 2004, NB5430, compact disc.

———. *The Simple Life*. Flaming Dame Records, 2018, compact disc.

———. *Until from This (Dream) I Wake*. Namoli Brennet, 2009, NB5434, compact disc.

———. *We Belong*. Flaming Dame Records, 2017, compact disc.

———. *We Were Born to Rise*. Flaming Dame Records, 2011, compact disc.

The Buffalo Gals. *Buffalo Moon*. The Buffalo Gals 1999, compact disc.

Burgess, Wilma. *Could I Have This Dance*. 51-West 1982, vinyl.

———. *Don't Touch Me*. Decca 1966, vinyl.

———. *Misty Blue* (compilation). MCA Coral 1973, vinyl.

———. *Parting Is Such Sweet Sorrow*. Decca 1969, vinyl.

———. *Tear Time*. Decca 1967, vinyl.

———. *The Tender Lovin' Country Sound of Wilma Burgess*. Decca 1968, vinyl.

———. *Wake Me Into Love* (with Buddy Logan). Shannon 1974, vinyl.

———. *Wilma Burgess Sings Misty Blue*. Decca 1967, vinyl.

Byrne, Mya. *As I Am*. 2015, compact disc.

Carlile, Brandi. *Bear Creek*. Columbia, 2012, 88691 96122 2, compact disc.

———. *Brandi Carlile*. Red Ink, Columbia, 2005, WK 97238, compact disc.

———. *By the Way, I Forgive You*. Low Country Sound, Elektra, 2018, 565226-2, compact disc.

———. *The Firewatcher's Daughter*. Brandi Carlile Band / ATO Records 0882223724, 2015, compact disc.

———. *Give up the Ghost*. Columbia, 2009, 88697 24740-2, compact disc.

———. *The Story*. Sony BMG Columbia 88697008022, 2006/7, compact disc.

Charlie Pacheo, the Castro Cowboy. *Here Come the Blues*. Castro Cowboy Records, 1999, compact disc.

Conley, Eli. *At the Seams*. Eli Conley, 2013, compact disc.

———. *Strong and Tender*. Eli Conley, 2017, compact disc.

Coyote, Ivan, and Rae Spoon. *You Are Here*. Washboard Records YAH2007, 2007, compact disc.

Coyote Grace. *Boxes & Bags*. Mile After Mile MAM0001, 2006, compact disc.

———. *Buck Naked*. Mile After Mile, 2010, compact disc.

———. *Ear to the Ground*. Mile After Mile MAM003, 2009, compact disc.

———. *Now Take Flight*. Mile After Mile Music MAM005, 2011, compact disc.

Coyote Grace and Courtney Robbins. *The Harvey Tour*. Mile After Mile MAM002, 2008, compact disc.

Dalhart, Vernon. *The Lavender Cowboy*. Bluebird B-8229, 1939.

The Deadly Nightshade. *The Deadly Nightshade*. Phantom/RCA 1975.

———. *Funky & Western*. Phantom/RCA 1976, vinyl.

———. *Never Never Gonna Stop*. 2012.

Diplo. *Chapter 1: Snake Oil*. Columbia, 2020, mp3.

DK and the Joy Machine. *(Shy One . . .)*. Positive Addiction Records, 2015, compact disc.

Dobkin, Alix. *Living with Lavender Jane*. Ladyslipper WWWA001/2, 1997, compact disc.

Doug Stevens and the Outband. *From Christopher to Castro*. 2000, compact disc.

———. *Out in the Country*. Longhorn Productions, 1993, compact disc.

———. *When Love Is Right*. Red Hill Records DS102, 1995, compact disc.

Down from the Mountain: Live Concert Performances by the Artists & Musicians of "O Brother, Where Art Thou?" Lost Highway 088170 221-2, 2001, compact disc.

Elliot, Beth. *Buried Treasure*. Beth Elliott 1450, 2005, compact disc.

Fink, Cathy, Marcy Marxer, and Sam Gleaves. *Shout and Shine*. Community Music Inc. CMCM213, 2017, compact disc.

Gauthier, Mary. *Between Daylight and Dark*. UMG Recordings / Lost Highway B0008965-02, 2007, compact disc.

———. *Dixie Kitchen*. Groove House Records / In the Black 48003-2, 1997, compact disc.

———. *Drag Queens in Limousines*. In the Black 41962, 1999, compact disc.

———. *Filth & Fire*. Mary Gauthier / In the Black Records SIG1273, 2002, compact disc.

———. *The Foundling*. 2011, compact disc.

———. *Live at Blue Rock*. In the Black ITB1006, 2013, compact disc.

———. *Mercy Now*. UMG Records / Lost Highway B0003570-02, 2005, compact disc.

———. *Trouble & Love*. In the Black ITB1007, 2014, compact disc.

Girlyman. *Everything's Easy*. Fine Feathered Music GM003, 2009, compact disc.

———. *Joyful Sign*. Girlyman Inc. GM 001, 2007, compact disc.

———. *Little Star*. Daemon Records DAM-19053, 2005, compact disc.

———. *Remember Who I Am*. Daemon Records DAM-19044, 2004, compact disc.

———. *Somewhere Different Now (live)*. Girlyman Inc. GM 002, 2008, compact disc.

Gleaves, Sam. *Ain't We Brothers*. Community Music CMCD301, 2015, compact disc.

Gleaves, Sam, and Tyler Hughes. *Sam Gleaves & Tyler Hughes*. Community Music CMCD211, 2017, compact disc.

Grudzien, Peter. *The Unicorn*. Peter Grudzien, [1974] Subliminal Sounds 2019, vinyl.

Haggerty, Patrick. *Lavender Country*. Gay Community Social Services of Seattle, Inc. PC-160, 1973.

———. *Lavender Country*. Paradise of Bachelors PoB-12, 2014, compact disc. http://www.paradiseofbachelors.com/pob-12/.

Hall, Vera. "Trouble So Hard." *Sounds of the South*. Atlantic, 1960, SD-1346.

Herndon, Ty. *Got It Covered*. BFD, Audium Nashville, 2019, BFD161, mp3.

———. *House on Fire*. BFD, 2016, BFD076, mp3.

———. *Lies I Told Myself*. Ty Herndon, 2013, mp3.

———. *Living in a Moment*. Epic, 1996, EK 67564, compact disc.

———. *What Mattered Most*. Epic, 1995, EK 66397, compact disc.

The Highwomen. *The Highwomen*. Elektra, Low Country Sound, 2019, 075678651748, compact disc.

Himan, Eric. *Playing Cards*. Thumbcrown Records TCR016, 2015, compact disc.

———. *Resonate*. Thumbcrown Records, 2008, compact disc.

———. *Supposed Unknown*. Thumbcrown Records TCR011, 2011, compact disc.

Howard, Brittany. *Jaime*. ATO Records, 2019, ATO0505.

Hughes, Tyler. *Wise County Jail*. RVR 12008, 2017, compact disc.

Humble Tripe. *Counting Stars*. 307 knox records 307029, 2010, compact disc.

———. *The Giving*. Harper Wells Music, 2013, compact disc.

Hurray for the Riff Raff. *Hurray for the Riff Raff*. Loose Music, 2011, compact disc.

———. *It Don't Mean I Don't Love You*. 2008, compact disc.

———. *Look Out Mama*. Born to Win Records BTW 003, 2012, compact disc.

———. *The Navigator*. ATO Records / Hurray for the Riff Raff ATO0366, 2017, compact disc.

———. *Small Town Heroes*. ATO Records AT00212, 2014, compact disc.

———. *Young Blood Blues*. Hurray for the Riff Raff, 2010, compact disc.

Indiana Queen. *How To Get from Here to There: Motion Picture Soundtrack.* 2018, compact disc.

——. *Hurts Like Hell.* Long Live the Queen Publishing, 2017, compact disc.

——. *Summon without Sorrow.* 2017, compact disc.

Indigo Girls. *Look Long.* Rounder, 2020, compact disc, 1166100867.

Kahn, Si. *New Wood.* Philo Records, 1974.

Karen and the Sorrows. *Guaranteed Broken Heart.* Ocean Born Mary Music, 2019, compact disc.

——. *The Names of Things.* 2014, compact disc.

——. *The Narrow Place.* Ocean Born Mary Music, 2017, compact disc.

k.d. lang and the Reclines. *Absolute Torch and Twang.* Sire 9 25877-2, 1989, compact disc.

——. *A Truly Western Experience: 25th Anniversary Edition.* Bumstead Productions BUM842A, 2010, compact disc.

k.d. lang and the Siss Boom Bang. *Sing It Loud.* Nonesuch 7559797695, 2011, compact disc.

Kiah, Amythyst. *Dig.* 2012, compact disc.

——. *Wary + Strange.* Rounder, 2021, 1166101236.

Krell, Elena Elías. *As Eli.* 2017, compact disc.

lang, k.d. *Shadowland.* Sire Records Company 9 25724-2, 1988, compact disc.

——. *Watershed.* Nonesuch 2-999082, 2008, compact disc.

Lavender Country and Other Artists. *Blackberry Rose and Other Songs.* 2019.

Lynch-Thomason, Saro, and Sam Gleaves. *I Have Known Women: Songs by Si Kahn Celebrating Women's Lives and Struggles.* Strictly Country Records, 2020, SCR-83, compact disc.

Mac and Strikeback. *Small Dog Songs.* 2017, compact disc.

Madsen Minax and the Homoticons. *Shipwrecks & Dreamboats.* Dame, 2009, compact disc.

Mattel, Trixie. *Barbara.* Producer Entertainment Group, 2020, compact disc.

——. *One Stone.* Trixie Mattel, 2018, compact disc.

——. *Two Birds.* Trixie Mattel, 2017, compact disc.

Mattel, Trixie Feat. Orville Peck. "Jackson." Trixie Mattel, 2021, AAC.

Moby. "Natural Blues." *Play.* V2, 1999, 63881-27049-2, compact disc.

Moby feat. Gregory Porter & Amythyst Kiah. "Natural Blues." *Reprise.* Deutsche Grammophon, 2021, mp3.

Mouths of Babes. *Brighter in the Dark.* Mouths of Babes WAM0003, compact disc.

——. *Faith & Fumes.* Mouths of Babes MOB001, 2014, compact disc.

My Gay Banjo. *Country Boys in the City.* 2014, compact disc.

——. "Jolene (Dolly Parton)." 2014, mp3.

——. *Limp Wrist & a Steady Hand.* Riot Grrrl Ink, 2012, compact disc.

——. *My Gay Banjo.* 2010, compact disc.

——. *To the Wolves.* 2017, compact disc.

Namoli Brennet Trio. *Live in Germany.* Flaming Dame Records in cooperation with Tucan Records TC81426, 2016, compact disc.

Novice Theory. *at the end we listen*. 2008, compact disc.

O Brother, Where Art Thou? Music from a Film by Joel Coen & Ethan Coen. Lost Highway 088 170 069-2 DG02, 2000, compact disc.

One Trick Rodeo. *You're a Nation*. One Trick Rodeo / Gung Ho Records OTRCD19691, 2017, compact disc.

O Sister! The Women's Bluegrass Collection. Rounder 11661-0499-2, 2001, compact disc.

Paisley Fields. *Electric Park Ballroom*. Don Giovanni Records, 2020, DG-205, mp3.

———. *Glitter & Sawdust*. Red Butterfly Records, 2018, mp3.

———. *Oh These Urban Fences*. Crazywim Publishing, 2015, compact disc.

Parton, Dolly. *Backwoods Barbie*. Dolly Records DP925, 2008, compact disc.

———. *Heartsongs: Live from Home*. Blue Eye Records CK 66123, 1994, compact disc.

Peck, Orville. "Born This Way (The Country Road Version)." Columbia 2021, mp3.

———. *Pony*. 2019, compact disc.

———. *Show Pony*. 2020, Columbia Records, mp3.

Ranch Romance. *Flip City*. Sugar Hill Records, 1993, compact disc.

———. *Western Dream*. Sugar Hill Records SH-CD-3799, 1992, compact disc.

Ray, Amy. *Goodnight Tender*. Daemon Records, DAM-19059-2, 2014, compact disc.

———. *Holler*. Daemon Records, DAM-19061-2, 2018, compact disc.

———. *The Tender Hour: Live from Seattle*. Daemon Records, DAM-19061-2, 2014, compact disc.

Reed, Dock, and Vera Hall Ward. *Spirituals with Dock Reed and Vera Hall Ward*. Folkways Records, 1953, FP 38.

Robbins, Courtney. *Red sky in morning*. Badge, 2006, compact disc.

Songcatcher: Music from and Inspired by the Motion Picture. Vanguard / Combustion Music 79586-2, 2001, compact disc.

Songs of Our Native Daughters. Smithsonian Folkways Recordings SFW CD 40232, 2019, compact disc.

Spencer, Sid. *Lovin' Strangers*. Amethyst Records AR9235, 1996, compact disc.

———. *Out -n- About, Again*. Amethyst Records, 1995, compact disc.

Spoon, Rae. *Armour*. Factor / Coax Records OAX333, 2016, compact disc.

———. *I Can't Keep All of Our Secrets*. Saved by Radio / Alberta Foundation for the Arts SBR009, 2012, compact disc.

———. *Love Is a Hunter*. RAWLCO Radio / Saved by Radio SBR007, 2010, compact disc.

———. *My Prairie Home*, SOCAN, 2013, compact disc.

———. *SuperiorYouAreInferior*. Washboard Records / Alberta Foundation for the Arts RS005, 2017, compact disc.

———. *White Hearse Comes Rolling*. Washboard Records / Spin Digital Media RS004, 2006, compact disc.

———. *Your Trailer Door*. Washboard Records, 2005, compact disc.

Spoon, Rae, and Rodney DeCroo. *Trucker's Memorial*. Northern Electric / Maximum MAX21532, 2006, compact disc.

Steele, Bethel. *Broken Record*. Bethel Steele Music, 2013, compact disc.

————. *Come Home*. 2009, compact disc.

————. *Of Love & Whiskey*. Trespass Music, 2012, compact disc.

————. *Shadows and Light*. Bethel Steele Music / Pig Iron Records, 2015, compact disc.

Stevens, Caitlin. *The Waterclock: Caitlin Stevens 2004 @ Cornish College of the Arts*, Joe Stevens BMI 2015, compact disc.

Stevens, Joe. *Last Man Standing*. Mile After Mile MAM006, 2014, compact disc.

Thunderbitch. *Thunderbitch*. Thunderbitch, 2019, 088236014, mp3.

Transamerica: Original Motion Picture Soundtrack. Nettwerk 0 6700 30475 24, 2006, compact disc.

Wallace, Ben. *Real Boy Vol. 1*. 2013. http://www.cdbaby.com/cd/benwallace.

Weigle, Mark. *The Truth Is*. Mark Weigle 656863-3066-21, 1998, compact disc.

Welch, Gillian. *Revival*. Acony Records ACNY-0101, 1996, compact disc.

Yola. *Walk Through Fire*. Easy Eye Sound, 2019, EES-0082019, mp3.

BIBLIOGRAPHY

Abernathy, Marti. "Transphobic Radical Hate Didn't Start with Brennan: The Sandy Stone–Olivia Records Controversy." *The Transadvocate*, 24 August 2011. https://www .transadvocate.com/transphobic-radical-hate-didnt-start-with-brennan-the-sandy -stone-olivia-records-controversy_n_4112.htm.

Aciman, Andre. "Afterword: Parallax." In *Alibis: Essays on Elsewhere*, 185–200. New York: Farrar, Straus and Giroux, 2011.

———. *Out of Egypt*. New York: Farrar, Straus and Giroux, 1994.

Adelson, Leslie A. "When Sincerity Fails: Literatures of Migration and the Emblematic Labor of Personhood." In *The Rhetoric of Sincerity*, edited by Ernst van Alphen, Mieke Bal, and Carel Smith, 174–94. Stanford, CA: Stanford University Press, 2009.

Adiseshiah, Siân. "Spectatorship and the New (Critical) Sincerity: The Case of Forced Entertainment's Tomorrow's Parties." *Journal of Contemporary Drama in English* 4, no. 1 (2016): 180–95.

Agnew, Vanessa. "Songs from the Edge of the World: Enlightenment Perceptions of Khoikhoi and Bushmen Music." In *Representing Humanity in the Age of Enlightenment*, edited by Alexander Cook, Ned Curtoys, and Shino Konishi, 79–93. London: Pickering and Chatto, 2013.

Ainley, Rosa, and Sarah Cooper. "She Thinks I Still Care: Lesbians and Country Music." In *The Good, the Bad and the Gorgeous: Popular Culture's Romance with Lesbianism*, edited by Diane Hamer and Belinda Budge, 41–56. London: Harper Collins, 1994.

Anastasia, Andrew. "Voice." *Transgender Studies Quarterly* 1, no. 1–2 (2014): 262–63.

Anderson, Jamie. *Drive All Night*. Tallahassee: Bella Books, 2014.

Balay, Anne. *Semi Queer: Stories of Gay, Trans, and Black Truck Drivers*. Chapel Hill: University of North Carolina Press, 2018.

Bealle, John. *Old-Time Music and Dance: Community and Folk Revival*. Bloomington: Indiana University Press, 2005.

Beauchamp, Toby. *Going Stealth: Transgender Politics and U.S. Surveillance Practices*. Durham, NC: Duke University Press, 2019.

Bendix, Regina. *In Search of Authenticity: The Formation of Folklore Studies*. Madison: University of Wisconsin Press, 1997.

Bennett, Jill. "A Feeling of Insincerity: Politics, Ventriloquy, and the Dialectics of Gesture." In *The Rhetoric of Sincerity: Cultural Memory in the Present*, edited by Ernst van Alphen, Mieke Bal, and Carel Smith, 195–213. Stanford, CA: Stanford University Press, 2009.

Bernstein, Jonathan. "Inside the Americana Genre's Burgeoning Identity Crisis." *Rolling Stone*, 13 September 2017.

Betts, Stephen L. "Billy Gilman Reveals He's Gay, Laments It's 'Not the Best Thing' for Country Career." *Rolling Stone*, 21 November 2014.

———. "Chely Wright, 'I Am the Rain' Album: Release Date, Special Guests Revealed." *Rolling Stone*, 6 July 2016.

Bidgood, Lee, and Irena Přibylová. "Bluegrass as Global Folk Music." In *The Oxford Handbook of Global Popular Music, edited by Simone Krüger Bridge*. London: Oxford University Press, forthcoming.

Bloechl, Olivia. "Race, Empire, and Early Music." In *Rethinking Difference in Music Scholarship*, edited by Olivia Bloechl, Melanie Lowe, and Jeffrey Kallberg, 77–107. Cambridge: Cambridge University Press, 2015.

Boellstorff, Tom. "Queer Studies under Ethnography's Sign." *GLQ: A Journal of Lesbian and Gay Studies* 12, no. 4 (2006): 637–39.

Boucher, Cindy. "Newly Imagined Audiences: Folkways' Gay and Lesbian Records." *Journal of Popular Music Studies* 20, no. 2 (June 2008): 129–49.

Bourdieu, Pierre. *Distinction: A Social Critique of the Judgment of Taste*. Translated by Richard Nice. Cambridge, MA: Harvard University Press, 1984.

Bowers, Jane, Zoe C. Sherinian, and Susan Fast. "Snapshot: Gendering Music." In *Garland Encyclopedia of World Music*, Volume 3, *The United States and Canada*. New York: Routledge, 2000. https://search.alexanderstreet.com/view/work/bibliographic _entity%7Creference_article%7C1000225776.

Brett, Philip. "Musicality, Essentialism, and the Closet." In *Queering the Pitch: The New Lesbian and Gay Musicology*, edited by Philip Brett, Elizabeth Wood, and Gary Thomas, 9–26. New York: Routledge, 1994.

Brett, Philip, Elizabeth Wood, and Gary C. Thomas, eds. *Queering the Pitch: The New Gay and Lesbian Musicology*. New York: Routledge, 1994.

Brubaker, Roger. *Trans: Gender and Race in an Age of Unsettled Identities*. Princeton, NJ: Princeton University Press, 2016.

Bruzzi, Stella. "Mannish Girl: k.d., from Cowpunk to Androgyny." In *Sexing the Groove: Popular Music and Gender*, edited by Sheila Whiteley, 191–206. London: Routledge, 1997.

Bryson, Bethany. "'Anything but Heavy Metal': Symbolic Exclusion and Musical Dislikes." *American Sociological Review* 61, no. 5 (October 1996): 884–99.

Butler, Judith. *Gender Trouble: Feminism and the Subversion of Identity*. New York: Routledge, 1990.

———. "Imitation and Gender Insubordination." In *Inside/Out: Lesbian Theories, Gay Theories*, edited by Diana Fuss, 13–31. New York: Routledge, 1991.

———. *Undoing Gender*. New York: Routledge, 2004.

Byrne, Mya. "The Case of the Missing Trans Country Artists—Country and Americana: Y'all Got a Trans Problem." *Country Queer*, n.d. https://countryqueer.com/article/the-case-of-the-missing-trans-country-artists/.

Campbell, Olive Dame, and Cecil Sharp. *English Folk Songs from the Southern Appalachians*. New York: G. P. Putnam's Sons, 1917.

Cantwell, Robert. *Bluegrass Breakdown: The Making of the Old Southern Sound*. Urbana: University of Illinois Press, 1984.

———. *When We Were Good: The Folk Revival*. Cambridge, MA: Harvard University Press, 1996.

Casarino, Cesare. "Can the Subaltern Confess? Pasolini, Gramsci, Foucault, and the Deployment of Sexuality." In *The Rhetoric of Sincerity*, edited by Ernst van Alphen, Mieke Bal, and Carel Smith, 121–43. Stanford, CA: Stanford University Press, 2009.

Catte, Elizabeth. *What You Are Getting Wrong about Appalachia*. Cleveland, OH: Belt Publishing, 2018.

Cavalcante, Andre. "Centering Transgender Identity via the Textual Periphery: *TransAmerica* and the 'Double Work' of Paratexts." *Critical Studies in Media Communication* 30, no. 2 (2013): 85–101.

———. *Struggling for Ordinary: Media and Transgender Belonging in Everyday Life*. New York: New York University Press, 2018.

Cerankowski, KJ. "Queer Pasts, Trans Longings: Being and Becoming in a Past That Is Yet to Come." Paper presented at the Trans* Studies Conference, Tucson, Arizona, September 2016.

Chauncey, George. *Gay New York: Gender, Urban Culture, and the Making of the Gay Male World, 1890–1940*. New York: Basic Books, 1994.

Ching, Barbara. "Going Back to the Old Mainstream: *No Depression*, Robbie Fulks, and Alt.Country's Muddied Waters." In *A Boy Named Sue: Gender and Country Music*, edited by Kristine M. McCusker and Diane Pecknold, 178–95. Jackson: University Press of Mississippi, 2004.

———. *Wrong's What I Do Best: Hard Country Music and Contemporary Culture*. New York: Oxford University Press, 2001.

Cholst, Rachel. "Amythyst Kiah Is Done Hiding: 'Black Myself' Singer-Songwriter Shares Her Journey Toward Her Truth." *Country Queer* n.d. (spring 2021) https://countryqueer.com/stories/interview/amythyst-kiah-the-making-of-a-grammy-nominee/.

———. "The Gay Ole Opry: Building a Queer Country Community," Wide Open Country, 2018, https://www.wideopencountry.com/the-gay-ole-opry-building-a-queer-country-community/.

Citron, Marcia. *Gender and the Musical Canon.* 1993; repr., Urbana: University of Illinois Press, 2000.

Clements, Mikaella. "Notes on Dyke Camp." *The Outline*, 17 May 2018. http://theoutline .com/post/4556/notes-on-dyke-camp.

Colanduoni, Christina. "'Moving Parts': Trixie Mattel's Country Performance and Gender Subversion." Paper presented at Balancing the Mix: A Conference on Popular Music and Social Justice, Memphis, Tennessee, March 2019.

Connor, Steven. "The Ethics of Voice." In *Critical Ethics: Text, Theory and Responsibility*, edited by Dominic Rainsford and Tim Woods, 220–37. New York: Palgrave Macmillan, 1999.

Constansis, Alexandros N. "The Changing Female-to-Male (FTM) Voice." *Radical Musicology* 3 (2008): 32 paras. http://www.radical-musicology.org.uk.

Corin, Amy. "Queer Country, Line Dance Nazis, and a Hollywood Barndance: Country Music and the Struggle for Identity in Los Angeles, California." In *Country Music Annual 2000*, edited by Charles K. Wolfe and James E. Akenson, 141–50. Lexington: University Press of Kentucky, 2000.

Coyote, Ivan, and Zena Sharman. *Persistence: All Ways Butch and Femme.* Vancouver: Arsenal Pulp Press, 2011.

Crazy Horse, Kandia. "Freak Show: Race Rock and the New Weird America." *Perfect Sound Forever.* Last modified February 2007. http://furious.com/Perfect/freakshow.html.

Creadick, Anna. "Banjo Boy: Masculinity, Disability, and Difference in Deliverance." *Southern Cultures* 23, no. 1 (2017): 63–78.

Crenshaw, Kimberlé. "Mapping the Margins: Intersectionality, Identity Politics, and Violence against Women of Color." *Stanford Law Review* 43, no. 6 (July 1991): 1241–99.

Cusick, Suzanne. "On a Lesbian Relationship with Music: A Serious Effort Not to Think Straight." In *Queering the Pitch: The New Gay and Lesbian Musicology*, edited by Philip Brett, Elizabeth Wood, and Gary C. Thomas, 67–83. New York: Routledge, 1994.

———. "On Musical Performances of Gender and Sex." In *Audible Traces: Gender, Identity, and Music*, edited by Elaine Barkin and Lydia Hamessley, 25–49. Zürich: Carciofoli Verlagshaus, 1999.

Davis, Heath Fogg. *Beyond Trans: Does Gender Matter?* New York: New York University Press, 2017.

D'Emilio, John. "Capitalism and Gay Identity." In *The Lesbian and Gay Studies Reader*, edited by Henry Abelove, Michèle Aina Barale, and David M. Halperin, 467–78. New York: Routledge, 1993.

De Savia, Tom. "k.d. lang's Truly Western Experience." *Cash Box Magazine*, 10 June 1989, 7.

Dews, Carlos, and Carolyn Leste Law, eds. *Out in the South.* Philadelphia: Temple University Press, 2001.

DiAngelo, Robin. *White Fragility: Why It's So Hard for White People to Talk about Racism.* Boston: Beacon Press, 2018.

Dickinson, Chris. "Country Undetectable: Gay Artists in Country Music." *Journal of Country Music* 21, no. 1 (1999): 28–39.

Dobkin, Alix. "The Emperor's New Gender." *Off Our Backs* 30, no. 4 (2000): 14.

———. "Minstrel Blood: (In)Famous Last Words (For Now)," *Windy City Times* (Chicago), 21 June 2000.

Doyle, J. D. "Lavender Cowboy—Charting a Song's History." *Queer Music Heritage* radio show, March 2005, http://www.queermusicheritage.com/mar2005lavender.html.

Du Bois, W. E. B. *The Souls of Black Folk.* Chicago: A. C. McClurg & Co., 1903.

Dyer, Richard. "In Defense of Disco." *Gay Left* 8 (1979): 20–23.

Edwards, Leigh H. *Dolly Parton, Gender, and Country Music.* Bloomington: Indiana University Press, 2018.

Eidsheim, Nina Sun. *The Race of Sound: Listening, Timbre & Vocality in African American Music.* Durham, NC: Duke University Press, 2019.

Erickson-Schroth, Laura, ed. *Trans Bodies, Trans Selves: A Resource for the Transgender Community.* New York: Oxford University Press, 2014.

Fausto-Sterling, Anne. *Sexing the Body: Gender Politics and the Construction of Sexuality.* New York: Basic Books, 2000.

Feigenbaum, Anna. 'Some Guy Designed This Room I'm Standing In': Marking Gender in Press coverage of Ani DiFranco," *Popular Music* (2005) Volume 24, no. 1: 37–56.

Fellows, Will, ed. *Farm Boys: Lives of Gay Men from the Rural Midwest.* Madison: University of Wisconsin Press, 1996.

Fenster, Mark. "Alternative Country." In *Continuum Encyclopedia of Popular Music of the World.* London: Bloomsbury, 2012.

Filene, Benjamin. *Romancing the Folk: Public Memory and American Roots Music.* Chapel Hill: University of North Carolina Press, 2000.

Fillingim, David. *Redneck Liberation: Country Music as Theology.* Macon, GA: Mercer University Press, 2003.

Foucault, Michel. *The History of Sexuality, Volume 1.* New York: Pantheon Books, 1978.

Fox, Aaron. *Real Country: Music and Language in Working-Class Culture.* Durham, NC: Duke University Press, 2004.

Fox, Pamela. *Natural Acts: Gender, Race, and Rusticity in Country Music.* Ann Arbor: University of Michigan Press, 2009.

Fox, Pamela, and Barbara Ching, eds. *Old Routes, New Routes: The Cultural Politics of Alt. Country Music.* Ann Arbor: University of Michigan Press, 2008.

Frith, Simon. "Music and Identity." In *Questions of Cultural Identity*, edited by Stuart Hall and Paul du Gay, 108–27. London: Sage Publications, 1996.

———. *Performing Rites: On the Value of Popular Music.* Cambridge, MA: Harvard University Press, 1996.

———. "Towards an Aesthetic of Popular Music." In *Music and Society: The Politics of Composition, Performance and Reception*, edited by Richard Leppert and Susan McClary, 133–49. Cambridge: Cambridge University Press, 1987.

Garafalo, Reebee. "Pop Goes to War, 2001–2004: U.S. Popular Music after 9/11." In *Music in the Post-9/11 World*, edited by Jonathan Ritter and J. Martin Daughtry, 3–26. New York: Routledge, 2007.

Garringer, Rae. "'Well, We're Fabulous and We're Appalachians, So We're Fabulachians': Country Queers in Central Appalachia." *Southern Cultures* 23, no. 1 (Spring 2017): 79–91.

Gay, Roxane. "The 'Roseanne' Reboot Is Funny. I'm Not Going to Keep Watching." *New York Times*, 29 March 2018. https://www.nytimes.com/2018/03/29/opinion/roseanne-reboot-trump.html.

Geertz, Clifford. "Making Experiences, Authoring Selves." In *The Anthropology of Experience*, edited by Victor W. Turner and Edward M. Bruner, 373–81. Urbana: University of Illinois Press, 1986.

Giddens, Rhiannon. "Keynote Address at IBMA Conference: Community and Connection." October 3, 2017. https://www.nonesuch.com/journal/rhiannon-giddens-keynote-address-ibma-conference-community-connection-2017-10-03.

Gilbert, Ronnie. *Ronnie Gilbert: A Radical Life in Song*. Oakland: University of California Press, 2015.

Glasberg, E. "'Fine with the Dark': Amy Ray Is the Butch Throat," in "The Butch Throat: A Roundtable, MoPop Conference, April 2018," *Journal of Popular Music Studies* 30, no. 4 (2018): 77–81.

Goffman, Erving. *Stigma: Notes on the Management of Spoiled Identity*. Englewood Cliffs, NJ: Prentice-Hall, 1963.

Goldin-Perschbacher, Shana. "Gay Country, TransAmericana, and Queer Sincerity." In *The Oxford Handbook of Music and Queerness*, edited by Fred E. Maus and Sheila Whiteley. Oxford: Oxford University Press, 2021.

———. "TransAmericana: Gender, Genre, and Journey." *New Literary History* 46, no. 4 (Autumn 2015): 775–803.

———. "The World Has Made Me the Man of My Dreams: Meshell Ndegeocello and the 'Problem' of Black Female Masculinity." *Popular Music* 32, no. 3 (2013): 471–96.

Gray, Mary L. *Out in the Country: Youth, Media, and Queer Visibility in Rural America*. New York: New York University Press, 2009.

Gray, Mary, Colin R. Johnson, and Brian J. Gilley, eds. *Queering the Countryside: New Frontiers in Rural Queer Studies*. New York: New York University Press, 2016.

Grow, Kory. "Laura Jane Grace Blasts Arcade Fire Over 'We Exist' Video," *Rolling Stone* 22 May 2014.

Gruning, Thomas R. *Millennium Folk: American Folk Music Since the Sixties*. Athens: University of Georgia Press, 2006.

Hajdu, David. "Queer as Folk." *New York Times*, 18 August 2002.

Halberstam, Jack. *Trans**: *A Quick and Quirky Account of Gender Variability*. Oakland: University of California Press, 2017.

Halberstam, Judith. *In a Queer Time and Place: Transgender Bodies, Subcultural Lives*. New York: New York University Press, 2005.

Halperin, David M. *How to Be Gay*. Cambridge, MA: Harvard University Press, 2012.

Hayes, Eileen M. *Songs in Black and Lavender: Race, Sexual Politics, and Women's Music.* Urbana: University of Illinois Press, 2010.

Heaney, Emma. "Women-Identified Women: Trans Women in 1970s Lesbian Feminist Organizing." *TSQ: Transgender Studies Quarterly* 3, no. 1–2 (2016): 137–45.

Herring, Scott. *Another Country: Queer Anti-urbanism.* New York: New York University Press, 2010.

Hochschild, Arlie Russell. *Strangers in Their Own Land: Anger and Mourning on the American Right.* New York: New Press, 2016.

Holloway, Pippa. "Manifesto for a Queer South Politics." *PMLA* 131, no. 1 (2016): 182–86.

Holt, Fabian. *Genre in Popular Music.* Chicago: University of Chicago Press, 2007.

hooks, bell. "Eating the Other: Desire and Resistance." In *Black Looks: Race and Representation,* 21–39. Boston: South End Press, 1992.

Howard, John. *Men Like That: A Southern Queer History.* Chicago: University of Chicago Press, 2001.

Hubbs, Nadine. "Country Music in Dangerous Times: IASPM-US Keynote, Cleveland, February 24, 2017." *Journal of Popular Music Studies* 30, no. 1–2 (2018): 15–26.

———. "'I Will Survive': Musical Mappings of Queer Social Space in a Disco Anthem." *Popular Music* 26, no. 2 (2007): 231–44.

———. "'Jolene,' Genre, and the Everyday Homoerotics of Country Music: Dolly Parton's Loving Address of the Other Woman." *Women and Music: A Journal of Gender and Culture* 19, no. 1 (2015): 71–76.

———. *The Queer Composition of America's Sound: Gay Modernists, American Music, and National Identity.* Berkeley: University of California Press, 2004.

———. *Rednecks, Queers, and Country Music.* Berkeley: University of California Press, 2014.

———. "'Redneck Woman' and the Gendered Poetics of Class Rebellion." *Southern Cultures* 17, no. 4 (Winter 2011): 44–70.

Huber, Patrick, Steve Goodson, and David Anderson, eds. *The Hank Williams Reader.* Oxford: Oxford University Press, 2014.

Hughes, Walter. "In the Empire of the Beat." In *Microphone Fiends: Youth Music and Youth Culture,* edited by Andrew Ross and Tricia Rose, 147–57. New York: Routledge, 1994.

Hutcheon, Linda. *Irony's Edge: The Theory and Politics of Irony.* London: Routledge, 1994.

Isenberg, Nancy. *White Trash: The 400-Year Untold History of Class in America.* New York: Viking, 2016.

Isherwood, Christopher. *The World in the Evening.* London: Methuen, 1954.

Jackson, Josh. "Brandi Carlile Interviews Amy Ray about Her New Solo Album *Holler.*" *Paste Magazine,* 26 September 2018. https://www.pastemagazine.com/articles/2018/09/brandi-carlile-interviews-amy-ray-about-her-new-so.html.

Jain, S. Lochlann. "Cancer Butch." *Cultural Anthropology* 22, no. 4 (2007): 501–38.

———. *Malignant: How Cancer Becomes Us.* Berkeley: University of California Press, 2013.

James, Robin. "Is the Post- in Post-identity the Post- in Post-genre?" *Popular Music* 36, no. 1 (2017): 21–32.

———. *Resilience and Melancholy: Pop Music, Feminism, Neoliberalism*. Winchester, UK: Zero Books, 2015.

Jennings, Dave. "The Twang's the Thang: k.d. lang." *Melody Maker*, May 26, 1990, 41.

Jensen, Joli. *The Nashville Sound: Authenticity, Commercialization, and Country Music*. Nashville, TN: Vanderbilt University Press, 1998.

Johnson, Colin R. *Just Queer Folks: Gender and Sexuality in Rural America*. Philadelphia: Temple University Press, 2013.

Johnson, E. Patrick. *Appropriating Blackness: Performance and the Politics of Authenticity*. Durham, NC: Duke University Press, 2003.

———. *Sweet Tea: Black Gay Men of the South*. Chapel Hill: University of North Carolina Press, 2008.

Karkazis, Katrina Alicia. *Fixing Sex: Intersex, Medical Authority, and Lived Experience*. Durham, NC: Duke University Press, 2008.

Karkazis, Katrina Alicia, Rebecca Jordan-Young, Georgiann Davis, and Silvia Camporesi. "Out of Bounds? A Critique of the New Policies on Hyperandrogenism in Elite Female Athletes." *American Journal of Bioethics* 12, no. 7 (2012): 3–16.

Kehrer, Lauron. "Goldenrod Distribution and the Queer Failure of Women's Music." *American Music* 34, no. 2 (Summer 2016): 218–42.

Kennedy, Elizabeth Lapovsky, and Madeline Davis. "'They Was No One to Mess With': The Construction of the Butch Role in the Lesbian Community of the 1940s and 1950s." In *The Persistent Desire: A Femme-Butch Reader*, edited by Joanne Nestle, 62–79. Boston: Alyson Publications, 1992.

Key, Susan. "Sound and Sentimentality: Nostalgia in the Songs of Stephen Foster." *American Music* 13, no. 2 (1995): 145–66.

King, Stephen A., and P. Renee Foster. "'Leave Country Music to White Folk?': Narratives from Contemporary African-American Country Artists on Race and Music." In *The Honky Tonk on the Left: Progressive Thought in Country Music*, edited by Mark Allan Jackson, 214–35. Amherst: University of Massachusetts Press, 2018.

Kirby, Jason. "Antimodernism and Genre from Country-Rock to Alt.Country, 1968–98." PhD dissertation, University of Virginia, 2016.

Kirshenblatt-Gimblett, Barbara. "Theorizing Heritage." *Ethnomusicology* 89, no. 3 (1995): 367–80.

Kisliuk, Michelle. *Seize the Dance! BaAka Musical Life and the Ethnography of Performance*. New York: Oxford University Press, 1998.

Knapp, Raymond. "The Straight Bookends to Camp's Gay Golden Age: From Gilbert and Sullivan to Roger Vadim and Mel Brooks." In *Music & Camp*, edited by Christopher Moore and Philip Purvis, 200–219. Middletown, CT: Wesleyan University Press, 2018.

Kraus, Carolyn. "Screening the Borderland: Transsexualism as Cinematic Metaphor." *CineAction*, no. 78 (Winter 2009): 17–22.

Krell, Elena Elias. "Contours through Covers: Voice and Affect in the Music of Lucas Silveira." *Journal of Popular Music Studies* 25, no. 4 (December 2013): 476–503.

———. "Trans/forming White Noise: Gender, Race, and Disability in the Music of Joe

Stevens." In *The Oxford Handbook of Voice Studies,* edited by Nina Sun Eidsheim and Katherine Meizel, 143–63. Oxford: Oxford University Press, 2019.

Kulick, Don, and Margaret Willson, eds. *Taboo: Sex, Identity and Erotic Subjectivity in Anthropological Fieldwork.* London: Routledge, 1995.

Kun, Josh. *Audiotopia: Music, Race, and America.* Berkeley: University of California Press, 2005.

LaVenture, Liz. "Interview: Namoli Brennet." *Vital Voice,* 25 October 2012. http://www.thevitalvoice.com/interview-namoli-brennet/.

Lawrence, Tim. *Love Saves the Day: A History of American Dance Music Culture (1970–79).* Durham, NC: Duke University Press, 2003.

Levine, Lawrence W. *Black Culture and Black Consciousness: Afro-American Folk Thought from Slavery to Freedom.* 30th anniversary ed. Oxford: Oxford University Press, 2007.

Lewin, Ellen, and William Leap, eds. *Out in the Field: Reflections of Lesbian and Gay Anthropologists.* Urbana: University of Illinois Press, 1996.

Lott, Eric. *Love and Theft: Blackface Minstrelsy and the American Working Class.* New York: Oxford University Press, 1995.

Mapes, Jillian. "Brittany Howard on Her Solo Debut, Her Black Heroes, and Owning Her Greatness," *Pitchfork,* 17 September 2019.

Markowitz, Fran, and Michael Ashkenazi, eds. *Sex, Sexuality, and the Anthropologist.* Urbana: University of Illinois Press, 1999.

Mason, Carol. *Oklahomo: Lessons in Unqueering America.* Albany: State University of New York Press, 2015.

Mattel, Trixie, and Katya Zamolodchikova. *Trixie and Katya's Guide to Modern Womanhood.* New York: Plume Books, 2020.

Mazor, Barry. *Ralph Peer and the Making of Popular Roots Music.* Chicago: Chicago Review Press, 2015.

McCracken, Allison. *Real Men Don't Sing: Crooning in American Culture.* Durham, NC: Duke University Press, 2015.

McCusker, Kristine M., and Diane Pecknold, eds. *A Boy Named Sue: Gender and Country Music.* Jackson: University Press of Mississippi, 2004.

Meyerowitz, Joanne J. *How Sex Changed: A History of Transsexuality in the United States.* Cambridge, MA: Harvard University Press, 2002.

Miller, Karl Hagstrom. *Segregating Sound: Inventing Folk and Pop Music in the Age of Jim Crow.* Durham, NC: Duke University Press, 2010.

Mock, Janet. *Redefining Realness: My Path to Womanhood, Identity, Love, and So Much More.* New York: Atria Press, 2014.

Mockus, Martha. "Queer Thoughts on Country Music and k.d. lang." In *Queering the Pitch: The New Gay and Lesbian Musicology,* edited by Philip Brett, Elizabeth Wood, and Gary C. Thomas, 257–71. New York: Routledge, 1994.

Moore, Allan. "Authenticity as Authentication." *Popular Music* 21, no. 2 (2002): 209–23.

Moore, Jennifer Grayer. *Fashion Fads through American History: Fitting Clothes into Context.* Santa Barbara, CA: Greenwood, 2015.

Morris, Bonnie J. *Eden Built by Eves: The Culture of Women's Music Festivals*. Los Angeles: Alyson Books, 1999.

Muñoz, José Esteban. *Disidentifications: Queers of Color and the Performance of Politics*. Minneapolis: University of Minnesota Press, 1999.

Nash, Jennifer C. "Intersectionality and Its Discontents." *American Quarterly* 69, no. 1 (March 2017): 117–29.

Negus, Keith. "Country, k.d. lang and Lesbian Style." In *Popular Music in Theory: An Introduction*, 130–33. Hanover, NH: Wesleyan University Press, 1996.

Negus, Keith, and Patria Román Velázquez. "Belonging and Detachment: Musical Experience and the Limits of Identity." *Poetics* 30, no. 1 (2002): 133–45.

Nestle, Joan, ed. *The Persistent Desire: A Femme-Butch Reader*. Boston: Alyson Publications, 1992.

Nettick, Geri (a.k.a. Beth Elliot). *Mirrors: Portrait of a Lesbian Transsexual*. Oakland, CA: CreateSpace 2011.

Newton, Esther. *Mother Camp: Female Impersonators in America*. Chicago: University of Chicago Press, 1979.

Nordmarken, Sonny. "Becoming Ever More Monstrous: Feeling Transgender In-Betweenness." *Qualitative Inquiry* 20, no. 1 (2014): 37–50.

Olson, Johanna. "Medical Intervention for Trans Children." In *Trans Bodies, Trans Selves: A Resource for the Transgender Community*, edited by Laura Erikson-Schroth, 442–43. Oxford: Oxford University Press, 2014.

Ortega, Teresa. "'My Name Is Sue! How Do You Do?': Johnny Cash as Lesbian Icon." In *Reading Country Music: Steel Guitars, Opry Stars, and Honky Tonk Bars*, edited by Cecilia Tichi, 222–33. Durham, NC: Duke University Press, 1998.

Packard, Chris. *Queer Cowboys and Other Erotic Male Friendships in Nineteenth-Century American Literature*. New York: Palgrave Macmillan, 2005.

Parker, Lyndsey. "Country Hitmaker Shane McAnally on Coming Out: 'I Was So Afraid of What it Would Mean to My Career.'" Yahoo Music 9 June 2020. https://www.yahoo .com/now/country-hitmaker-shane-mc-anally-on-coming-out-i-was-so-afraid-of-what -it-would-mean-to-my-career-225156865.html.

Pearson, Stephen. "How to Pronounce Appalachia." *Yappalachia*. Last modified 30 April 2018. https://yappalachia.com/2018/04/30/how-to-pronounce-appalachia-or-white man-thou-shalt-not-steal/.

Pecknold, Diane, ed. *Hidden in the Mix: The African American Presence in Country Music*. Durham, NC: Duke University Press, 2013.

———. *The Selling Sound*. Durham, NC: Duke University Press, 2007.

Pecknold, Diane, and Kristine M. McCusker, eds. *Country Boys and Redneck Women: New Essays in Gender and Country Music*. Jackson: University Press of Mississippi, 2016.

Pedelty, Mark. "This Land: Seeger Performs Guthrie's 'Lost Verses' at the Inaugural." *Popular Music and Society* 32, no. 3 (2009): 427–28.

Pellegrini, Ann. "After Sontag: Future Notes on Camp." In *A Companion to Lesbian, Gay,*

Bisexual, Transgender, and Queer Studies, edited by George E. Haggerty and Molly McGarry, 168–93. Oxford: Wiley-Blackwell, 2007.

Pennington, Stephan. "Transgender Passing Guides and the Vocal Performance of Gender and Sexuality." In *The Oxford Handbook of Music and Queerness*, edited by Fred E. Maus and Sheila Whiteley. Oxford: Oxford University Press, 2021.

Peraino, Judith A. *Listening to the Sirens: Musical Technologies of Queer Identity from Homer to Hedwig.* Berkeley: University of California Press, 2006.

Peterson, Richard A. *Creating Country Music: Fabricating Authenticity.* Chicago: University of Chicago Press, 1997.

———. "The Dialectic of Hard-Core and Soft-Shell Country Music." In *Reading Country Music: Steel Guitars, Opry Stars, and Honky Tonk Bars*, edited by Cecelia Tichi, 234–55. Durham, NC: Duke University Press, 1998.

Peterson, Richard A., and Bruce A. Beal. "Alternative Country: Origins, Music, World-View, Fans, and Taste in Genre Formation." *Popular Music and Society* 25, nos. 1–2 (Spring 2001): 233–49.

Pittelman, Karen. "Another Country: On the Relationship between Country Music and White Supremacy—and What We Can Do about It." *Medium*, 17 December 2018. https://medium.com/@Pittelman/another-country-80a05dd7fc15.

Powers, Ann. "Songs We Love: Brandi Carlile, 'The Joke,'" *NPR*, 13 November 2017, https://www.npr.org/2017/11/13/563358018/songs-we-love-brandi-carlile-the-joke.

Queer Appalachia. *Electric Dirt: A Celebration of Queer Voices and Identities from Appalachia and the South.* Bluefield, WV: Queer Appalachia, 2017.

Ray, Amy. "Queer and Fucked." IndigoGirls.com, 5 September 2002. http://indigogirls .com/?p=1571.

Raymond, Diane. "Popular Culture and Queer Representation: A Critical Perspective." In *Gender, Race, and Class in Media: A Critical Reader*, edited by Gail Dines and Jean M. Humez, 98–110. Thousand Oaks, CA: Sage Publications, 2018.

Rodnitzky, Jerry. *Feminist Phoenix: The Rise and Fall of a Feminist Counterculture, 1960–1995.* Westport, CT: Praeger, 1999.

Rogers, Bradley. "The Queer Pleasures of Musical Theater." In *Oxford Handbook of Music and Queerness*, edited by Sheila Whiteley and Fred E. Maus. Oxford: Oxford University Press, forthcoming.

Root, Deane. "Foster, Stephen C. (1826–1864), Songwriter." In *Grove Music Online*, 2013. http://www.oxfordmusiconline.com.

Rosenberg, Neil, ed. *Transforming Tradition: Folk Music Revivals Examined.* Urbana: University of Illinois Press, 1993.

Royster, Francesca T. "Black Edens, Country Eves: Listening, Performance, and Black Queer Longing in Country Music." *Journal of Lesbian Studies* 21, no. 3 (2017): 306–22.

———. *Sounding Like a No-No? Queer Sounds and Eccentric Acts in the Post-soul Era.* Ann Arbor: University of Michigan Press, 2013.

Rubin, Gayle S. *Deviations: A Gayle Rubin Reader.* Durham, NC: Duke University Press, 2011.

Salamon, Gayle. *Assuming a Body: Transgender and Rhetorics of Materiality*. New York: Columbia University Press, 2010.

Samson, Jim. "Genre." In *Oxford Music Online*. Edited by Deane Root. Accessed 20 January 2016. http://www.oxfordmusiconline.com:80/subscriber/article/grove/music/40599.

Scherr, Rebecca. "(Not) Queering 'White Vision' in *Far from Heaven* and *Transamerica*." *Jump Cut* 50 (2008). https://www.ejumpcut.org/archive/jc50.2008/Scherr/index.html.

Schilt, Kristen. *Just One of the Guys: Transgender Men and the Persistence of Gender Inequality*. Chicago: University of Chicago Press, 2010.

Sears, James T. *Rebels, Rubyfruit, and Rhinestones: Queering Space in the Stonewall South*. New Brunswick, NJ: Rutgers University Press, 2001.

Sedgwick, Eve Kosofsky. *Touching Feeling: Affect, Pedagogy, Performativity*. Durham, NC: Duke University Press, 2003.

Segarra, Alynda. "Open Letter to Folk Musicians: Fall in Love with Justice (Op-Ed)." *Bluegrass Situation,* 19 May 2015. Originally http://thebluegrasssituation.com/read/alynda-lee-segarras-call-folk-singers-fall-love-justice-op-ed, now https://web.archive.org/web/20150523010759/http://www.thebluegrasssituation.com/read/alynda-lee-segarras-call-folk-singers-fall-love-justice-op-ed.

Shank, Barry. "'That Wild Mercury Sound': Bob Dylan and the Illusion of American Culture." *boundary 2* 29, no. 1 (2002): 97–123.

Shelburne, Craig. "Gender Identity and Country Music Merge in *Transamerica*." 3 March 2006. http://www.cmt.com/news/1525363/gender-identity-and-country-music-merge-in-transamerica/.

Skeggs, Beverley. "Exchange, Value and Affect: Bourdieu and 'The Self.'" *Sociological Review* 52, no. 2 (2004): 75–95.

———. "Uneasy Alignments, Resourcing Respectable Subjectivity." *GLQ: A Journal of Lesbian and Gay Studies* 10, no. 2 (2004): 291–98.

Slobin, Mark. *Folk Music: A Very Short Introduction*. New York: Oxford University Press, 2011.

Slominski, Tes. "Doin' Time with Meg and Cris, Thirty Years Later: The Queer Temporality of Pseudonostalgia." *Women and Music: A Journal of Gender and Culture* 19, no. 1 (2015): 86–94.

———. "Queer as Trad: LGBTQ Performers and Irish Traditional Music in the United States." In *The Oxford Handbook of Music and Queerness*, edited by Fred Everett Maus and Sheila Whiteley. Oxford University Press, 2021.

Sloop, John M. "'So Long, Chaps and Spurs, and Howdy—er, *Bon Jour*—to the Wounded Songbird': k.d. lang, Ambiguity, and the Politics of Genre/Gender." In *Disciplining Gender: Rhetorics of Sex Identity in Contemporary U.S. Culture*, 83–103. Amherst: University of Massachusetts Press, 2004.

Small, Christopher. *Musicking: The Meanings of Performance and Listening*. Middletown, CT: Wesleyan University Press, 1998.

Smith, Patrick. "Brittany Howard: 'I didn't want to end up back in the trailer park.'" *Independent*, 20 September 2019.

Sontag, Susan. "Notes on 'Camp.'" *Partisan Review* 31, no. 4 (Fall 1964): 515–30.

Spade, Dean. "Mutilating Gender." In *The Transgender Studies Reader,* edited by Susan Stryker and Stephen Whittle, 315–32. New York: Routledge, 2006.

———. *Normal Life: Administrative Violence, Critical Trans Politics, and the Limits of the Law.* Durham, NC: Duke University Press, 2015.

Spanos, Brittany. "Drag Queen Trixie Mattel on Her Country Albums, Kacey Musgraves Obsession." *Rolling Stone,* 29 March 2018.

Spoon, Rae. *First Spring Grass Fire.* Vancouver: Arsenal Pulp Press, 2012.

———. *How to (Hide) Be(hind) Your Songs.* Vancouver: Kolakovsky Press, 2017.

Spoon, Rae, and Ivan E. Coyote. *Gender Failure.* Vancouver: Arsenal Pulp Press, 2014.

Stephens, Vincent. "Open Secrecy: Self-Presentation by Queer Male Musicians." In *Masquerade: Essays on Tradition and Innovation Worldwide,* edited by Deborah Bell, 145–55. Jefferson, NC: McFarland & Company, 2015.

———. *Rocking the Closet: How Little Richard, Johnnie Ray, Liberace, and Johnny Mathis Queered Pop Music.* Urbana: University of Illinois Press, 2019.

———. "Shaking the Closet: Analyzing Johnny Mathis's Sexual Elusiveness, 1956–82." *Popular Music and Society* 33, no. 5 (December 2010): 597–623.

Stewart, Susan. "Notes on Distressed Genres." *Journal of American Folklore* 104, no. 411 (Winter 1991): 5–31.

Stimeling, Travis. "Narrative, Vocal Staging, and Masculinity in the 'Outlaw' Country Music of Waylon Jennings." *Popular Music* 32, no. 3 (2013): 343–58.

Stone, Sandy. "The Empire Strikes Back: A Posttranssexual Manifesto." In *Body Guards: The Cultural Politics of Sexual Ambiguity,* edited by Kristina Straub and Julia Epstein, 221–35. New York: Routledge, 1996.

Stryker, Susan. "Another Dream of Common Language: An Interview with Sandy Stone." *TSQ: Transgender Studies Quarterly* 3, no. 1–2 (2016): 294–305.

———. *Transgender History.* Berkeley, CA: Seal Press, 2008.

———. "Transing the Queer (In)Human." *GLQ: A Journal of Lesbian and Gay Studies* 21, no. 3–4 (2015): 227–30.

Stryker, Susan, and Aren Aizura, eds. *The Transgender Studies Reader 2.* New York: Routledge, 2013.

Stryker, Susan, and Stephen Whittle, eds. *The Transgender Studies Reader.* New York: Routledge, 2006.

Sukop, Sylvia. "Transamericana: From Folk Roots Up and Out." *Huffington Post,* 18 March 2010.

Sullivan, John Jeremiah. "Rhiannon Giddens and What Folk Music Means." *New Yorker,* 12 May 2019.

Taylor, Jane. "'Why Do You Tear Me from Myself?': Torture, Truth, and the Arts of the Counter-Reformation." In *The Rhetoric of Sincerity,* edited by Ernst van Alphen, Mieke Bal, and Carel Smith, 19–43. Stanford, CA: Stanford University Press, 2009.

Toynbee, Jason. *Making Popular Music: Musicians, Creativity and Institutions.* London: Arnold, 2000.

Trilling, Lionel. *Sincerity and Authenticity.* Cambridge, MA: Harvard University Press, 1971.

Valentine, David. *Imagining Transgender: An Ethnography of a Category*. Durham, NC: Duke University Press, 2007.

Välimäki, Susanna. "The Audiovisual Construction of Transgender Identity in *Transamerica*." In *The Oxford Handbook of New Audiovisual Aesthetics*, edited by John Richardson, Claudia Gorbman, and Carol Vernallis, 372–88. Oxford: Oxford University Press, 2013.

———. "Listening to Transgender Utopia in Boys Don't Cry." *SQS: Journal of Queer Studies in Finland* 1–2 (2013): 1–17.

van Alphen, Ernst, and Mieke Bal. Introduction to *The Rhetoric of Sincerity*, edited by Ernst van Alphen, Mieke Bal, and Carel Smith, 1–16. Stanford, CA: Stanford University Press, 2009.

Vander Wel, Stephanie. "The Lavender Cowboy and 'The She Buckaroo': Gene Autry, Patsy Montana, and Depression-Era Gender Roles." *Musical Quarterly* 95, no. 2–3 (2012): 207–51.

Voss, Brandon. "Lucas Silveria: Trans Rock." BrandonVoss.com. Last modified 1 April 2007. http://brandonvoss.com/blog/lucas-silveria-trans-rock.

Wald, Elijah. *Dylan Goes Electric! Newport, Seeger, Dylan, and the Night That Split the Sixties*. New York: Harper Collins, 2015.

———. *Escaping the Delta: Robert Johnson and the Invention of the Blues*. New York: Amistad, 2004.

Wallace, David Foster. "E Unibus Pluram: Television and U.S. Fiction." *Review of Contemporary Fiction* 13, no. 2 (Summer 1993): 151–94.

Warner, Michael. *The Trouble with Normal*. New York: Free Press, 1999.

Watson, Jada E., in consultation with WOMAN Nashville. "Gender Representation on Country Format Radio: A Study of Published Reports from 2000–2018." SongData, 26 April 2019.

Watson, Jada E. "Redlining in Country Music: Representation in the Country Music Industry (2000-2020)." *SongData Reports*, 12 March 2021. Ottawa, Ontario, Canada.

Weiss, Margot. "The Epistemology of Ethnography." *GLQ: A Journal of Lesbian and Gay Studies* 17, no. 4 (2011): 649–64.

Whiteley, Sheila. "k.d. lang, a Certain Kind of Woman." In *Women and Popular Music: Sexuality, Identity and Subjectivity*, 152–70. London: Routledge, 2000.

Wilde, Oscar. "The Truth of Masks." In *Intentions*. London: Methuen, 1891.

Wilkerson, Jessica. "Living with Dolly Parton." *Longreads,* October 2018. https://longreads.com/2018/10/16/living-with-dolly-parton/.

Williams, Cristan. "Radical Inclusion: Recounting the Trans Inclusive History of Radical Feminism." *TSQ: Transgender Studies Quarterly* 3, no. 1–2 (2016): 254–58.

Wong, Deborah. *Speak It Louder: Asian Americans Making Music*. London: Routledge, 2004.

Films

Birleffi, Bobbie, and Beverly Kopf, dirs. *Chely Wright: Wish Me Away*. 2012, 96 minutes.

Coen, Joel, dir. *O Brother, Where Art Thou?* 2001, 103 minutes.

Davis, Kate. *Southern Comfort*. HBO, 2001, 90 minutes.

Deitch, Donna, dir. *Desert Hearts*. Desert Heart Productions, Samuel Goldwyn Company, 1986, 91 minutes.

Dupuis, Isabelle, and Tim Geraghty, dirs. *The Unicorn: A Documentary about Peter Grudzien*. Aonbheannach Productions LLC, 2017, 93 minutes.

Greenwald, Maggie, dir. *Songcatcher*. 2000, DVD, 109 minutes.

Haas, Shaleece, dir. *Real Boy*. 2016, DVD, 72 minutes.

Lerner, Murray, dir. *Festival!* Patchke Productions/Eagle Rock Entertainment EE391019R2, 1967, DVD, 97 minutes.

———, dir. *The Other Side of the Mirror: Live at the Newport Folk Festival 1963–1965*. Colombia/Legacy, 2007, DVD, 83 minutes.

McMullan, Chelsea, dir. *My Prairie Home*. Montreal: National Film Board of Canada C9913425, 2013, DVD, 76 minutes.

Minax, Madsen, dir. *Riot Acts: Flaunting Gender Deviance in Music Performance*. New York: Outcast Films, 2010, DVD, 76 minutes.

Taberski, Dan, dir. *These C*cksucking Tears*. 2016. Vimeo video, 15:50. http://www.these cocksuckingtears.com/.

Tucker, Duncan, dir. *Transamerica*. Belladonna Productions, 2005; Weinstein Company, 2006, 79039, 103 minutes.

Interviews

Brennet, Namoli. San Francisco, 2010; Rhode Island, October 2014; Philadelphia, October 2018.

Ciaccio, Haseldon, Sam Gleaves, and Tyler Hughes. Ann Mitz's Philadelphia house concert, December 2, 2017; at author's home, December 3, 2017.

Conley, Eli. Queer Country seminar, Temple University, April 11, 2019.

DK and the Joy Machine. "Another Country" festival, at Come On Y'all, Brooklyn, July 2, 2017.

Firkus, Brian. Conversation by video with Queer Country seminar, Temple University, October 22, 2018.

Gleaves, Sam. Phone conversation with Queer Country seminar, Temple University, February 14, 2019.

Gleaves, Sam, and Tyler Hughes. Queer Country Quarterly, Branded Saloon, Brooklyn, November 19, 2016.

Gleaves, Sam. The Philadelphia Folk Song Society, October 22, 2017.

Haggerty, Patrick. Brooklyn, September 22, 2017; Philadelphia, June 8, 2018, June 13, 2018, and October 2019. By phone June 14, 2021.

Ingrid Elizabeth and Tylan Greenstein. November 2016, Music in American Society class, Temple University.

Spoon, Rae. Conversation by phone, December 2015, and in person, May 2016.

Steele, Bethel, and Joe Stevens. Philadelphia, March 19, 2017.

Stevens, Joe. Palo Alto, California, April 2010; Pittsburgh, August 2010; Newport, California, September 2010; in author's Gender Transgression class at Stanford University with Ingrid Elizabeth, October 2010; Santa Rosa, California, October 2010; 5 Guys 6 Strings in San Francisco, 2011; Queer Christian Climate event, Manhattan, 2014; "Music in History" and "American Roots Music and Identity," Temple University, 2015, 2016.

Stevens, Joe, with Ben Wallace and Shaleece Haas. "American Roots Music and Identity," Temple University, 2016.

Strikeback, Simon. Phone, 4 March 2018.

Performers Observed in Person

Alabama Shakes, Namoli Brennet, Mya Byrne, Brandi Carlile, Che Apalache, Haseldon Ciaccio, Eli Conley, DK and the Joy Machine, Cathy Fink and Marcy Marxer, Girlyman, Sam Gleaves, Coyote Grace, Patrick Haggerty, Tyler Hughes, Hurray for the Riff Raff, Eric Hyman, Indigo Girls, Karen and the Sorrows, Amythyst Kiah, Elena Elias Krell, A.J. Lewis and Friends, Mac and Strikeback, Trixie Mattel, Mouths of Babes, My Gay Banjo, Orville Peck, Paisley Fields, The Amy Ray Band, Elana Redfield, Rae Spoon, Joe Stevens, Spider John Dubek, Ben Wallace

Performers Observed through Virtual Concerts

Jake Blount, Namoli Brennet, Della Mae, Indigo Girls, Justin Hiltner, Mary Gauthier and Jaimee Harris, Tatiana Hargreaves, Mouths of Babes, Secret Emchy Society

INDEX

Page references in italics refer to illustrations.

Aciman, Andre, 63
Actor Slash Model, 74, 114; audience of, 132; "TN Tranny Two-Step," 24, 131–32, 151, 219n14
Acuff, Roy: sincerity of, 212n20
Adams, Sheila Kay, 106
Adelson, Leslie A., 51
Adiseshiah, Siân, 54–55
Against a Trans Narrative, 212n11
Against Me!, 165
Agnew, Vanessa, 75, 212n13, 212n14
Alabama Shakes, 103, 215n80
Allen, Julia, 106, 158
Almanac Singers, social justice issues of, 100
alt.country, 99; politics of, 100
Americana music: country-punk-rock sound of, 13; gender/genre relationships in, 118; gender/sexuality politics of, 121; identity crisis of, 99–100; lack of Black musicians, 100; lang's, 69, 86; relationship to gender/sexuality, 69; in *Transamerica*, 145–48
Americana Music Association (AMA): Americana Trailblazer Award of, 69; attention to minority musicians, 69; hon-
oring of Carlile, 93; honoring of lang, 69, 86
Americana music industry, 86; marketing in, 13–14; middlemen of, 15; version of country music history, 176
American Roots Music, 100
America's Got Talent, gay country musicians on, 214n56
Amy Ray Band, *128*; eclectic country influences, 127
anger, gendered expression of, 124
Annenburg Inclusion Initiative: "No Country for Female Artists," 5
Anohni, on transition, 149
Appalachian music, 1, 102, 106, 107
Appalachian musicians: gay/lesbian, 52, 104–9; political image of, 104; queer/trans, 104
Appalachian people: inaccurate depictions of, 219n5
appropriation: colonialist, 157–58; musical, 153, 155, 162
appropriation, cultural: of Blackness, 163; of fashion, 159–60; of identity, 153, 155; for material gain, 162; of Otherness, 160; social inequity and, 155; of voice, 160, 161; by white middle class, 154, 170

Arcade Fire, 163; performance at Coachella, 166–67, 169; *Reflektor*, 164; Spoon on, 164; stage makeup of, 166–67, 169; use of masks, 170. See also *We Exist*; "We Exist"

Ariel, *Funky & Western*, 85

art music: female singers of, 216n93; omission of women from, 75; vocal technique for, 217n101

authenticity: Black, 161, 163, 170; countering of stereotypes, 163; as discursive formation, 53; in early modern European society, 42; essentialism and, 40, 171; false, 158–59, 161, 162; hybridity and, 161–62; in journey narratives, 133–34; need for, 54; in North American culture, 53; of Otherness, 154; postmodern critique of, 53–55; as unchanging, 40; and violence against nonnormative people, 41; vulnerability in, 53; yearning for meaning in, 162–63. *See also* sincerity; truth

authenticity, musical: in blues music, 161; boy bands', 194; of country music, 6, 30, 34, 41, 172, 175–76; of folk music, 30, 116, 160–61; in honky-tonk, 58; lived proof of, 64; in musical genres, 78; problematic, 196; of queer/trans country music, 3, 27, 42, 199

Baez, Joan: activism of, 29, 206n21; authenticity of, 29; bisexuality of, 93; and Eve Morris, 29–30; solemnity of, 30. Works: "Altar Boy and the Thief," 206n21; "Joe Hill," 77

Bal, Mieke, 43

Baldwin, James, 95

Bandy, Moe: "Honky Tonk Queen," 82

bathroom usage, transgender, 6, 202n13

Beal, Bruce, 99

Beauchamp, Toby: *Going Stealth*, 202n14

Bendix, Regina, 53, 160, 161; on authenticity, 162–63

Benjamin, Harry, 138–39

ben Miriam, Faygele, 26, 205n10

Bermuda Triangle, 103

Bernstein, Jonathan, 100

Betts, Stephen, 87–88

bigotry: class and, 215n73; in mainstream country music, 34, 147, 194; working-class, 111, 221n37

Billboard: Hot 100 chart, 192; removal of "Old Town Road," 189, 190–91

BIPOC musicians: lack of opportunity for, 197, 199

Black Americans: cowboys, 191, 193; soul in culture of, 52; stereotypes of, 40

Blackberri, "Eat the Rich," 36

blackface minstrelsy, 11, 162, 225n22; audiences of, 147–48; cultural fluidity of, 147

Blackfoot Diner, 68; Spoon's performances at, 66

Black Lives Matter movement, 187

Black musicians: contributions to bluegrass, 102, 203n33; country music narratives of, 195, 196; country queer/trans, 103, 197; folkloric recordings of, 196–97; folk music, 30, 76; omitted from Americana, 100; racial impersonation of, 155; white artists' sampling of, 196–97

Blackness: authenticity of, 170; cultural appropriation of, 163; cultural value of, 161; as invented category, 163

Blanco, 226n22

Bloechl, Olivia, 155

Bloomfield, Mike, 161, 169

Blount, Jake, 227n48; genrequeer music of, 98, 124; on identity categories, 98–99

bluegrass: authority of, 141; Black Americans' contributions to, 102, 203n33; genre of, 220n26; secular gospel song in, 151

Bluegrass Pride, 14, 21; community building by, 173

Bluegrass Situation, 172; Segarra's open letter to, 100–102

blues music, authenticity in, 161

Boomers, 118

Boorman, John: *Deliverance*, 129

Boucher, Cindy, 85

Bowie, David, 38

Boy George, 82

Boyland, Jennifer Finney, 6

Bradley, Owen, 86, 213n35

Brandt, Pamela, 85

breast cancer, gender-confirming surgery for, 208n63

Brennet, Namoli, 69, 121; audience of, 122; *Boy in a Dress*, 119–20; compositions of, 119–20; disruptions of gender binary, 120; folk music of, 72; gender assigned at birth,

119–20; genre/gender identity of, 119; musical genres of, 119; rural imagery of, 120; tours of, 121, 133; transgender identity of, 118–19; transition of, 119, 120; use of yodel, 217n103; vocal changes of, 217n104

Briggs, Billy: "The Sissy Song," 81

Briggs Initiative, 206n21

Brooks, Garth, 77; venues of, 52; "We Shall Be Free," 64, 82

Brooks, Mel: use of camp, 52

Brothers Osborne, 172, 199

Bruce, Lenny: arrest of, 206n16

Bryant, Anita, 82

Bryson, Bethany, 194

Burgess, Wilma, 2; "Ain't Got No Man," 83; *Could I Have This Dance*, 83

Burkholder, Nancy Jean, 94–95

Burns, Ken: country music documentary, 2, 162

Butler, Judith, 8; on "bad copy" homosexuality, 41; *Gender Trouble*, 78, 155, 211n1; theory of performativity, 156

Butler, Win, 166; on Jamaica, 164–65

Butterfly Conservatory, 111, 216n89

Byrne, Mya: "The Case of the Missing Trans Country Artists," 111–12

Cacciolo, Hasse (Haselden), 106

Calgary Stampede, 65, 143–44

Cameron, Loren: *Body Alchemy*, 134–35

camp: characteristics of, 19; coded communication in, 52; "dyke," 61; experimentation in, 18, 20; in gender nonidentification, 116; genre of, 18; irony in, 52; mainstreaming of, 52; in *Oxford English Dictionary*, 52; radical queer politics of, 52; as reparative, 19; sincerity and, 53; as strategy, 52

camp humor, queer/trans, 3, 24, 60; in music, 6. *See also* humor

Camp Trans, 95

Cantwell, Robert, 11, 151

Cargill, Jeremy, 31

Carlile, Brandi, 2, 14, 197; band of, 92; genres of, 92–93. Works: "If She Ever Leaves Me," 198; "The Joke," 93, 214n59; "The Story," 92, 214n59

Carlin, George: "Seven Words You Can Never Say on Television," 28

Carter, Dave: transgender identification of, 216n89

Carter, "Mother" Maybelle, 176

Carter Family, 41, 82; hybrid music of, 162

Casarino, Cesare, 51

Cash, Johnny, 185, 210n94

Cash, June Carter, 185

Cash, Roseanne, 88, 148

Cashier, Albert, 45, 208n62

Cavalcante, Andre, 45, 78

Chicks (Dixie Chicks), blacklisting of, 204n41

Cho, Margaret, 18

Cholst, Rachel, 79, 98, 196

Christianity, relationship of country music industry to, 34

cisgender people: gender identity questions of, 73; interrogation of trans people, 43–44; vocal character of, 44–45

cisgender straight men: cross-dressing for comedy, 178

cisgender women: country musicians, 5; perceived threats to, 202n13

Citron, Marcia, 10, 75

The Civility of Albert Cashier, 208n62

civilization, European ideals of, 75

class, essentialism of, 188. *See also* working class

class habitus, regional moves in, 63

classical music, exclusion of women composers from, 10

classification, colonialist practices of, 8, 9

classification, musical: population management through, 10. *See also* genres, musical

class mobility, anxiety over, 43

Clear Channel Communications, censorship by, 204n41

Clear Channel Radio, monopolies of, 75

Clements, Mikaella, 61

Clemmons, Ginni: *Gay and Straight Together*, 85

Clifftop Bluegrass Festival, gay competition winners, 172

Cliks, 122

Cline, Patsy: repertoire of, 58–59

Coachella: violent atmosphere of, 223n32; *We Exist* at, 166–67, *167*, *168*

Cobain, Kurt, 186

Cobb, Dave, 197, 214n59

"cocksucking," audience offence at, 207n28

Coe, David Allan: "Fuck Aneta Briant," 82; "Take This Job and Shove It," 77, 212n12

Coen Brothers, *O Brother, Where Art Thou?*, 99, 100, 146–47

Cohen, Michael: *What Did You Expect?*, 84

Colanduoni, Christina: "Moving Parts," 224n12

colonialism: classification practices of, 8, 9; complicity in, 170; settler, 98

Concert for Love and Acceptance: community building by, 173; Indigo Girls at, 90; rainbow imagery of, 89

Conley, Eli, 1, 79

Connolly, Michael, 70, 141

Connor, Steven, 160

Constansis, Alexandros N., 114, 217n101

Coon Creek Girls, 82

Cooper, Leonie, 225n22

Coroneos, Kyle "The Triggerman," 226n29; on "Old Town Road," 191, 192; *Saving Country Music* website, 177, 191

country music: alternative, 99; alternative historiographies of, 19; alternative understandings of, 95; appeal to queer/trans people, 5, 19; archetypes of, 71; audience expectations of, 117; authenticity of, 6, 30, 34, 41, 172, 175–76; biases in, 4–5; bigoted audience of, 34, 147, 194; boundaries of genre, 14, 191; censorship of, 81, 204n41; countrypolitan, 58–59, 60, 61; cowpunk, 99; definitions of, 191; discourses of, 71; as emotionally intellectual, 178; essentializing of truth, 3–5; feelings of displacement in, 64; folk music and, 30, 72, 76–77; gender/genre rules of, 118; genre trouble of, 8–11, 70, 75–80, 87–89; grassroots values of, 11; heterosexual lyrics of, 197; hillbilly humor in, 59; homophobic, 3, 81; honesty in, 38–45; honky-tonk versus Nashville sound, 58; humor in, 5–6, 57–60; hybridity of, 162; identity in, 72, 127, 191; identity struggle in, 72; inception as "hillbilly," 190–91; Jewish themes in, 51; loneliness in, 183–84; marginalized identities of, 226n22; middle-class listeners, 184; misuse of Othered people, 152; myths of, 161; in North American identity, 111; objectification of

women in, 4–5; "originary," 77–78; Otherness in, 152, 184, 198; outlaw, 192, 226n32; outsiders in, 127; patriotism in, 111; political, 80; pop sound in, 212n20; queerness in, 81–82, 184; queer/trans audiences of, 5–6; racist exclusions from, 103, 191; rhetoric of, 39–40; rockabilly, 58; rural imagery of, 127–28; sad, 51–52; self-parody in, 59; sexual politics of, 30; sincerity in, 3, 6, 22–23, 38–45, 172–73; social justice and, 72; soft-shell versus hard-core, 77–78, 99, 176, 188; stigma in, 184; transgender people's welcome in, 110–12; trap, 189, 192; travelers in, 127; urban audience of, 184; urbanized, 40, 57–58, 60; values of, 5–6; working-class identity in, 4, 14, 39, 76, 77, 127; yodel technique in, 59, 131, 217n103

country music, commercial, 40, 141; invention of, 76, 77

country music, mainstream: bigotry in, 34, 147, 194; Gay Ole Opry and, 1; lesbians artists in, 3, 87–93; marketing of, 99, 176; perceived honesty in, 206n27

country music, queer/trans, 15; alliances in, 16; assimilation into social norms, 130; audiotopias of, 199; authenticity of, 27, 42, 199; Black, 103, 197; boundaries of, 14; categorization of, 75; communication of truth, 68; during COVID-19 pandemic, 20–21; creation myths of, 170; definitions of, 13; ethnicity of, 16; expectations of truth for, 41; gender discourse of, 16; genres of, 8–13; history of, 80–82; identity in, 8, 80; intergenerational gay solidarity in, 181; irony in, 51–55; labels supporting, 14; listeners' support for, 201n7; marginalized voices of, 7; media coverage of, 21; messages of, 16; narratives of self, 199; Otherness of, 30, 198; performance of, 55; priorities of, 27; production of, 205n4; radical politics of, 16; sexual identity of, 16; sincerity in, 6, 42, 55, 110; social media following of, 20; as socioaesthetic phenomenon, 13, 69, 199, 211n117; stage banter of, 89; straight/cisgender audience of, 173; stranger character in, 181; understandings of country music in, 95; values of, 8; venues for, 14 country music, traditional, 78, 111; audience of, 118; images of, 175; instruments, 175, 176; versus popular, 77

Country Music Against White Supremacy, 69

Country Music Association (CMA): leaders of, 204n41; listeners of, 69

country musicians: ahistorical, 71; class pretentions among, 41; connections to rural culture, 39; political expression by, 34; regional/class backgrounds of, 41

country musicians, bisexual. *See* Segarra, Alynda

country musicians, gay: communication of sincerity, 173; personae of, 173; on rodeo circuit, 86–86; sincerity of, 199

country musicians, lesbian: mainstream, 87–93; narratives of, 199; sincerity of, 3; stardom of, 93. *See also* country musicians, women; country musicians, transgender

country musicians, lesbian/gay: anomalous position of, 1–2; out, 2–3, 83–84

country musicians, nonbinary. *See* Evil; Fields, Paisley; gender, nonbinary; Spoon, Rae

country musicians, queer/trans: activist, 30; closeted, 13; exclusions from industry, 2–3, 16; gender journeys of, 133; journey narratives of, 124, 125–33, 197; modalities of living, 133; narratives of, 6, 8, 199; performance of genre, 80; performance of self, 6; power brokers' interest in, 14; queer/trans politics of, 80; relationship to genre, 14; rural, 23–24, 124; sincerity of, 6, 42, 55, 110; touring experiences, 133; unwelcome reception of, 77; versus cisgender/straight, 71

country musicians, transgender: breaking of rules, 118; process of becoming, 109–12; sincerity of, 3; white men, 112. *See also* country musicians, men; country musicians, nonbinary; country musicians, women

country musicians, women: Black, 195–97; cisgender, 5; femininity of, 175, 176. *See also* country musicians, lesbian; country musicians, transgender

country music industry: CEOs of, 34–35; conservative imagery of, 38; exclusions from, 2–3, 16, 24; heteronormative stakeholders, 33; on *Lavender Country*, 33–34; Nashville sound in, 58; power brokers in, 191; processes of, 191–92; queer/trans discrimination in, 5; racism in, 191; relationship to Christianity, 34; relationship to gender/sexuality, 69; stereotypes in, 40

Country Queer, 14, 21, 172

Country Queer concert, 92

COVID-19 pandemic: cancellations during, 178–79, 194; effect on marginalized musicians, 199; virtual concerts during, 20

cowboys: Black, 191, 193; homoeroticism of, 182; Spoon's identification with, 63–65, 159; "yeehaw agenda," 190

Cowell, Simon, 214n56

cowpunk music, 99

Cox, Laverne, 112

Coyote, Ivan, 116

Coyote Grace, 14, 50; *Boxes & Bags*, 134, 136; business card of, 136; commercial music of, 141; conveying of identity, 46; genre trouble of, 70; income of, 47; journey songs of, 133–34; Mile After Mile label of, 133; repertoire of, 49; "roots" performance of, 141; Stevens's tour with, 47; touring experiences of, 133; venues of, 47

Creadick, Anna, 219n5

Crenshaw, Kimberlé, 71

crooning, 183

Crosby, Bing, 183

"The Cuckoo," 97–98; intersectional analysis of, 98; queer/trans trope of, 7

cuckoos, as queer birds, 97

culture: hybrid, 161, 162; progressive changes in, 34–35. *See also* appropriation, cultural

Cusick, Suzanne, 112, 216n91

Cyrus, Billy Ray, 190, 194; outlaw status of, 192

Dalhart, Vernon, 81

dance: "heels technique," 170; in *We Exist*, 166, 167, 169–70

dance clubs, gay, 12

dancing, straight male cultural anxiety about, 194

Daughters of Bilitis, 85

Davis, Stephanie: "We Shall Be Free," 82

Deadly Nightshade, 85

Decoupigny, Alexandre, 153, 157

Deliverance, 129; "Dueling Banjos," 42; rural Georgians in, 219n5

Democrats, gay, 36

DiAngelo, Robin: *White Fragility*, 222n5

Dickey, James: *Deliverance*, 129

Dickinson, Chris, 36, 85, 87

difranco, ani, 123

Diplo (Thomas Wesley), 37, 192, 225n22; "Do Si Do," 226n22

discos, as space of refuge, 222n9

disidentification, as queer strategy, 220n17

Dobkin, Alix: *Lavender Jane Loves Women*, 84, 144; "View from Gay Head," 144–45

Doyle, J. D.: *Queer Music Heritage*, 212nn29–30

Doug Stevens and the Out Band, *Out in the Country*, 87

drag: in folk music, 177–78, 179; lip syncing in, 20; Parton imitation in, 20

Dubeck, Spider John, 132

Dupuis, Isabelle, 85

Dust Bowl migration, 134, 137

Dylan, Bob, 28, 170

Elizabeth, Ingrid, 47, 48, 49; on "Daughter-son," 141; on genre, 70, 78

Elliot, Sam, 194

Elliott, Beth: stalker experience of, 85–86. Works: *The Bucktooth Varmints*, 86; *Kid, Have You Rehabilitated Yourself?*, 85; *Mirrors*, 213n42

Emch, Cindy, 21

engineering, recording, 224n1

essentialism: appropriation and, 154; authenticity and, 40, 171; of class, 188; in gender/sexuality, 41; of Otherness, 163; postmodern critique of, 24; social roles in, 43; ties of sincerity to, 22, 39; of truth, 3; in understanding of identity, 156, 159, 162, 191; view of gender/sexuality, 208n52

Evil (musician), 225n22

Farmer, Frances, 205n3

Feigenbaum, Anna, 123–24

Ferrick, Melissa, 47

Festival!, 101

Fields, Paisley, 37

Filene, Benjamin, 11, 175; on folk music, 75, 76, 161; *Romancing the Folk*, 198; on roots music, 99

Fink, Cathy, 104, 106, *108*

Fire, Kathy: *Songs of Fire*, 84–85

Firkus, Brian (Trixie Mattel), 2, 28, 173–81; audience of, 175, 178, 224n9; authenticity of, 176–77; autoharp playing, 176; camp humor of, 175; collaboration with Peck, 185; cosmetic line of, 181; drag comedy videos, 181; experience of homophobia, 177; gay camp performance, 177; Haggerty and, *179*, 179–80, *180*; intellectual/political discourse of, 178; as Other, 181; at Philadelphia Folk Festival, 178–79; queer country politics of, 185; in *RuPaul's Drag Race All Stars*, 173, *174*; sincerity of, 24, 177, 178–79, 185, 186, 188–89; success of, 181; at Temple University, *180*; trans listeners of, 178; use of humor, 178; venues played, 194–95; vocals of, *174*; as working-class gay male artist, 179; working-class upbringing of, 181. Works: *Barbara*, 179; "Goner," 181; "Mama Don't Make Me Put On the Dress Again," 178; *Two Birds*, 174, *174*–75

Floyd, George: murder of, 187

folklore: invention of, 160–61, 163; urban middle class and, 161

folk music: agrarian past of, 101; alternative historiographies of, 19; as alternative to corporate media, 100; archetypes of, 71; authenticity of, 30, 116, 160–61; Black Americans', 30, 76; Black Lives Matter movement and, 100, 102; class struggle in, 76; collectors of, 11; conventions of, 203n39; country music and, 30, 72, 76–77; as cultural invention, 75; development as genre, 11; discourses of, 71; distinctions from popular music, 100; in drag, 177–78, 179; effect of anticommunism on, 76; genre trouble of, 75–76; German, 116, 157; identity in, 10, 72, 127; intimacy of, 124;

market share of, 13; myths of, 161; naturalized, 12; naturalness of, 197; origins of, 75;
outsider populism of, 76, 161; outsiders in,
127; postrevival purposes of, 185; purpose
of, 30; queer/trans relationships to, 18;
sexual politics of, 30; socialism and, 100;
social justice and, 72, 100–102; soft/femi-
nine, 124; travelers in, 127; US-centric, 30;
"white racial heritage" in, 76
folk music collectors, 75; selectivity of, 30, 41
folk musicians, gay/lesbian: albums of,
84–86
folk musicians, lesbian, 82–86; women-focused venues for, 93
folk musicians, queer/trans, 121; versus cis-
gender/straight, 71; journey narratives
of, 124, 125–33
folk music industry: queer/trans people in,
13; relationship to gender/sexuality, 69
folk music revival, 76, 82; New Left consumption of, 155
Folkway Records, gay/lesbian records of,
84–85
Foster, Stephen: "Beautiful Dreamer," 147,
148; blackface minstrel songs of, 147, 148
Foucault, Michel, 9
Frith, Simon, 12, 78; on musical identity,
156; on musical production, 112–13; on
rule-breaking, 186
Fure, Tret, 124

Garafalo, Reebee: "Pop Goes to War," 204n41
Garfield, Andrew: in *Angels in America*,
223n27; in *We Exist*, 165–66, 169, 224n35
Garringer, Rae, 111
gas stations, 131; queer/trans meetings at,
219n13
Gauthier, Mary, 2, 112, 205n4; artists covering, 92; awards of, 91, 92–93; Dixie
Kitchen restaurant of, 91; early life of, 91;
on empathy through vulnerability, 199; at
Grand Ole Opry, 91–92; virtual concerts
of, 92. Works: *Drag Queens and Limousines*, 91; "I Drink," 91; *Rifles and Rosary
Beads*, 92, 113, 216n95; "When a Woman
Goes Cold," 92
Gay Community Social Services (Seattle),
sponsorship of *Lavender Country*, 25

gay/lesbian rights, 44; intersectionality
with other movements, 84; radicalism
in, 26
Gay Ole Opry, 1, 3; concern over irony, 51.
See also Pittelman, Karen; Queer Country Quarterly
gay people: lack of power, 36; Latinx, 158;
mentoring for, 170; structural oppression
of, 26. *See also* country musicians, gay
Geiser, Nell, 97
Geist, Dale Henry, 21
gender: ambiguity of, 73–74; assumptions of
fixity, 10; based on sexual desire, 9; deployment for self-valuation, 159; dysphoria, 141,
220n25; equation with genitalia, 149; essentialist view of, 208n52; ideological shaping
of, 44; nonbinary, 2, 15, 16, 22, 48, 65, 72,
74, 98, 116, 131, 141, 142, 154, 215n84, 218n111,
225n22; performance of, 74, 176, 182; race in
in (mis)representation of, 164; relationship
to genre, 8–13, 65, 72, 78, 79, 100, 117–18, 122;
representation on country radio, 227n45;
retirement from, 116–18, 157; social construction of, 10, 203n20, 208n52; stationary,
44, 74; vocal performance of, 217n104
gender binary: disruptions to, 120; heterosexually defined, 141; musical, 124; resistance
to, 116; in transgender narratives, 142
gender identity, 8–9; genre shifts and, 72–73;
nonnormative, 73–74; racial factors affecting, 142; versus sexual identity, 44. *See
also* identity
Genius, 192
genre: assumptions of fixity, 10; etymology
of, 8; nonnormative musicians' defining
of, 211n1; relationship to gender, 8–13, 65,
72, 78, 79, 100, 117–18, 122; social construction of, 10, 11
genres, musical: authenticity in, 78; cogenerative with identity, 122–24; determina-
tion of, 190; effect on human categorization, 75; expression of community in, 10,
11; gendered exclusions from, 11; gender
in, 8–9, 65, 117–19; gender/sexuality politics of, 80; identity in, 11, 12, 23, 70–71,
78, 79, 100, 153–56; identity politics of,
13, 20, 70, 71; intersectionality with identity categories, 71; juxtaposition in, 20;

genres, musical (*continued*): limiting, 70–71; performance of self in, 11; performers suitable for, 113; policing of, 71, 75; post-identity, 12; queer/trans peoples', 4, 8–13, 80; queer/trans relations to, 14; relationship of musicians to, 110–11; stereotypes in, 11–13

Gentry, Bobbie: "Fancy," 187

Geraghty, Tim, 85

Giddens, Rhiannon, 33, 203n33; IBMA keynote address (2017), 102; on musical hybridity, 162; "Rhiannon Giddens and What Folk Music Means," 162

Gilbert, Ronnie, 82; bisexuality of, 93; feminism of, 83

Gilbert and Sullivan, camp in, 52

Gilkyson, Eliza, 92

Gillman, Billy, 3

Girlyman, 16–19; American experience of, 19; bluegrass influence on, 18; identity politics of, 20; members of, 17; repertoire of, 17–18; sexuality of, 17; vocal harmony-folk-pop of, 18

Glasberg, E., 126

Gleaves, Sam, 2, 52; *Ain't We Brothers*, 7; Appalachian musical style, 106–7; banjo playing of, 106; "fabulachian" music of, 107; at Queer Country Quarterly, 104, 106; on queerness, 106

Goffman, Erving, 43; on spoiled identity, 52

Goldenrod, 31

Goldin-Perschbacher, Shana: "The World Has Made Me," 211n1

Grace, Laura Jane, 165–66, 169

Grammar, Tracy, 111

Grand Ole Opry, 1; exclusion of gay musicians, 2; Gauthier at, 91–92

Gravity Lounge, 16–17

Gray, Mary, 6–7, 111; on rural communities, 126, 130, 169, 170; on rural queer spaces, 168–69

Greaves, Brendan, 36

Greene, Jayson, 28, 29–30

Greenstein, Tylan, 18, 78; on musical genre, 70

Grelle, Jack, 32

Grindley, Lucas, 169

Grudzien, Peter: *The Unicorn*, 85

Gruning, Thomas: folk music ethnography of, 76; *Millennium Folk*, 203n39

Guthrie, Woody, 82; class struggle in music of, 76, 77

Haas, Shaleece, 49; *Real Boy*, 45, 115, 139, *139*, 218n106

Haggerty, Patrick, 24, 31; activism of, 34; appeal of country music to, 34, 42; authenticity of message, 35; careers of, 30; and censorship, 28, 205n14; choice of country music, 77; cisgender men and, 36, 69; on class struggle, 77; collaborators of, 32; country music industry on, 33–34; as elder gay icon, 37–38; family of, 25, 31; Firkus and, *179*, *179*–80, *180*; on folk/country music divisions, 76–77; on gay activism, 26, 84; gay Marxism of, 35, 36, 38, 53, 67; institutionalization of, 25, 204n3; interview with Goldin-Perschbacher, 33–38; male music producers' discovery of, 87; on meaning of gayness, 25–26, 205n10; at Nashville, 84; in Peace Corps, 25; Peck and, *186*; performances of, 32–33; political goals of, 37, 38; radicalness, 38; on stardom, 37; StoryCorps interview, 32; and tenant dairy farmers, 25, 204n2; on truth in music, 38–39; venues for, 35–36. See also *Lavender Country*

Hail, Ewen: "Lavender Cowboy," 81

Hajdu, David, 93, 95

Halberstam, Jack, 8, 9; *Trans**, 45

Hall, Ryman, 99, 100

Hall, Vera: "Trouble So Hard," 196

Halperin, David, 170

Hanseroth, Tim and Phil, 92, 198

Hargreaves, Tatiana, 102

Harlan Howard Songs, Gauthier with, 91

Harris, Jaimee, 92

Harris, J. P., 32

Hart, Rod: *Breakeroo*, 81; "CB Savage," 81–82

Hays, Lee, 82

Hee Haw, 3, 4

Heffington, Ryan, 170, 224n35

Hellerman, Fred, 82

Hemby, Natalie, 197, 198

Henry, Joe, 88

Herder, Johann Gottfried von, 10; on nation-state, 160; theory of folk, 75, 212n13

Herndon, Ty, 3; coming out, 89, 186; Concert for Love and Acceptance, 89, 90, 173; Foundation for Love and Acceptance, 89; LGBT advocacy, 89–90; pop country style of, 88–89; visibility politics of, 186
Hersey, Harold: "Lavender Cowboy," 81
heteronormativity: for breast cancer patients, 208n63; in country music industry, 33; medical maintenance of, 208n63; for transgender people, 48; urban standards of, 129
Highwaymen, 197
The Highwomen, 24, 103, 197–98; "Crowded Table," 198
Hill, Montero Lamar. *See* Lil Nas X
hillbilly music: country music's inception as, 190–91; distinction from "race records," 103; humor in, 59; sincerity in, 39; stereotypes of, 11, 61
hip hop, 159, 190, 225n22; distaste for, 191, 194
hobos, folk persona of, 134
Holt, Fabian, 99
homelessness, among nonnormative people, 126, 133, 165, 223n26
Homo Latte series (Chicago), 14
homophobia, 177; in country music, 3, 81; Jamaican, 164–65
homosexuality: "bad copy" theory of, 41–42; as species, 9; "spoiled identity" of, 52
honesty: in country music, 38–45; cultural notions of, 6. *See also* authenticity; sincerity
honky-tonk, 99; authenticity in, 58; bars, 58; versus countrypolitan, 60; hillbilly stereotypes in, 61; male viewpoint in, 58; vulnerability in, 58
The Hook, 16
hormone therapy, 220n17; and agricultural growth hormones, 132; effect on voice, 113–14, 217nn101–3
House, Son, 161, 169
Howard, Brittany, 215n73; *Jaime*, 103; "Leather Jacket," 103; whiteface performances, 103
Howard, Harlan, 5, 39, 92, 207n39
Hubbs, Nadine, 60, 82; on class and bigotry, 215n73; on cultural omnivores, 4, 118; *Rednecks, Queers, and Country Music*, 4,

221n37; on socioeconomic status, 193–94; on working-class bigotry, 111, 221n37; on working-class queerness, 4, 14, 39, 76, 77, 127, 130, 184
Huffman, Felicity, 145, 220n34
Hughes, Tyler, 52; Appalachian musical training, 106–7; at Queer Country Quarterly, 104, *106*; on queerness, 106
humor, in country music, 5–6, 57–60. *See also* camp humor, queer/trans
Hurray for the Riff Raff, 100, *101*

Ian, Janis, 106, 206n21
identity: appropriation of, 153, 155; bodily, 44; cogenerative with musical genre, 124; in country music, 4, 8, 16, 72, 80, 111, 127, 191; cultural ideas about, 12; disguised, 173; essentialist understandings of, 156, 159, 162, 191; fixed, 39; in folk music, 10, 72, 127; genre categories and, 70; heteronormative, 9; homosexual, 52; industrial capitalism and, 9; in journey narratives, 134; middle-class standards of, 129–30; mobile, 127; musical classification of, 10; in musical genres, 11, 12, 23, 70–71, 78, 79, 100, 153–56; music in formation of, 208n54; national, 24; North American understanding of, 24; performance of, 12, 23, 78, 156; post-, 12, 78–79; "real," 41; role of music in, 8–13, 208n54; social construction of, 18, 155, 156, 170; stereotypes of, 40; "truth" of, 44. *See also* self
identity, queer/trans: in country music, 8; gender, 9; musicians' engagement with, 7, 8; terminology for, 15–16
identity, transgender: genre changes and, 72; risks in, 216n98; vocal music and, 112–15
identity, working-class: in country music, 4, 14, 39, 76, 77, 127; queered gender and, 4, 14. *See also* working class
indie rock music: audience expectations of, 117; gender phobia in, 116–17
Indigo Girls, 2, 13, 24; Carlile with, 92; at Concert for Love and Acceptance, 90; with Epic Records, 94; political stances of, 94; Stevens and, 47–48; support from women's music community, 14
Innocente, Bobby, 31

International Association for the Study of Popular Music: Spoon's appearance at, 143

International Bluegrass Music Association (IBMA), 203n33; Diversity Showcase of, 15; Giddens's address to (2017), 102; Shout and Shine Showcase, 102, 107

International Gay Rodeo Association, 86

"Iron Hoof Outlaws: Orville Peck Fan Club," 185

irony, queer: in camp aesthetics, 52; in queer/trans country music, 51–55

Isbell, Jason: "If She Ever Leaves Me," 198

Isherwood, Christopher: on camp, 53; *The World in the Evening*, 52

Ives, Burl, 81

Jain, S. Lochlann, 208n63

James, Robin, 12, 187, 225n22; on post-genre, 78

Jennex, Craig, 143

Jennings, Dave, 55, 61

Jennings, Waylon, 192

Jensen, Joli, 58–59, 64

Jim Reeves Enterprises, 83

Joel, Billy: "New York State of Mind" tour, 85

Johnson, E. Patrick, 163

Jordan, Leslie, 199

Journal of Country Music, 87

journey narratives: authenticity in, 133–34; identity in, 134; queer/trans, 124, 125–33, 197; rural, 128–33; train, 134; of *Transamerica*, 145, 149, 150, 151

Kahn, Si: *New Wood*, 85

Kang, Danny, 190

Karen and the Sorrows, 32–33, 80, *105*; sadness in repertoire, 51

Karkazis, Katrina, 44

Keil, Charles, 52

Kentucky, queer/trans youth in, 167

Key, Susan, 147

Kiah, Amythyst, 2, 14; Black American narratives of, 195, 196; Grammy nomination, 195; navigations of genre, 197; at Queer Country Quarterly, 104, 107, *108*, 109;

Rounder Records label, 196, 197; solo shows of, 196; stage banter of, 195. Works: "Black Myself," 109, 195–97; "Trouble So Hard" cover, 196; *Wary + Strange*, 196

Kienzle, Rich, 55

Kio, Young, 190

Kirby, Jason, 99

Kisliuk, Michelle, 204n40, 211n117

Knapp, Raymond, 52

Koenig, Ryan, 32

Krell, Elena Elias, 123; "Contours through Covers," 217nn102–3; on gender and genre, 79

Kun, Josh, 199

labeling: oppression through, 9; of transgender people, 169

labor songs, 1, 86, 104

Lafser, Jesse, 103

lang, k.d.: ambiguity of gender, 59–60; Americana of, 86; audience of, 60–61; awards of, 69, 210n89; Canadianness of, 67; coming out of, 61–62; country music of, 2, 6, 55–61, 68; countrypolitan influence on, 59; gender/sexuality in music of, 210n89, 210n98; honesty of, 67; influences on, 62; Lone Ranger poses of, 55, *56*, 57, 61; performance art studies, 55; popularity of, 62; shift from country music, 61, 62; sincerity of, 23, 55, 122; support for honky-tonk, 58; support for Nashville Sound, 58; on urbanized music, 57; use of humor, 55, 57, 59, 60; work with Bradley, 213n35. Works: *Absolute Torch and Twang*, 57; *Angel with a Lariat*, 86; "Bopalena," 86, 213n44; *Even Cowgirls Get the Blues* soundtrack, 86; "Pollyann," 60; *Shadowland*, 86; *A Truly Western Experience*, 59, 86

Lavender Country, 2, 23, 25–29, *27*; banned songs of, 28; censorship of, 205n14; country music industry on, 33–34; "Cryin' These Cocksucking Tears," 28–29, 31–33, 181, 205n14; distribution of, 31; goal of, 37; honesty of, 39; intersectionality of, 28; production of, 26; rediscovery of, 31–33, 35; reissue of, 31–32,

88, 172; release of, 25; sales of, 30. *See also* Haggerty, Patrick
Lavender Country band, 31, 36, 199; dissolution of, 84; "I Can't Shake the Stranger (out of You)," 179, 181
Lavender Country Revisited, 31
LaVenture, Liz, 118, 120
Leap, Braden, 4
Ledbetter, Huddie (Leadbelly), 76
Lee, Ang: *Brokeback Mountain*, 144
Leiber, Jerry, 225n21; "Jackson," 185
Lerner, Murray, 101, 161
Lesbian and Gay Country Music Association, 87
lesbians: folk musicians, 82–86; socialization in country bars, 209n70; working-class, 61. *See also* country musicians, lesbian
Lewis, A. J., 7–8, 19; at Another Country Festival, 96; on "The Cuckoo," 97–98; "Darling Corey," 95–96; morphine songs of, 97; queer theory of old-time music, 96–97
Lil Nas X (Montero Lamar Hill), 188–93; authenticity of, 193; awards for, 194; coming out, 192; costume of, *189*; country/trap music combination, 189; cowboy persona of, 189, 192–93, 194; dance moves, 194; evasion of country music process, 191; gay camp humor of, 24; as outlaw musician, 192; pandemic cancellations, 194; queerness of, 193; remixes of, 192; removal from *Billboard* country chart, 189, 190–91; social media following of, 189–90, 191; trap music of, 191. Works: "Old Town Road," 2, 173, 189–93; "34 Ghosts IV" sampling, 190
Lomax, Alan, 82, 196
Lomax, John, 76
Longwood Gardens, *109*
Lynn, Loretta, 198

Maass, Micha, 121
Mac and Strikeback, 114, *115*
Maguire, Martie, 204n41
Maines, Nathalie, 204n41
Makeba, Miriam, 145

Mancari, Becca, 103
manhood, North American ideals of, 48. *See also* heteronormativity
Mapes, Jillian, 215n73
Marcus, Greil, 97–98
marginalized people: artistic representation of, 154–55; categorization of, 156; dance clubs of, 158; distrust of, 40; by gender/sexuality, 71; identities of, 156–57; queer/trans narratives of, 27; vulnerability of, 197. *See also* nonnormative people; Othered people
Marxer, Marcy, 106, *108*
Massek, Sue, 86
Mattel, Trixie. *See* Firkus, Brian
Mayo, Danny: "Feed Jake," 82
McAnally, Shane, 89
McCall, C. W.: "Convoy," 81
McCracken, Allison, 183
McIntire, Reba: "Fancy" cover, 187–88
McKenna, Lori, 198
McMullen, Chelsea, 65; *My Prairie Home*, 65–66, 157
Meyerowitz, Joanne, 205n10; on transgender narrative, 138–39
Michigan Womyn's Music Festival: trans women at, 94–95
middle class: as intolerant, 4; as "normal," 163, 184; as tolerant, 13, 166, 169; as tourists, 220n15; consumption of blackface, 147–48; country music listeners, 147, 184; cultural appropriation by, 154, 159, 170; cultural omnivorism of, 4, 165, 194; folklore and, 161; standards of gender/sexuality 132, 142
Milk, Harvey: assassination of, 206n21
Miller, Karl Hagstrom, 11, 76
Minax, Madsen: *Riot Acts*, 74, 212n11, 217n102
Moby: accusations of appropriation against, 196–97. Works: "Natural Blues," 196; *Play*, 196–97, 227n42
Mock, Janet: *Redefining Realness*, 45
Mockus, Martha, 60–61
Morris, Eve, 28, 206n19; and Baez, 29–30; lesbian feminism of, 29
Morris, Maren, 197
Morris, Shane, 191, 226n29

Mouths of Babes, 72; genre trouble of, 70
music: categorization of, 75, 196; communication through, 157; cultural appropriation of, 153, 155; as labor, 21, 207n42; ownership of, 153, 155; post-genre, 12; racial impersonation in, 155; role in identity, 8–13, 208n54; shared knowledge through, 26; as socioaesthetics, 204n40; transgenre, 79; truth in, 3–5, 38–39, 41, 68, 156; unity in, 9. *See also* country music; names of musical genres
music, queer/trans: by cisgender musicians, 153; rebelliousness in, 12
music festivals, women's: queer/trans participants in, 12
musicians: addiction among, 207n42; coming out, 46; gender-marginalized, 71; gender nonnormative, 211n1; Generation X/Y, 104; inauthentic costumes of, 161; negotiation of self, 71; physical performance of, 207n42; post-genre, 78. *See also* country musicians; folk musicians
musicians, cisgender: male privilege among, 117; queer/trans music by, 153
musicians, gay: gay press coverage of, 94; marketing of, 94
musicians, queer/trans: Appalachian, 104; autobiographical work, 170; coalitional politics of, 23; engagement with country music, 80; engagement with identity, 7; gender/genre transitions of, 23; gender identity of, 9; mentoring by, 172; music/genre relationships for, 12–13, 80; narratives of, 27; negotiations with country music, 23; paying audience for, 79–80; in progressive festivals, 15; rural/working-class symbols of, 129; straight allies of, 172; straight/cisgender audiences of, 80; "trans" genre of, 79. *See also* country musicians, queer/trans
musicians, transgender: identity/genre changes of, 72; singers, 112–15; transgenre music of, 79
"musicking," 3, 201n4
My Gay Banjo, 20, 36–37; audiences of, 104; explicit queerness of, 46; framing of genre, 80; members of, 104, 106; queer-

ness of, 104; queer/trans audience of, 106. Works: "Bombs Away," 158; *Country Boys in the City*, 105
My Prairie Home, 65–66, 157, 223n24; audience reactions in, 66, 67, 68. *See also* Spoon, Rae

Nashville, 92
Near, Holly, 83
Negus, Keith, 156
Nelson, Willie, 118, 210n109
New Left: consumption of folk revival, 155; failure of, 170
Newport Folk Festival, gay roots showcase, 15
Newton, Esther, 52
Nine Inch Nails: "34 Ghosts IV," 190
nonnormative people: categorization of, 157; homelessness among, 126, 133, 165, 223n26; as "unheard," 101–2; violence against, 41. *See also* marginalized people; Othered people
Nordell, Justin, 179
Nordmarken, Sonny, 44, 73–74
Now This News, Mattel/Firkus interview, 181

O Brother, Where Art Thou?, 99, 100; country/folk music of, 146–47
Okies, folk persona of, 134
Oklahoma Cyclone, 81
old-time music: death in, 96–97; queerness of, 19, 95–99; Southern, 98
Orbison, Roy, 183, 210n89
O'Rourke, Beto: senatorial campaign of, 64, 211n109
Othered people: as common people, 161; country music's misuse of, 152; relationship to identity categories, 155; sincerity for, 43–44. *See also* marginalized people; nonnormative people
Otherness: appropriation of, 160, 199; as authentic, 154; in country music, 152, 184, 198; essentialized notions of, 163; individuation and, 157–58; performance of, 154–55; sincerity in, 24; tokenized, 102; vulnerability to appropriation, 160
Our Lady J, 224n35

Our Native Daughters, 24, 109

Owen, Taylor, 104, 106. Works: "Bombs Away," 158; "Country Boys in the City," 106

Paisley, Brad, 89, 186

Paradise of Bachelors, 31, 172

Parton, Dolly, 1, 4, 118; autoharp playing, 175; drag queens imitating, 20; "hillbilly humanism" of, 151. Works: "Travelin' Thru," 24, 150–51; "Wayfaring Stranger" recording, 222n48

Paycheck, Johnny: "Take This Job and Shove It," 212n12

Peck, Orville, 2, 182–88, *183*; artistic agenda of, 182, 186; childhood of, 183; Coachella booking (cancelled), 194; collaborations of, 185, 225n22; desire for anonymity, 182, 224n13; disguise of, 173; fans of, 185; gender performance of, 182; Haggerty and, *186*; identity of, 224n13; "indie" music elements, 188; loneliness in music of, 183–84; Lone Ranger persona of, 182, 186; pandemic cancellations, 194; post-identity/post-genre opportunities, 187; queer country politics of, 185; sincerity of, 24, 184, 185, 186, 188–89; singing style of, 182–83; use of gesture, 185; use of masking, 182, 184–85. Works: "Fancy" cover, 187–88; "Legends Never Die," 188; *Pony*, 173, 184; *Show Pony* EP, 187–88

Pecknold, Diane, 11

Peer, Ralph, 162

Pellegrini, Ann, 53, 55

Pennington, Stephan, 44; on marginalized people's identity, 156–57; on transgender risks, 142; on transgender voices, 112; on vocal performance, 217n104

performance: critically sincere, 54; fictional aspects of, 22; of self, 6, 11, 199. *See also* identity, performance of

Peter, Paul, and Mary, 28

Peters, Gretchen, 92

Peterson, Clyde, 116, 212n20

Peterson, Richard, 6, 11, 161, 175; *Creating Country Music*, 39–40; on musical genre, 99; on traditional country music, 176; on traditional versus popular style, 77

Philadelphia Folk Song Society, 37

PhilaMOCA (Philadelphia Mausoleum of Contemporary Art), 37

Pierce, Webb, 213n44

Pittelman, Karen, 1, 201n6; Another Country festival, 95; Appalachian musicians and, 104; concern over irony, 51, 52; and Country Music Against White Supremacy, 69; experiences as Jewish woman, 51; on homophobia, 3; on political use of "country," 80; QCQ audience of, 209n70; Trans Justice Funding Project, 95; and Wright, 90–91. *See also* Gay Ole Opry; Queer Country Quarterly

popular music: distinctions from folk, 100; transgender voices in, 217n101

populism, outsider, 76, 161, 169, 198–99

postmodernism: critique of authenticity, 53–55; critique of essentialism, 24; role-playing in, 43; sincerity in, 54

Presley, Elvis, 210n94

Progress, Eurocentric narrative of, 160

progressive music: human rights in, 34–35; marketability of, 15

Proulx, Annie: "Brokeback Mountain," 144

Pulse Nightclub (Orlando), mass shooting at, 158

"queer," etymologies of, 41

Queer Country Quarterly, 1, 7, 14; audience appreciation at, 51–52, 209n70; community building by, 173; queer/trans musicians at, 79; radicalism of, 91, 199; sexual/gender identifications and, 104. *See also* Gay Ole Opry; Pittelman, Karen

Queer Country West, queer/trans musicians at, 79

Queer Folk Fest, 92

Queer Music Heritage, 212nn29–30

queerness: in country music, 81–82, 184; of My Gay Banjo, 46; of old-time music, 19, 95–99; at Queer Country Quarterly, 106; queer/trans musicians' deniability of, 78; regional difference in, 131–32; revolutionary, 23; in rural spaces, 168–69; visibility politics of, 168; working-class, 4, 14, 39, 60, 76, 77, 97, 127, 130 queer/trans people: appeal of country music to, 5, 19; assumptions concerning, 111; camp humor of, 3; cisgenders' interrogation of, 43–44; concept of truth for, 45; demographics of, 15; depiction in country music, 211n4; diversity of practices among, 135; exclusions from the normative, 197; explanations of self, 6; mainstream assumptions concerning, 78; music genres of, 4, 8–13, 80; narratives of, 23; negative experiences of, 126; "queered" social position, 97; surveillance of, 202n14; terminology of, 15. *See also* country musicians, queer/trans; musicians, queer/trans; transgender people

queer/trans people, rural, 6–7, 125–33, 168–69, 170; danger for, 130; ethics of familiarity, 7; scholarship on, 202n16; Southern experiences of, 125–27

race, in (mis)representation of gender, 164
race music, 11; stereotypes in, 40
racism, structural, 222n5
radical faerie communes (Tenn.), 132, 220n15
Rainbow Squad, 89
Ramsey, Mason, 192
Ray, Amy, 24, 47; antiracist activism of, 125, 127, 151; "butch throat" of, 126; negotiation of boundaries, 125–26; northern Georgia home of, 127; on women's music scene, 93–94. Works: "Oyster and Pearl," 129; "Sure Feels Good Anyway," 125–27
Raymond, Janice: *The Transsexual Empire*, 202n13
Reagan, Toshi, 14
Real Boy, 45, 115, 139, 139, 218n106
The Reclines, 58
Red Dead Redemption, 190
Reel World String Band, 86, 104
Reeves, Mary, 83
Rich, Ruby, 209n70
Riot Acts, 74, 212n11, 217n102
RM, 192
Robbins, Courtney, 47
Roberts, Brian, 147
Roberts, Paddy: "Lavender Cowboy," 81
Robinson, Tom: "Lavender Cowboy" cover, 81
rockabilly music, 58, 210n94

rock music: dark/masculine, 124; queer country musicians' use of, 80; rule breaking in, 78
Rodgers, Jimmie, 40; hybrid music of, 162
Rogers, Jimmie N., 39
Rolling Stone, on "Old Town Road," 190
Román Velázquez, Patria, 156
Root, Deane, 147
roots music, 98–100
Roseanne, reboot of, 45
Rosenberg, Neil, 11
Ross, Kameron, 213n44
Rosskam, Jules, 212n11
Rubin, Gayle: on gender/sexuality division, 141–42
Ru Paul's Drag Race, 2, 170, 181, 195
Ru Paul's Drag Race All Stars: Mattel/Firkus in, 173, 174
rural life: country music imagery of, 127–28; familiarity in, 7, 169; journey narratives of, 128–33; oppression in, 41; queer/trans people in, 125–33, 168–69, 170; in *Transamerica*, 128
rural spaces: danger in, 130; environmental damage to, 130; mutual help in, 126; queerness in, 168–69; as spaces of death, 129, 142–43; transgender women in, 170; venues of, 117; visibility in, 169

Saliers, Emily, 2, 47
Sanders, Bernie: presidential campaign (2016), 36
Sandifer, Elizabeth: "The Wasted Daughter of the Moon," 216n89
Scherr, Rebecca, 149
Schilt, Kristen, 208n59
Schwarzenegger, Arnold, 17
Sedgwick, Eve Kosofsky, 19
Seeger, Pete, 82
Segarra, Alynda, 100, 185; definition of folk music, 102; "Fall in Love with Justice," 100–102; Puerto Rican roots of, 101, 102; train journeys of, 134; on voicelessness, 101–2
self: cultural markers of, 155; display of resources for, 159; performance of, 6, 11, 199; queer/trans country musicians' performance of, 6; sung performances of, 112–13. *See also* identity

Self, Ronnie, 213n44

sexuality: deployment for self-valuation, 159; essentialist view of, 208n52; ideological shaping of, 44; social construction of, 208n52; versus gender identity, 44

Shakira, 20

Shank, Barry, 154–55, 170

Shannon Records, 83

Sharp, Cecil, 203n31; *English Folk Songs from the Southern Appalachians*, 75–76, 103

Shepard, Matthew: murder of, 130

Shires, Amanda, 197, 198

Silveira, Lucas, 69; audience perception of, 123, 124; coming out as transgender, 122–23; reception of his music, 123; roots imagery of, 123; shift to rock music, 72; suppression of self, 124

sincerity: actors' conveying of, 42–43; as aesthetic mode, 54; as affective process, 54; antiessentialism in, 54; audiences', 51; camp and, 53; corporeal, 43; in country music, 3, 6, 22–23, 38–45, 172–73; critical, 54; in early modern European society, 42; essentialism of, 22, 39; in hillbilly music, 39; inner truth in, 42; irony within, 54; as mode of self-expression, 40–41; in North American culture, 53; for Othered people, 43–44; in Otherness, 24; in postmodernism, 54; queer, 6, 24, 55, 110, 143; in queer/trans country music, 6, 42, 55, 110; as unchanging, 40. *See also* authenticity

singing. *See* vocal music; voice

Skeggs, Beverley, 159, 160, 161

Sloop, John, 60, 61–62

Small, Christopher, 201n4

Smith, Christopher, 36

snake oil, 225n22

social justice: folk music and, 72, 100–102; politics of revival, 176

Sons of Erin, "Lavender Cowboy" cover, 81

Sontag, Susan, 51, 52

South: queer activism in, 126; recording industry in, 98; rural queer/trans experiences in, 125–27. *See also* rural spaces

Spade, Dean, 141

Spencer, Brittney, 198

Spencer, Sid, 86; albums of, 87; death of, 87

Spoon, Rae, 2, 62–69, 67, 68; Alberta experiences of, 62–63, 65; art grants to, 205n4;

audiences of, 66, 67, 118; authenticity of, 158–59, 171; autobiographies of, 144; banjo playing, 157; childhood of, 62–64; critique of racism, 155; departure from country music, 69; discrimination facing, 117, 118; electronic music techniques of, 116; family of, 62, 63, 64–65, 66; feelings of misplacement, 64; on folk myth, 161; on gender-based violence, 131; on gender/genre, 65, 110; on genre change, 72–73; on German folk music, 116; identification as songwriter, 117–18; identification with cowboys, 63–65, 159; on indie rock, 116–17; influences on, 64; at International Association for the Study of Popular Music, 143; move from Alberta, 62–63; on musical identity, 157; nonbinary identity of, 154, 218n111, 218n113; Otherness in work of, 155; "performance art" albums of, 65; pronoun preferences, 217n103; on queer sincerity, 110; retirement from gender, 116–18, 157; on rural spaces, 142–43; sense of self, 65–66; sincerity of, 23, 65; song writing, 157; "Tourism Alberta" parody, 144; transgender identification of, 62–63; use of appropriation, 155; use of humor, 110, 131; venues of, 65, 66, 67, 68, 117; and *We Exist*, 163–64. Works: *Armour*, 153; "Come On Forest Fire, Burn the Disco Down," 157–58, 170; "Cowboy," 65–66; *Gender Failure*, 64, 109, 116, 218n111; *How to (Hide) Be(hind) Your Songs*, 65, 158–59; "Keep the Engine Running," 24, 131; "A Message from the Queer Trans Prairie Tourism Co.," 24, 143–45, 220n32; "Stolen Song," 24, 153, 157, 163–64, 170; "Sunday Dress," 62. *See also My Prairie Home*

Stallings, L. H., 132

Stamply, Joe: "Honky Tonk Queen," 82

Staples, Mavis, 93

Stephens, Vincent, 62, 78; *Rocking the Closet*, 213n36

Stevens, Doug, 87

Stevens, Joe, 2, 24; alcohol addiction, 47, 48; bluegrass influences on, 141; on *Body Alchemy*, 134–35; Christians' criticism of, 140; earned identity of, 47; family of, 49; former name of, 49; gender identity of, 48, 49; gender transition of, 46, 47;

Stevens, Joe (*continued*): girlhood of, 140; at girls' reform school, 47–48; great grandfather's home, 137; interest in bondage, 134; life on the road, 133, 134, 138, 151; pre-transition life of, 47–48, 49; queer/trans-themed songs of, 47; in *Real Boy*, 115, 139, *139*; relationship with listeners, 115; #RoadDog handle of, 133; socialization as female, 46; Songs of the People project, 113; Sprinter van of, *138*; stage banter of, 48; tour with Coyote Grace, 47; transgender experiences of, 46, 151; and transition, 134–35, 140, 149; workshops of, 115; XX tatoo of, 49, *50*. Works: "Daughter-son," 140–41, 221n41; "A Guy Named Joe," 47; "Man in the Moon," 115

Stone, Sandy: "The Empire Strikes Back," 139–40

Stonewall Rebellion (1969), 26, 84

Stowe, Harriet Beecher: *Uncle Tom's Cabin*, 147

straight men, 97; crossdressing of, 178; Haggerty's relation to, 28, 36, 69; homophobia of, 181

Strange Fire, 14, 21

Strikeback, Simon Fisher: packer of, 132; singing voice of, 114. Works: *Riot Acts*, 74, 212n11; "TN Tranny Two-Step," 131–32, 151, 219n14

Sukop, Syliva, 133–34

Sweet Violet Boys (Prairie Ramblers), 182; "I Love My Fruit," 5, 82

Tambor, Jeffrey, 220n34

Taylor, Jane, 40–41, 44

teachers, gay/lesbian: banning of, 206n21

Teena, Brandon: murder of, 130

Telecommunications Act (1996), 204n41

Thornton, Kevin James, 21

Three Women and the Truth, 92

Thunderbitch, 103

Tillis, Mel, 213n44

Tompkins, Chris, 198

Tower Records, roots room of, 100

Toynbee, Jason, 11

Trans 101, 47

Transamerica: Americana music in, 145–48, 150–51; characters of color in, 147; cisgen-der audience of, 147, 151; editing of, 148; ending of, 149; gendered speaking voice in, 150; journey theme of, 145, 149, 150, 151; poster for, *146*; queer/trans humanity in, 151; racial politics in, 221n38; rural life in, 128; surgery in, 145, 149; transition in, 145; use of Otherness, 152; vocal agency in, 221n47; white working class in, 148–49

transgender children, family support for, 215n84

transgender men: acceptance in cisgender society, 216n98; reward for transitioning, 208n59; testosterone levels of, 114; ties with queer community, 216n98; voices of, 150, 217n101; in women-only spaces, 48

transgender narratives, 138–40; assimilation versus revolution in, 142; gender binary in, 142; medicalized, 132, 133, *139*, 141; "wrong body" in, 139

transgender people: appeal of ordinary life to, 45; contingency in lives of, 216n89; as deceptive, 44, 48, 49; ethnography of, 78; former names of, 49; gender dysphoria diagnosis for, 141; heteronormative, 114; heterosexual gender binary of, 217n100; labeling by aid workers, 169; means of communication among, 205n10; media engagement of, 78; risks for, 142; sharing of experiences, 46; stereotypes of, 74; upholding of heteronormativity, 48; use of mixed-gender references, 48; violence against, 48, 131; vocal adaptations of, 113–14; welcome in country music, 110–12. *See also* country musicians, transgender; musicians, transgender; queer/trans people

transgender women: Americana singer-songwriters, 120; exclusion from feminism, 213n42; in lesbian feminist organizations, 121; risks for, 216n98; in rural spaces, 170; vocal persona of, 45; voices of, 114. *See also* women

"Transitioning Together," 47

Transparent, 220n34

travel, danger in, 129. *See also* journey narratives

Travis, Randy, 64; gay song elements of, 19

Trevor Project, 223n26
Trigger. *See* Coroneos, Kyle "The Trigger-man"
Trilling, Lionel: on sincerity, 42–43
trucker hats, as class markers, 159
Trump, Donald, 52
truth: in art, 23; bodily expression of, 43, 44; essentializing of, 3; gender assigned at birth perceived as, 44; of identity, 44; in music, 3–5, 38–39, 41, 68, 156; "possession" of, 73; queer theory and, 45; in queer/trans country music, 68; sincerity and, 42. *See also* authenticity
Tucker, Duncan: *Transamerica*, 145–52
Tucker, Tanya, 93
Twain, Sania, 188

Uncle Tupelo, 99
U.S. Transgender Population Health Survey, 223n26

Vadim, Roger: use of camp, 52
Valentine, David, 169
Välimäki, Susanna, 146, 221n41
Vallee, Rudy, 183
van Alphen, Ernst, 43
Vegan, Brooklyn, 224n13
vocal music: performance of self in, 112–13; transgender identity and, 112–15
Vogel, Lisa, 95
voice: cultural appropriation of, 160, 161; cultural construction of, 112; effect of hormone therapy on, 113–14, 217nn101–3; gendered tendencies in, 113, 217n104; politics of, 160; socioaesthetic analysis of, 217n104
Volk: eighteenth-century concept of, 75. *See also* folklore
Volkslieder, 10

Wald, Elijah, 11; on roots music, 99
Wallace, Ben, 49; in *Real Boy*, 45, 115, 139, 218n106; on transition journey, 149
Wallace, Henry Agard: presidential campaign, 82
Wallen, Morgan, 226n22
Watson, Jada, 197; "Gender Representation on Country Format Radio," 4–5

The Weavers: repertoire, 82–83; social justice issues of, 100–101
We Exist, 163–70; at Coachella, 166–67, *167, 168*; conflation between gay and transgender people, 169; criticisms of, 165–66, 169; dance in, 166, *167*, 169–70; dream sequence of, *167*; masking in, 170; narrative stereotypes of, 165; Spoon and, 163–64; transgender abuse in, 166, 169; transgender character of, 165–67, 169–70; visibility in, 169. *See also* Arcade Fire; "We Exist"
"We Exist," 223n24; narrator of, 164
Welch, Gillian, 41
Wheeler, Billy Edd: "Jackson," 185
white flight, 154
Whiteley, Sheila, 62
Whole Foods, labor practices of, 165
Wilde, Oscar: on masks, 53
Williams, Hank, 159; authenticity of, 64; loneliness in music of, 183; "Lovesick Blues," 192; on sincerity, 39; spina bifida occulta of, 39
Williams, Lucinda, 112
Williams Institute, 223n26
Wilson, David, 165, 167
Wish Me Away, 89, *90*
womanhood, folk singing and, 119, 124
women: music festivals, 12; objectification in country music, 4–5; omission from classical music canon, 75; "rounders," 95–96; "womyn-born," 48, 95; working-class, 129. *See also* cisgender women; country musicians, women; lesbians; transgender women
women composers, exclusion from classical music, 10
women's music: audience of, 121–22, 124; emotional palette of, 123–24; festivals, 12; venues of, 93–95
working class: assumptions of bigotry concerning, 111, 221n37; identities in country music, 4, 14, 39, 76, 77, 127; lesbian, 61; markers of, 159–60; as nonnormative, 61; queerness, 4, 14, 39, 76, 77, 97, 127, 130; queerness of, 60; "realness" of, 45; suffering, 39
Wright, Chely (Richell Renee), 2, 3, 14, *90*; activism of, 91; at AmericanaFest, 88;

Wright, Chely (Richell Renee) (*continued*): awards of, 89; charity activity, 89; coming out, 122, 186; genre shift of, 88, 122; Kickstarter fundraising, 88, 205n4; with MCA Nashville Records, 88; Unispace position of, 89; visibility politics of, 186. Works: *I Am the Rain*, 88; *Like Me*, 89
Wyeth, Geo, 217n102

Yola, 103, 198
Young, Brett: "Lady," 90
Young, Robin, 148
Young Thug, 192

Zamolodchikova, Katya, 181, 195
Zapf, Amy, 121

Shana Goldin-Perschbacher is an assistant professor of music studies in the Boyer College of Music and Dance at Temple University.

MUSIC IN AMERICAN LIFE

Only a Miner: Studies in Recorded Coal-Mining Songs *Archie Green*
Great Day Coming: Folk Music and the American Left *R. Serge Denisoff*
John Philip Sousa: A Descriptive Catalog of His Works *Paul E. Bierley*
The Hell-Bound Train: A Cowboy Songbook *Glenn Ohrlin*
Oh, Didn't He Ramble: The Life Story of Lee Collins, as Told to Mary Collins
    Edited by Frank J. Gillis and John W. Miner
American Labor Songs of the Nineteenth Century *Philip S. Foner*
Stars of Country Music: Uncle Dave Macon to Johnny Rodriguez
    Edited by Bill C. Malone and Judith McCulloh
Git Along, Little Dogies: Songs and Songmakers of the American West *John I. White*
A Texas-Mexican *Cancionero*: Folksongs of the Lower Border *Américo Paredes*
San Antonio Rose: The Life and Music of Bob Wills *Charles R. Townsend*
Early Downhome Blues: A Musical and Cultural Analysis *Jeff Todd Titon*
An Ives Celebration: Papers and Panels of the Charles Ives Centennial Festival-
    Conference *Edited by H. Wiley Hitchcock and Vivian Perlis*
Sinful Tunes and Spirituals: Black Folk Music to the Civil War *Dena J. Epstein*
Joe Scott, the Woodsman-Songmaker *Edward D. Ives*
Jimmie Rodgers: The Life and Times of America's Blue Yodeler *Nolan Porterfield*
Early American Music Engraving and Printing: A History of Music Publishing in America
    from 1787 to 1825, with Commentary on Earlier and Later Practices *Richard J. Wolfe*
Sing a Sad Song: The Life of Hank Williams *Roger M. Williams*
Long Steel Rail: The Railroad in American Folksong *Norm Cohen*
Resources of American Music History: A Directory of Source Materials from Colonial
    Times to World War II *D. W. Krummel, Jean Geil, Doris J. Dyen, and Deane L. Root*
Tenement Songs: The Popular Music of the Jewish Immigrants *Mark Slobin*
Ozark Folksongs *Vance Randolph; edited and abridged by Norm Cohen*
Oscar Sonneck and American Music *Edited by William Lichtenwanger*
Bluegrass Breakdown: The Making of the Old Southern Sound *Robert Cantwell*
Bluegrass: A History *Neil V. Rosenberg*
Music at the White House: A History of the American Spirit *Elise K. Kirk*
Red River Blues: The Blues Tradition in the Southeast *Bruce Bastin*
Good Friends and Bad Enemies: Robert Winslow Gordon and the Study of American
    Folksong *Debora Kodish*
Fiddlin' Georgia Crazy: Fiddlin' John Carson, His Real World, and the World
    of His Songs *Gene Wiggins*
America's Music: From the Pilgrims to the Present (rev. 3d ed.) *Gilbert Chase*
Secular Music in Colonial Annapolis: The Tuesday Club, 1745–56 *John Barry Talley*
Bibliographical Handbook of American Music *D. W. Krummel*
Goin' to Kansas City *Nathan W. Pearson Jr.*
"Susanna," "Jeanie," and "The Old Folks at Home": The Songs of Stephen C. Foster from
    His Time to Ours (2d ed.) *William W. Austin*

Songprints: The Musical Experience of Five Shoshone Women   *Judith Vander*

"Happy in the Service of the Lord": Afro-American Gospel Quartets in Memphis
   Kip Lornell

Paul Hindemith in the United States   *Luther Noss*

"My Song Is My Weapon": People's Songs, American Communism, and the Politics of
   Culture, 1930–50   *Robbie Lieberman*

Chosen Voices: The Story of the American Cantorate   *Mark Slobin*

Theodore Thomas: America's Conductor and Builder of Orchestras, 1835–1905
   Ezra Schabas

"The Whorehouse Bells Were Ringing" and Other Songs Cowboys Sing
   Collected and Edited by Guy Logsdon

Crazeology: The Autobiography of a Chicago Jazzman   *Bud Freeman,*
   as Told to Robert Wolf

Discoursing Sweet Music: Brass Bands and Community Life in Turn-of-the-Century
   Pennsylvania   *Kenneth Kreitner*

Mormonism and Music: A History   *Michael Hicks*

Voices of the Jazz Age: Profiles of Eight Vintage Jazzmen   *Chip Deffaa*

Pickin' on Peachtree: A History of Country Music in Atlanta, Georgia   *Wayne W. Daniel*

Bitter Music: Collected Journals, Essays, Introductions, and Librettos   *Harry Partch;*
   edited by Thomas McGeary

Ethnic Music on Records: A Discography of Ethnic Recordings Produced in the United
   States, 1893 to 1942   *Richard K. Spottswood*

Downhome Blues Lyrics: An Anthology from the Post–World War II Era   *Jeff Todd Titon*

Ellington: The Early Years   *Mark Tucker*

Chicago Soul   *Robert Pruter*

That Half-Barbaric Twang: The Banjo in American Popular Culture   *Karen Linn*

Hot Man: The Life of Art Hodes   *Art Hodes and Chadwick Hansen*

The Erotic Muse: American Bawdy Songs (2d ed.)   *Ed Cray*

Barrio Rhythm: Mexican American Music in Los Angeles   *Steven Loza*

The Creation of Jazz: Music, Race, and Culture in Urban America   *Burton W. Peretti*

Charles Martin Loeffler: A Life Apart in Music   *Ellen Knight*

Club Date Musicians: Playing the New York Party Circuit   *Bruce A. MacLeod*

Opera on the Road: Traveling Opera Troupes in the United States, 1825–60
   Katherine K. Preston

The Stonemans: An Appalachian Family and the Music That Shaped Their Lives
   Ivan M. Tribe

Transforming Tradition: Folk Music Revivals Examined   *Edited by Neil V. Rosenberg*

The Crooked Stovepipe: Athapaskan Fiddle Music and Square Dancing in Northeast
   Alaska and Northwest Canada   *Craig Mishler*

Traveling the High Way Home: Ralph Stanley and the World of Traditional
   Bluegrass Music   *John Wright*

Carl Ruggles: Composer, Painter, and Storyteller   *Marilyn Ziffrin*

Never without a Song: The Years and Songs of Jennie Devlin, 1865–1952
    Katharine D. Newman

The Hank Snow Story   *Hank Snow, with Jack Ownbey and Bob Burris*

Milton Brown and the Founding of Western Swing   *Cary Ginell,*
    with special assistance from Roy Lee Brown

Santiago de Murcia's "Códice Saldívar No. 4": A Treasury of Secular Guitar Music
    from Baroque Mexico   *Craig H. Russell*

The Sound of the Dove: Singing in Appalachian Primitive Baptist Churches
    Beverly Bush Patterson

Heartland Excursions: Ethnomusicological Reflections on Schools of Music   *Bruno Nettl*

Doowop: The Chicago Scene   *Robert Pruter*

Blue Rhythms: Six Lives in Rhythm and Blues   *Chip Deffaa*

Shoshone Ghost Dance Religion: Poetry Songs and Great Basin Context   *Judith Vander*

Go Cat Go! Rockabilly Music and Its Makers   *Craig Morrison*

'Twas Only an Irishman's Dream: The Image of Ireland and the Irish in American Popular
    Song Lyrics, 1800–1920   *William H. A. Williams*

Democracy at the Opera: Music, Theater, and Culture in New York City, 1815–60
    Karen Ahlquist

Fred Waring and the Pennsylvanians   *Virginia Waring*

Woody, Cisco, and Me: Seamen Three in the Merchant Marine   *Jim Longhi*

Behind the Burnt Cork Mask: Early Blackface Minstrelsy and Antebellum American
    Popular Culture   *William J. Mahar*

Going to Cincinnati: A History of the Blues in the Queen City   *Steven C. Tracy*

Pistol Packin' Mama: Aunt Molly Jackson and the Politics of Folksong   *Shelly Romalis*

Sixties Rock: Garage, Psychedelic, and Other Satisfactions   *Michael Hicks*

The Late Great Johnny Ace and the Transition from R&B to Rock 'n' Roll
    James M. Salem

Tito Puente and the Making of Latin Music   *Steven Loza*

Juilliard: A History   *Andrea Olmstead*

Understanding Charles Seeger, Pioneer in American Musicology   *Edited by Bell Yung*
    and Helen Rees

Mountains of Music: West Virginia Traditional Music from *Goldenseal*
    Edited by John Lilly

Alice Tully: An Intimate Portrait   *Albert Fuller*

A Blues Life   *Henry Townsend, as told to Bill Greensmith*

Long Steel Rail: The Railroad in American Folksong (2d ed.)   *Norm Cohen*

The Golden Age of Gospel   *Text by Horace Clarence Boyer;*
    photography by Lloyd Yearwood

Aaron Copland: The Life and Work of an Uncommon Man   *Howard Pollack*

Louis Moreau Gottschalk   *S. Frederick Starr*

Race, Rock, and Elvis   *Michael T. Bertrand*

Theremin: Ether Music and Espionage   *Albert Glinsky*

Poetry and Violence: The Ballad Tradition of Mexico's Costa Chica   *John H. McDowell*

The Bill Monroe Reader   *Edited by Tom Ewing*

Music in Lubavitcher Life   *Ellen Koskoff*

Zarzuela: Spanish Operetta, American Stage   *Janet L. Sturman*

Bluegrass Odyssey: A Documentary in Pictures and Words, 1966–86   *Carl Fleischhauer and Neil V. Rosenberg*

That Old-Time Rock & Roll: A Chronicle of an Era, 1954–63   *Richard Aquila*

Labor's Troubadour   *Joe Glazer*

American Opera   *Elise K. Kirk*

Don't Get above Your Raisin': Country Music and the Southern Working Class
   Bill C. Malone

John Alden Carpenter: A Chicago Composer   *Howard Pollack*

Heartbeat of the People: Music and Dance of the Northern Pow-wow   *Tara Browner*

My Lord, What a Morning: An Autobiography   *Marian Anderson*

Marian Anderson: A Singer's Journey   *Allan Keiler*

Charles Ives Remembered: An Oral History   *Vivian Perlis*

Henry Cowell, Bohemian   *Michael Hicks*

Rap Music and Street Consciousness   *Cheryl L. Keyes*

Louis Prima   *Garry Boulard*

Marian McPartland's Jazz World: All in Good Time   *Marian McPartland*

Robert Johnson: Lost and Found   *Barry Lee Pearson and Bill McCulloch*

Bound for America: Three British Composers   *Nicholas Temperley*

Lost Sounds: Blacks and the Birth of the Recording Industry, 1890–1919   *Tim Brooks*

Burn, Baby! BURN! The Autobiography of Magnificent Montague   *Magnificent Montague with Bob Baker*

Way Up North in Dixie: A Black Family's Claim to the Confederate Anthem
   Howard L. Sacks and Judith Rose Sacks

The Bluegrass Reader   *Edited by Thomas Goldsmith*

Colin McPhee: Composer in Two Worlds   *Carol J. Oja*

Robert Johnson, Mythmaking, and Contemporary American Culture
   Patricia R. Schroeder

Composing a World: Lou Harrison, Musical Wayfarer   *Leta E. Miller and Fredric Lieberman*

Fritz Reiner, Maestro and Martinet   *Kenneth Morgan*

That Toddlin' Town: Chicago's White Dance Bands and Orchestras, 1900–1950
   Charles A. Sengstock Jr.

Dewey and Elvis: The Life and Times of a Rock 'n' Roll Deejay   *Louis Cantor*

Come Hither to Go Yonder: Playing Bluegrass with Bill Monroe   *Bob Black*

Chicago Blues: Portraits and Stories   *David Whiteis*

The Incredible Band of John Philip Sousa   *Paul E. Bierley*

"Maximum Clarity" and Other Writings on Music   *Ben Johnston, edited by Bob Gilmore*

Staging Tradition: John Lair and Sarah Gertrude Knott   *Michael Ann Williams*

Homegrown Music: Discovering Bluegrass   *Stephanie P. Ledgin*

Tales of a Theatrical Guru   *Danny Newman*

The Music of Bill Monroe   *Neil V. Rosenberg and Charles K. Wolfe*

Pressing On: The Roni Stoneman Story   *Roni Stoneman, as told to Ellen Wright*

Together Let Us Sweetly Live   *Jonathan C. David, with photographs by Richard Holloway*

Live Fast, Love Hard: The Faron Young Story   *Diane Diekman*

Air Castle of the South: WSM Radio and the Making of Music City   *Craig P. Havighurst*

Traveling Home: Sacred Harp Singing and American Pluralism   *Kiri Miller*

Where Did Our Love Go? The Rise and Fall of the Motown Sound   *Nelson George*

Lonesome Cowgirls and Honky-Tonk Angels: The Women of Barn Dance Radio
    Kristine M. McCusker

California Polyphony: Ethnic Voices, Musical Crossroads   *Mina Yang*

The Never-Ending Revival: Rounder Records and the Folk Alliance   *Michael F. Scully*

Sing It Pretty: A Memoir   *Bess Lomax Hawes*

Working Girl Blues: The Life and Music of Hazel Dickens   *Hazel Dickens
    and Bill C. Malone*

Charles Ives Reconsidered   *Gayle Sherwood Magee*

The Hayloft Gang: The Story of the National Barn Dance   *Edited by Chad Berry*

Country Music Humorists and Comedians   *Loyal Jones*

Record Makers and Breakers: Voices of the Independent Rock 'n' Roll Pioneers
    John Broven

Music of the First Nations: Tradition and Innovation in Native North America
    Edited by Tara Browner

Cafe Society: The Wrong Place for the Right People   *Barney Josephson,
    with Terry Trilling-Josephson*

George Gershwin: An Intimate Portrait   *Walter Rimler*

Life Flows On in Endless Song: Folk Songs and American History   *Robert V. Wells*

I Feel a Song Coming On: The Life of Jimmy McHugh   *Alyn Shipton*

King of the Queen City: The Story of King Records   *Jon Hartley Fox*

Long Lost Blues: Popular Blues in America, 1850–1920   *Peter C. Muir*

Hard Luck Blues: Roots Music Photographs from the Great Depression   *Rich Remsberg*

Restless Giant: The Life and Times of Jean Aberbach and Hill and Range Songs
    Bar Biszick-Lockwood

Champagne Charlie and Pretty Jemima: Variety Theater in the Nineteenth
    Century   *Gillian M. Rodger*

Sacred Steel: Inside an African American Steel Guitar Tradition   *Robert L. Stone*

Gone to the Country: The New Lost City Ramblers and the Folk Music Revival
    Ray Allen

The Makers of the Sacred Harp   *David Warren Steel with Richard H. Hulan*

Woody Guthrie, American Radical   *Will Kaufman*

George Szell: A Life of Music   *Michael Charry*

Bean Blossom: The Brown County Jamboree and Bill Monroe's Bluegrass Festivals
    Thomas A. Adler

Crowe on the Banjo: The Music Life of J. D. Crowe   *Marty Godbey*

Twentieth Century Drifter: The Life of Marty Robbins   *Diane Diekman*

Henry Mancini: Reinventing Film Music   *John Caps*

The Beautiful Music All Around Us: Field Recordings and the American
    Experience   *Stephen Wade*

Then Sings My Soul: The Culture of Southern Gospel Music   *Douglas Harrison*

The Accordion in the Americas: Klezmer, Polka, Tango, Zydeco, and More!
    Edited by Helena Simonett

Bluegrass Bluesman: A Memoir   *Josh Graves, edited by Fred Bartenstein*

One Woman in a Hundred: Edna Phillips and the Philadelphia Orchestra
    Mary Sue Welsh

The Great Orchestrator: Arthur Judson and American Arts Management
    James M. Doering

Charles Ives in the Mirror: American Histories of an Iconic Composer   *David C. Paul*

Southern Soul-Blues   *David Whiteis*

Sweet Air: Modernism, Regionalism, and American Popular Song   *Edward P. Comentale*

Pretty Good for a Girl: Women in Bluegrass   *Murphy Hicks Henry*

Sweet Dreams: The World of Patsy Cline   *Warren R. Hofstra*

William Sidney Mount and the Creolization of American Culture   *Christopher J. Smith*

Bird: The Life and Music of Charlie Parker   *Chuck Haddix*

Making the March King: John Philip Sousa's Washington Years, 1854–1893
    Patrick Warfield

In It for the Long Run   *Jim Rooney*

Pioneers of the Blues Revival   *Steve Cushing*

Roots of the Revival: American and British Folk Music in the 1950s   *Ronald D. Cohen*
    and Rachel Clare Donaldson

Blues All Day Long: The Jimmy Rogers Story   *Wayne Everett Goins*

Yankee Twang: Country and Western Music in New England   *Clifford R. Murphy*

The Music of the Stanley Brothers   *Gary B. Reid*

Hawaiian Music in Motion: Mariners, Missionaries, and Minstrels   *James Revell Carr*

Sounds of the New Deal: The Federal Music Project in the West   *Peter Gough*

The Mormon Tabernacle Choir: A Biography   *Michael Hicks*

The Man That Got Away: The Life and Songs of Harold Arlen   *Walter Rimler*

A City Called Heaven: Chicago and the Birth of Gospel Music   *Robert M. Marovich*

Blues Unlimited: Essential Interviews from the Original Blues Magazine
    Edited by Bill Greensmith, Mike Rowe, and Mark Camarigg

Hoedowns, Reels, and Frolics: Roots and Branches of Southern Appalachian Dance
    Phil Jamison

Fannie Bloomfield-Zeisler: The Life and Times of a Piano Virtuoso   *Beth Abelson Macleod*

Cybersonic Arts: Adventures in American New Music   *Gordon Mumma,*
    edited with commentary by Michelle Fillion

The Magic of Beverly Sills   *Nancy Guy*

Waiting for Buddy Guy   *Alan Harper*

Harry T. Burleigh: From the Spiritual to the Harlem Renaissance   *Jean E. Snyder*

Music in the Age of Anxiety: American Music in the Fifties   *James Wierzbicki*

Jazzing: New York City's Unseen Scene   *Thomas H. Greenland*

A Cole Porter Companion   *Edited by Don M. Randel, Matthew Shaftel, and Susan Forscher Weiss*

Foggy Mountain Troubadour: The Life and Music of Curly Seckler   *Penny Parsons*

Blue Rhythm Fantasy: Big Band Jazz Arranging in the Swing Era   *John Wriggle*

Bill Clifton: America's Bluegrass Ambassador to the World   *Bill C. Malone*

Chinatown Opera Theater in North America   *Nancy Yunhwa Rao*

The Elocutionists: Women, Music, and the Spoken Word   *Marian Wilson Kimber*

May Irwin: Singing, Shouting, and the Shadow of Minstrelsy   *Sharon Ammen*

Peggy Seeger: A Life of Music, Love, and Politics   *Jean R. Freedman*

Charles Ives's *Concord*: Essays after a Sonata   *Kyle Gann*

Don't Give Your Heart to a Rambler: My Life with Jimmy Martin, the King of Bluegrass   *Barbara Martin Stephens*

Libby Larsen: Composing an American Life   *Denise Von Glahn*

George Szell's Reign: Behind the Scenes with the Cleveland Orchestra   *Marcia Hansen Kraus*

Just One of the Boys: Female-to-Male Cross-Dressing on the American Variety Stage   *Gillian M. Rodger*

Spirituals and the Birth of a Black Entertainment Industry   *Sandra Jean Graham*

Right to the Juke Joint: A Personal History of American Music   *Patrick B. Mullen*

Bluegrass Generation: A Memoir   *Neil V. Rosenberg*

Pioneers of the Blues Revival, Expanded Second Edition   *Steve Cushing*

Banjo Roots and Branches   *Edited by Robert Winans*

Bill Monroe: The Life and Music of the Blue Grass Man   *Tom Ewing*

Dixie Dewdrop: The Uncle Dave Macon Story   *Michael D. Doubler*

Los Romeros: Royal Family of the Spanish Guitar   *Walter Aaron Clark*

Transforming Women's Education: Liberal Arts and Music in Female Seminaries   *Jewel A. Smith*

Rethinking American Music   *Edited by Tara Browner and Thomas L. Riis*

Leonard Bernstein and the Language of Jazz   *Katherine Baber*

Dancing Revolution: Bodies, Space, and Sound in American Cultural History   *Christopher J. Smith*

Peggy Glanville-Hicks: Composer and Critic   *Suzanne Robinson*

Mormons, Musical Theater, and Belonging in America   *Jake Johnson*

Blues Legacy: Tradition and Innovation in Chicago   *David Whiteis*

Blues Before Sunrise 2: Interviews from the Chicago Scene   *Steve Cushing*

The Cashaway Psalmody: Transatlantic Religion and Music in Colonial Carolina   *Stephen A. Marini*

Earl Scruggs and Foggy Mountain Breakdown: The Making of an American Classic   *Thomas Goldsmith*

A Guru's Journey: Pandit Chitresh Das and Indian Classical Dance in Diaspora   *Sarah Morelli*

Unsettled Scores: Politics, Hollywood, and the Film Music of Aaron Copland
    and Hanns Eisler   *Sally Bick*
Hillbilly Maidens, Okies, and Cowgirls: Women's Country Music, 1930–1960
    Stephanie Vander Wel
Always the Queen: The Denise LaSalle Story   *Denise LaSalle with David Whiteis*
Artful Noise: Percussion Literature in the Twentieth Century   *Thomas Siwe*
The Heart of a Woman: The Life and Music of Florence B. Price   *Rae Linda Brown,*
    edited by Guthrie P. Ramsey Jr.
When Sunday Comes: Gospel Music in the Soul and Hip-Hop Eras   *Claudrena N. Harold*
The Lady Swings: Memoirs of a Jazz Drummer   *Dottie Dodgion and Wayne Enstice*
Industrial Strength Bluegrass: Southwestern Ohio's Musical Legacy
    Edited by Fred Bartenstein and Curtis W. Ellison
Soul on Soul: The Life and Music of Mary Lou Williams   *Tammy L. Kernodle*
Unbinding Gentility: Women Making Music in the Nineteenth-Century South
    Candace Bailey
Punks in Peoria: Making a Scene in the American Heartland   *Jonathan Wright*
    and Dawson Barrett
Homer Rodeheaver and the Rise of the Gospel Music Industry   *Kevin Mungons*
    and Douglas Yeo
Americanaland: Where Country & Western Met Rock 'n' Roll   *John Milward,*
    with Portraits by Margie Greve
Listening to Bob Dylan   *Larry Starr*
Lying in the Middle: Musical Theater and Belief at the Heart of America   *Jake Johnson*
The Sounds of Place: Music and the American Cultural Landscape   *Denise Von Glahn*
Peace Be Still: How James Cleveland and the Angelic Choir Created a Gospel
    Classic   *Robert M. Marovich*
Politics as Sound: The Washington, DC, Hardcore Scene, 1978–1983   *Shayna L. Maskell*
Tania León's Stride: A Polyrhythmic Life   *Alejandro L. Madrid*
Elliott Carter Speaks: Unpublished Lectures   *Elliott Carter, edited by Laura Emmery*
Interviews with American Composers: Barney Childs in Conversation   *Barney Childs,*
    edited by Virginia Anderson
Queer Country   *Shana Goldin-Perschbacher*

The University of Illinois Press
is a founding member of the
Association of University Presses.

University of Illinois Press
1325 South Oak Street
Champaign, IL 61820-6903
www.press.uillinois.edu